Virtual Teams That Work

Virtual Teams That Work

Creating Conditions for Virtual Team Effectiveness

Cristina B. Gibson
Susan G. Cohen

Editors

the Autonomous Management School
of Ghent University and Katholieke Universiteit Leuven

Reep 1 B-9000 Gent +32(9)2109711

JOSSEY-BASS
A Wiley Imprint
www.josseybass.com

Published by Jossey-Bass
A Wiley Imprint
989 Market Street, San Francisco, CA 94103-1741   www.josseybass.com

Jossey-Bass books and products are available through most bookstores. To contact Jossey-Bass directly call our Customer Care Department within the U.S. at 800-956-7739, outside the U.S. at 317-572-3986 or fax 317-572-4002.

Jossey-Bass also publishes its books in a variety of electronic formats. Some content that appears in print may not be available in electronic books.

Library of Congress Cataloging-in-Publication Data

Virtual teams that work : creating conditions for virtual team effectiveness / Cristina B. Gibson, Susan G. Cohen, editors.
     p. cm. — (The Jossey-Bass business & management series)
     Includes bibliographical references and index.
     ISBN 0-7879-6162-0 (alk. paper)
     1. Virtual work teams. 2. Teams in the workplace. 3. Leadership. 4. Computer conferencing. I. Gibson, Cristina B. II. Cohen, Susan G. III. Series.
     HD66 .V57 2003
     658.4'02—dc21
                                            2002151295

Printed in the United States of America
FIRST EDITION
HB Printing   10 9 8 7 6 5 4 3

The Jossey-Bass Business & Management Series

Cristina dedicates this book to her lifelong collaborator, Stephen Gibson, who has tolerated an often virtual spouse with the greatest of patience and has made life a truly grand cross-cultural adventure.

Susan dedicates this book to her husband, Steve Lampert, and her son, Danny Lampert, who make everything worthwhile.

CONTENTS

TABLES, FIGURES, AND EXHIBITS

TABLES

FIGURES

EXHIBITS

ACKNOWLEDGMENTS

This book is the result of numerous virtual collaborations among funding sources, valued colleagues, and superb support staff. The National Science Foundation's Innovation and Organization Change Division provided funding to our research team at the Center for Effective Organizations (CEO) (Grant 9975612) and to the Laboratory for Information Technology and Culture at Wayne State University. Special thanks go to Mariann Jelinek, past program officer at the National Science Foundation, for supporting (and attending!) the project conference that brought together the chapter authors so that we could share ideas with each other and with practitioners. We at CEO also received supplemental funding from the Center for Innovation and Management Studies at the University of North Carolina, Chapel Hill, and the Laboratory for Information Technology and Culture received funding from the Wayne State University Targets of Opportunity Program.

We extend warm gratitude to all of the chapter authors for their insights, creativity, and willingness to craft their ideas in such a manner that resulted in an integrated book. We sincerely appreciate their patience during our hiatus and their flexibility in meeting a dynamic set of deadlines. It has been a great pleasure working with each and every author. In particular, we thank Marietta Baba and Julia Gluesing for their coleadership of the Wayne State team and their valuable help in shaping this book.

We acknowledge all of the company participants and industry representatives who have participated in our research. In addition to providing research funding and the generous gift of their time, they sparked our imagination, helped us to test out ideas in many forums, and motivated us to pursue the issues addressed in this book. In particular, we extend our deep appreciation to Jude Olson, Larry Mestad, Michael Mueller, Ron Sacchi, Bruce Pasternack, Gary Huyssee, Mark Capper, Simon McPherson, and Raghu Kolli.

We thank our colleagues and coauthors on related projects who have fueled our explorations, provided feedback, and supported our endeavors. We are deeply indebted to Alec Levenson and Arjan Raven, two special members of our virtual teams research team at CEO, who have provided so many valued contributions to our project, our thinking, and our lives. We are tremendously grateful for our colleagues Sue Mohrman, Jim O'Toole, Jay Conger, and Edy Greenblatt at CEO and David Finegold, formerly at CEO, for their ongoing support, encouragement, and corroboration. We especially acknowledge Ed Lawler for his personal support and for creating the conditions at the center that stimulate us to write books that bridge the gap between theory and practice. In addition, Cristina extends special thanks to Julian Birkinshaw, Chris Earley, Richard Hackman, Brad Kirkman, Kristi Lewis-Tyran, Martha Maznevski, Chris Porath, Ben Rosen, Paul Tesluk, Freek Vermuelen, and Mary Zellmer-Bruhn.

Susan was being treated for breast cancer as we held the project conference, wrote, and edited this book. She is indebted to friends and colleagues who provided intellectual and emotional support during a very difficult time. She especially thanks Brenda Eskenazi, Don Mankin, Yvonne Herrera, Claudia Olivares, Hazel Rosin, Sue Mohrman, Gretchen Spreitzer, Molly Smith-Olsson, Jean Bartunek, and Richard Hackman. She owes special thanks to her oncologist, James Waisman, and his nurse, Laurie Feinstein, and all the others at Norris Cancer Care Center at the University of Southern California for helping her make the transition from breast cancer patient to survivor. She also thanks her support group at the Wellness Community and the many other survivors who shared their experiences with her, making hers a little bit easier to bear. It feels good to be able to write and edit a book!

Finally, we would be remiss if we did not acknowledge the support from our amazing staff at CEO. With supreme dedication and good humor, they made our conference a success, assisted us in keeping our data in order, maintained our complex accounts, provided endless hours of editorial and administrative assistance, and genuinely made this project possible. Special thanks to Alice Mark, Annette Yakushi, Lydia Arakaki, Patty Trinidad, Dan Canning, and Arienne McCracken. We value their (often virtual) help more than words can say.

January 2003   CRISTINA B. GIBSON
Los Angeles   SUSAN G. COHEN

THE AUTHORS

Cristina B. Gibson is associate research professor with the Center for Effective Organizations, Marshall School of Business, University of Southern California. She received her Ph.D. in organizational behavior from the Graduate School of Management at the University of California, Irvine, and her bachelor's degree in psychology from Scripps College. Gibson's research interests include communication, interaction and effectiveness in teams, the impact of culture and gender on work behavior, social cognition, and international knowledge management. She is coauthor with P. Christopher Earley of *Multinational Teams: A New Perspective*. Her research has appeared in many scholarly journals, including *Administrative Science Quarterly, Academy of Management Journal,* and *Academy of Management Review*. She is the recipient of numerous awards recognizing her research, including grants from the Thomas J. Watson Foundation, the Carnegie Bosch Institute for Applied International Management, the Center for Innovation and Management Studies, and the National Science Foundation.

Susan G. Cohen is a senior research scientist at the Center for Effective Organizations, Marshall School of Business, University of Southern California. She received her B.A. in psychology from the State University of New York, Buffalo, her M.A. in applied behavioral science from Whitworth College, and her M.Phil. and Ph.D. in organizational behavior from Yale University. She has done research on a variety of approaches to improving organizational effectiveness, self-managing teams, and team effectiveness, particularly in knowledge work and virtual settings. She has published widely and is coauthor of *Designing Team-Based Organizations: New Forms for Knowledge Work* and *Teams and Technology: Fulfilling the Promise of the New Organization.* She has won awards recognizing her research from the National Science Foundation and Center for Innovation and Management Studies.

Tara C. Alcordo is a research technician with the Globally Distributed Teams Project through the Institute for Information Technology and Culture, Wayne State University. She received her M.A. in anthropology from the Business and Industrial Anthropology Graduate Program at Wayne State University and her bachelor's degrees in anthropology and English from the University of Michigan. Her research interests include intercultural communication, virtual teaming, organizational culture, identity and entrepreneurship in East Asian countries, and the application of social science research methodologies to corporate issues. She received the Leadership in Excellence Award for her work as president of the Wayne State University Anthropology Club.

Nicholas A. Athanassiou is associate professor at Northeastern University's College of Business Administration. Previously, he held a number of senior executive positions throughout the world with major corporations. His research interest is international business strategy, with a focus on the international business capabilities of top management teams, global teams, global innovation, social networks, and social capital. His research has been published widely. He holds a B.S. degree from the Naval Academy of Greece, an M.S.E.E. from Georgia Institute of Technology, an M.B.A. from the University of Michigan, and a Ph.D. from the University of South Carolina.

Marietta L. Baba is dean of the College of Social Science and professor of anthropology at Michigan State University. She was the founding director of the Business and Industrial Anthropology initiative at Wayne State University and served as program director of the National Science Foundation's industry-funded research program entitled *Transformations to Quality Organizations.* She is the author of more than sixty-five scholarly and technical publications in the fields of organizational culture, technological change, and evolutionary processes. In 1998, she was appointed to serve on Motorola's global advisory board of anthropologists, the first of its kind in the United States. She holds an M.B.A. from Michigan State University's Eli Broad School of Management and a Ph.D. in physical anthropology from Wayne State University.

Richard Blackburn is an associate professor of organizational behavior at the University of North Carolina at Chapel Hill's Kenan-Flagler Business School. He received his Ph.D. in organizational behavior from the University of Wisconsin-Madison, where he also earned his M.B.A. He has a bachelor's degree in mathematics from Carleton College. His research interests include organizational and individual creativity and innovation, the meaning and motivation of work in the twenty-first century, and managing in the virtual environment. His research work has been published widely. He serves on the editorial review boards of the *Academy of Management Journal* and the *Human Resources Management Journal* and the board of governors of the Southern Management Association. He is coauthor with W. A. Randolph of *Managing Organizational Behavior.*

David Britt, professor and chair of sociology at Wayne State University, has been working on two lines of research: the development of a perspective for using models as a vehicle for increasing the dialogue between qualitative and quantitative researchers and summarizing what is tentatively understood about what concepts are important, how they are related to one another, and what their nature is. Among the issues with which he has been concerned is the overriding importance of context for understanding meaning and causal implications.

Catherine Durnell Cramton is associate professor in the School of Management at George Mason University. She received her Ph.D. in organizational behavior from Yale University and her bachelor's degree from Harvard-Radcliffe. Her research explores contemporary issues of collaboration and leadership, including distributed work, interorganizational collaboration, project team leadership, and the impact of technology on collaboration. Currently she is focusing on information-sharing processes, attribution processes, and cross-national dynam ics in distributed work groups. Her work has appeared in scholarly and pedagogical journals and has been featured in *Business Week Online.*

Efrat Elron is an assistant professor with the School of Business Administration, Hebrew University. She received her Ph.D. in organizational psychology from the University of Maryland, and her bachelor's degree in biology from Hebrew University. Her research interests include multinational organizations and the ways that cultural diversity affects them, team processes and effectiveness, and the impact of gender on work behavior.

David Finegold is an associate professor of management at the Keck Graduate Institute. He received his D.Phil. in politics from Oxford University. His research projects include the impact of the Internet on organizational design and human resources, managing technical excellence, the career paths of temporary workers, and the design of effective corporate boards. He is widely published, and his most recent book is *Corporate Boards: Adding Value at the Top.* He is a Forum Fellow of the World Economic Forum, a member of the Academy of Management, and a reviewer for a number of journals.

Stacie Furst is a doctoral candidate in the organizational behavior program at the Kenan-Flagler Business School, University of North Carolina at Chapel Hill. Her research interests include the impact of managerial influence tactics on employees' commitment to organizational change initiatives, the relationship between organizational values and employee work behaviors, and the dynamics of virtual versus colocated teams.

Julia C. Gluesing is president of Cultural Connections, a research, training, and consulting firm. She is experienced in the practical application of the theory and methods of anthropology, cross-cultural communication, and organizational culture to the understanding of business issues and the development and implementation of solutions to strategic business problems. Her specialization is global virtual teams in product development. She is currently the interim director of the Institute for Information Technology and Culture at Wayne State University. She received her Ph.D. in business and industrial anthropology from Wayne State University, her M.A. from Michigan State University in organizational and intercultural communication and research, and her B.A. in French and Russian languages from the University of California. She has published professionally and in scholarly journals and is currently working on a grant from the National Science Foundation.

Terri L. Griffith is a professor of management in the Leavey School of Business at Santa Clara University. Her research and consulting interests include the implementation and effective use of new technologies and organizational practices, most recently focusing on virtual teams and negotiated implementation. Her recent field research includes sites within the Sutherland Group, a major imaging company, and two major high-tech organizations. Her work has been widely published and she is a coeditor with M. A. Neale and E. A. Mannix of *Research on Managing Groups and Teams: Technology* (2000). She is a senior editor for *Organization Science* and an associate editor for *MIS Quarterly.* She received her Ph.D. from Carnegie Mellon University.

Pamela J. Hinds is an assistant professor with the Center on Work, Technology, and Organization in the Department of Management Science and Engineering, Stanford University. She conducts research on the effects of technology on group dynamics and on the way work is coordinated, and she studies information sharing across distance, disciplinary boundaries, and levels of expertise. She is coauthor with Sara Kiesler of *Distributed Teams,* and her research has appeared widely in scholarly journals. She received her Ph.D. in organization science and management from Carnegie Mellon University.

Nelson King received his Ph.D. in industrial and systems engineering from the University of Southern California. He also has an M.S. from the University of

Arizona and a B.S. from Columbia University School of Engineering. His research interests include information system architectures for knowledge management and collaboration among virtual teams, particularly in new product development. He has worked as a systems engineer on numerous projects for over twenty years, with an emphasis on integrating information technology into planning activities. His information systems research has appeared in several journals. He is also the recipient of numerous corporate awards.

Janice A. Klein is senior lecturer at the Massachusetts Institute of Technology's Sloan School of Management. Her research focuses on teams, work design, team leadership, employee empowerment, and organizational change. She is the coeditor with Jeffrey Miller of *The American Edge: Leveraging Manufacturing's Hidden Assets* and has published widely in journals. She received her B.S. in industrial engineering from Iowa State University, her M.B.A. from Boston University, and her Ph.D. in industrial relations from the Sloan School.

Astrid Kleinhanns is consulting with the Boston Consulting Group in Vienna, Austria. As a visiting research affiliate at the Program on Negotiation at Harvard University, she did research on collaboration in virtual teams, with an emphasis on maximizing the diverse contributions of intellectual capital and negotiating the differences in globally dispersed, high-performance teams. She was also a research fellow at the Massachusetts Institute of Technology's Sloan School of Management and the Business School of the National University of Singapore and has taught in the Program of Instruction for Lawyers at Harvard Law School. She received her Ph.D. in social and economic studies from the Johannes Kepler University in Austria in collaboration with the Sloan School.

Edward E. Lawler III is Distinguished Professor of Business and director of the Center for Effective Organizations (of which he is the founder) in the Marshall School of Business at the University of Southern California. He has consulted with over one hundred organizations on employee involvement, organizational change, and compensation and has been honored as a top contributor to the fields of organizational development, organizational behavior, and compensation. He is the author of over three hundred articles and thirty books, and his works have been translated into seven languages. His most recent books are *Tomorrow's Organization, Strategies for High Performance Organizations— The CEO Report, The Leadership Change Handbook, Rewarding Excellence, Corporate Boards: New Strategies for Adding Value at the Top,* and *Organizing for High Performance.*

Alec R. Levenson is a research scientist at the Center for Effective Organizations, University of Southern California. He received his M.A. and Ph.D. in economics from Princeton University and his B.A. in economics and Chinese language from the University of Wisconsin, Madison. His research focuses on personnel and the economics of human resources. He is coeditor with Lewis C. Solmon of *Labor Markets, Employment Policy, and Job Creation* and a member of the editorial board of *Small Business Economics.* He has received research grants from the Russell Sage Foundation, the Rockefeller Foundation, the National Science Foundation, and the National Institute for Literacy.

Ann Majchrzak is professor of information systems at the Marshall School of Business, University of Southern California (USC). She received her Ph.D. in social psychology from the University of California, Los Angeles, and has since worked as an organizational consultant as well as taught at USC's Institute for Safety and Systems Management, Purdue's Krannert School of Management, and USC's Industrial and Systems Engineering Department. Her research interest is in the organizational impacts and design of computer-automated work environments. She has published widely and has received awards that include MIS Quarterly Paper of the Year (2000), Best Paper Academy of Management Organizational Communication and Information Systems Division (2001), and Society for Information Management First Place Paper Competition (2000).

Elizabeth A. Mannix is an associate professor of management and organizations at Cornell University's Johnson Graduate School of Management. She is also the director of the Center for Leadership in Dynamic Organizations. Her current research projects include work on patterns of conflict over time, the performance of virtual teams, and negotiation behavior in Japan and China. She is the coeditor of the book series *Research on Managing Groups and Teams* and is widely published.

Jennifer A. Manuel is completing her M.Phil. in international relations with the Centre for International Studies at the University of Cambridge. She obtained an undergraduate degree in psychology and business from the University of Southern California (USC). For her honors thesis, she collaborated with the Center for Effective Organizations investigating trust and communication in virtual teams. She won first prize at the USC Symposium for Scholarly and Creative Work and presented this work at the Stanford University 2001 Psychology Conference. Her current research at Cambridge investigates state constraints on foreign ownership in a global age.

Martha L. Maznevski is a professor at the International Institute for Management Development, in Lausanne, Switzerland, engaged in management and executive development in the areas of international management and leadership. She is also affiliated with the firms Human Factors and Multicultural Management Solutions and with the Institute for International Business at the

Stockholm School of Economics. She received her Ph.D. in business administration from the University of Western Ontario, specializing in international and cross-cultural organizational behavior. Prior to that, she received degrees in anthropology and linguistics and in education. She has published her research on global and diverse teams in academic and management journals and books, presented it in many conferences and other settings, and used the results to facilitate team performance in organizations throughout the word. Her current research expands the earlier work to focus on virtual teams and on teams as networks within larger networks.

Willie McKether is a lecturer in the Department of Anthropology and assistant director of the Douglas A. Fraser Center for Workplace Issues at Wayne State University. He is also a Ph.D. candidate in the Department of Anthropology, where he has studied globally dispersed teams. He has focused specifically on developmental patterns and the emergence of trust among culturally diverse work teams. Other research interests include interest-based bargaining and the use of technology to prepare high school students for entry-level employment. He holds an undergraduate degree in economics and has graduate degrees in business administration and industrial relations.

Susan Albers Mohrman is senior research scientist at the Center for Effective Organizations, Marshall School of Business, University of Southern California (USC). She received her Ph.D. in organizational behavior from Northwestern University and has served on the faculty of the Management and Organization Department in the business school at USC. Her research focuses on management and human resource innovations, including employee involvement and Total Quality Management, organizational change, organizational design processes, and team design and the lateral organization. She has researched and consulted to a variety of organizations that are redesigning structures and systems to create high performance. She is active in the Organization Development and Change Division of the Academy of Management and serves on the review and editorial boards of several management journals.

Leslie Monplaisir is an assistant professor in the Department of Industrial and Manufacturing Engineering at Wayne State University. He received his Ph.D. in 1996 from University of Missouri-Rolla, specializing in engineering management. His research interest spans collaborative engineering and computer-integrated manufacturing system designs. His funded research involves the design and development of a distributed product design and development systems for cross-functional teams virtually colocated, the development of appropriate measures to track the performance of such teams, and laboratory and field-testing of the impact of computer-supported collaborative work technologies on the output of the engineering project team distributed in time and space. He is a senior member of the Institute of Industrial Engineers and the Society of Manufacturing Engineers.

Margaret A. Neale is the John G. McCoy–Banc One Corporation Professor of Organizations and Dispute Resolution at Stanford University. Her major research interests include bargaining and negotiation, distributed work groups, team composition, learning, and performance. She is the author of over seventy articles on these topics and mostly recently coauthored, with L. Stroh and G. Northcraft, the third edition of *Organizational Behavior: A Management Challenge.* She serves on the editorial boards of the *Journal of Applied Psychology, Organizational Behavior and Human Decision Processes,* and *Human Resource Management Review.*

Kara L. Orvis is a doctoral candidate in the industrial/organizational psychology program at George Mason University and currently employed as a senior research fellow at the U.S. Army Research Institute in Alexandria, Virginia. She received her M.A. in industrial/organizational psychology from George Mason University and her B.A. from Ohio Wesleyan University. Her main research interests have been in the realms of teams, multiteam systems, and leadership, concentrating on team training and development. Her current research focuses on teamwork and leadership issues regarding dispersed teams and computer-supported collaborative learning. With the Army Research Institute, she is concluding a series of evaluations and controlled experiments on the training effectiveness of distance-learning technology.

Hilary Horn Ratner is professor of psychology and interim dean of the Graduate School at Wayne State University. She completed her Ph.D. in psychology at the University of Massachusetts and a postdoctoral fellowship at the University of Chicago. Her research interests include memory and cognitive development, collaborative learning, and social cognition. Her work has been funded by the National Science Foundation, National Institute on Aging, Maternal and Child Health, and the McGregor Foundation. She is a fellow of the American Psychological Association.

Arjan Raven is an assistant professor in the Computer Information Systems Department at Georgia State University, Robinson College of Business. He received his Ph.D. in business administration from the University of Southern California. He also holds degrees in computer science from the University of Amsterdam and electrical engineering from the Utrecht School of Engineering. His current research interests center around the management of knowledge and collaboration within virtual groups and communities of practice, with an emphasis on supporting technologies. He also conducts research on the development of on-line courses and the use of instructional technologies. He has published widely and is a coprincipal investigator for a multiyear research grant from the National Science Foundation.

Kenneth Riopelle is a cofounder and principal of Cultural Connections. He received a Ph.D. in adult education from the University of Michigan, an M.A. from Eastern Michigan University in educational leadership, and a B.A. in communication from Michigan State University. He is a faculty member and leadership project adviser in the Ford Motor Company and Wayne State University Engineering Management master's program teaching the management of technology change in the global enterprise. His professional experience spans over twenty-five years using qualitative and quantitative research designs and methods to help companies develop and target their products and services and evaluate their performance with customers.

Benson Rosen is Hanes Professor of Management at the Kenan-Flagler Business School, University of North Carolina. He holds a Ph.D. in social and industrial psychology from Wayne State University. He is a fellow of the American Psychological Association and a member of the Academy of Management and the Society for Human Resources Management. His research interests include virtual teams, empowerment, and career success. He is the coauthor of two books and over ninety articles that have appeared in leading academic and professional journals. He serves on the editorial review board of the *Academy of Management Executive* and the *Human Resource Management Journal* and has consulted on many management issues, including Total Quality Management, organizational change, employee empowerment, diversity management, and conflict management.

Morgan Shepherd is an associate professor of information systems at the University of Colorado at Colorado Springs. His research focuses on improving the performance of distributed groups. His teaching interests are in telecommunications, decision support for virtual teams, and e-commerce. Morgan helped develop the distance M.B.A. program at the University of Colorado and teaches several sections each year. He received his B.S. in mechanical engineering from the University of Virginia and his Ph.D. in management information systems from the University of Arizona. His work has been published in journals and national and international conference proceedings.

Craig K. Tyran is an associate professor in the Department of Decision Sciences in the College of Business and Economics at Western Washington University. He received his Ph.D. from the University of Arizona in management information systems, his M.B.A. from the University of California, Los Angeles, and his bachelor's and master's degrees in petroleum engineering from Stanford

University. His research focuses on the ways that technology can be used to support collaboration, learning, and information systems development. His work has been published in numerous journals, and he has made many research presentations at national and international conferences.

Kristi Lewis Tyran is an assistant professor in the Department of Management in the College of Business and Economics at Western Washington University. She received her Ph.D. in organizational behavior from the University of California, Irvine, and her M.B.A. and bachelor of science degree from the University of Washington. Her research interests include exploring the role of values and emotion in leadership and teams. Her interest in cross-cultural impacts on leadership is reflected in her current research exploring leadership in virtual teams. She has published several articles in leading journals.

Eran Vigoda is a faculty member in the Department of Political Science, University of Haifa, Israel. His current research interests include behavior and performance in the public sector, organizational politics, organizational citizenship behavior, and citizenship behavior outside organizations. He is the head of the master's program of local government administration and a member of several consulting committees working closely with public institutions and local municipalities in Israel. He is the author and coauthor of more than twenty-five articles and book chapters, as well as many other scholarly presentations and working papers. He received his Ph.D. from the University of Haifa.

Kimberly Harris Wagner is a Ph.D. candidate in organizational behavior and human resources at the Anderson School at the University of California, Los Angeles. She is investigating conflict in global virtual teams and is involved with the Wayne State University research project on globally distributed teams.

Suzanne P. Weisband is an associate professor in management information systems at the University of Arizona. She received her B.A. in psychology at San Diego State University and a Ph.D. in social and decision sciences and policy analysis from Carnegie Mellon University. Her research examines social and technological aspects of knowledge sharing in distributed work groups and how that information affects collaboration, leadership, and learning over time. She has published her work in leading management and information systems journals and is editing a book on the challenges of leading distributed teams.

CHAPTER ONE

In the Beginning

Introduction and Framework

Susan G. Cohen, Cristina B. Gibson

The objective was to get the savings to satisfy Wall Street. Our strategic decision to give clearly assigned common goals to people on both sides of the organization really helped integration in the postmerger environment. We were very successful in a short period of time with the use of virtual teams. We could not have done this in any other way.
—Leader of a procurement management team

The cost and risk are much greater. The risk of success is very much hindered by the system. I'm not sure you are going to gain success by having all these people working together on the same program. I'm not sure that they are even aware of the culture differences. Then there are monetary costs. We are losing time on certain design processes that would be so much easier if we were colocated. We lose 50 percent by teaming virtually. With the tools that we have right now and the people we have managing those fixes, it is going to be really bad. We are in the crawling stage on the virtual technology stuff.
—Engineer for a new product design team

Both of these people are describing their experiences with virtual teams. The leader of the procurement management team views the use of virtual teams as critical to his company's postmerger success. In procurement, commodity specialists work together across countries and languages to achieve common savings goals. They are developing new procurement strategies from the best practices of their former companies. In their first year of operation, these procurement teams have met their savings goals more quickly and more efficiently than expected. Similarly, other postmerger virtual teams in new product development, manufacturing, and sales and service are determining integrated strategies to position this organization for competitive success.

In contrast, the engineer on the virtual new product design team is skeptical about his company's purported claims for virtual work. He feels that the costs and risks far outweigh the benefits. As a working member of this team that combines engineers from different organizations and countries, he finds the cultural differences to be insurmountable. He resents the time that has been wasted trying to work with unfriendly technology that does not work as advertised and is frequently down. Based on the experience of his team, he believes that virtual teaming is 50 percent more expensive due to time delays, support needs, and coordination inefficiencies.

So what is the truth? How successful are virtual teams? In this fast-paced global economy, can their achievements propel organizations to competitive success? Or are virtual teams just another fad whose claims of effectiveness far outweigh reality?

This book shows that virtual teams can be either dramatic successes or dismal failures—or anywhere in between. Virtual teams amplify both the benefits and the costs of teamwork. Virtual teams that are designed, managed, and implemented effectively can harness talent from anywhere in the globe to solve business problems, service customers, and create new products. But if little attention is paid to how they are designed, managed, or supported, they will fail. Organizations must create the conditions for effective virtual teamwork. How to do so is the subject of this book.

Each of the chapter authors conducted in-depth research on virtual teams. They interviewed members, leaders, and support personnel. Some observed these groups as they go about their work. Others collected empirical data from questionnaires and archival data from organizational records, and they tested research hypotheses. The authors are from a variety of academic disciplines: psychology, sociology, engineering, information technology, political science, and economics. However, it is not the theories, hypotheses, or disciplinary frameworks that are the focus of this book. Rather, our focus is the application of these perspectives to real problems that practitioners experience when they serve as members and leaders of virtual teams. The book's chapters respond to questions that practitioners face when they use virtual teams—for example:

- How do people who speak different languages and are from different cultures develop effective ways of sharing knowledge when there is little opportunity to meet face-to-face?
- How can trust be built in virtual teams? Is trust necessary for performance?
- What should managers look for in selecting members for virtual teams?
- What reward systems support virtual work?
- How can return on investment be measured for virtual teams? Should it be measured?
- What can leaders do to coordinate and motivate virtual teams to high performance?

- How do organizations determine which technologies best fit a variety of virtual team tasks?
- How can virtual teams effectively manage conflict?
- What are virtual organizational politics? Can virtual politics be managed?
- How do virtual teams develop over time? What can leaders do to promote effective development?

The chapter authors addressed these questions at "Creating Conditions for Effective Virtual Teams: A Meeting of Minds and Sharing of Practices," a conference held April 3–4, 2001, hosted by the Center for Effective Organizations at the University of Southern California and Wayne State University. A unique feature of the conference was that following several presentations on a theme, a practitioner facilitated a discussion about the applicability of the research presented to practice. The five practitioners represented Intel (computer technology), Procter & Gamble (consumer products), Lockheed Martin (aerospace), Herman Miller (workplace design), and Rush Medical Center (health care). The practitioners challenged the authors to make their work relevant to their concerns. The chapters in this book reflect the practitioners' input. In addition, we as editors have integrated their comments into our introductions and summaries for each part of the book.

Before getting into the content of the book, we address three matters: we define the domain of the research, addressing what a virtual team is, describe our framework, and provide a brief road map to the book's structure and content.

WHAT IS A VIRTUAL TEAM?

Two problems plague the use of the term *virtual team*. First, people casually use it to apply to a wide variety of social and organizational phenomena. This is misleading, particularly for those who struggle with creating the conditions for effectiveness. Consider the difference between a virtual new product development team and an engineering Web-based learning network, both of which may be labeled virtual teams.

In the first case, there is clear interdependence among the geographically dispersed members of the team and shared responsibility for producing deliverables by a certain time and at a certain cost. The members use shared design tools to do work and stay in touch with frequent e-mails. How well they coordinate their activities can make a difference between successfully introducing a new product within the market window or not. In the second case, people are sharing knowledge, but there are no clear deliverables. Membership is voluntary, and people join or leave the discussion as they wish. People learn from each other, but there is no task interdependence. If a member feels that she has something particular to learn from another member, then she is likely to initiate e-mail correspondence with that person. Designing the new product development team for success is likely to be quite different from designing the learning network for success.

Second, several other terms are used to describe what may be the same phenomenon. Are geographically dispersed teams the same as virtual teams? Are *global teams, virtual transnational teams,* or *multicultural teams* different names for the same work unit? When people talk about virtual collaboration, are they talking about working in virtual teams?

We need to be precise about our definition of virtual teams. By clearly specifying our research domain, we can determine the practices that organizations should implement to create the conditions for effectiveness. To be considered virtual to some degree, a team must have the following three attributes:

- It is a functioning team—a collection of individuals who are interdependent in their tasks, share responsibility for outcomes, see themselves and are viewed by others as an intact social unit embedded in one or more social systems, and collectively manage their relationships across organizational boundaries (Hackman, 1987; Alderfer, 1977).
- The members of the team are geographically dispersed.
- The team relies on technology-mediated communications rather than face-to-face interaction to accomplish their tasks.

The requirement to be a team constrains our research domain. Learning networks, communities of practice, Web-based interest groups, and other loosely formed collectives are not real teams. Communicating with others electronically does not transform a collection of people into a team. Teams must have real tasks to perform, interdependent members, and shared outcomes.

What makes virtual teams virtual is geographical dispersion and the use of technologically mediated communications. The members of virtual teams are not colocated; their primary work sites are different from one another. They may be located in different buildings, cities, states, nations, and even continents. Team members may belong to the same organization or multiple organizations. Thus, these teams may be transnational or global and multiorganizational.

Virtual teams also rely on electronically mediated communication to stay in touch and get their work done. They use a variety of technologies that range in sophistication, such as telephone, faxes, teleconferences, e-mail, videoconferences, collaborative design tools, and knowledge-management systems. These teams may meet face-to-face from time to time, but they could not do their work and effectively coordinate their activities without technological support. Of course, teams that are colocated also use telephones, e-mail, and computers. But just the use of technology does not make a team virtual, because all teams use technology. It is the degree of reliance on electronic communication that increases virtuality. Virtual teams often have no choice; they must communicate electronically. Colocated teams typically have more discretion about whether and when to use technology.

We see virtuality as a continuum. Virtual teams range in their degree of virtuality, from slightly virtual to extremely virtual. Where a team exists on this continuum is a function of the amount of dependence on electronically mediated communication and the degree of geographical dispersion. A team that does all its work through e-mail, text exchanges, and teleconferences, never meeting face-to-face, is more virtual than a team that meets monthly face-to-face. A team that spans multiple continents and time zones is more virtual than one whose members are located in the same city. As the cases discussed in this book suggest, increased virtuality adds complexity that must be managed.

So far we have discussed what is a virtual team. Now we need to explore what it is not. A virtual team is not the same thing as a cross-functional team, a multiorganizational team, or a multicultural team. This is because it is possible for a team to be colocated and comprise members from different functions, organizations, and cultures. Given our definition, it is possible for a virtual team to consist of members from the same function, organization, and culture. That said, many of the virtual teams studied in our research had members from multiple functions, organizations, and national cultures. The greater the geographical dispersion on the team is, the more likely it is that the team will comprise members quite different from one another. Like degree of virtuality, these differences increase the complexity that must be managed. However, they do not define virtual teams. These same differences can and do occur in colocated teams.

By specifying our research domain, we limit the scope of the generalizability of our findings: they apply to real virtual teams. Although bounded, this domain is still relatively large, encompassing virtual management teams, new product development teams, service and support teams, manufacturing teams, and others. Among the virtual teams that the chapter authors studied are these:

- A virtual team prototyping a new wireless device enabling children and families to transmit pictures to one another, drawn from representatives of six organizations from four European countries

- A virtual team with representatives of five aerospace companies (three American, one British, and one Dutch) that tests new collaborative technologies and demonstrates that the development of a new fighter airplane does not have to incur costs beyond those of the traditional development process

- A virtual team of Israeli information system specialists from a high-technology company with subsidiaries in the United States, Europe, and Asia asked to recommend a new information system that can expedite data transfer across locations

- An American-based company that reconstitutes its French customer team so that it can create and execute a global strategy for building relationships with French customers not only in France but around the world

In a couple of instances in this book, however, the authors describe collective work units that fall outside the boundaries of our definition—for example:

- A consulting company establishes a loosely linked network to develop intellectual capital for the firm.

- A newly merged company creates a series of knowledge-management forums (communities of practice) so that best practices can be widely disseminated.

By standing outside and looking in, we see what we are studying from another perspective. Comparing these examples to real virtual teams helps us to understand better the design elements and management practices needed for virtual team success.

ORIENTING FRAMEWORK

None of the chapter authors began their research with a totally blank slate. Each was familiar with the emerging literature on virtual teams as well as the broader literature on team development and performance (Cohen and Bailey, 1997). In addition, the authors have been influenced by the theoretical paradigms from their academic disciplines. They used their knowledge of the team literature and their disciplinary perspectives to shape their research studies of virtual teams. As the authors talked to one another at our conference, they were surprised by the degree of overlap among their perspectives. The authors shared five major assumptions about what enables virtual teams to be effective and focused their attention on a set of key factors that fit within the preliminary research framework developed by our research team at USC.

Key Assumptions

A key assumption is that teams are more likely to be effective when certain enabling conditions exist. Teams in general, and virtual teams more specifically, are complex social forms, and effectiveness is the result of multiple practices, often redundant with one another. Many factors working together determine effectiveness. In addition, the same outcome can be produced by several different methods. For these reasons, trying to identify specific causal relationships between one factor and team effectiveness may not be fruitful (Hackman, 1990).

A more promising approach is to identify the conditions that promote virtual team effectiveness. What should leaders and managers do to create these enabling conditions? How can leaders create a context for virtual teams so that they are more likely to perform well? What managers and leaders actually do is to create the conditions that support effectiveness. They use multiple techniques, just as teams use multiple performance strategies to achieve their goals. Thus, this approach is consistent with how leaders and teams actually behave in organizations.

Our second key assumption stems from the first. We believe that there are multiple design and implementation factors that help to create the conditions supporting virtual team effectiveness. We use a broad net to identify these factors. We look at the organizational context, team and task characteristics, technology use, team member characteristics, and work and team processes. Several factors are embedded in each of these categories. For example, selection, training, and reward systems are part of the organizational context. How an organization's reward system is structured, how its policies are designed, and how its practices are implemented may make it more likely (or less likely) that its virtual teams will succeed. Those who establish, lead, and support virtual teams can influence organizational systems, structures, policies, and practices. These are the levers that can be pulled to promote effectiveness.

The third assumption highlights how virtuality amplifies the challenges that teams face. Given a certain set of inputs, all teams have to overcome barriers in order to create the enabling conditions that lead to effectiveness. We believe that teams range in their degree of virtuality from slightly virtual to extremely virtual. As teams become more virtual, they confront greater uncertainty and complexity, increasing the difficulty of the information processing and sense-making tasks that they do. Virtual teams face an upward climb, needing to overcome powerful barriers to effectiveness. This puts a premium on using all the design and implementation levers at their disposal to create highly enabling conditions. If leaders and managers have shied away from using teams because of potential effectiveness problems, they should not consider the use of virtual teams.

The fourth assumption is related to the third. Virtual teams are frequently composed of members who are quite different from one another. They may represent different disciplines, functions, professions, business units, organizations, countries, and cultures. Virtual teams vary in the number and depth of differences they confront. The greater the number and depth of differences that need to be managed, the greater are the barriers to effectiveness. If a team is both highly virtual and must cope with multiple and deep differences, then the uphill climb is even steeper. These teams must be designed, supported, and led in a superb manner to be successful.

Our next assumption is the converse of what we have just said. What we have emphasized are the barriers to virtual team effectiveness. We have said that the mountain that virtual teams have to climb is high. However, what happens if they successfully climb that mountain? What happens if they are effective despite all the obstacles?

Our fifth assumption is that virtual teams can amplify the benefits of teamwork. The greater the degree of virtuality and differences, the higher the potential benefit is. Virtual teams enable the best talent regardless of location to be applied to solve business problems, create products, and deliver services. Cross-organizational teams can be set up to capitalize on each organization's unique competencies. When organizations compose virtual teams with people from different perspectives and knowledge bases (high degree of differences), innovation is more likely to occur. Problems can be framed in ways that allow for innovative solutions when people can apply knowledge from one domain to another (Pinchot, 1985). Thus, virtual teams have the potential for producing high-quality, innovative business solutions. At the same time, relying on electronically mediated communication reduces the cost of coordination. Face-to-face meetings can be scheduled when needed, but people can do most of the work from their primary, distant work settings. Thus, virtual teams offer efficiency benefits as well. The potential to produce high-quality, innovative solutions at lower cost offers organizations competitive advantage. How can organizations harness the potential of virtual teams? How can virtual teams be designed and supported for success? What can be done to build enabling conditions?

Enabling Conditions

For virtual teams to perform well, three enabling conditions need to be established:

• *Shared understanding* is the degree of cognitive overlap and commonality in beliefs, expectations, and perceptions about a given target. Virtual teams need to develop this shared understanding about what they are trying to achieve (their goals), how they will achieve them (work and group processes), what they need to do (their tasks), and what each team member brings to the team task (member knowledge, skills, and abilities). When teams involve people from different disciplines, business units, organizations, and cultures, their members will have different ways of perceiving their tasks, key issues, and making sense of their situation. Dougherty (1992) described new product development team members as inhabiting different "thought worlds" because of these differences. By developing shared understandings, virtual teams learn how to bridge the chasm between thought worlds (see Chapter Two).

- *Integration* is the process of establishing ways in which the parts of an organization can work together to create value, develop products, or deliver services. The parts of the organization (or organizations) represented by virtual team members are likely to be highly differentiated in response to global competitive pressures and uncertain business environments. This differentiation across organizational units means that they are likely to have different policies, organizational structures, and systems. These differences can hinder effective collaboration in virtual teams both directly and indirectly. When organizational units have different information technology infrastructures, for example, connectivity can be a real problem. At the most basic level, virtual team members may not be able to send e-mails to team members from other business units. In a more subtle way, business unit policies, structures, and systems influence employee behaviors, providing incentives for certain behaviors and disincentives for others. Incentives for cross-unit collaboration may be lacking. Policies, structures, and systems also shape employee perspectives and worldviews on what is and is not important. The greater the degree of differentiation in an organization, the greater is the need for integration. The formation of virtual teams is one mechanism to encourage integration.

In essence, integration refers to organizational structures and systems, while shared understanding refers to people's thoughts. Integration is a structural variable; shared understanding is cognitive. However, the two covary together. The greater the differentiation among business units, the more likely it is that team members will inhabit different thought worlds, making it more difficult to develop shared understanding. At the same time, the lower the level of integration, the greater the difficulty of developing shared understanding. Chapter Three describes this relationship. It examines the set of activities needed to develop shared understanding in differentiated global new product development networks.

- *Mutual trust* (or collective trust) is a shared psychological state characterized by an acceptance of vulnerability based on expectations of intentions or behaviors of others within the team (Rousseau, Sitkin, Burt, and Camerer, 1998; Cummings and Bromiley, 1996). Teams that have established mutual trust are safe environments for their members, who are thereby willing to take risks with one another and let their vulnerabilities show. As discussed in Chapter Four, trust is difficult to establish in virtual teams. Members are geographically dispersed and are likely to have different backgrounds, experiences, and cultures. People tend to trust those whom they perceive as similar to themselves. Electronically mediated communication lacks the interpersonal cues that are so important for building trust. Special steps need to be taken to build trust in virtual teams.

In general, managers and teams cannot simply command a high rating on the enabling conditions. Giving the right instructions does not create shared understanding, integration, and trust. It is how the team is designed and managed that creates the enabling conditions. This is a cyclical process that is ongoing.

Design Factors

The systems and structures that make up the organizational context are important for virtual team success. We examine selection, education and training, and performance evaluation systems in Chapter Five, consider reward systems for virtual teams in Chapter Six, and look at performance measurement for virtual teams and how to establish return-on-investment metrics in Chapter Seven.

The virtual team structure should promote task accomplishment. Are there clear goals? Is the task designed so that the group is held accountable for a meaningful piece of work? Do group members receive feedback on their progress (Hackman and Oldham, 1980)? How is information shared and processed in virtual teams (see Chapter Ten)? What is the structure of social relationships in virtual teams? Can social capital be built over communications technologies rather than through face-to-face interaction (see Chapter Nine)? We expect that these elements of team structure that are critical in face-to-face settings will also be important in virtual settings. In addition, leadership is key. How do leaders emerge in virtual teams? What should virtual team leaders do to ensure effectiveness? Emergent leadership is the focus of Chapter Eight.

Information technology provides the infrastructure for virtual collaboration. It should enable virtual team members from any location to communicate and coordinate their work effectively. Technology should also support virtual team development and work on tasks. Many commercialized products exist to support collaboration in virtual teams. The challenge for practitioners is to figure out which technologies are most appropriate for their teams. Three chapters address information technology needs. Chapter Eleven identifies the technologies appropriate for teams operating in different contexts and looks at how networking and communication infrastructure influence their use. This chapter also considers the role of technology in the development of virtual teams over time. Chapter Twelve examines technological support for knowledge work, recommending that systems be flexible and adaptable. Chapter Thirteen looks at the fit between the structure of the team and information technology support and discusses how communities of practice have different information requirements from virtual teams.

The people who work in virtual teams need to possess certain capabilities in order to work effectively with their teammates. First, they need sufficient task-related knowledge and skills. They also need to have the skills to work collaboratively in virtual space. We believe that they need lateral skills to work with people quite different from themselves. Team members need to have a tolerance for ambiguity to deal with the unstructured communication that characterizes much of virtual teamwork. The personality dimensions and skills that team members possess will influence the establishment of enabling conditions. Although we view member characteristics as important, we do not have a separate part devoted to it. Chapter Five identifies the knowledge, skills, and abilities for virtual team members on which team selection can be based.

Finally, the team and work processes that are followed can help or hinder the creation of enabling conditions. Conflict can have both positive and negative effects on virtual-team performance. Chapter Fifteen presents strategies for recognizing, managing, and using conflict so that it is productive. Chapter Sixteen looks at developmental processes in virtual teams and examines what can be done to promote effective development. Chapter Seventeen looks at the competing time pressures that members of virtual teams face and examines what can be done to close the time gap. Communication processes are discussed in many other chapters, for example, Chapter Ten on information processing and Chapter Four on trust. What leaders can do to help build effective group processes is discussed Chapter Eight.

Outcomes

We consider both business outcomes and human outcomes as virtual team effectiveness measures. Possible business outcomes are goal achievement, productivity, timeliness, customer satisfaction, organization learning, innovation, and cycle time. Possible human outcomes are team member attitudes such as commitment, satisfaction, and longevity, that is, the capacity to work together in the future. For example, as discussed in Chapter Seven, the key business outcome for a future planning team may be acceptance of alternative design scenarios generated by the team. For a systems engineering team, the key outcome may be the functionality of the tools developed. Essentially, selecting the appropriate performance measure depends on the team and its task. Often, judgments of performance are subjective and are best done by the team's manager or other stakeholders in its social system.

Research Framework

Figure 1.1 presents our research framework. It shows that effectiveness outcomes are a function of the enabling conditions. It categorizes and lists the design factors that contribute to the establishment of enabling conditions. It shows that degree of virtuality and degree of differences moderate the relationship between design factors and enabling conditions. Stated another way, degree of virtuality and degree of differences amplify the effects of the design factors on the enabling conditions. The greater the degree of virtuality and degree of differences, the more difficult it will be to establish supportive enabling conditions. This framework does not make specific causal predictions. It summarizes where we began our research. It is not where we expect to conclude our research. We expect to go beyond our framework and present some cross-cutting themes and learnings we did not expect from the outset.

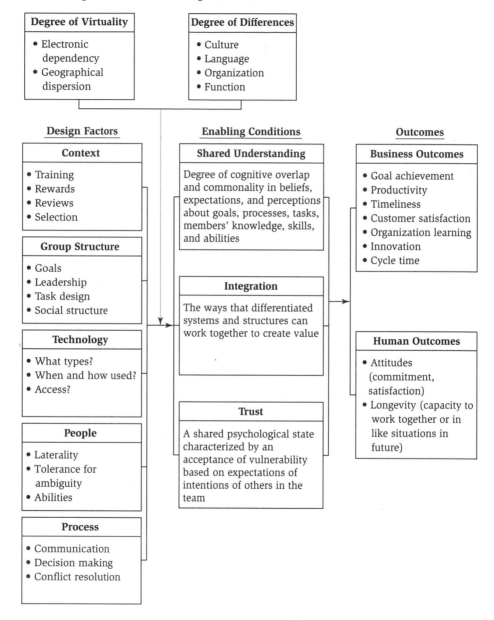

Figure 1.1 Research Framework.

Note: Variables listed under each category are meant as examples; they do not constitute an exhaustive listing.

ROAD MAP TO THE BOOK

This introduction begins this book, followed by five major parts corresponding to our research framework. Part One addresses the enabling conditions and Part Two the supportive organizational contexts for virtual teams. Part Three examines the design of effective virtual teams, Part Four explores implementing information technology to support virtual teams, and Part Five looks at virtual processes and group development. Each part consists of three or four chapters with case studies, anecdotes, and ample examples to demonstrate how the principles identified in the authors' research play out in actual virtual teams. At the end of each chapter are the implications for practice and recommendations for best practices. We as editors provide an introduction and summary to each part to frame the issues, discuss cross-cutting themes, and intersperse practitioner reflections. The book ends with a conclusion and implication chapter that highlights what is special about virtual teams and their advantages and disadvantages, and recommends best practices for leaders, members, and facilitators.

Let the (virtual) fun begin!

References

Alderfer, C. P. "Group and Intergroup Relations." In J. R. Hackman and J. L. Suttle (eds.), *Improving the Quality of Work Life.* Palisades, Calif.: Goodyear, 1977.

Cohen, S. G., and Bailey, D. E. "What Makes Teams Work: Group Effectiveness Research from the Shop Floor to the Executive Suite." *Journal of Management,* 1997, *23*(3), 239–290.

Cummings, L. L., and Bromiley, P. "The Organizational Trust Inventory (OTI): Development and Validation." In R. M. Kramer and T. R. Tyler (eds.), *Trust in Organizations: Frontiers of Theory and Research.* Thousand Oaks, Calif.: Sage, 1996.

Dougherty, D. "Interpretive Barriers to Successful Product Innovation in Large Firms." *Organization Science,* 1992, *3*(2), 179–202.

Hackman, J. R. "The Design of Work Teams." In J. W. Lorsch (ed.), *Handbook of Organizational Behavior.* Upper Saddle River, N.J.: Prentice Hall, 1987.

Hackman, J. R. "Work Teams in Organizations: An Orienting Framework." In J. R. Hackman (ed.), *Groups That Work (and Those That Don't): Creating Conditions for Effective Teamwork.* San Francisco: Jossey-Bass, 1990.

Hackman, J. R., and Oldham, G. R. *Work Redesign.* Reading, Mass.: Addison-Wesley, 1980.

Pinchot, G., III. *Intrapreneuring.* New York: HarperCollins, 1985.

Rousseau, D. M., Sitkin, S. B., Burt, R. S., and Camerer, C. "Not So Different After All: A Cross-Disciplinary View of Trust." *Academy of Management Review,* 1998, *23*(3), 393–404.

ESTABLISHING THE FOUNDATION

*Shared Understanding,
Integration, and Trust*

INTRODUCTION

Shared understanding was not a predictor of anything except effectiveness.
It was an outcome of the way you do work. If you want to create shared
understanding, the thing to operate on is the way that you do work and the
way you work together. You can't just bring people in a room and create shared
understanding. You have to have the work processes that bring people together
continually to share their understanding of what's going on.
—Conference attendee describing shared understanding as a result
of how people work together

Shared understanding, integration, and trust are three enabling conditions for virtual team effectiveness. They cannot be commanded into place but rather must emerge from how virtual teams are designed and managed. Each chapter in Part One examines one of the enabling conditions.

In Chapter Two, Hinds and Weisband assert that shared understanding can have a significant impact on the ability of teams to coordinate work and perform well. They suggest that team members need to have shared understanding and mutual expectations among several dimensions: goals, tasks, work and team processes, and member characteristics and roles. Similar backgrounds and shared experiences help build shared understanding. It is difficult to reach shared understanding in virtual teams because team members are often from different backgrounds and have limited opportunities to have common experiences, as described by a conference attendee who works with a complex virtual team:

> When you're in a colocated context, there's a lot of sharing and shared understanding. Knowledge creation is natural and unrecognized. People don't even know how it's happening or that it's happening. Then when you disrupt that and you put people in different contexts, shared understanding disappears. Why virtual teams are different is that you have to somehow create that inner virtual context. It's very difficult to do that when you don't even know what the context is because it's unrecognized.

Even when shared understanding is reached, it is likely to be in some areas and not in others and to be fleeting. Developing shared understanding in virtual teams is a dynamic process, and managers and team leaders have a key role in facilitating that process. The practitioners and academics at our conference recognized this and agreed with what the following participant voiced:

> So we can't just go in and pour shared understanding in people's heads at the beginning. That helps to jump-start it, but if we then diverge and never reconnect around it, we'll just break apart again in terms of how we understand what we're doing. It's an ongoing task.

In Chapter Three, Mohrman, Klein, and Finegold use a systemic perspective to examine global new product development. They assert that global new product development is more than the sum of multiple virtual and colocated teams; it is a system composed of a set of complex and overlapping task networks, linking multiple product lines, technical knowledge, geographies, and customers. They provide an in-depth case analysis of global product development at an integrated electronics business headquartered in Europe.

Their intriguing argument provides a conceptual link between the requirements for structural integration and the sense-making activities needed to develop shared understanding. In essence, the collaboration they describe is a highly differentiated business entity, with two major product lines, multiple products, modules, subsystems that often vary by country, and multiple innovation and development activities. Given customer needs and the capabilities of software tools and computer systems, integration is a key part of the company's strategy. In order to achieve this integration, people in the differentiated units need to develop shared understandings about the company's strategy, organization, and competency development. Ironically, the opportunity to meet face-to-face and collaborate informally is critical for the sense-making process. Electronically mediated communication does not suffice. A practitioner in our conference from a technology-based firm describes the importance of meeting face-to-face for building shared understanding and for trust:

> Product development teams would rather sacrifice information systems than they would their travel budget. A lot of that has to do with the front-end stuff of forming the team building, the relationship, the social capital, and then at the very end, the whole synergy of moving forward as a team. What we're finding is that relationships based in face-to-face tend to last much longer. The person who is a human link for the team comes with a network of relationships and allows the network of relationships to build that trust with the team.

In Chapter Four, Gibson and Manuel examine trust in multicultural virtual teams. They define collective trust as a shared psychological state on a team characterized by an acceptance of vulnerability (based on Rousseau, Sitkin, Burt, and Camerer, 1998). They provide preliminary evidence for their assertion that the greater the cultural differences, the lower the level of trust on virtual teams. They argue that multiculturalism on virtual teams leads to suboptimal levels of risk and interdependence, which reduces trust.

The practitioners and academics at our conference had much to say about trust. They debated its very definition, but nobody challenged its importance:

When you're virtual, how do you go ahead and establish those shared meanings and that level of intimacy when you don't have the opportunity to meet? And does that mean that there is higher risk to building trust because you don't want to let anyone out of your sight? [conference attendee working with virtual teams].

We have found that task notions of trust based on reliability and responsiveness are likely the most critical in virtual teams.

There are so many different definitions of trust out there. I want to highlight that there are also different perceptions of trust within a virtual team across cultures. So there is cultural variance in terms of what trust is, what is evidence of trust, and how important trust is [conference attendee and academic researcher examining trust].

Gibson and Manuel propose several intercultural communication strategies designed to build trust. The approaches they suggest are the building blocks of effective communication for any setting, virtual or face-to-face. What they argue, however, is that these communication skills are absolutely critical in multicultural virtual settings.

Reference

Rousseau, D. M., Sitkin, S. B., Burt, R. S., and Camerer, C. "Not So Different After All: A Cross-Disciplinary View of Trust." *Academy of Management Review,* 1998, *23*(3), 393–404.

CHAPTER TWO

Knowledge Sharing and Shared Understanding in Virtual Teams

Pamela J. Hinds, Suzanne P. Weisband

Teams by their very nature are interdependent. Although they assign roles, differentiate responsibilities, and hire members with complementary skills, the purpose of teams is to coordinate work toward a common goal. To do so, they must have a shared understanding of the goal toward which they are working and the processes that will help them to achieve that goal. In virtual teams, separated by geographical distance, the process of developing a shared understanding is more challenging. Members of virtual teams rely heavily on mediating technologies for their day-to-day communications, do not share the same work context, and are not geographically proximate. All of these factors conspire to inhibit knowledge sharing and shared understanding on virtual teams. In this chapter, we discuss the importance of shared understanding, the factors that lead to shared understanding, and how these factors may differ on virtual teams. The chapter ends with a discussion of how managers might design and lead virtual teams that are able to triumph over these limitations.

WHY SHARED UNDERSTANDING IS IMPORTANT

Shared understanding—a collective way of organizing relevant knowledge—can have a significant impact on the ability of teams to coordinate work and perform well. There are several ways that shared understanding contributes to

---

This research was supported by National Science Foundation grant IIS9872996.

performance, although these ways are not completely understood. First, having a shared understanding enables people to anticipate and predict the behaviors of their team members and the behavior of the group. When behavior is predictable, more assumptions can be made about what is being done and what needs to be done so that work can move forward without constant monitoring and consultation. Team members can take action without having to check what other team members are doing because they have reached a common understanding of the team's needs. Such independent action enables teams to work like finely tuned machines in which members are acting independently but contributing to the good of the team. Shared understanding also ensures that team members are using resources efficiently and collective effort is minimized. In teams without a common understanding, team members are more likely to hedge their bets against the errors anticipated from others on the team, thus duplicating efforts and increasing the likelihood of rework.

Imagine a situation where a team gets together, discusses a problem, and arrives at a decision—or so they think. A common occurrence on teams is that members think they have come to agreement, but the agreement they believe they have reached is viewed differently by different team members. This can wreak havoc at the time of implementation, with each team member taking actions that may be inconsistent with the actions of others. One famous example of this was with the Mars Climate Orbiter. Team members in different locations (Denver, Colorado, and Pasadena, California) thought that they were all using the same unit of measurement but found out after the spacecraft failed to push itself into orbit that some team members were using English while others were using metric units (Lloyd, 1999). Had the Mars Orbiter team members had a common understanding of their work processes, this multimillion-dollar disaster could have been averted. With a shared understanding of the work processes used and agreements that are reached, team members are more likely to take actions that are consistent with those of others on the team and are likely to result in more rapid and successful implementations.

Shared understanding also can contribute to performance by increasing the satisfaction and motivation of team members. A shared understanding of goals and work processes serves to focus team members on behaviors that will contribute to their success. Goal-directed behavior and a sense of self-efficacy increase people's willingness to work toward the goal. For example, when all members on a software development team understand exactly what function is needed in a system, how the client will be using the system, and the time frame in which it needs to be built, they are better able to focus their energy on building the requested system and believe that they are more likely to succeed.

Predictability, ability to implement agreed-on decisions, and increased motivation all result from shared understanding and contribute to improved team performance. In the absence of shared understanding, negotiation, consultation, and monitoring of what others are doing must take place. Continual negotiation and consultation, especially if done piecemeal and not with the entire team, can lead to conflicts, heightened frustration, and mistrust among team members. In summary, shared understanding among team members has these benefits:

- Enables people to predict the behaviors of team members
- Facilitates efficient use of resources and effort
- Reduces implementation problems and errors
- Increases satisfaction and motivation of team members
- Reduces frustration and conflict among team members

DIMENSIONS OF SHARED UNDERSTANDING

Shared understanding is a collective way of organizing and communicating relevant knowledge, as a way of collaborating. In his book *No More Teams!* (1995), Schrage defines the act of collaboration as "two or more individuals with complementary skills interacting to create a shared understanding that none had previously possessed or could have come to on their own" (p. 33). Collaboration is more than exchanging information. As Schrage notes, "Collaboration creates a shared meaning about a process, a product, or an event. . . . It can occur by mail [or e-mail], over the phone lines, and in person" (p. 33).

To develop a shared understanding among members of a team, people need to learn together, relate to one another, and develop mutual expectations along several dimensions, including the nature of their goals, their job or task, the processes required to perform their task, the team interactions that support task accomplishment, and information about the characteristics and activities of team members themselves.

A common understanding of the goals and objectives of a team is crucial for an effective team. Clear, unambiguous goals define the work content of the task, provide a basis for clear communication, focus attention on the desired goal, make clear how each team member can contribute to the goal, and challenge the team to make progress toward the goal (Katzenbach and Smith, 1993). It is important not only to share a common goal, but also to have a common understanding of it. For example, on one engineering project, the U.S. and European teams had different definitions of product quality goals, and these differences caused unexpected conflicts and delays. The team members were never able to overcome the mistrust between them and the project failed. A shared understanding of the team's goals ensures that the team is moving together toward a common vision.

Related to common goals is a shared understanding of the task itself. A satellite design team may share a goal of putting a satellite into space but have different views of what is required to do that. What are the dimensions of the task? How do different aspects of the task relate to others? Shared understanding of the task is akin to team members' mental model of the activity in which they are engaged. To the extent that teams have a shared understanding of the task, they will be able to anticipate with confidence the decisions of other team members and know that those decisions will complement their own activities on the task.

Team members benefit from a shared understanding of the interaction anticipated among team members, including roles and responsibilities, interdependencies, communication patterns, and expectations for the flow of information. Having a common understanding of how the team will interact contributes to a more effective team process, including coordination, communication, and cooperation among team members (Mathieu and others, 2000). Team members who are confident about whom to go to, what information to provide to other team members, the media expected for various communications, and so forth are more likely to have a mutually shared perspective for anticipating and predicting the actions of others. Furthermore, such predictability in team member behaviors is likely to engender trust among members.

Teams also benefit from having a shared understanding about the characteristics and activities of team members themselves. For example, teams that learn where the expertise resides on the team are much more efficient at accessing that expertise (Liang, Moreland, and Argote, 1995). It is also helpful to know what team members are doing on an ongoing basis. This is so that team members can gauge progress against a goal, know when their help may be needed, and know when team members are out sick, on vacation, or having personal problems that may have an impact on the team's performance.

There is some evidence that all of these types of shared understanding can contribute to team performance, especially for teams that are highly interdependent, working on more ambiguous tasks, and need to move quickly and be adaptable. For example, Mathieu and his colleagues (2000) demonstrated that teams using an advanced computer-generated program to simulate missions with the F-16 fighter aircraft performed better at meeting their mission objectives if they had a shared understanding of both the way the team worked together and of the task itself.

WHAT LEADS TO SHARED UNDERSTANDING

A number of factors contribute to shared understanding, including having similar backgrounds, having a base of shared experiences, having the opportunity to learn about each other over time, communicating and sharing information, and developing a team spirit.

Not surprisingly, having a similar background or perspective to begin with helps to develop a shared understanding. To the extent that team members are trained in the same field (for example, civil engineering or finance), have worked in the same organization, and have been involved in similar activities, they will more likely begin the project with a more common understanding of the task, the expected team interactions, and the project goals. Diversity on any dimension, including demographic diversity, is likely to detract from shared understanding because diversity leads to different perspectives even when the objective information remains the same. For example, in our work with construction teams, we found that architects and construction engineers often had completely different perspectives on and proposed quite different solutions to the same problem.

Sharing experiences also builds shared understanding. For example, training teams together builds a shared understanding of a task and of the location of the expertise on the team. Because shared understanding often results from shared experiences, more shared experiences can contribute to higher levels of shared understanding. For example, a blind or no-look pass in basketball (where one player throws the ball to a teammate without looking) depends in part on the passer's shared experiences with the team, allowing the passer to predict where teammates are likely to be (Cannon-Bowers and Salas, 2001). Thus, the longer the team has been working together, the easier it should be to create shared understanding.

Communication and information sharing among team members also contribute to shared understanding. Communication provides the opportunity to talk through problems, share perspectives, get feedback, and answer questions that arise among team members. Collaboration among team members is required for shared meaning and shared understanding to develop (Donnellon, Gray, and Bougon, 1986). Without communication, misunderstandings are more frequent and more difficult to resolve.

SHARED UNDERSTANDING IN VIRTUAL TEAMS

On virtual teams, shared understanding is more difficult to generate. Members of virtual teams rely heavily on technology to mediate their interactions, often have different environments in which they are working and technologies supporting their work, and are geographically distant from one another. Each of these factors affects shared understanding. The relationship between these factors and the antecedents to shared understanding are summarized in Figure 2.1. To illustrate these relationships, we draw on data and examples from two laboratory studies (a study of student project teams and a field study of colocated and geographically distributed product development teams) and examples from the literature. The laboratory studies compared distributed

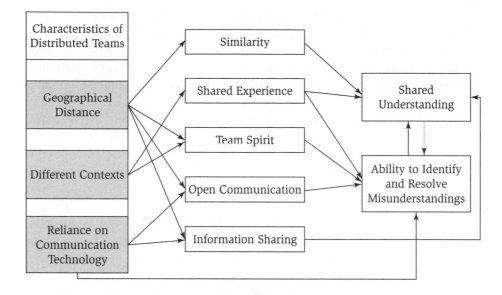

Figure 2.1 The Effects of Team Characteristics on Shared Understanding.

versus colocated dyads whose task was to separately collect environmental data within a building (for example, temperature, humidity, light levels, and air movement) and together determine the condition of the building. It is important to note that dyads are not typically thought of as teams. However, by conducting laboratory studies with dyads, the complexity of the studies is reduced, and questions of interest can more easily be isolated. What we learn from these laboratory studies can then be applied to help us explain what we observe in virtual teams.

EFFECTS OF GEOGRAPHICAL DISTANCE

Virtual teams, because of the geographical distance separating members, rely more heavily on communication and information technologies to facilitate interaction and coordinate work than members who share a common physical environment. Physical proximity—how closely people are located to one another—makes it easy for people to gather together to work on tasks or hold formal project meetings. People in a common environment are also more likely to engage in casual conversations, thereby allowing them to identify common interests and goals.

Teams are more successful at coordinating their activities if they can keep aware of how the team is doing. This may include knowing whether team members will complete their part of the work on time, do the work they said they would do, or be available to work over an upcoming weekend. When people share a physical work environment, feedback about what others are doing is immediate and can be accomplished with very little effort. Group members, for instance, can observe who attends meetings or participates in hallway conversations in which the group's progress is discussed. They can glance at another person to see if he or she is working, or they can hear the sound of a particular machine and know what work is being done.

The presence of others increases familiarity along multiple dimensions. When we are present with others on a day-to-day basis, we get to know about their family life, vacation plans, favorite books, feelings about the organization, and attitudes toward work. This knowledge about and familiarity with one another increases rapport and shared identity. For example, in our study comparing colocated and virtual product development teams, we found that members of colocated teams were more strongly identified with the team and with the company but less identified with their profession than were members of virtual teams. Although rapport does not directly affect shared understanding, it is likely to improve knowledge sharing and make it easier to identify and resolve issues that arise. People who are distant from one another are less likely to share information freely and less likely to pay attention to information from their distant team members. Thus, members of virtual teams can be expected to have more difficulty developing a shared group identity and attending to the information that flows among team members. Such a lack of attention may reduce shared understanding in virtual teams.

Another reason to expect a link between distance and shared understanding is that distance makes it less likely that informal, unintentional information will be shared. For example, many of the project teams we have observed have common bulletin boards and team spaces that display information (such as schedules and accomplishments) relevant to the team. They frequently meet in the hallways, have lunch together, and overhear and participate in conversations at the coffee machine. Although some of these information-laden interactions are intentional, many of them are not planned, and people often are not even aware of the information that has been shared. Because these interactions are unplanned and opportunistic, they occur far less frequently with distant colleagues. In one study of students performing a measurement task, we found that people who were distant knew less about what their team members were doing and the way they were gathering measurement information. Although those in distant dyads as compared with colocated dyads talked more about their individual process, less understanding was reached. This is largely because colocated workers can see what their teammates are doing. They can observe their activities and develop, without communicating directly, a deep understanding of their team members' work process.

Physical distance also often brings with it dissimilarity. Because distance often means different regional or national cultures, different organizational cultures, and different perspectives on work, members of teams raised and trained in different environments often have different views of how the work should be performed and may use different work processes (an example is metric versus English measurements). Distant teams also are more likely to be demographically dissimilar than colocated teams. In our study of product development teams, we found that the greater the distance, the greater the demographic dissimilarity among team members: virtual teams had more ethnic diversity and more diversity in educational background. Teams with high levels of diversity bring different perspectives, and thus start out with a narrower base of shared understanding than teams similar on many demographic dimensions, such as ethnicity, culture, and gender.

EFFECTS OF UNSHARED CONTEXT

Along with physical distance often come differences in context. Contextual differences are revealed in different work and geographical environments, different technologies, and different cultures. For example, in a project described by Davenport and Prusak (1998), drilling equipment experts at British Petroleum headquarters remotely assisted engineers on a mobile drilling ship in the North Sea. The work, weather conditions, and close quarters on a drilling ship undoubtedly created a different work atmosphere from what would be expected at headquarters. These contextual differences can make it more difficult to develop a shared understanding. When using new machines in a factory, for example, engineers and users had trouble resolving equipment problems over the telephone because the engineers needed to see firsthand the technology and the way it was being used in context (Tyre and von Hippel, 1997). Shared understanding is more difficult to achieve in teams with different contexts because they do not share the same experiences.

Only part of the problem of different work contexts concerns the shared physical environment. Distance often means different regional, national, and organizational cultures. For example, team members from more individualistic (such as the United States) as compared with collectivist (such as Japan and Singapore) cultures often have different attitudes toward hierarchies and different beliefs about how dissenting opinions are expressed. To the extent that virtual team members are embedded in dissimilar social structures, the context influencing their behavior is likely to be different. For example, Karnoe (1995) observed that Danish and American workers used different paradigms for understanding problems and potential solutions and attributed these differences to disparities in local routines and behavioral norms. Operating in different cultures with different norms and expectations can interfere with the development of shared understanding because communication misunderstandings are more likely.

To compound the problems of different work contexts, people with different perspectives often neglect to share information that would help their partners understand the context in which they are working. They may not think to mention that a winter storm is approaching or that a power outage occurred the day before. They rarely mention the type of technology they are using to perform their work or the measurement units they used to calculate equations. Thus, not only do contextual differences exist for virtual teams, they also may be particularly difficult to identify. In face-to-face teams, this is less of an issue because people are able to observe the work of others casually, thus informally and inadvertently sharing contextual information. For example, a manager of a virtual software development group told us about the difficulties he had in getting all of the information he needed from distant sites:

> You really miss out on the informal discussions that happen in a hallway or at lunch, having a cup of coffee—you know, someone finds out something and it's, "Oh, I needed to know that." It avoids problems ahead of time. When you're not colocated, it becomes harder to have this type of communication. I would call the primary task leader on one job every day, maybe a couple of times a day, and he would call me. There still at times would be things that we should have communicated to each other but we did not, and I think if we had been in the same building and ran into each other at various times during the day, it would have happened.

EFFECTS OF TECHNOLOGIES

Communication technologies such as telephone, voice mail, e-mail, videoconferencing, and instant messaging all help members of virtual teams stay in touch with one another and share information. However, these technologies have limitations that can easily lead to misinterpretation. They cannot provide the same richness as face-to-face interaction. Because of delays in transmission and the lack of social and nonverbal cues, communication technologies can interfere with open communication, knowledge sharing, and the ability of teams to identify and resolve misunderstandings.

Face-to-face interaction provides rich social information not available through most communication technologies. The social information that flows among team members increases the comfort and ease of communication, thus enabling more self-disclosure. Communicating face-to-face is also physically easier than communicating over media that require typing or holding a telephone. Therefore, people are more likely to talk longer and do so with more ease when face-to-face.

For this reason, knowledge sharing is less likely to take place when people must type out complex ideas or try to hold a telephone conversation for an extended period of time.

Knowledge sharing also takes place less often over mediated technologies because people have more difficulty sharing complex knowledge. Although basic information may be shared, there is less elaboration on the meaning of the information, and therefore less understanding is reached. When interacting face-to-face, people rely heavily on voice intonation, facial expressions, and gestures for cues to help interpret meaning. For example, when troubleshooting an electronic component, people often will point to the circuit board or a diagram and gesture to describe how the circuits are built and where the problems lie. They point to these objects of reference and use them to develop shared understanding and confirm that a shared understanding has been reached. In the absence of rich auditory and visual cues, reaching understanding is inhibited.

Mediated communication also makes it more difficult to identify and resolve misunderstandings that arise. Visual and auditory cues provide important indicators that help us to understand when meaning is and is not being conveyed. For example, a puzzled look tells communication partners that their communication may not have been fully understood. This signal gives an opportunity for the communicator to repair the communication and ensure understanding. Without these cues, misunderstandings may never be identified or addressed.

There are, of course, differences among technologies in the amount of information that can be conveyed and the ease with which miscommunication can be detected and resolved. E-mail, for example, affords the exchange of vast amounts of detailed, archivable information. However, people generally read their e-mail without the benefit of the sender's observing their reaction and identifying points of possible misunderstanding. E-mail allows little in the way of real-time feedback and can lead to extensive information sharing without the same level of shared understanding. In fact, it can lead to the illusion of shared understanding because team members believe that the information has been shared. For example, in the measurement experiment, dyads communicating by e-mail often incorrectly assumed that they were using the same process as their partner when gathering data independently. As a result, the dyads interacting using e-mail as compared with face-to-face demonstrated less of a shared understanding of the task they were performing.

The telephone is a somewhat better technology for reaching shared understanding because more social cues are available and both parties are participating at the same time. However, the telephone lacks visual cues and does not comfortably enable more than two people to participate at once. Conference calls are notoriously difficult to manage and tend to preclude extensive information sharing. In one team spread throughout the United States, a team member described their monthly conference calls as effective for decision making, but indicated that little knowledge was shared and few questions asked because interactions were heavily constrained by a facilitator. Still, some evidence shows that the telephone may be better than text-based systems for detecting and resolving misunderstandings. For example, one team member told us that talking face-to-face or by telephone helped her to understand her team members better: "For myself it helps a lot to have met the people in person rather than just sending e-mails or even talking over the phone because then you sort of know how that person expresses himself or herself."

The most promising communication media for developing shared understanding appear to be high-quality videoconferencing and shared work spaces. With videoconferencing, more of the social cues are available, so visual information like gestures can be conveyed, understanding can be evaluated through unspoken feedback like facial expressions, and repairs can be made. Evidence for this was found in a study in which one participant told another where to draw a path on a map (Veinott, Olson, Olson, and Fu, 1999). When members of the pair had a less common background, video helped them to understand the instructions being given and participants more accurately recreated the path. Another benefit of videoconferencing is that more parties can participate, thus making it more likely that all team members will receive the same information at the same time. However, videoconferencing brings with it a new set of problems. Often, virtual teams do not use videoconferencing because it is not reliable, technical support and training are not readily available, conversation is awkward because the quality of the image and sound are poor or out of sync, and the cost is prohibitive, causing team members to hang up without sharing essential information or avoiding the technology altogether. A recent study of the introduction of desktop videoconferencing into a large organization also reported that concerns about others' videotaping or listening in on their conversations discouraged the use of videoconferencing (Webster, 1998).

Although training and privacy may still be concerns, shared work or team spaces may be fairly promising technologies for alleviating some of the problems with shared understanding in virtual teams. Shared work spaces are electronic spaces in which team members can work together on documents or objects. They can see the actions of others and draw or write their own comments during a common session. Shared work spaces provide a limited amount of shared context, at least with regard to a particular activity. Shared team spaces provide the team with an electronic place, generally on the Web, in which they can communicate, share, and store documents. For example, researchers at Lucent Technologies have developed a presence awareness and instant messaging tool that they call Rear View Mirror (RVM). RVM enables informal communication between team members by one-to-one or group chat, information about who is available and where, and awareness of others' work activities (Atkins and others, 2000). Although the information-sharing component of these team spaces may prove to be valuable, we believe that one of the most valuable aspects of the team spaces is the team identity and team spirit that can be triggered. In addition, shared workspaces provide some shared experience that may translate into greater shared understanding over time.

IMPLICATIONS FOR PRACTICE

The picture portrayed so far is not a positive one. We have argued that virtual teams will share less information and develop less shared understanding than colocated teams and that this may have negative effects on performance. However, there are ways to ameliorate these effects.

To increase shared understanding in virtual teams, managers can start by composing teams with members who have similar backgrounds. Teams that have similar backgrounds—professional or demographic—are likely to find it easier to identify and resolve differences that arise. For example, a member of one of the silicon chip design teams we studied told us that one of the reasons that their virtual team was successful was that all team members had the same disciplinary background, which contributed to a deeper friendship than would have otherwise existed given their geographical distance.

Of course, it is not always practical to compose teams of similar members, and doing so can interfere with other objectives. For example, in product development teams, cross-functional expertise is often desired to spur innovation. Also, creating cross-cultural teams can be an important way to ensure that product designs take into account the diverse needs of different cultural groups. But even when team diversity is desired or managers do not have the luxury of selecting from a large pool of qualified candidates, the team members can view themselves as similar. One strategy is to make sure that team members are aware of their similarities. Especially if their common background is not apparent, a manager can help to establish common ground by identifying and pointing out to team members where they share interests or experiences. For instance, managers can point out shared hobbies, shared family situations, and so forth. These similarities can go a long way toward establishing rapport among team members. On this foundation, shared understanding can be built.

In addition to pointing out similarities at the start of a project, managers can facilitate shared understanding by continuing to facilitate the sharing of task, team, and personal information. For example, Weisband (forthcoming) found that teams that shared information about where they were and what they were doing performed better than teams that did not share this information. In a research study of geographically dispersed student project teams, four-person teams had just thirty-six days to complete the project: deciding what they would work on and how it would be carried out, and then moving forward to accomplish their group goals and produce a successful joint outcome. The project consisted of selecting a policy topic, and researching and writing a five-page policy paper. The project was designed to simulate work in short-term distributed teams. All discussions took place on a Web-based conferencing system or using e-mail, and all teams had one project leader. The results from this study showed that teams performed better when team members were more aware of what others were doing by asking others on the team for information about their whereabouts, availability, and progress. Such active, intentional sharing of task and contextual information, though effortful and time-consuming, can be critical to project success. Weisband's study also showed that leaders who shared "awareness" information acted as role models, setting a pattern that encouraged their team members to behave similarly. Leaders who kept the team on task and created awareness about the team members' progress in doing their work were more successful.

The team members and the manager should be sensitive to sharing the right information at the right time. One of the most critical points is at the beginning of a project. At the start of a project, managers can improve shared understanding by encouraging the sharing of personal information (for example, on expertise, personal interests, and work habits) and ensuring that high-level goals are agreed on. As the project progresses, the manager should encourage team members to share information about day-to-day activities, especially any deviations (no matter how small) from the agreed-on plan. Managers who are aware of the knowledge that does and does not reside at each site can make a significant contribution by ensuring that essential knowledge is transferred among sites.

One of the ways to ensure information sharing in virtual teams is to have face-to-face meetings among team members. In our study of product development teams, team members consistently told us that they gained tremendous benefits from the face-to-face meetings they had with their team members from other sites. It is especially important that these meetings take place early in the process so that rapport and common ground can be established before misconceptions arise.

We caution against the strategy of staging an off-site retreat. One of the benefits to be gained from face-to-face meetings is the sharing of contextual information. For that reason, we recommend meetings at project sites or meetings that enable team members to visit each others' work locations. The benefits of on-site meetings were evidenced in one of the virtual product development teams we studied. The team was split between Canada and Mexico. Prior to meeting face-to-face, the Canadian team members thought that their Mexican colleagues were lazy and unresponsive. When the teams met on-site in Mexico, the Canadian team members were embarrassed to discover that although they all worked for the same company, the Mexican office had far fewer resources (such as administrative support and technology) and the Mexican team members' level of productivity was quite high given their work context. This new understanding resulted in more trust between team members and a fairer allocation of work.

Where possible, we also believe that significant benefit can be gained if team members can work at the distant site for a short period of time to develop a deeper understanding of their team members' work context. One of the semiconductor firms we studied made a habit of doing this. Their teams would convene for a month or more at one of the project sites and work together. The managers of these teams felt that the teams were much better able to coordinate work after having worked closely together at a single site.

Other opportunities for face-to-face interaction include team training sessions and customer visits. Training teams together is an effective way to establish a shared base of experience, common work practices, and a clear understanding of where the expertise resides in the group. Such a foundation will contribute to the building of shared understanding over time. One member of a product development team we interviewed described the benefit he received by visiting a customer with his distant team members: "We were actually out in the field, all of us together in one place. We were there for an entire week, down in Georgia, and working long hours and really putting in a lot of effort to pull something together. A lot of interaction and bonding went on there."

It is important to note that the benefits of face-to-face meetings and training sessions will degrade over time. It is beneficial to facilitate these interactions early but also important to sustain the bonds that are established. Therefore, managers, particularly on fast-paced, highly interdependent projects, should stage regular (annual at least) meetings and encourage team members to visit the other sites periodically.

Another way to facilitate shared understanding in virtual teams is to increase team spirit or team identity. Managers can increase team identity by ensuring that the team has an overriding goal in which team members believe. In addition, selecting a meaningful team name and creating a shared electronic work space can convey a sense of team spirit and act as a constant reminder of team identity.

One of the other phenomena that present a particular problem for shared understanding in virtual teams is turnover. When team members leave, their replacements have none of the shared experience built up by the team. All of the initial work of building a solid foundation is costly and time-consuming to reestablish in virtual teams. Managers must strive to retain team members and ensure stability in virtual teams.

CONCLUSION

Shared understanding in teams can lead to improved performance by helping teams to anticipate the behavior of others, better coordinate their work by improving implementation, and increase team members' motivation. However, it can be more difficult to achieve shared understanding in virtual teams. One of the project managers of a virtual software development team we interviewed summarized the problems she has experienced in managing a virtual team: "When you break it down, it's really information flow. How do you keep everybody in sync on strategies and the priorities of effort and make sure you've got the right folks who are doing the job and are putting forth the effort? It's a major challenge for the engineering community to keep up."

Some of these problems stem from reliance on communication technologies, some from having different contexts, and some from simply being miles (or thousands of miles) away from one another. Taken together, being virtual can lead to reduced similarity, fewer shared experiences, less team spirit or identity, less open communication, and less information sharing—all factors that reduce shared understanding on teams either directly or because differences become too difficult to identify and resolve.

Members and managers of virtual teams can combat these problems to some extent. Members can make a point of sharing information and intentionally keeping their distant team members in the loop, and managers can facilitate this process by being aware of where information resides and what should be shared. Managers also can help build rapport and provide opportunities for interaction among team members as a way to increase commitment and comfort with information sharing and identification of misunderstandings.

In summary, we recommend the following practices for facilitating shared understanding in virtual teams:

- Compose teams in which members have similar backgrounds.
- Highlight and emphasize similarities among team members.
- Facilitate sharing of personal information, especially early in the project.
- Facilitate sharing of information about day-to-day activities throughout the project.
- Identify essential knowledge that is needed on the project, and make sure that this knowledge is shared, especially across sites.
- Encourage face-to-face meetings with team members early in the project and periodically throughout longer, more difficult projects.
- Encourage team members to visit the work locations of other team members.
- Build a strong team identity.
- Keep turnover low.
- Provide easy access to and support for (including training and technical support) videoconferencing and on-line team spaces.

References

Atkins, D., and others. "Achieving Speed in Globally Distributed Project Work." Paper presented at the Human-Computer Interaction Consortium meetings, Winterpark, Colo., 2000.

Cannon-Bowers, J., and Salas, E. "Reflections on Shared Cognition." *Journal of Organizational Behavior,* 2001, *22,* 195–202.

Davenport, T. H., and Prusak, L. *Working Knowledge: How Organizations Manage What They Know.* Cambridge, Mass.: Harvard Business School Press, 1998.

Donnellon, S., Gray, B., and Bougon, M. G. "Communication, Meaning, and Organized Action." *Administrative Science Quarterly,* 1986, *31,* 43–55.

Karnoe, P. "Competence as Process and the Social Embeddedness of Competence Building." *Academy of Management Journal Best Paper Proceedings,* 1995, pp. 427–431.

Katzenbach, J., and Smith, D. "The Discipline of Teams." *Harvard Business Review,* 1993, *71,* 111–120.

Liang, D. W., Moreland, R., and Argote, L. "Group Versus Individual Training and Group Performance: The Mediating Factor of Transactive Memory." *Personality and Social Psychology Bulletin,* 1995, *21,* 384–393.

Lloyd, R. "Metric Mishap Caused Loss of NASA Orbiter." [http://www10.cnn.com/TECH/space/9909/30/mars.metric.02]. Sept. 30, 1999.

Mathieu, J., and others. "The Influence of Shared Mental Models on Team Process and Performance." *Journal of Applied Psychology,* 2000, *85,* 273–283.

Schrage, M. *No More Teams! Mastering the Dynamics of Creative Collaboration.* New York: Doubleday, 1995.

Tyre, M., and von Hippel, E. "The Situated Nature of Learning in Organizations." *Organization Science,* 1997, *8,* 71–83.

Veinott, E., Olson, J., Olson, G., and Fu, X. "Video Helps Remote Work: Speakers Who Need to Negotiate Common Ground Benefit from Seeing Each Other." Paper presented at the Computer-Human Interaction (CHI) Conference Proceedings, Pittsburgh, Pa., 1999.

Webster, J. "Desktop Videoconferencing: Experiences of Complete Users, Wary Users, and Non-Users." *MIS Quarterly,* 1998, *22*(3), 257–286.

Weisband, S. "Maintaining Awareness in Distributed Team Collaboration: Implications for Leadership and Performance." In P. Hinds and S. Kiesler (eds.), *Distributed Work.* Cambridge, Mass.: MIT Press, forthcoming.

CHAPTER THREE

Managing the Global New Product Development Network

A Sense-Making Perspective

Susan Albers Mohrman, Janice A. Klein, David Finegold

Firms developing products with global applications must build competencies to connect and leverage knowledge on a worldwide basis (Bartlett and Ghoshal, 1998). This means reaching out globally to secure the best talent available at the most reasonable cost. It also requires new organizational approaches to manage knowledge, products, geographies, and customers simultaneously (Galbraith, 2000). Traditional bureaucratic designs that are built around vertical control and the partition of work into lateral segments such as functions and country units are no longer sufficient. Instead, new organizational models have emerged that facilitate work that occurs through dynamic configurations of teams (Jelinek and Schoonhoven, 1990; Brown and Eisenhardt, 1997) and cross-cutting processes that extend across diverse and dispersed knowledge centers (Mohrman, Cohen, and Mohrman, 1995; Nonaka and Takeuchi, 1995).

Global new product development takes place through a complex network of relationships and interdependencies that cut across countries. It cannot simply be conceived of as the aggregation of multiple virtual and colocated teams; rather, it must be viewed as a system composed of a set of complex and overlapping task networks, typically linking multiple product lines and several geographies. The system is saturated with work process and knowledge interdependencies (Pava, 1983). Accomplishing the strategic intent of the global firm depends on the sense-making processes in the organization: it requires that shared meanings guide these many activities.

This chapter draws on an in-depth case study of a firm that is doing global new product development to explore the role of sense making in new product development organizations.

SENSE MAKING AND GLOBAL PRODUCT DEVELOPMENT

To take maximum advantage of the innovation-creating capabilities of the global firm, the different elements of the new product development system must be aware of and connected to the larger system, and the larger system must be responsive to and able to incorporate the knowledge that is generated in its various subunits. Organizations must therefore develop the capacity to innovate in dispersed development centers and diffuse new knowledge among local units and back to the center (Bartlett and Ghoshal, 1998; Nohria and Ghoshal, 1997). Operating in this way is easy to describe at the macrolevel but requires building a great deal of shared understanding throughout the system.

Product development organizations have been described as sense-making systems that connect technological capability to market uses (Dougherty, Borrelli, Munir, and O'Sullivan, 2000). Their effectiveness depends on how well the system imports, interprets, shares, applies, and generates new technological and market knowledge. That knowledge is a combination of information, experience, context, interpretation, and reflection (Davenport, De Long, and Beers, 1998). It is socially constructed and emerges from social processes through which shared understandings are developed and become incorporated into beliefs and activities. Therefore, innovation is a collective process that entails making sense of new and diverse information and incorporating this knowledge into new methodologies, products, and services (Nonaka and Takeuchi, 1995; Dougherty, 2001; Leonard-Barton, 1995).

New product development entails both tacit and codified, articulated knowledge. Innovative ideas may stem from individuals who go beyond codified knowledge as they learn from their experiences dealing with particular technical challenges and addressing particular customer needs. Their tacit knowledge can become organizational knowledge as it is interpreted by and embedded in the work of teams. These teams in turn interact and further diffuse the knowledge to affect work throughout the organization (Nonaka and Takeuchi, 1995). It becomes part of the articulated knowledge of the organization as it is embedded in product concepts, methods and procedures, technology and product evolution maps, and strategies.

Sense making in the new product development system is by necessity virtual. It occurs simultaneously within and across different levels and elements of the organizational system. New customer understanding that emerges from experiences developing a product for a particular customer set may become incorporated into corporatewide or business unit strategies and product concepts. Changing business strategies often infuse the work of particular teams or individuals with new meaning. Sense making also occurs within and across different streams of activities by those who operate in different geographies, carry out different processes, and attend to different customers and markets. For example, as a new approach to product testing and validation is developed in response to the requirements of a particular customer set, this approach may become incorporated into the practice of other business units and product lines. Knowledge of a particular customer gained by one product line may enrich another product line unit's understanding of the same customer and result in new and perhaps coordinated approaches.

Sense making typically occurs through either interactive collaboration or alignment frameworks.[1] Using interactive collaboration, groups interpret information, such as by jointly exploring novel approaches to solving technical problems or collectively defining solutions and applications. Organizations also use alignment frameworks to create contextually embedded shared understandings about such matters as roles, rules and routines, strategies, and product concepts. These generic frameworks shape meaning through the organization without requiring participation in an interactive interpretative process. The organization's innovative capacity depends on maintaining a dynamic interchange between these two kinds of sense making. The sense making that occurs through the interactive collaboration pertaining to particular situations and activities can be incorporated into the alignment frameworks such as strategy and the architecture of systems of products. The meaning embedded in these alignment frameworks in turn provides meaning that infuses the sense making in particular new product development activities (see Figure 3.1).

Our case analysis examines three domains where sense making is needed to foster global product development: the linking of product development activities to strategy, the integration of knowledge related to the ongoing technical task of generating new products, and the enhancement of the organization's new product development capabilities.[2] In all three domains, we will see the use of both interactive collaboration and alignment frameworks and will examine barriers to and enablers of the sense making required for successful global new product development.

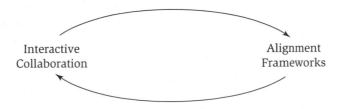

Interactive Collaboration   Alignment Frameworks

Figure 3.1 Iterative Sense Making.

THE GLOBAL NEW PRODUCT DEVELOPMENT SYSTEM: A CASE EXAMPLE

Techco, an integrated electronics business headquartered in Europe, contains a global knowledge network with many different innovation and development activities that must unfold in an integrated manner. It has two major product lines, each focusing on different types of electronic devices that are often used by the same customers but for different purposes. Techco's products have evolved from mechanical to computerized devices, with the vast majority of value delivered embedded in software. In the past, these product line business units were able to operate independently of one another, although sharing some common services and technology. Given the capabilities of today's software tools and computer systems, planning for the integration of the products of these two business units has begun, and integration is part of Techco's long-range strategy.

Each of the product line organizations designs and produces multiple products, modules, and subsystems, which often vary by country. Because of the variety of industries making up the customer base and the large differences in the user systems across industries and geographies, there are many variations in the applications that are provided. New modules and products are being developed within an overarching architecture to enable integration and global application. The company is moving toward a new generation of devices that represents a discontinuous development path, entailing costly development that must be recouped by increasing its global market share. Given the magnitude of customers' investment in existing devices and the cost to change technologies, Techco feels that the new generation must be designed in a modular manner that enables gradual migration from the existing systems, another strategy that requires an integrated global development network.

Through a series of acquisitions, Techco has developed a global presence, including development capabilities on multiple continents, occurring in close proximity to customers around the world. The largest concentration of development activities resides in two European cities, each the headquarters for one of the product line businesses. They are located within easy commuting distance, allowing easy access for face-to-face interactions. The software development teams include members from other locations, in Europe, North America, and Asia, which are viewed as global centers for specific technical competencies. Several recent global acquisitions provided new, overlapping, and sometimes redundant product capabilities. Each business went through a strategy process of deciding how best to integrate these globally dispersed development capabilities, including articulating a development path to an integrated product line, eliminating redundant technological development, and determining what development work would be done in which locations or by teams that cut across the locations.[3]

Techco is experiencing growth in its worldwide business and is successfully introducing a new generation of products. However, it is having more difficulty than expected to integrate its development activities and take advantage of newly acquired talent and the proximity of development activities to customers outside its home base. Growth outside Europe has been slower than planned, and management is questioning whether they are receiving adequate return from their investment in worldwide product development capabilities.

By examining the sense-making processes Techco employs and the challenges it has experienced, we can better define the requirements for the global integration of new product development activities.

Sense Making Around Strategy

Strategy for successful new product development includes the value proposition of the firm, the outcomes sought, the investments that will be made in pursuit of the capability to deliver on the value proposition, and deployment of resources (Dougherty, 2001). Strategy is a core alignment framework in the knowledge system: it relates the loose configuration of teams and projects to the larger system, provides direction and meaning to work, and determines what knowledge needs to be acquired, generated, and leveraged (Nonaka and Takeuchi, 1995; Zack, 1999). Sense making for innovation entails linking strategic understanding across locations and simultaneously focusing on established and emerging technology and market requirements (Jelinek and Schoonhoven, 1990). This is especially true at Techco because its strategy entails building the capability to make the transition from the current hard-wired devices to the emerging distributed, software-based technology that is being developed in large part in its subsidiaries. Four aspects of the strategy domain emerged from the interviews as particularly vital to the integration of the global network and yet posing considerable challenges: achieving understanding and awareness of strategy throughout the network, gaining shared understanding of the organizational strategy to support it, integrating local and global customers and markets, and balancing development of current versus disruptive technology.

Understanding and Awareness of Strategy. In the headquarters location, all levels, including the individual engineers, expressed a clear sense of the strategy and understood the need for a dual strategy of extending the reach of the current product to new geographies while developing the solutions and technologies that will cannibalize the market:

> We can't live on our current product family and technology forever. It's become a kind of commodity product, and we have price erosion. We're giving a lot of consideration to how we go about maintaining our business while coming up with these new solutions. There's a paradigm shift. We're starting a new s-curve and moving to component-based architecture [executive in Europe].

It was not just the executives in Europe who were able to articulate the strategy and feel that they knew what it meant for their activities. The European engineers working on product development were remarkably consistent in their renditions of the strategy and their belief that it was clear. They reported meetings and discussions where the strategy was discussed, and decisions were guided by it. An engineer in Europe reported, "There is a clear strategy. We have a vision of what is going to happen ten to twenty years out, and that's why we have projects trying to picture systems that run without any of our current products. Someone is going to cannibalize them, and it may as well be us."

By contrast, both managers and engineers in North America expressed strategic confusion. "I'm in a microcosm," said a manager in North America. "It seems as if there is some vision coming from here and some vision coming from Europe. I really am not privy to them, but I don't think that they are always the same."

Shared Understanding of the Organizing Strategy. A strategic activity core to building the innovative capabilities of Techco's global network was determining the role of each of the dispersed units in the organization in contributing to corporate strategy. The organizational strategy emerged in discussion and negotiation with the engineering directors from all the subsidiaries. North American sites were to be competency centers, tasked with taking the lead in developing key aspects of the new technology:

> There are some principles that we have created in the last year, and we've transported them to all locations. It's very important to give each global development center a known identity in terms of competence. If you try to use global development centers like many other companies using software engineers from India or test engineers in Japan, it won't work. The United States is the country of software and personal computers, so we decided to build on that expertise with a North American center of excellence [senior manager in Europe].

Yet given Techco's technology migration strategy, these North American sites were faced with the challenge of managing a unit tasked with innovating while having strong connections to the larger system:

> It is disruptive technology to our existing business. It would never see the light of day if done in Europe, as it's too threatening to them. Yet ideas come from the current devices family. We've been set up as a separate group and are seeding our work with some key technical people from the existing product family to transfer their know-how [executive expatriate working in North America who had been involved in the original strategy development].

But North American line engineers, who had not been privy to the strategic discussions, could not make sense of this nuanced strategy and felt they were receiving mixed messages. One of these engineers said, "The original intent that we would be a center of excellence brought excitement. The company was to be driven by technology and rapidly changing market needs. But I have seen very little change. We are just responding to requirements set by a massive organization in Europe that are defined slowly."

Integrating Global and Local Customers and Markets. In Techco, there is a tension inherent in the attempt to develop a globally integrated approach that will have application in diverse local and industry markets and across existing and disruptive technologies. The European business units understand the importance of being close to the customer and in fact have introduced an elaborately defined set of formal processes for collecting customer information. They involve marketing as a key player in the product definition process, establishing close codevelopment relationships with key customers, tracking field issues, and introducing new functionalities and components in response to customer feedback.

The highly centralized and coordinated manner of making sense of and dealing with this market complexity results in a great deal of input into overarching product definition frameworks and provides guiding direction. But it also creates tensions with the North American subsidiary. The North Americans are operating in a very different kind of marketplace, one that in comparison with the European marketplace is diverse in customers' current capabilities and systems and their expressed needs. Furthermore, the customers in Europe are in fact quite different, they employ highly trained technicians who can take advantage of complex products that require high sophistication from users. North American customers are looking for turnkey solutions that do not demand a great deal of local engineering:

> In Europe, the product can be difficult to learn and doesn't need to be user friendly because they have highly skilled employees. What they consider good, we consider unmarketable. They think their product is perfect, and only customers need to learn how to use it. Nationalization of product is not just language; it is customizing the product to the user base. It is very difficult to learn customer needs outside North America; that is our biggest challenge [senior manager in North America].

The gap in sense making about the customer has a strong impact on motivation in the subsidiaries because personal meaning in the product development network focuses on using technology to bring value to the marketplace:

> The biggest problem is that we need a vision to grow the business with a viable product. There is not a lot of entrepreneurial spirit here. Everything we do is from Europe. When you have an idea and it is taken to Europe, it gets squashed.

They essentially say, "Do what you are told to do." There is not a lot of interaction in our group with the customer. It is a very confined group [engineer in North America].

Balancing Current Versus Disruptive Technology. Another tension arises from efforts to make sense of market applications for the North American unit's disruptive technology with the same centralized sense-making approaches that are being used to evolve generations of the current technological approaches:

Europe has a very rigorous development process with input from sales and product marketing to make a product spec that fits in the road map. It is a highly coordinated process. Because we are starting a new business with the North American products, we're still trying to figure out where to focus. We get a product marketing person who wants one thing, and then the next day it changes. It's very reactive to the market and depends on which customer we met last and what they need [senior manager in North America].

In part, confusion about role reflects the dual identity common in today's global, matrixed organizational structures. Units are part of a global product line organization designed to leverage knowledge and take advantage of dispersed competencies to promote innovation. North American locations are viewed not only as solutions developers for the local market, but also as the global competency center for the development of the new systems. At the same time, they are located in a home country business unit held accountable for profit and loss at the local level. This leads to activities designed to bring in revenue, such as taking on project work loosely related to the competency mission. At the same time, direction and funding to support the local innovation mission are often slow to materialize, since development strategy and funding is controlled from headquarters. This leads to more mixed messages:

Senior managers in Europe care very little about whether we're making money. They care about market penetration and technological advancement. But unfortunately, the subsidiary tends to focus more on the business unit point of view. We can spend only as much on R&D as a percentage of the revenue we bring in [executive in North America].

The center of excellence designation also contributed to confusion in the North American units, as the European development units tended to farm out project work to them that fit the technical competencies of the center of excellence. In the view of the North American employees, this detracted from their ability to enact their defined strategic role by placing a drain on their limited technical resources and treating them more as a job shop than a driver of innovation. From the viewpoint of the Europeans, however, these requests enable the integration of the overall architecture of the system, including the ability to link different generations and components together, as well as to link the hard-wired technology to the emergent PC and Web-based technology so that customers can mix and match and determine their own migration path. Thus, individuals in the global subsidiaries often experience as fragmented what the headquarters organization conceived as an elaborate and elegant alignment serving as the framework for the strategy and organizational approach. This was particularly true for the lower-level North American engineers, who are often enmeshed in and making sense of a web of interdependent technical connections and interactions without the larger strategic and system perspective.

Sense Making Around Technical Work

New product development entails defining product concepts that meet customer needs and market opportunities and solving technical problems to design and deliver products and solutions. In the global corporation, this requires linking knowledge about technology and markets across many dispersed units within the overall umbrella of the strategic intent of the corporation. Product integrity (Clark and Fujimoto, 1991) demands that various elements of the product fit with each other and with customer needs. Shared understanding is required to coordinate and make sense of the ongoing juxtaposition of the emerging and existing technology, the interdependent work being done by many teams and units, and the multiple perspectives of numerous disciplines and functions (Dougherty, 2001; Iansiti, 1995). Shared understanding derives from both alignment frameworks and interactive collaboration as new insights and knowledge emerge in the process of doing the work. The latter must feed back into the former if the organization is to build new knowledge into its alignment frameworks. Three aspects posed particular sense-making challenges for Techco: involving the subsidiaries in the ongoing sense-making activities, communication and coordination modalities, and language and translation issues.

Involving Subsidiaries in Ongoing Sense Making. Although Techco tries to differentiate units operationally by creating projects and subprojects that develop whole products or systems, many projects include work done in multiple competency centers and consequently entail teams with geographically dispersed members. Because Techco's business strategies call for integrating components into a compatible system and enabling customers to migrate between product generations and discontinuous technologies, an overall architecture framework is required. High-level integration of these many dispersed projects and teams is accomplished in part through multiple alignment frameworks, such as the establishment of technical road maps, system architectures, and standard processes for change management and maintenance of the source code. These form the guiding context for the work being carried out in any particular team. But it is also recognized that the system architecture, although the glue that holds the system together, is dynamic and must respond to what is learned in the development activities. For this purpose, interactive collaboration is also required:

> The managers of the technology group and marketing define the strategy for the business's products and the road map. There is a road map on the intranet. There's a meeting every year where we get updates to the road map: markets and products. But architecture is a living thing, and doing implementation changes the architecture. Ideas on the white board may not be implementable, so we need to change the architecture [manager in Europe].

Both the development of the architecture for each generation and its updating must be done through interactive collaboration. To take advantage of knowledge gained throughout the global network, collaborative sense making must involve various parts of that network. A formal process involves all competence centers in the initial definition of each new generation's architecture. However, much of the ongoing interaction to make sense of how the products are unfolding and the frameworks are changing occurs in the European headquarters unit. Thus, there is an ongoing process of weaving emergent understandings into the formal framework:

> One team makes the systems architecture for the software and the hardware. If there are special problems or functions, normally there are meetings. Project leaders or coordinators get together. Information is exchanged in meetings about the whole family of products. We have project leader meetings and project family meetings to exchange information. Architecture groups share as well in their meetings [project leader in Europe].

Although North American representatives may attend key events, in person or electronically, the subsidiary units feel distant from these sense-making processes, which often leads to a frustration that the subsidiary is always on the receiving end of a stream of changes determined in Europe:

> There is a group of systems engineers in Europe who maintain the specs for the interfaces. We implement what they define. Sometimes we are involved in the definition, and sometimes we are not. I got an e-mail this morning asking what impact a change would make. If we are lucky, the specs are in English, but they are usually in [native language], so we have to get them translated. There is also a communications problem in Europe across the sites. We have on-line specs, and they give us notification of changes. But the changes come at such a rate and they are in [native language], so it is hard to keep up with them [engineer in North America].

Sense making about the technical-market interface is particularly attenuated at the lower level of the subsidiaries. Higher-level managers typically have the opportunity to attend road map meetings and other framework-building activities; however, the line engineers developing products are generally on the receiving end, feeling disconnected from the logic that went into decisions and plans and feeling that these plans are disconnected from their experience in developing solutions for their local customers. These line engineers attribute this tension to cultural and values differences between the Europeans and North Americans:

It's a classic example of the difference between Europe and North America. In Europe, they stand at the top, work through the thought process in advance, and then let it trickle down. In North America, we just do it and see what happens. There is no culture for exchange between Europe and North America about customer requirements. We do have an electronic system for field problems, and it has worked out well, but it is slow and there are language barriers [engineer in North America].

Communication and Coordination Modalities. Even when working within the structure of alignment frameworks, the requirements for interactive collaboration for sense making increase for virtual projects in which dispersed team members need to work out ongoing task interdependencies. In Techco, this entails electronic coordination, translation, and frequent face-to-face meetings:

I'm working on a project that is being codeveloped: they are doing the hardware in Europe, and I'm doing the firmware. It is working well. I met the folks there when they were here for a meeting. My partner in Europe has the same design tools as I do, and he has emulated my firmware to test it there. Language is the toughest part. He speaks good English, but I still need to talk slowly and avoid slang. We share documents. He writes up the requirements documentation and then translates it and sends it to me. His English is good enough for translating the base requirements, but I've had to have his comments translated. We both understand the function of the module, so it works well. We communicate back and forth and work as a team. We exchange e-mails daily. He checks with me if he makes any little change to see if it is a problem. I was over there last month and will probably go again next month [engineer in North America].

The information technology infrastructure is a key part of linking together geographically dispersed activities. Techco's European management feel that the key step of implementing a compatible information infrastructure to support and manage distributed development activities has been accomplished. European employees are also quite positive about the electronic availability of information to link the activities of all projects and see these as living documents influenced by two-way interaction. This attitude in part reflects their ease of supplementing electronically available frameworks with interpersonal interaction:

> It all comes together in the source code—every engineer can look to the source code of all the projects. We have one system test group for our engineering tool, and they make sure it fits. But it's easier to call them by phone than to look at the source code [engineer in Europe].

In contrast, North American employees are not as positive about the electronic systems. They often experience obstacles due to system incompatibility, language, time lags in updating information, or limited access (partly due to document control) that cause delays and confusion. In addition, these employees perceive that they are not allowed to feed information into the system:

> We can get parts lists and drawings and all the documentation of the product. It is read-only, however, not two-way. There's a technical incompatibility with their accessing our drawings. We don't even know if they care to see our stuff. We should be able to indicate changes when we see a problem. When we see problems in the code, there is no formal way to tell them [engineer in North America].

In addition, North American employees did not find it as easy to supplement the electronic system with person-to-person interaction. Differences in the size, organization, and complexity of the subsidiary and home country units result in different operating styles, which, although fitting local requirements, result in subsidiary members' being poorly connected to the product line sense making. The European development group was so large and concentrated that it had resorted to regular weekly meetings and other impromptu sessions to communicate and exchange information when there was a sense that new information had emerged and collaborative interaction was required. People in subsidiaries had less access to the ongoing stream of sense-making activities in the home location and did not always know whom to call to get information. An engineer in North America said, "They have a huge bureaucracy, and it is hard to know who to talk with. They have many layers. It is difficult to just figure out how to get specifications. It's not a language issue; it's the distance and the large organization and not knowing who to talk to."

Language and Translation. Language issues clearly exacerbated the difficulty of collaborative interaction between the subsidiaries and the home country. Managers and engineers both acknowledge the issue of multiple languages and talk about the difficulties in sense making that result. The company had adopted

English as its official language in order to accommodate developers from many countries. Nevertheless, developing cross-cultural communication capabilities about technical issues was an extreme challenge:

> English is the language we've decided to use. From our development side, we are a typical European department, and everything is in our native language, and now we have global development and have to react. They cannot understand our language, and each specification has to be translated. A big challenge is to find a way to be efficient to get information back and forth. If English is not your native language, it's hard to write specifications in English; you miss nuances within the language. You have to be in North America and England and practice it for two or three weeks at a time. It's not possible to send all five hundred European engineers to do this [manager in Europe].

This same translation issue was mirrored in a number of comments by North American employees and managers, who recalled, "We got what we asked for but found out that we asked for the wrong thing." The translation of documents also caused work delays.

While sophisticated communication and group work technologies are extensively applied in Techco, there is a general sense that this is insufficient to establish shared meaning through either the sharing of alignment frameworks or attempts at mediated interactive collaboration. There was general consensus among the interviewees that face-to-face interactions are essential for that purpose:

> It starts with personal relationships and a lot of travel back and forth. You lose a lot of time traveling. We meet a couple of times a quarter at first—have to tune the road map and truly learn to understand each other—and have weekly videoconferences. For us in Europe, videoconferencing is not so easy, as we're not too familiar with it. On the North American side, they're used to it [manager in Europe].

Whether used to videoconferencing and other electronic communication forms or not, North American employees were just as convinced that shared meaning is more easily established in face-to-face interaction. They were aware that much collaborative sense making was occurring in just that manner in Europe, greatly limiting their ability to contribute to the ongoing evolution of knowledge and new products.

Across all aspects of sense making around technical work, gaps in awareness and involvement created a performance pattern that in many ways led to a self-fulfilling prophecy in some subsidiary locations—a belief that they are no longer active contributors to knowledge in the innovating network but passive recipients of work.

Sense Making Around Competency Development

A key task of the global network is to ensure the development and enhancement of the competencies required to enact the global strategy. This includes identifying and developing deep expertise in individuals and teams and embedding knowledge in articulated methods, processes, and formal knowledge repositories. In Techco, the concept of centers of competence underlies an organizational strategy that clusters knowledge in units that become deep experts in particular technologies or applied contexts. Emergent aspects of the organization's competencies stem from the development of new knowledge through interactive collaboration. This knowledge can then be articulated and applied across the organization, enabling the leveraging of innovation and integration of the network's new product development activities. Because of the integrated nature of new product development work at Techco, emerging discipline knowledge and the broader product and customer knowledge need to be accessible throughout the organization as soon as possible and incorporated into the processes, methods, and understandings of product developers. Three aspects posed particular challenges to sense making in the Techco network: differences in job design and staffing patterns, cultural differences in work processes, and limited access in subsidiaries to common development experiences.

Job Design and Staffing Patterns. Job design and staffing patterns are formal alignment mechanisms that have an impact on the way in which knowledge is distributed in the organization and the patterns of sense-making interaction required to connect knowledge. Patterns of use of specialists versus generalists reflect underlying assumptions about knowledge and how it is best created and applied. Differences in staffing patterns can make it difficult to identify where knowledge lies and may reflect differences in worldviews that present obstacles to the development of shared meaning (Dougherty, 1992). In Techco, the European emphasis on deep specialty knowledge and the North American tendency toward more generalist knowledge bases and roles create such a lack of symmetry:

> In Europe, there is a lot more specialization. A person is in a job function, and there is pride in doing that job well. In North America, we are more generalists, and there is more innovation. Both work well within their context. If there is a problem in Europe, you know the person whose job it is to be an expert by the organization chart. The cultures tend to clash. There have been conflicting expectations in both directions. We expected innovation, and they expected compartmentalized professionals [engineer in North America].

Work Processes. Work processes are formal alignment mechanisms that are another key element of an organization's competencies. In Techco, even the processes that guide development reflect the difference in cultures and complexity in various subsidiary units and the differing approaches to work design. The Europeans stress uniformity of process that guides well-choreographed interactions among many different specialty groups and interdependent projects. In North America, the emphasis is on collaborative interaction to create processes owned by the people doing the work and on stimulating innovation and the capture of innovative ideas. As a result, processes crafted for the North American sites have to be rationalized with the European processes through interactive processes:

> We have a formal process for the knowledge management side of things. We started with a team to document the process, and that's what we're running to now. For me, the management of technical product innovation and knowledge capture is crucial. We had a conscious set of conversations about how we do it. We have talked with Europe about how to synchronize our process with what they are doing [executive in North America].

Subsidiary Access to Development. The European discipline groups in the matrix organization take an active role in all aspects of competency development, applying systematic approaches to training and development, new process development and training, technology scanning and importing, and using job assignments and career rotation purposefully to support competency development:

> There are issues where it's necessary to have the same skill level for the people. They all need to know a particular tool. Then we do in-house courses right here in our location. When they need to learn something about our own products, training in our headquarters training center works best. We try also to use external training companies so our engineers get exchange with other people and get outside of this organization [manager in Europe].

Although development is also stressed in the North American locations, these units are smaller and do not have the infrastructure to support the extensive development activities and forums available in Europe. Although development experiences that are offered in person in Europe may be made available electronically for other locations, the North American sites are seemingly unaware of these offerings. Much development in the subsidiaries occurs through attendance at public seminars, which may build individual competencies but are unlikely to enhance the sense-making process within the firm:

> Developers go at least once a year to a software developers' conference. They can see that we're not just milking them but investing in them. No one is left to struggle by himself. They can talk to peers and supervisors. If the issue is simple, it's solved right away. If the issue is more general, the lead engineer will organize an internal seminar and share the knowledge [senior manager in North America].

The discipline groups in Europe also set up regular meetings to share learning and create knowledge among developers across the product lines. These forums are most prevalent in Europe, although one product line's intent is to have them occur in different locations:

> In Europe, there are meetings—events where people give reports about experiences, such as special tools or experience with a new technology. Sometimes any developers can come; sometimes it's a smaller team depending on what the issue is. For example, if there is something about using a new tool, one or two people from each project may come [engineer in Europe].

As a result, the carefully planned and integrated development offerings in Europe promote a shared understanding of the technical and business environment, while the experiences in North America appear to be somewhat more diffuse, impromptu, and individualized.

Techco creates electronic access to the information from discipline group meetings and from courses so that individuals who are not in attendance can have access to the learning. In addition, a number of learning-oriented databases are regularly maintained and available to developers globally. Despite efforts to translate these databases, the inevitable delay and difficulty of intranet access cause them to be less useful to North American developers. Again, the structured approaches to competency development in Europe encourage frequent and intense collective sense-making processes in Europe, with North American contributors being only loosely connected, if at all.

Throughout Techco, person-to-person knowledge transfer is intentionally used to carry knowledge and create a common understanding from team to team and location to location by moving people with relevant knowledge to locations that need to acquire that knowledge. Learning takes place through the interactive collaboration that occurs naturally when people work together to solve technical problems. Although long-term expatriate assignments are more common for Europeans coming to North America than vice versa, a considerable number of North American engineers pay short visits to the European locations. Whereas North Americans are viewed as coming to Europe to learn, however, the expatriates from Europe are viewed as transporting knowledge of the European technology, work processes, and product lines that the North American locations need to gain:

> When we find that there is a gap in skills, then one expatriate will organize an internal class and try to bring people up to speed. We usually have an expatriate who has good knowledge and can get documentation and use the network back in Europe to find any missing information [senior manager in North America].

Within Europe, transfer of people is also used to carry technical knowledge to the other product lines, to foster reuse and the building of compatible features into the new system. The North Americans are often not effectively linked into these exchanges, however, and learning in the various North American sites aligns almost exclusively with their product line units. As a result, the North American developers are very dependent on building a network of contacts to link them into the developing knowledge base and complex network of specialized expertise of the European development community:

> It would definitely be a problem for the kind of work we're doing if didn't have expatriates here. Much of the important information isn't written. If we don't have contacts back to mainstream development, we won't be able to get work done. There are hundreds of developers back in Europe. You need to know the key people and know who the expert is who is buried in the organization. It's not always those who are managers whom you need to contact. You need to know who has the real knowledge. We use personal relationships. Those come from the projects you've worked on and friends you've made [engineer in North America].

Despite Techco's conscious efforts to align and integrate new product development activities across the globe, physical dispersion coupled with time zone, language, and cultural differences have led to both real and perceived gaps in understanding, sense of involvement, and perceived value between European and North American units. As shown in Figure 3.2, people who are physically located at headquarters or are within a short commute from headquarters have more access to those interactions, either because these interactions are done face-to-face or because prior face-to-face interactions have led to the establishment of personal networks that promote interactive collaboration. This is true for all new product development processes from strategy formation to competency development.

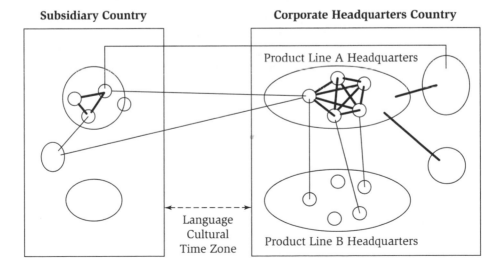

Figure 3.2 Interactive Collaboration.

IMPLICATIONS FOR PRACTICE

Designing knowledge-creation networks for highly integrated large systems is a complicated process. Aligning all aspects is difficult even when all parties involved in new product development are located on one site. When time zone, language, and cultural differences are added to physical dispersion, this task becomes more difficult. Some might hope that more time spent on the development and use of alignment frameworks would reduce the need for some of the informal sense making. But as we have seen at Techco, the alignment frameworks are formulated and evolve through interactive collaboration in meetings or informal interactions.

One of the most interesting study findings is that none of the sense making was done purely virtually, that is, electronically mediated. New product development is dynamic work, and thus alignment frameworks, such as architectures, specifications, and even interfaces, cannot stay static while each element carries out its part. Interactive collaboration enables these frameworks to be dynamic and responsive. This sense making occurs primarily through meetings or informal interactions. In other words, alignment frameworks are created through interactive collaboration, and then those frameworks become the foundation for further interactive collaboration. As shown in Figure 3.2, there is a continuous iterative process between electronically mediated and person-to-person interaction in all three domains described in the Techco case.

Geographically dispersed members of the network are disadvantaged with respect to participation in this sense making. Lateral access to information about the dynamic unfolding of particular technical developments requires lateral connections and communication among contributors. With employees located across multiple sites around the globe, person-to-person interactions must move from ad hoc meetings and informal hallway discussions to a combination of synchronous and asynchronous electronically mediated communications. Synchronous interactions, both face-to-face and virtual, must be scheduled in advance and can lengthen the time required for interactive collaboration in all areas. Time delays and distance create discontinuities where misalignments can grow.

Virtual teams exist at every level of an organization's hierarchy, and each must develop its own knowledge creation network. The global knowledge creation network therefore is the overarching framework within which teams can work through their own sense making. As such, it plays a pivotal role in the development and maintenance of effective virtual teams by providing a basis for developing shared understanding within the teams relative to the teams' goals and objectives. Virtual team members within organizations that are effective global networks tend to have fewer struggles in understanding their role and how their team adds value to the business. Conflicts between local and global priorities will still exist (Klein and Barrett, 2001), but the context will be set for finding meaningful accommodation of local needs and global objectives since both team members and their local supervisors are part of a larger infrastructure that supports and nurtures global interaction.

BEST PRACTICES

Based on the Techco case, we believe that the establishment of formal and informal networks is a key in creating deeper understanding of alignment frameworks and more symmetrical interactive collaboration on a global basis. Among the best practices that we have observed to enhance global sense making across time, distance, and language differences are these:

• *Ensure full connectivity and familiarity across site locations.* It is critical that company, product, competitor, and customer information is communicated to employees throughout the organization. General managers play an important role in linking the global network (Nohria and Ghoshal, 1997), but as the Techco case illustrates, they are essential but not necessarily sufficient. Building bridges upward and laterally is not enough. Translating global frameworks and integrating them with local norms and cultural assumptions can be an even bigger task. For example, all the people we interviewed in Europe described a corporate strategy that included the North American subsidiaries' playing a central role in the development of future products. Yet many employees within the North American sites question their role in the company's strategy.

• *Do not assume that there will be shared understanding across the global knowledge-creation network of alignment frameworks created and maintained primarily at headquarters.* Managers of global knowledge-creation networks need to ensure that each location has full input into the processes and systems for defining products, architectures, and strategies and ongoing feedback and influence as the product line evolves. Interactive collaboration brings together two sets of alignment frameworks: one for the global network and the other at the local site. Each local site has a set of cultural norms and processes built around the site's mission (for example, development of discontinuous technologies), stage in the product life cycle, size, and historical context. These local assumptions need to be considered in the development of global alignment mechanisms, and vice versa.

• *Devote time in meetings and during travel to personal network building.* Communications occur between people who either know one another or are referred to each other by someone they know. As we saw at Techco, language, cultural, and time zone differences inhibit connections that would typically occur between engineers working side by side. Hence, building relationships is a critical part of creating a global knowledge-creation network. These relationships develop naturally when people are colocated but need to become part of meeting and travel agendas for people working on geographically dispersed projects.

• *Rotate people in and out of headquarter locations to develop a working network of contacts and an understanding of the bigger picture.* Unfortunately, many companies use expatriate assignments only as a leadership development tool rather than a knowledge management and sense-making mechanism. Techco's expatriates played a pivotal role in bridging European and North American locations by providing a conduit for interactive collaboration. They used their personal networks to link technical and business resources and build extended networks for individuals who have not had the opportunity to travel to or interact with other sites. In addition, they helped managers and engineers within newly acquired groups make sense of the new organizational norms and processes.

• *Use competency building, especially training, to further global networks.* Techco's use of competency development across the European locations clearly shows the value of using training and development, as well as project assignments, to build networks across multiple locations. This typically happens by osmosis rather than consciously planning and leveraging the networks that are built during classroom or knowledge exchanges. By carefully selecting and building learning cohorts, organizations can create both formal and informal networks that can be used to extend and promote future knowledge transfer and sense making throughout the global organization.

• *Minimize cultural and language barriers to electronic connectivity.* As the Techco case illustrates, it is all too easy to assume that a locally friendly information technology infrastructure will be accessible and accepted on a global basis. Information systems are an extreme case of where the local versus global cultural assumptions come into play. Each site has its own norms around technology use and information sharing. Furthermore, a hidden cost of many acquisitions is incompatibility of legacy systems. Hence, organizations need to develop and implement information technology to complement both local and global sense making.

CONCLUSION

Building the global knowledge creation network for new product development requires a focus on the overall global system. It is not sufficient to connect top managers to one another or to concentrate on building each virtual team. The overall network of activities and interactions shapes the sense-making capabilities of the system and creates the context for each team and the activity within it. Failure to attend to the attributes of the global network has performance consequences in terms of time lost, redundancy, and rework, as well as the failure to incorporate learning throughout the organization into the strategies and competencies of the firm. Perhaps more important, the characteristics of the global network determine the level of engagement that people have with the purposes of the firm.

Notes

1. Weick (1995) identified two kinds of sense making: "intersubjective sense-making" and "generic sense-making" (pp. 71, 170). For the purposes of this chapter, we have renamed these two concepts *interactive collaboration* and *alignment mechanisms.*

2. These relate to the multiple practices that Dougherty (2001) has identified that go on simultaneously within the new product development organization. Because we are focusing on innovation from the perspective of the technical community, we have grouped the activities somewhat differently than Dougherty did.

3. The data reported in this chapter were collected as part of a larger study examining the conditions for technical excellence in large, geographically distributed firms. In Techco, we conducted thirty-six interviews with senior and middle-level managers and individual contributors and six focus groups of three to four technical employees each. The interviews were conducted in two European and three North American locations. Each interview and focus group was guided by a standard protocol and lasted between one and two hours.

References

Bartlett, C., and Ghoshal, S. *Managing Across Borders: The Transnational Solution.* Boston: Harvard Business School Press, 1998.

Brown, S., and Eisenhardt, K. "The Art of Continuous Change: Linking Complexity Theory and Time Paced Evolution in Relentless Shifting Organizations." *Administrative Science Quarterly,* 1997, *42*(1), 1–35.

Clark, K., and Fujimoto, T. *Product Development Performance.* Boston: Harvard Business School Press, 1991.

Davenport, T. H., De Long, D. W., and Beers, M. C. "Successful Knowledge Management Projects." *Sloan Management Review,* 1998, *39*(2), 43–59.

Dougherty, D. "Interpretive Barriers to Successful Product Innovation in Large Firms." *Organization Science,* 1992, *13*, 77–92.

Dougherty, D. "Re-Imagining the Differentiation and Integration of Work for Sustained Product Innovation." *Organization Science,* 2001, *12*(5), 612–631.

Dougherty, D., Borrelli, L., Munir, K., and O'Sullivan, A. "Systems of Organizational Sensemaking for Sustained Product Innovation." *Journal of Engineering Technology Management,* 2000, *17*(3), 321–355.

Galbraith, J. R. *Designing the Global Corporation.* San Francisco: Jossey-Bass, 2000.

Iansiti, M. "Shooting the Rapids: Managing Product Development in Turbulent Environments." *California Management Review,* 1995, *38,* 37–58.

Jelinek, M., and Schoonhoven, C. *The Innovation Marathon: Lessons from High Technology Firms.* Oxford: Basil Blackwell, 1990.

Klein, J., and Barrett, B. "One Foot in a Global Team, One Foot at the Local Site: Making Sense Out of Living in Two Worlds Simultaneously." In M. Beyerlein (ed.), *Advances in Interdisciplinary Studies of Work Teams.* Vol. 8: *Virtual Teams.* Greenwich, Conn.: JAI-Elsevier, 2001.

Leonard-Barton, D. *Wellsprings of Knowledge: Building and Sustaining the Sources of Innovation.* Boston: Harvard Business School Press, 1995.

Mohrman, S. A., Cohen, S. G., and Mohrman, A. M. *Designing Team-Based Organizations: New Forms for Knowledge Work.* San Francisco: Jossey-Bass, 1995.

Nohria, N., and Ghoshal, S. *The Differentiated Network: Organizing Multinational Corporations for Value Creation.* San Francisco: Jossey-Bass, 1997.

Nonaka, I., and Takeuchi, H. *The Knowledge-Creating Company.* New York: Oxford University Press, 1995.

Pava, C. *Managing New Office Technology: An Organizational Strategy.* New York: Free Press, 1983.

Weick, K. *Sensemaking in Organizations.* Thousand Oaks, Calif.: Sage, 1995.

Zack, M. H. "Developing a Knowledge Strategy." *California Management Review,* 1999, *41*(3), 125–145.

CHAPTER FOUR

Building Trust

Effective Multicultural Communication Processes in Virtual Teams

Cristina B. Gibson, Jennifer A. Manuel

I need to understand that people are working to stated objectives, that they are able to meet the objectives, and that they are competent. Technical competence is easier to yield than behavioral competence. To understand the internal and stated needs of each company and how this interacts within the team is important. Our counterparts are really being buffeted by their home organizations. There has to be a lot of trust that they are trying to do the job that they have agreed to do and to the best of their ability.
—Member of a virtual team in the aerospace industry

Collective trust is a crucial element of virtual team functioning. As exemplified by the opening quotation, collective trust can be defined as a shared psychological state in a team that is characterized by an acceptance of vulnerability based on expectations of intentions or behaviors of others within the team (Rousseau, Sitkin, Burt, and Camerer, 1998; Cummings and Bromiley, 1996). Collective trust is challenged by the often prominent differences in culture and lack of face-to-face interaction in virtual teams. In this chapter, we draw on research in organizational behavior and cultural anthropology to examine why cultural differences reduce trust in virtual teams and then focus on the role of communication processes in building trust. Specifically, we examine the communication techniques and strategies that can be used to reconcile intercultural communication challenges in order to draw on the strengths of each culture represented within a multicultural virtual team. Our key point in this chapter is to increase the precision of thinking pertaining to the source and reconciliation of the communication difficulties that prevent the development of virtual collective trust.

In addition to reviewing previous research, our arguments in this chapter are based on evidence from a research project on virtual teams conducted through the Center for Effective Organizations at the University of Southern California.

This larger study began in July 1999 and had two phases: in-depth qualitative case analysis with two different virtual teams from each of eight organizations and a comprehensive quantitative survey that will be administered in each firm and analyzed as to statistical predictors of virtual team effectiveness. In developing the sample for this study, we gathered teams that had members representing many different cultures, with culture being broadly defined as characteristic ways of thinking, feeling, and behaving shared among members of an identifiable group (Earley and Gibson, 2001). Defined in this way, cultures exist at many different levels: national (French culture as compared to German culture), organizational (General Electric's culture as compared to Daimler-Chrysler's culture), and functional (engineering culture as compared to human resource management culture). Culture is a source of shared understandings and sense making and shapes the beliefs, expectations, and behaviors of members of the cultural group (Schein, 1993). Some cultures have a more individualistic (focus on self-interest) versus collectivistic (focus on group interests) orientation (Chatman and Jehn, 1994). Some are high context and feature strong cultural characteristics, while others are low context, meaning that assumptions and values are not widely shared in the group and vary from individual to individual or unit to unit (Gordon, 1991). Cultures also differ in the extent to which they focus on communal (for example, nurturing) versus rationalistic (agency oriented) values (Kabanoff, Waldersee, and Cohen, 1995) and in the extent to which hierarchy is emphasized (Hofstede, Neuijen, Ohayv, and Sanders, 1990).

We focus on examples drawn from three of the virtual teams from phase one of our study. Each of these teams consisted of a different composition of cultures participating in the team. The first virtual team, which we call Europe Connect, consisted of twelve members representing six organizations from four European countries: England, the Netherlands, Austria, and Finland. There were two corporations involved, two universities, one nonprofit institute, and one small consulting company. Team members were from multiple disciplines: industrial design, graphic design, user interface design, design engineering, software engineering, computer science, usability research, and sociology. This team has the greatest amount of diversity in terms of culture.

The second virtual team, which we refer to as Aerospace Alliance, consisted of twenty-one team members and five stakeholders (that is, internal customers) from four different corporations. Three of the firms are U.S. based, and one is based in the United Kingdom. All of the corporations were aerospace firms with different specialties, but all participants were in the same industry. This team had a moderate amount of diversity in terms of cultures.

The third virtual team, which we refer to as Auto Unification, consisted of ten members representing two global automotive organizations that recently merged, one U.S. organization, and one German organization. This team has the least amount of diversity in terms of cultures.

We conducted a comprehensive analysis of interviews with leaders, members, and stakeholders of each team to determine cultural differences and then examined incidences in which participants discussed evidence of trust or lack of trust (see the chapter appendix for a description of the research methods). Finally, we analyzed these instances to determine the processes that had an impact on development of trust and to look for clues as to how to reconcile intercultural breakdowns in trust.

TRUST IN VIRTUAL TEAMS

Trust is important in any type of team, but it is a critical enabling condition in virtual teams (Chapter One, this volume; Jarvenpaa, Knoll, and Leidner, 1998). Research has demonstrated that it can increase confidence and security in relationships and promote open and influential information exchange (Earley, 1986), as well as reduce transaction costs, negotiation costs, and conflict (Zaheer, McEvily, and Perrone, 1998). Trust has also been related to the performance of interorganizational collaborations in terms of goal fulfillment, quality, timeliness, and flexibility (Zaheer, McEvily, and Perrone, 1998).

In virtual collaborations, trust is harder to identify and develop, yet may be even more critical, because the virtual context often renders other forms of social control and psychological safety less effective or feasible. Furthermore, other factors known to contribute to social control and coordination, such as geographical proximity, similarity in backgrounds, and experience, are often absent (Jarvenpaa, Knoll, and Leidner, 1998). Because of the infrequency of face-to-face communication, direct observation and monitoring of team members is not possible. Furthermore, computer-based communication media differ from traditional face-to-face communication in that they eliminate cues about interpersonal affections such as warmth, attentiveness, and trust.

In fact, research has demonstrated that communicators use physical and linguistic copresence (that is, physical colocation) to make inferences about one another's knowledge (Hollingshead, 1998). This implies that lack of face-to-face contact in electronic communication may have a negative impact on message understanding. Indeed, electronically mediated groups have been found to have more difficulty establishing meaning of information and managing feedback in discussion (DeSanctis and Monge, 1999). Other studies show that individuals take longer to form impressions of one another when conversing electronically because it takes longer to decode social cues (Sproull and Kiesler, 1986). Some theories suggest that face-to-face encounters are irreplaceable for building and repairing trust in traditional collaboration. Recently, researchers have argued that this is also true in virtual collaborations (Jarvenpaa and Leidner, 1999). In a virtual environment, according to

O'Hara-Devereaux and Johansen (1994, p. 243), "Trust is the glue of the global workspace."

To date, research has shed little light on the underlying mechanisms that explain the particular difficulties in establishing trust in organizational virtual teams. Our basic argument is that the degree and type of cultural differences represented on the virtual team matter a great deal. Specifically, we propose that in ongoing virtual teams, the number of cultural differences represented on the team is negatively associated with the establishment of trust.

CHALLENGES TO FORMATION OF TRUST

Reviewing several decades of trust research across disciplines, Rousseau, Sitkin, Burt, and Camerer (1998) surmise that two conditions are necessary for building trust: risk and interdependence. Risk, that is, the perceived probability of loss, as interpreted by the decision maker, is considered essential in psychological, sociological, and economic conceptualizations of trust (Coleman, 1990; Chiles and McMackin, 1996). Some minimal level of risk necessitates trust, but too much risk counters the propensity to trust. At a basic level, trust would not be needed if actions could be undertaken with complete certainty and no risk (Lewis and Weigert, 1985). Uncertainty regarding whether the other intends to and will act appropriately is the source of risk. Risk creates an opportunity for trust. Only if some initial risk is taken is it possible for the trustee to demonstrate his or her trustworthiness. For example, a member of Aerospace Alliance explained:

> When you are performing your design task, nothing is going to work right the first time. People who may be working on adjacent parts come to you with their parts. It is frustrating, but it forces you to work with that other person. It is not something that people are used to. You almost just can't stand to find someone looking over your shoulder. There may be some risk of embarrassment when revealing your sketches before you are ready to unveil your best one. The minute you know something, you have to put it down. You might feel bad about being wrong.

However, too much risk can be detrimental. Social norms and social categorization processes shape both the behaviors parties engage in and their beliefs regarding the intentions of others (Whitener, Brodt, Korsgaard, and Werner, 1998). Distrust and suspicion often arise between individuals from different groups, such as cultures, purely on the basis of group membership. In addition to our own interview excerpts, evidence for the existence of such category-based distrust has been provided by ethnographic research on in-group and out-group dynamics. This research demonstrated that categorization of individuals into distinct groups often resulted in individuals' evaluating out-group members as less honest, reliable, open, and trustworthy than members of their own group (Spears and Lea, 1994). In virtual teams, natural subgroups often form based on national, organizational, or functional cultures. Due to in-group and out-group distinctions, perceptions of risks in terms of information sharing across these cultural subgroups are likely to be exaggerated, particularly when members of one subgroup have inadequate information about the other subgroup. This may result in superoptimal levels of risk perceptions that prohibit trust. A member of Aerospace Alliance describes this:

> When you have teams, this is something you will experience in a lot of them. You have a lot of pride. You don't want to admit that I screwed up and that it is going to cause a lot of problems with your partners. We find a problem with a model and immediately jump to conclusions about the other guys. This creates mistrust. If you had more of an understanding of it, perhaps you wouldn't have finger-pointing going on in the back room. You don't want to say too soon, "The sky is falling." There's an issue of when you have to let someone know and when you are letting them know too soon. You need to pull back and ask, "What have I done here, and how it is affecting you?"

Larkey (1996) argued that the categorization process is related to the degree of divergence, defined as adherence to cultural communication patterns in the face of differences. Divergence is a reaction to perceived risk and is illustrated in the first part of the previous quotation. This can be contrasted with convergence, defined as adjustment of communication style to match one's partner. Convergence helps to counterbalance risk and is illustrated in the following quotation from an Auto Unification team member:

> We had a couple of communications, and then we decided we needed to get out to the suppliers and show them we are one company. And what would happen is that first we would brief each other, and then we would drive and spend a couple of hours talking in the car. He sees things in a similar manner—the same strengths, the same opportunities—so I can have confidence and trust in this guy.

Research on institution-based trust is also relevant here. Scholars in this domain maintain that trust reflects the security one feels about a situation because of guarantees, safety nets, or other organizational control structures (Shapiro, 1987). In the absence of such structures, perceived risk is likely to be higher and trust is likely to be lower. For example, a member of Aerospace Alliance said:

> I cannot stand it when my part interferes with your part, and people are looking at this immature part. There is nothing wrong with going ahead except for your own reluctance. When people put something out there, there is a threat that

people are going to do something with it. Everyone is looking at the same data in real time, and they are changing. And you have to be comfortable that what is there today isn't going to be the same tomorrow, and that bothers people.

At the same time, the more cultures represented on the virtual team, the greater is the tendency to establish strict control mechanisms. Some controls actually appear to signal the absence of trust and therefore can hamper its emergence. Institutional controls can also undermine trust when legal mechanisms give rise to rigidity in response to conflict and substitute high levels of formalization for more flexible conflict management (Sitkin and Bies, 1994). For example, one member of Team Europe Connect mentioned the following:

> I don't fully understand what we can talk about and what we cannot talk about. They haven't specified that we can't talk about the technical specifications of the product, because there aren't any technical inventions involved. It is, I think, the concept that is a problem to talk about, but this is confusing.

On a related note, another member stated,

> The contracts were pretty vague, and they're not so specific, because the more specific you are, the harder it is to meet your goals! So it took me a lot longer to actually figure out what we were doing, like a year or something, which is too long. And then it is hard to motivate people into going in the right direction if you don't know what the direction is.

Beyond an optimal level of risk, interdependence is also critical in establishing trust in virtual teams. There are various types of interdependence in organizations, including task interdependence, outcome interdependence, and resource interdependence, but essentially interdependence captures the degree to which one party depends on the actions or information of another in order to accomplish work (Wageman, 1995). The way in which work is designed places some minimum requirements on levels of interdependence. Beyond that, members often have some flexibility in terms of with whom they interact. Development of collective trust requires opportunities to interact and exchange information, which occur less frequently when interdependence is low. In fact, some scholars have argued that the key to effective collaboration is high interdependence (Marshall and Novick, 1995). Yet often the more cultures that are represented in a virtual collaboration, the more difficult it is to maintain interdependence, and thus the less trust. A member of Aerospace Alliance said:

> Collaboration can be enabled by the process and tools that you use. Human interaction is dependent on the personalities of the people involved. There needs to be a desire to interact and a fundamental ability to interface. One of the ways

to build trust was to help out with each other's task as much as possible. Do it in a subtle way. Take something off-line, and make some suggestions; then you're not threatening their position and are building collaboration.

The logistics of interaction across cultural boundaries usually means that members within a cultural subgroup (for example, within an organization or a function) will have greater interdependence than will members across cultural subgroups. In other words, it is much easier for me to share information and interact on the task with members of my own culture than with members of the other cultural subgroups. However, if I do not interact with members of other cultural subgroups, how will I know that I can trust them? Thus, lower overall levels of interdependence result when more cultures are represented on a virtual team, and this reduces trust. A member of Aerospace Alliance noted the importance of interdependence:

If they had a deadline for the deliverable, you'd get the deliverable on the deadline despite the quality of the product. In return, if we didn't meet a particular deadline after receiving their part of the product, then it looked like our fault. There was blame cast behind our back. We had a discussion about this several times. I think it got better as we learned to work better together interdependently. The individuals concerned needed to trust each other more.

Trust is critical in virtual teams and is often threatened by suboptimal levels of risk and interdependence in a multicultural setting. The psychological dynamics that occur when multiple cultures work together make it difficult to establish comfortable levels of risk and interdependence that facilitate trust and, subsequently, team effectiveness. We obtained direct evidence of these relationships in our interview data.

EVIDENCE FOR LINKS BETWEEN CULTURAL DIFFERENCES AND TRUST

Our exploratory interview analysis suggests that teams with greater cultural differences (Team Europe Connect) were characterized by a greater proportion of negative expressions of trust than teams with fewer cultural differences (Aerospace Alliance and Auto Unification). In fact, statistical analysis (analysis of variance, or ANOVA) demonstrated that the mean number of negative responses per individual on a team varied significantly across teams ($F = 21.72$, $p < .001$; see Tables 4.1, 4.2, and 4.3). Even compensating for variation in length of the interviews, the same results were obtained with an analysis of covariance (ANCOVA), entering number of words per interview as the covariant. For example, members of Team Europe Connect had this to say about building trust in a

Table 4.1. Comparison of Negative Trust Excerpts per Team

	Mean Number of Individual Negative Expressions of Trust	Standard Deviation
Europe Connect	10.88	5.38
Aerospace Alliance	2.88	2.52
Auto Unification	2.00	1.67
Total	4.39	4.69

Table 4.2. Analysis of Variance

Negative Expressions of Trust	Sum of Squares	df	Mean Square	F	Significance
Between groups	437.916	2	218.958	21.722	.000
Within groups	332.640	33	10.080		
Total	770.556	35			

Note: Similar results were obtained with an analysis of covariance using number of words per interview as the covariate.

Table 4.3. Multiple Comparisons: Mean Number of Individual Negative Expressions of Trust

(I) Team	(J) Team	Mean Difference (I − J)	Standard Error	Significance
Europe Connect	Aerospace Alliance	*7.9926	1.361	.011
	Auto Unification	*8.8750	1.475	.006
Aerospace Alliance	Europe Connect	*−7.9926	1.361	.011
	Auto Unification	.8824	1.229	.620
Auto Unification	Europe Connect	*−8.8750	1.475	.006
	Aerospace Alliance	−.8824	1.229	.620

*The mean difference is significant at the .05 level.

highly diverse multicultural environment in which multiple countries, organizations, and functions are represented:

> I think trust is being personal with people and honest and direct about things.
> I haven't seen this very personal approach. I see only political ways—convincing
> first the one and then the other but not directly, the natural way. Maybe trust
> has something to do with knowing what the other one is talking about. I think

that people should be honest and critical, but the Team Europe Connect people aren't.

There has to be a level of trust and understanding. People have to know how to take what people say. There was a constant, ongoing communication problem that began because certain parties simply have different ways of saying things, and they always sound so much harsher than they actually mean it.

Trust has been very difficult on this project, because partners have their own interests, and they pull the project toward their interests. I guess trust is something that you stick to the plan in some way, but you leave room for separate interests.

I don't think [company name] trusts the people at [university name] more than they trust those at [a second university], but I'm sure the relationship is better between [the company and the first university] because they share a common language.

[University name and company name] are pretty close as far as I understand because they're physically close and speak the same language. [Research institute] gets along pretty well with [design institute] because the people share a designer background. There are three cultural blocks from North to South: Scandinavia, Anglo-Saxon, and Vienna. There's national culture, the skills the person has, and the type of organization that they work in.

In contrast, members of Aerospace Alliance, which had far fewer cultural differences represented on the team, said the following:

In some cases, it doesn't matter that they are different. In some cases, it matters a lot. This is an issue with the United States and the United Kingdom. We in the United Kingdom assume that we are communicating, but often we are not. In some ways, it is easier when there is a different language. The interesting thing from our point of view is that in the United States, there are differences between California and the Midwest. We in the United Kingdom feel closer to the Californians, and I think sometimes the Californians feel closer to us than they do to the midwesterners. We have more similarities, particularly when you get to those tricky issues of humor. British humor has a sarcastic edge to it. It often is misconstrued in the Midwest.

You have to be careful not to let the IT [information technology] geeks run the show. Engineers have a similar profile. IT people are different. They have far less need for peer approval. They have less need for interaction. They are remarkably unresponsive to the bigger picture and need reminding of what this is all about. That is tricky. It is almost like you need the experts, but you need translators in the middle—people who can talk to the geeks in the language they understand. I have one or two people who are quite skilled at that.

We do need a modicum of translation. We have different words for things. When we talk about systems, we mean utility systems on the aircraft. When [one company] talks about systems, they could mean anything. Some of the phrases for individual components are different. The United Kingdom works on a metric system and the United States on a different system. But these are very small differences here.

We got to see and know the people outside the Alliance environment. That helps a lot to bridge the differences. We have common interests and hobbies. Talk about that means that you are more relaxed when you approach somebody and say that the work is incorrect. Makes it easier and more relaxed to be able to do this. We can talk more frankly about real issues and real problems. If you don't know the person, you are not sure whether you should mention the issue.

Finally, members of Auto Unification, which had the fewest cultural differences represented on the team, had proportionately the least negative expressions of trust. The establishment of commonalities and emphasizing similarities was often mentioned alongside the cultural differences. A member of this team explains:

It seems that the younger Germans are much more like us. The stereotypes might be true about the older Germans, but the younger Germans are very international. They think more along the American mind-set.

Another team member chuckled when we asked about cultural differences between the Germans and the members from the United States:

I laugh because people here who haven't had a lot of interaction with the Germans assume that they are going to be stubborn and stiff, but they speak English better than you do! They like Coke and have traveled the world. Does it sound like those are culture clashes?

The Germans appeared to agree, viewing culture as an opportunity rather than a challenge. One German stated, "I never felt that the cultural differences were a real problem. In mostly every case, those differences are known by the partners and accepted by the partners. Those things don't make any problems." Another commented:

Systems costs, cycle time, human resources, and technologies: those are the four key areas. We are using a similar logic to get to our objective, and what we are trying to decide on is our joint objectives. There should be integration across cultures. There is a lot of opportunity to work closer together than we have.

Thus, we have preliminary evidence that the greater the cultural differences, the more negative expressions of trust there are. While we view this evidence as an important first step, it will be informative for future research to examine the impact of specific aspects of culture on the building of trust more closely.

For purposes of this research, we examined the number of cultures represented, assuming each culture has unique characteristics that are different in some respects than the other cultures on a team. It will be important for future research to determine the nature of each culture and to look for themes regarding how different cultures interact.

BRIDGING THE DIFFERENCES: COMMUNICATION PROCESSES IN VIRTUAL TEAMS

Communication is the process of transferring information, meaning, and understanding from sender to receiver (Gibson, 1996). It is fundamental to any form of organizing and provides the basic building blocks on which people collaborate, make decisions, and act to achieve organizational objectives. Communication is particularly critical in virtual collaboration, enabling parties to link across distance, time, departments, organizations, and nations (O'Hara-Devereaux and Johansen, 1994). Electronic communication in particular loosens constraints of proximity and structure, making it possible for distant parties to exchange messages with one another (Feldman, 1987). Some authors have argued that the real power of virtual forms of collaboration is realized only when communication processes are effective (Ring and Van de Ven, 1994; DeSanctis and Monge, 1999). The exact nature of communication processes in virtual teams, that is, their antecedents and consequences, is as yet unknown; nevertheless, we can examine basic communication research, as well as research examining intercultural and electronic communication, for clues as to the nature of these processes.

Communication Builds Trust

Communication processes are the key underlying mechanisms for establishing trust. There are several reasons that communication and information processing play important roles in trust building. Communication engenders cooperative relationships, provides insightful information about the personalities of team members, lays a basis for developing common values, and encourages continued interaction.

First, open and prompt communication among members is believed to be an indispensable characteristic of trusting relationships (Kanter, 1994). Without proper communication, cooperative relationships tend to suffer. Only if members can constantly sound off their differences (and there are always some in any relationship) will they be able to avoid fatal conflicts. Thus, communication irons out the potential kinks in daily operations and makes for a satisfactory working relationship.

Second, members of virtual teams need to collect evidence about other members' credibility and trustworthiness, and communication facilitates that process. Without information exchange, this process would take a long time. Sharing information among members of collaborative efforts leads to information symmetry rather than information asymmetry (Hart and Saunders, 1997). Members of virtual teams may deliberately provide unsolicited—including even somewhat sensitive—information to other members as a way of showing both goodwill and intimacy. As the reciprocal process engenders credibility, sustained information flow among members creates a trusting environment (Das and Teng, 1998).

Third, communication helps build trust because it provides the basis for continued interaction, from which members further develop common values and norms. Sustained interaction is a crucial mechanism for holding the members together. Through information exchange, members identify and develop more commonalities, reinforcing a sense of trust. Indeed, in a study of seventy-five teams, consisting of four to six members residing in different countries who were interacting for eight weeks, Jarvenpaa, Knoll, and Leidner (1998) found that the level of participation in exercises focusing on increasing information exchange among team members was positively associated with antecedents of trust such as perceived ability, integrity, and benevolence of team members, although they had no effect on overall trust.

Although the research was groundbreaking and insightful, a limitation of it is that the participants were students, not virtual team members collaborating on behalf of different organizations. Furthermore, within a team, the participants in the research had no history of working together and did not anticipate a future in which they would continue to interact. Thus, our study extends the careful groundwork they laid by examining trust in ongoing teams that differed in the number of cultures represented on the team.

Cultural Differences in Communication Processes

It has been suggested that the five phases of the communication process are universal; that is, they exist whenever communication takes place regardless of the specific culture or organization in which it takes place. At the same time, research suggests that similarity in culture between a sender and a receiver can facilitate successful communication at each phase of the process (see Erez and Earley, 1993, for a review). Stated another way, the greater the cultural differences are between sender and receiver, the greater is the expected difficulty in communicating. When such differences are prevalent, we might expect a disruption in the work flow and errors in work performance. These intercultural differences in communication are most evident during the first two phases of the communication process when messages are constructed and transmitted and are often then reconciled during the third, fourth, and fifth phases of the process, during which receivers acquire, interpret, and respond to messages (Gibson, 1996).

During encoding, communicators vary in the extent to which they use an implicit versus an explicit style of language. Implicit language carefully imbues messages with a more positive tone in order to decrease the chances of unpleasant encounters, direct confrontations, and disagreements. Explicit language communicates exactly what is meant in a much more direct manner, even if the message is negative or somewhat harsh. This characteristic is likely related to the extent to which the sender's culture emphasizes a collectivistic versus individualistic value orientation (Gibson, 1996). Collectivism encourages the use of an implicit style of communication, in which the communicator makes frequent use of qualifiers and ambiguous words such as *maybe, perhaps,* and *somewhat* in order to avoid confrontation, and members of these cultures tend to avoid negative responses while communicating with members of their own work group in order to preserve the sense of harmony within the group (Adler, Brahm, and Graham, 1992).

Messages also vary in the extent to which they are context free or context specific. Based on anthropological research investigating high- versus low-context cultures (Hall and Hall, 1987), it is likely that communicators from low-context cultures tend to use external sources of information more often than internal sources when constructing messages (Gibson, 1996). A third way in which messages vary is the degree to which they contain rational material based on facts versus highly emotional material based on intuition and personal perspective (Glenn, Witmeyer, and Stevenson, 1977). Cultures vary in the extent to which they tend to emphasize either rationalistic or more communal (emotional) values, thus encouraging one type of message style over the other.

A final important cultural difference often occurs during transmission. At this stage of the communication process, use of formal versus informal channels of communication likely depends on the attitudes toward hierarchy in the communicator's culture (Gibson, 1996). Communicators from contexts in which hierarchy is explicit and revered are more likely to use formal communication channels that are authorized, planned, and regulated by the organization and are directly connected to its official structure. Communicators from contexts in which hierarchy is minimized are more likely to use informal communication channels as routes that are not prespecified by the organization but develop through the typical and customary interpersonal activities of people at work.

IMPLICATIONS FOR PRACTICE

Given our findings, we searched our case studies and the literature to define key implications for practice regarding the building of trust across cultures through the use of communication strategies. Many of the virtual teams in our study are highly effective, and their practices for developing trust are revealing. Based on our exploratory research and that of others, these implications for practice can be identified in three general areas: participating as a member of a virtual team, developing virtual teams, and structuring and managing virtual teams.

Participating in Virtual Teams

At a more microlevel, there are several communication strategies that members of virtual teams can use in order to overcome intercultural communication barriers to trust. Most of these contribute to what has been referred to as a supportive communication climate as opposed to a defensive communication climate, which results in a pattern of conflict that is either functional or dysfunctional (Lumsden and Lumsden, 1993). In a supportive climate, ideas are shared freely, conflict is based on the task, conflict resolution is open and perceived as fair, and problem solutions are well understood and mutually accepted. In a defensive climate, ideas are suppressed, conflict becomes related to personality issues, conflict resolution is behind the scenes and unsatisfying to many, and problem solutions are not understood or well accepted by all. To create a supportive climate, previous research indicates that generally proactive information exchange (Thomas and Trevino, 1993), regular and predictable communication (Crisp and Jarvenpaa, 2000), and explicit verbalization of commitment, excitement, and optimism (Jarvenpaa and Leidner, 1999) are key. For example, a member of Team Europe Connect suggested that a supportive climate may have helped them build trust: "I don't think that there has been any 'wow, good job' type of things that would have built trust to other people's capabilities." Another suggested that a supportive climate can help to bridge differences: "There are different cultures among the partners; there are creatives and technology-oriented folks and human factors. Sometimes this doesn't combust. If the basic energy of the group is not dissipated by the differences in chemistry and if the basic story they are exploring together is good, then it keeps them motivated to work through the problems."

Beyond these more general strategies, members of virtual teams can also employ basic communication techniques such as those described by Gibson (1996). For example, active listening can help to overcome difficulties experienced in receiving ambiguous messages that may result in low trust. One member of Auto Unification said this about message ambiguity: "It is much more difficult to communicate now that we are virtual. I'm not able to write e-mails with content. It is not as smooth as I would like. Sometimes we are very direct in our e-mails. In my experience, sitting at a table had good results in terms of trust."

Active listening (Morgan and Baker, 1985) has also been referred to as interaction management, degree of involvement in the conversation, and expressiveness (Spitzberg and Cupach, 1984). Basically, being an active listener requires requesting elaboration and clarification whenever the message being sent is not clear. A member of Auto Unification said, "You must have a personal relationship. You can see how your counterpart reacts. How direct or not? How to deal with disagreements? Is he open with feedback? What is his character? It is not necessary to become friends with him, but we must understand character and behavior by really listening."

Active listening is particularly helpful in teams when some members come from high-context organizations (strong cultures) and others come from low-context organizations (weak cultures; Gibson, 1996). Recall that in low-context organizations, members tend to prefer external sources of information, while those in high-context organizations tend to prefer internal sources of information when constructing messages. A low-context receiver who gets a message from a high-context communicator may be initially uncomfortable with the lack of external social referents within the message. Rather than completely discounting the message, if the receiver is aware of the cultural differences and practices active listening, she can request clarification by asking the communicator to verify her internally deduced information using external sources of information. The receiver might ask the communicator, for instance, whether other team members have similar information, opinions, or experiences. The additional clarification is expected to help overcome the initial frustration. A member of Aerospace Alliance captures this technique:

> I trust the guys here more than the others, because I know I can call them up and say, "I see something here," and they listen carefully and say, "Yeah, that is screwed up." They don't try to hide things. One person isn't dominating the teleconferences. I got a lot from going through the training systems. I trained a lot of those guys on this stuff. But I don't think that is always going to be true.

A second technique, listening for ideas (Morgan and Baker, 1985), can help overcome difficulties attributable to collectivistic versus individualistic value orientations in organizations. Communicators with a collectivistic value orientation tend to use an implicit style of communication, while communicators with an individualistic value orientation tend to use an explicit style of communication. Members from a more individualistic organization (explicit communicators) may have difficulty recognizing the gist of a message sent by members of a more collectivistic organization (implicit communicators). However, if she is aware of the intercultural differences, the individualist can carefully listen and extract the ideas couched within the implicit message. Indeed, in one study of the patterns of success and failure in cross-cultural adjustment, listening skills were found to be closely related to interactional effectiveness (Nishida, 1985). A member of Team Europe Connect commented on the importance of this skill in building trust: "There has to be a level of trust and understanding. People know how to take what people say. There was a constant ongoing communication problem that began because certain parties simply have different ways of saying things; they always sound so much harsher." A member of Auto Unification said: "Informal communication is very important for trust. My counterpart told me some problems and some internal issues from his side, and I did the same this way."

The technique of framing can help to overcome the challenge of decoding messages sent across communicators with very different perspectives. Decoding is the process by which a receiver interprets a message to derive meaning from it. Research suggests that in message interpretation, a key method for avoiding intercultural miscommunication is framing. Framing has also been referred to as the ability to empathize with the communicator (Gudykunst and Kim, 1984). Basically, framing involves taking the other's frame of reference (Hammer, 1989). A member of Team Europe Connect mentioned the importance of this technique: "I would say that what I have learned is that you have to communicate information to designers in a completely different way than for researchers. I learned how they think and the kinds of information they need and expect. I certainly would do my work completely differently than I did before." Another member of Europe Connect stated:

> The kind of objective language that researchers use is direct and practical.
> I think there are more ways to discuss the project and to discuss innovation.
> Including emotions and metaphors is important. You mustn't be afraid to use
> emotion with researchers and other people. I see people who are used to working in a business context, and they get into this design and research context and
> lose their bearings. They don't dare to talk about emotional things—about
> history, the future, visionary things.

Framing can help reconcile intercultural communication difficulties that are attributable to communal versus rationalistic values in organizations. Communicators from organizations that emphasize communal values are likely to construct messages with emotional content. Receivers from rationalistic organizational cultures may initially feel uncomfortable with such messages, but by using the framing technique, the receiver may better understand the message by adopting a communal frame of reference (Gibson, 1996). In this spirit, DeSanctis and Monge (1999) recommend that virtual teams provide rich contextual information to communicating parties to help heighten message understanding and shorten the time that might otherwise be required to establish interdependence. One member of Team Europe Connect had this to say about framing:

> I find it very hard to get a frame of reference. I think it really needs a sense of
> direction. You have to develop an image of how context changes. Maybe we

need more sociologists and more ethnic stories to give our project more context so that everyone knows, "Oh, we're going that way," and in that sense, the vision should be a frame of reference. You can define it in very different ways, but everyone should have the same frame of reference.

Responses to others' messages are also critical (Jarvenpaa and Leidner, 1999). A response is an endorsement that another person is willing to take the risk of interpreting the first person's message and, if necessary, supplying the missing elements to make it understandable. Because computer-mediated communication entails greater uncertainty than face-to-face communication, there tends to be an intense need for responses (Hawisher and Moran, 1993). Responses are trusting behaviors that indicate involvement, and involvement conveys attraction, intimacy, attachment, and affection (Jarvenpaa and Leidner, 1999). For example, one member of Aerospace Alliance said, "There is a very high level of trust on this team. Trust is notification—people contacting you when they need to. People tell you what they are going to do, and they do it. There is predictability and following through with what you say you're going to do."

The technique of following up can be extremely helpful in this regard. Following up involves accurately repeating the communicator's message (Gibson, 1996). Doing so quickly appears to be especially effective (Hammer, 1989). A member of Auto Unification said this about following up:

> In all honesty, this positive, trusting relationship did not hold true early on at the buyer level. They haven't had the same opportunity to have the time with each other. They are still a little concerned. My guys were very critical early on. When they would get something back, they would say, "This makes no sense." I agreed and then put it in German and sent it back to them. Then they would realize that the language is English and this is their second language, and they need to follow up.

In the final feedback phase of communication, the following-up technique may help to reconcile intercultural differences attributable to differences across organizations regarding hierarchy and structure. Such differences are associated with communication patterns. Members from organizations with strong hierarchies are likely to prefer communication patterns that follow the chain of command. In contrast, those from low hierarchy may become frustrated with this process, actively bypassing it. Balancing the two by following up with whichever channel is not used first—effectively becoming fluent in the use of formal and informal channels—can reduce the stress associated with the unfamiliar channels of communication. Although trust was high on the Auto Unification team, there were still issues to be resolved regarding hierarchy. One member explained it like this: "We have a high level of trust between the two groups, yet we are not totally there. We are still a little bit hesitant about sharing information. What we still do is that we tend to make sure that we discuss things first with our superior before we truly communicate with each other."

Developing and Supporting Virtual Teams

Team developers and facilitators can assist virtual teams in communicating these norms in advance, including procedures for reconciling differences in communication practices that emerge as members do business across multiple boundaries. As business processes are redesigned, organizations will have to find ways to preserve the beneficial norms that have been established while promoting newer ones that are more appropriate to the redesign (DeSanctis and Monge, 1999).

Some teams develop procedural templates for communicating using electronic media (Winograd and Flores, 1986), and this is beneficial for reducing risk and ensuring interdependence. Knowledge management systems can also help in this regard. For example, electronic communication products, such as conversations and documents stored in knowledge repositories, can provide stability to otherwise dynamic and uncertain relationships. A transactive memory system—knowledge about who knows what—can be formalized, documented, and reapplied (DeSanctis and Monge, 1999). A member of Aerospace Alliance talked about the importance of ensuring that learnings will be accessible and passed on to others in future collaborative efforts:

> The trust issue is pretty sensitive, because almost all the folks on this team will not be going to [a future new product development initiative]. We don't understand the intelligence of that. You have a system of people who have gone through the program and now are going to other areas. There are only one or two people who will be going onto the [new initiative]. That takes the trust and just throws it all away. They [on the new initiative] are going to start all over and make the same mistakes that we did.

Finally, ensuring that equity, fairness, and sense of procedural justice are maintained can increase trust. For example, one member of Team Europe Connect had this to say about procedures early in the project:

> Development of the first concepts was done by all the partners. Right now, I'm not sure, but maybe that's a mistake, because when the researchers are making concepts and also have to evaluate them later, it's a little bit hard. For me, it was really interesting. But from the methodological point of view, it was a bit of a problem. Some partners lost a little bit of reputation with other partners because they tried to do that work and were more or less amateurs. So I'm not sure about that.

Ironing out lateral communication appears to be particularly critical because it helps to create interpersonal relationships that often carry over into social life outside the business environment, and this is important for building trust. For example, in an important study that bridges communication theory and multinational organizational theory, Ghoshal, Korine, and Szulanski (1994) found that interpersonal relationships developed through lateral communication mechanisms such as joint work in teams, task forces, and meetings increased the communication effectiveness of virtual teams. The interpersonal relationships often spilled over into social connections made outside work. This idea was also evident in our interviews. A member of Auto Unification said, "We've spent time with each other outside a business environment. People lower their guard a little. It happens only by spending time together. We've had specific projects that we have had to work together on. Working on those types of things has helped us to instill trust." A member of Aerospace Alliance commented:

> Anything that you can do to get people together socially is good, even a ball game. When we were there for training, I think we went to dinner one evening. That builds extra trust. When you build that into a team and there is a crisis, the social interaction is the reserve. That is pretty cheap; the cost is minimal. On a small project, you can get away with not doing it. On a large program, the cost as compared to the gain is incredible. The more that you can bring together people in the beginning has an exponential impact in the end.

At the same time, addressing procedural justice may mean paying special attention to expectations regarding hierarchy. Decentralized approaches coupled with strong and explicit leadership roles may be well advised. In support of this, Hinds and Kiesler (1995) found better lateral communication in less hierarchical virtual work groups. For example, members of Team Europe Connect recognized the power of hierarchy and personal relationships in stating:

> You can't have one inexperienced person leading a partner organization working with a very experienced person. It was one of the problems.

> I would say that the team is more or less task related. There are some friends, some personal friends, and those relationships truly influence Team Europe Connect because it's clear that those people communicate more than people who aren't friends.

Structuring and Managing Virtual Teams

At the organizational level, establishing an optimal level of risk and increasing interdependence can increase trust. Locating organizations with a good reputation seems to be an effective starting point. A firm with a reputation of being honest, fair, and trustworthy gives members of other organizations the needed first piece of evidence to take some initial risk. Incremental resource commitments on the part of all organizations may also be a relevant strategy when risk and uncertainty levels are high (Bowman and Hurry, 1993). Structures, processes, and routines can then create a stable context that constrains risk to management levels so that interpersonal trust can develop and persist (Zaheer, McEvily, and Perrone, 1998). A member of Team Europe Connect said this about the importance of a structure that works:

> When we got down to the nitty-gritty of the work—the details of development of concepts—the communication broke. There was kind of a drop in the levels that people have to work together. What finally ended up happening is that we split the project up into chunks so that people could work on it in separate countries in order to try to find what they were supposed to be looking for.

Institutional factors can act as broad supports for the critical mass of trust that sustains further risk taking and trust behavior. These supports can exist at the organizational level, in the form of teamwork culture (Whitener, Brodt, Korsgaard, and Werner, 1998), and at the societal level through such cultural supports as legal systems that protect individual rights and property (Fukuyama, 1995). The caveat here is that too much control or legal barriers that are difficult to interpret or are applied haphazardly can be highly counterproductive to developing trust. Managers of virtual collaborative efforts need to simultaneously consider costs of control mechanisms, costs of failing to reach minimal levels of trust, and costs of trust building; a higher level of trust does not automatically dictate a lowering of the control level, and vice versa. All it means is more confidence in cooperation among members of the various organizations.

For example, certain members of Team Europe Connect based their definition of trust on the skills and capabilities of project members. One stated, "I trust certain partners because they have the skills. I'm not sure we're trusted." One solution to this problem, cited by a member of Team Europe Connect, would have been to increase the stability of the team. In her words, "Other projects always have priority, and so I think that people get pulled off the project and a lot of people get dumped on the project, so a key problem has been the constant turnover of members on the team." In a similar vein, a member of Aerospace Alliance said, "I had some built-in credibility because I worked with these guys before. Trust had developed between us—credibility and belief in the honesty of the other person. Does he know what he is talking about? Will he tell me the truth? If I've worked with him in the past, there is more of a chance I will believe this."

Another solution is to increase the strength and clarity of leadership. As one member of Team Europe Connect stated,

I think that the problem with Team Europe Connect in the first year was that there wasn't a real project leader because they tried to give us as much freedom as possible. For some of the partners, this might have been a problem because this freedom might have been too much, and we didn't have any help in where to go. But I think that in the second year, one of the partners fulfilled the task as leader better than in the first year. In the first year, it was a problem that Team Europe Connect was more or less leaderless.

Providing a positive example of the trust-building power of clear leadership, the U.S. leadership representative in Auto Unification stated, "If my German leadership counterpart and I had not hit it off as well as we did, we would not be able to do what we did. We respect each other, and we determined very early on that neither one of us had a hidden agenda. He and I are providing the example, and they are following it. The key is to learn from each other in a non-threatening way."

CONCLUSION

Our findings should not be interpreted as discouraging intercultural teaming. In fact, several of the teams in our study were highly effective, or at least effective in obtaining some portion of their outcomes, because they were able to overcome barriers to trust. For example, one member of Team Europe Connect stated:

> If you look at the outcome—the products or concepts coming out of it—it is not very high. If you look at the outcome of the project—what the network in Europe is developing, how the people are interconnecting—then the outcome is very high. People are learning very much about each other and different cultures and how people deal with problems. And I'm not entirely sure, but I think it must be one of the reasons that these projects even happen. Because these kinds of findings are valuable.

It should make virtual team participants aware of challenges that they may face through intercultural teaming and should compel future research to explore further how best to overcome diversity and use the strengths that initiated the partnering of the cultures. We briefly summarize a few guidelines for practice:

Implications for Virtual Team Members

- Develop a supportive communication climate by:

    Using active listening techniques to overcome differences in high-context versus low-context organizations

    Using listening for ideas to overcome differences in implicit versus explicit cultures

Using framing techniques to overcome differences in communal versus rational cultures

Using follow-up techniques to overcome differences in emphasis on hierarchy and chain of command

Implications for Virtual Team Developers

- Reduce risk and increase interdependence during the development process by:

    Establishing communication norms

    Developing templates for using technology

    Creating knowledge-management systems

Implications for Virtual Team Managers

- Establish appropriate hierarchy and leadership that instills a sense of procedural justice.

- Manage risk through careful selection of organizations for virtual team membership and incremental resource commitments.

- Develop interdependence through stable structures arranged by flexible but explicit contracts.

APPENDIX: RESEARCH METHODS

In each team, structured interviews with a sample of team members, team sponsor or leader (or both), and two or three internal customers (stakeholders) were conducted. A majority of the interviews were conducted face-to-face but supplemented by telephone. The questions relative to this research appear in Exhibit 4A.1. All interviews were taped and transcribed. Archival data available about the teams were also collected: background information about the organizations, e-mail or other electronic transcripts, previous evaluations of the teams, project plans, and written mission statements.

All of this information was compiled into an electronic textual database, and we then used computer-facilitated qualitative data analysis (CQDA; for recent examples of the more comprehensive procedures, see Mohrman, Gibson, and Mohrman, 2001; Gibson and Zellmer-Bruhn, 2001). CQDA aids in reviewing, categorizing, comparing, and discerning relationships within text by using search, retrieval, and collation routines. To examine evidence of trust, we needed to identify interview excerpts that contained this evidence. Following previous research, a category of key words pertaining to trust was created based on a comprehensive list of trust words compiled from various trust survey

Exhibit 4A.1 Sample Interview Questions.

1. On a scale of 1 to 10 (1 very low and 10 very high), how much trust is there on the team? How do you know?

2. How much do you trust others?

3. How much do others trust you?

4. If there are any discrepancies, why?

5. How much trust is there that time and money will be used in the best interest of the team? That they will be used in a fair and equitable way?

6. Do people trust each other to contribute worthwhile ideas?

7. Do people trust each other to do what they say they will do?

8. How did the team develop trust among its members? What factors hinder trust?

9. How do differences in culture, discipline, home organization, or some other area influence the way members work together?

10. Do problems occur because of these differences? If so, how do you resolve them?

11. Do individuals act as "interpreters" or "translators" between different functional areas?

12. Do members of the team have similar work values?

instruments, the research articles referenced in this chapter regarding trust, and dictionaries and thesauri to identify synonyms. A final test of the intercultural applicability of this list was conducted by asking a panel of experts represent ing all of the countries included in the three teams to review the list and add any additional terms that might imply trust or a lack of trust. The final list of trust words appears in Exhibit 4A.2.

We then searched for any word in this category in the three text databases. Three excerpt files were created containing only interview excerpts that held evidence of trust. Next, two independent raters coded the excerpts. One of three codes as assigned to each excerpt: NA (irrelevant), 1 (indicating trust among team members), or 0 (indicating a lack of trust among team members). Any excerpts deemed irrelevant by either of the raters was eliminated from the excerpt pool. Of the 595 excerpts retrieved by TACT, 377 were maintained as relating to trust. An initial estimate of inter-rater reliability among the two raters was .84. Any discrepancies between positive and negative codes were discussed and reconciled. A spreadsheet was generated from the results of the qualitative analysis consisting of information for each team member indicating the number of positive and negative expressions articulated by each virtual team member. These data were then entered into the SPSS statistical analysis program, along

Exhibit 4A.2 Trust Words.

able	confidentiality	presumptive
abilities	contemplative	presumptuous
ability	contemptuous	reliable
arrogance	credibility	reliability
arrogant	credible	reliant
assume	depend	rely
assumed	dependent	relying
assuming	depending	respect
assumption	depends	respected
assumptions	disagree	respectful
belief	disagreed	respective
beliefs	disagreement	respond
believe	disagreements	responding
believes	disagrees	response
believing	disbelieve	responses
benevolence	disdainful	responsible
benevolent	distrust	responsibilities
care	distrustful	responsibility
cared	distrusting	responsive
careful	egotistical	responsiveness
carefully	expert	selfish
carefulness	expertise	selfishness
caring	experts	sensible
caution	faith	sensitive
cautious	fight	sensitivity
cohesion	fighting	share
cohesive	flighty	shared
collaborate	friction	sharing
collaboration	genuine	sincere
collaborative	genuinely	sincerity
collaboratively	harmony	suspect
compatible	honest	suspecting
compatibility	honesty	suspicion
compete	honored	trust
competence	insecure	trustable
competencies	insecurities	trusted
competency	insecurity	trustful
competent	insensitive	trusting
competing	insolent	trusts
competition	integrity	trustworthiness
competitive	loyal	trustworthy
competitors	loyalty	unbelievable
conceited	mistrust	unreliable
confide	overbearing	unreliability
confidence	overconfidence	vulnerabilities
confident	overconfident	vulnerable
confidential		

with basic statistics about each team member (national background, organization, function), to determine the statistical relationships in the data.

References

Adler, N. J., Brahm, R., and Graham, J. L. "Strategy Implementation: A Comparison of Face-to-Face Negotiations in the People's Republic of China and the United States." *Strategic Management Journal*, 1992, *13*, 449–466.

Bowman, E. H., and Hurry, D. "Strategy Through the Option Lens: An Integrated View of Resource Investments and the Incremental-Choice Process." *Academy of Management Review*, 1993, *18*, 760–782.

Chatman, J. A., and Jehn, K. A. "Assessing the Relationship Between Industry Characteristics and Organizational Culture: How Different Can You Be?" *Academy of Management Journal*, 1994, *37*(3), 522–553.

Chiles, T. H., and McMackin, J. F. "Integrating Variable Risk Preference, Trust, and Transaction Cost Economics." *Academy of Management Review*, 1996, *21*, 73–99.

Coleman, J. S. *Foundations of Social Theory.* Cambridge, Mass.: Belknap Press, 1990.

Crisp, C. B., and Jarvenpaa, S. L. "Trust Over Time in Global Virtual Teams." Paper presented at the Academy of Management Meeting, Toronto, Canada, 2000.

Cummings, L. L., and Bromiley, P. "The Organizational Trust Inventory (OTI): Development and Validation." In R. M. Kramer and T. R. Tyler (eds.), *Trust in Organizations: Frontiers of Theory and Research.* Thousand Oaks, Calif.: Sage, 1996.

Das, T. K., and Teng, B. "Between Trust and Control: Developing Confidence in Partner Cooperative Alliances." *Academy of Management Review*, 1998, *23*(3), 491–512.

DeSanctis, G., and Monge, P. "Communication Processes for Virtual Organizations." *Organization Science*, 1999, *10*(6), 693–703.

Earley, P. C. "Trust, Perceived Importance of Praise and Criticism and Work Performance: An Examination of Feedback in the U.S. and England." *Journal of Management*, 1986, *12*, 457–473.

Earley, P. C., and Gibson, C. B. *Multinational Work Teams: A New Perspective.* Mahwah, N.J.: Erlbaum, 2001.

Erez, M., and Earley, P. C. *Culture, Self-Identity, and Work.* New York: Oxford University Press, 1993.

Feldman, M. S. "Electronic Mail and Weak Ties in Organizations." *Office: Technology and People*, 1987, *46*, 443–467.

Fukuyama, F. *Trust: The Social Virtues and the Creation of Prosperity.* New York: Free Press, 1995.

Ghoshal, S., Korine, H., and Szulanski, G. "Interunit Communication in Multinational Corporations." *Management Science*, 1994, *40*, 96–110.

Gibson, C. B. "Do You Hear What I Hear? A Framework for Reconciling Intercultural Communication Difficulties Arising from Cognitive Styles and Cultural Values." In M. Erez and P. C. Earley (eds.), *New Perspectives on International Industrial Organizational Psychology.* San Francisco: Jossey-Bass, 1996.

Gibson, C. B., and Zellmer-Bruhn, M. "Metaphors and Meaning: An Intercultural Analysis of the Concept of Teamwork." Working paper, University of Southern California, 2001.

Glenn, E., Witmeyer, D., and Stevenson, K. "Cultural Styles of Persuasion." *International Journal of Intercultural Relations,* 1977, *1,* 52–56.

Gordon, G. G. "Industry Determinants of Organizational Culture." *Academy of Management Review,* 1991, *16*(2), 396–415.

Gudykunst, W. B., and Kim, Y. Y. *Communicating with Strangers: An Approach to Intercultural Communication.* New York: Random House, 1984.

Hall, E. T., and Hall, M. R. *Hidden Differences: Doing Business with the Japanese.* New York: Doubleday, 1987.

Hammer, M. R. "Intercultural Communication Competence." In M. K. Asante and W. B. Gudykunst (eds.), *Handbook of International and Intercultural Communication.* Thousand Oaks, Calif.: Sage, 1989.

Hart, P., and Saunders, C. "Power and Trust: Critical Factors in the Adoption and Use of Electronic Data Interface." *Organization Science,* 1997, *8,* 23–42.

Hawisher, G. E., and Moran, C. "Electronic Mail and the Writing Instructor." *College English,* 1993, *55,* 627–643.

Hinds, R., and Kiesler, S. "Communication Across Boundaries: Work, Structure, and Use of Communication Technologies in a Large Organization." *Organization Science,* 1995, *6*(4), 373–393.

Hofstede, G., Neuijen, B., Ohayv, D. D., and Sanders, G. "Measuring Organizational Cultures: A Quantitative Study Across Twenty Cases." *Administrative Science Quarterly,* 1990, *35,* 286–316.

Hollingshead, A. B. "Communication, Learning, and Retrieval in Transactive Memory Systems." *Journal of Experimental Social Psychology,* 1998, *34,* 423–442.

Jarvenpaa, S. L., Knoll, K., and Leidner, D. E. "Is There Anybody Out There? Antecedents of Trust in Global Virtual Teams." *Journal of Management Information Systems,* 1998, *14*(4), 29–64.

Jarvenpaa, S. L., and Leidner, D. E. "Communication and Trust in Global Virtual Teams." *Organization Science,* 1999, *10*(6), 791–815.

Kabanoff, B. R., Waldersee, R., and Cohen, M. "Espoused Values and Organizational Change Themes." *Academy of Management Journal,* 1995, *38*(4), 1075–1104.

Kanter, R. M. "Collaborative Advantage: The Art of Alliances." *Harvard Business Review,* 1994, *72*(4), 96–108.

Larkey, L. K. "Toward a Theory of Communicative Interactions in Culturally Diverse Workgroups." *Academy of Management Review,* 1996, *21*(2), 463–491.

Lewis, J. D., and Weigert, A. "Trust as a Social Reality." *Social Forces,* 1985, *63,* 967–985.

Lumsden, G., and Lumsden, D. *Communicating in Groups and Teams: Sharing Leadership.* Belmont, Calif.: Wadsworth, 1993.

Marshall, C., and Novick, D. "Conversational Effectiveness and Multi-Media Communications." *Information Technology and People,* 1995, *8*(1), 54–79.

Mohrman, S. A., Gibson, C. B., and Mohrman, M. "Doing Research That Is Useful to Practice: An Empirical Investigation." *Academy of Management Journal,* 2001, *44,* 357–375.

Morgan, P., and Baker, K. "Building a Professional Image: Improving Listening Behavior." *Supervisory Management,* Nov. 1985, pp. 34–38.

Nishida, H. "Japanese Intercultural Communication Competence and Cross-Cultural Adjustment." *International Journal of Intercultural Relations,* 1985, *9*(3), 247–269.

O'Hara-Devereaux, M., and Johansen, R. *Globalwork.* San Francisco: Jossey-Bass, 1994.

Ring, P. S., and Van de Ven, A. "Developmental Processes of Cooperative Interorganizational Relationships." *Academy of Management Review,* 1994, *19,* 90–118.

Rousseau, D. M., Sitkin, S. B., Burt, R. S., and Camerer, C. "Not So Different After All: A Cross-Disciplinary View of Trust." *Academy of Management Review,* 1998, *23*(3), 393–404.

Schein, E. H. *Organizational Culture and Leadership.* (2nd ed.) San Francisco: Jossey-Bass, 1993.

Shapiro, S. P. "The Social Control of Interpersonal Trust." *American Journal of Sociology,* 1987, *93,* 623–658.

Sitkin, S. B., and Bies, R. J. (eds.). *The Legalistic Organization.* Thousand Oaks, Calif.: Sage, 1994.

Spears, R., and Lea, M. "Panacea or Panopticon? The Hidden Power in Computer-Mediated Communication." *Communication Research,* 1994, *21*(4), 427–459.

Spitzberg, B. H., and Cupach, W. R. *Interpersonal Communication Competence.* Thousand Oaks, Calif.: Sage, 1984.

Sproull, L., and Kiesler, S. "Reducing Social Context Cues: Electronic Mail in Organizational Communication." *Management Science,* 1986, *31*(11), 1492–1512.

Thomas, J. B., and Trevino, L. K. "Information Processing in Strategic Alliance Building: A Multiple-Case Approach." *Journal of Management Studies,* 1993, *30,* 779–814.

Wageman, R. "Interdependence and Group Effectiveness." *Administrative Science Quarterly,* 1995, *40,* 145–180.

Whitener, E. M., Brodt, S. E., Korsgaard, A. M., and Werner, J. M. "Managers as Initiators of Trust: An Exchange Relationship Framework for Understanding

Managerial Trustworthy Behavior." *Academy of Management Review,* 1998, *23*(3), 513–530.

Winograd, T., and Flores, F. *Understanding Computers and Cognition: A New Foundation for Design.* Norwood, N.J.: Ablex, 1986.

Zaheer, A., McEvily, B., and Perrone, V. "Does Trust Matter: Exploring the Effects of Interorganizational and Interpersonal Trust on Performance." *Organization Science,* 1998, *9*(2), 141–159.

PART ONE

SUMMARY

*As a team begins to establish greater trust and more shared understanding,
when you sort of know who everybody is and you know who knows what,
you have achieved the Zen state of collaboration.*
—Consultant working with virtual teams

*The ideal is that these enabling conditions might be separate, but then there's
some overlap among them, and one needs all three to actually work together.*
—International executive

The authors in Part One have examined shared understanding, integration, and trust—the enabling conditions for virtual team effectiveness. Three key points emerge from these chapters:

- All three enabling conditions are important for virtual team performance.
- They are difficult to establish.
- They are positively related to one another.

Hinds and Weisband demonstrate in Chapter Two that shared understanding contributes to virtual team performance through multiple mechanisms. Shared understanding aligns effort, increases member satisfaction and motivation, reduces implementation problems and errors, and reduces frustration and conflict. Mohrman, Klein, and Finegold assert in Chapter Three that the different elements of the product development system in a global firm must be integrated in order for innovation to occur. Gibson and Manuel assert in Chapter Four that trust is important in any type of team, but is critical for virtual teams. Trust promotes open and influential information exchange, reduces negotiation costs and conflict, and is related to achieving performance goals.

Each of the chapters suggests how difficult it is to establish the enabling conditions. Hinds and Weisband highlight how physical distance, personal dissimilarity, contextual work differences, and technology-mediated communication act as barriers to developing shared understanding on virtual teams. Mohrman, Klein, and Finegold examine the sense-making activities that occur across differentiated new product development sites and repeatedly point out how the North American sites had different understandings than the European sites do. Gibson and Manuel find that the greater the cultural differences on a virtual team, the lower the level of trust is. The research conducted by these authors suggests that establishing enabling conditions and overcoming the barriers to effectiveness is more difficult in virtual teams than in traditional teams.

Finally, these three enabling conditions are not independent of each other. They are related to one another and share some antecedents. The relationship between integration and shared understanding is explicitly discussed by Mohrman, Klein, and Finegold. The more activities that occur to enable the differentiated parts of the global new product development organization to work together (for example, full connectivity, personal networks, minimizing cultural and language barriers), the more likely that shared understanding will result. Network members engage in dialogue with one another and conduct joint sense-making activities, which result in a common understanding of business strategy, technical requirements, and product organization. Similarly, Gibson and Manuel recommend that cross-cultural virtual teams build trust through developing a supportive communication climate. They recommend communication skills such as active listening or framing techniques to help develop trust. What they do not explicitly say is that these are the same communication techniques that characterize productive sense-making activities and can help build shared understanding in multicultural virtual teams. We believe that integration, shared understanding, and trust are positively related; when one is in place, it is likely that the others are too.

Trust has been called the glue of the virtual workplace (O'Hara-Devereaux and Johansen, 1994). We believe that integration, shared understanding, and trust are equally important in establishing an effective foundation for virtual teaming. Integration is the structural underpinning, establishing the systems, policies, and forums that enable people across time and space to work together. Shared understanding provides the cognitive linkage, enabling people to understand where they are going and how they are going to get there. Trust provides the emotional connection, allowing people to be vulnerable with one another. Pasting together the virtual workplace means paying attention to structure, cognition, and emotion.

More research needs to be done to understand fully how the enabling conditions are related to one another and to effectiveness. What antecedents do they share? Are they equally important for performance outcomes? One thing we do know is that the design of the organizational context can strongly contribute to, or detract from, establishing these enabling conditions. We turn to this next.

Reference

O'Hara-Devereaux, M., and Johansen, R. *Globalwork*. San Francisco: Jossey-Bass, 1994.

THE RAW MATERIALS
People and Context

PART TWO

INTRODUCTION

We had a telecommunications group that was all over the world, and we brought them together. There were sixteen countries and five different acquisitions that we'd had. We started by setting strategy for them, to get them aligned on strategy. Then we talked about processes and systems because you basically have to redesign the entire system when you go virtual. Then below that, what skills, capabilities, or competencies do you require from your team members in operating within these processes and systems? What reward systems are you going to design? It took us three to four days just to get the fundamental foundations in place. Clearly, the system drives how they operate. What we were doing is creating a whole different way of doing business, so we saw that in some of the selection criteria. We had the capabilities in terms of the technology. It was the interpersonal area we had to work on. There's a whole system you've got to build around that. The requirements for support, much less for the team to succeed, are huge.
—Practitioner commenting on creating support systems for virtual teams

The people involved in a team effort and the organizational context in which they exist constitute two key sets of inputs into virtual collaboration. The chapters in Part Two address the knowledge, skills, and abilities necessary for individuals and teams that collaborate virtually, as well as the selection systems, training systems, and performance management systems that help support virtual teams. The chapter authors challenge us to think about how best to set up virtual teams for success.

In Chapter Five, Blackburn, Furst, and Rosen delineate the knowledge, skills, and abilities (KSAs) necessary for effective virtual team participation. They suggest, for example, that team members need the skills to use a variety of communication media and must understand when to use which. As a second set of KSAs, they describe team-level abilities such as establishing goals, agreeing on norms, and resolving conflicts. Following a discussion of virtual team KSAs, these authors delineate several KSAs for virtual team leaders, such as resolving relationship-based conflict. The importance of this set of KSAs was mentioned several times during our conference, as illustrated by the following comment by a consultant working with virtual teams:

> One of the interesting things I've been lucky enough to get involved in is an organization that has agreed that it will put only leaders who are relationship focused into virtual teams, which is kind of the opposite of how we promote people in our organizations. I think that's worth looking at.

After discussing the KSAs necessary for effective virtual teaming, Blackburn, Furst, and Rosen delineate and review many options for the design of selection and training systems that support virtuality. In terms of selection, they suggest profiling previous performance on virtual teams, situational interviews, and simulations that require candidates to interact virtually. In the area of training, they emphasize technology training and cross-cultural training because the meaning and interpretation of many behaviors is culturally bound.

A final topic addressed in Chapter Five is setting the organizational context for performance management. The need for such an effort was mentioned by several practitioners at our conference as a critical challenge, as exemplified in this comment by a practitioner discussing virtual assessment:

> I'm finding that turnover is an outcome of virtuality. People who are virtual a lot are saying, "I don't know where I belong, I don't know where my identity is, and I think I'm going to leave." What goes hand in hand is evaluation and the reward structure. Who's supposed to evaluate these people, especially in this team? They belong to different organizations, they have different bosses, and so on. Evaluation seems to be an issue; people are saying, "People who are evaluating me don't really know my work; they don't see me, and I don't see them."

In this regard, Blackburn, Furst, and Rosen argue that the key difference between virtual and face-to-face teams is that virtual performance management measures must capture process dimensions, for example, the extent to which individuals are able to resolve conflicts virtually. Finally, they develop the notion of a performance management system designed to look like an airplane cockpit that would contain and track in virtual space the measures of greatest strategic importance to the virtual team.

Many of these same themes are more fully developed in Chapter Six. Lawler argues that different types of virtual teams (for example, project teams versus production teams) have different operating systems and thus need somewhat different reward systems. Furthermore, to have an impact on outcomes such as attracting and retaining employees, motivating performance, or promoting skill and knowledge development, managers in organizations must make two critical decisions: whether to pay based on job descriptions or skills and competencies and how (if at all) to pay for performance. These challenges were expressed by many practitioners in our research, as exemplified in the following comment by a virtual team manager concerned about rewards for virtual teams:

> We have these high-achieving individuals located around the world, and they are delivering for their customer or their team great results without being able to calibrate their results versus anybody else. When I've been in situations like that, I think I'm doing great. Well, you then become impatient and want to move on, and I think a reward system could help address the uniqueness of, for example, a French national living in China, delivering great results for his team but not really feeling part of any social system.

Lawler argues that skill-based pay fits well in companies that want a flexible, relatively permanent workforce oriented toward learning, growth, and development; many team-based manufacturing plants use this approach. However, skill-based pay is more difficult to administer than job-based pay because there are no well-developed systems for determining the worth of individuals in the marketplace. Thus, given the variation among the skills needed for different virtual teams, Lawler argues that skill-based pay may be most effective for virtual teams that require cross-training in work processes, managerial tasks, or technical expertise. Skill-based pay, he suggests, is less effective for parallel teams because these teams are only a part-time commitment for many members.

The second fundamental question that Lawler addresses is whether organizations should pay virtual teams and their members for performance. He argues that in general, bonus plans do a better job of motivating employees than do pay raises and salary increase plans (because the latter become an annuity); that objective performance measures like sales volume are better than subjective measures such as supervisor ratings; and that group and organizational plans generally work best in creating integration and teamwork needed for virtual teams. In addition, Lawler makes the important point that determining what each virtual team values is a critical challenge that should be systematically addressed, and this is exacerbated the more that national, cultural, or other differences are represented on the team. Establishing objective metrics for successful team-level performance and linking rewards to team success is far more effective, particularly if team members are highly interdependent.

Chapter Seven, by Levenson and Cohen, focuses attention on the return on investment in virtual teaming. Not all organizations have a choice regarding whether to use virtual teams, but when decisions need to be made about how best to leverage virtuality, many issues arise, as illustrated in this quotation from a conference participant—a practitioner concerned about return on investment in virtual teams:

> The people involved in the project sometimes are not in the right position to support the cost. That can be addressed if there's clarity of commitment to the

objectives at the beginning. Often a team will say, "I need more, more, more," but if you can get the dialogue on return on investment at the beginning, that can be helpful. To the point of cost, I don't believe management understands the cost of virtual teams. They say, "We'll stop travel. We'll have a virtual team." We need to identify areas of cost that are missed. We've talked about getting on a plane when there's a crisis, so that needs to be built in. There needs to be some learning time for people. We talked about facilitation help; that's an extra resource from somewhere. I think you can help the whole process by quantifying the cost of having a virtual team. Then we'd be clearer on when to use them and when not.

Levenson and Cohen provide a framework for calculating return on investment (ROI) in virtual teams, develop a model for doing so, and highlight the specific issues that practitioners will confront in determining these returns. For example, the basic formula for ROI is benefits minus costs. However, a central issue for virtual teams is that it can be difficult to assign monetary values to costs and benefits that are not easily quantified. On the cost side, this may include opportunity costs associated with internal resources devoted to the team. Here, they recommend that simply calculating the costs of team members' time and support persons' time based on average salary is a good start. On the benefits side, a key challenge is moving beyond explicit revenue to understanding ancillary benefits that may emerge elsewhere in the organization as a result of a virtual team's work. Levenson and Cohen recommend that the focus here should be on identifying outcomes that stand to provide material benefit to the firm and can be expected to occur with some positive probability. Finally, these authors recommend using ROI data in a comparative mode to compare different projects using the same metric. Calibrating a prospective ROI value against prior projects allows for a more realistic assessment. In the end, Levenson and Cohen emphasize that the goal is to determine if a virtual team's charter is consistent with a company's bottom-line objectives. Given the substantial resources necessary to support virtual teams outlined in this part of the book, these are important questions to address in designing virtual teams and setting them up for success.

CHAPTER FIVE

Building a Winning Virtual Team

KSAs, Selection, Training, and Evaluation

Richard Blackburn, Stacie Furst, Benson Rosen

Technological advances have enabled many companies to assemble teams of employees from across the country or around the world into virtual teams to solve complex organizational problems (Lipnack and Stamps, 1998). Such teams are sometimes temporary, culturally diverse, geographically dispersed, and electronically communicating collections of individuals (Kristof, Brown, Sims, and Smith, 1995). They allow organizations to increase efficiency and effectiveness by tapping the knowledge, skills, and expertise of employees around the globe, increasing opportunities for information or knowledge exchange through expanded social networks (Wellman and others, 1996).

Virtual teams have the potential to contribute substantially to organizational effectiveness. However, there are no guarantees that virtual teams will reach their full potential. Experts suggest that as many fail as succeed (Lipnack and Stamps, 1998). And it may not even be obvious to virtual team leaders and members when a team is succeeding or in difficulty. To help managers develop a better appreciation for what is required to build a high-performance virtual team, we consider the critical knowledge, skills, and abilities (KSAs) needed to lead and work virtually, suggest how organizations can build effective virtual teams by selecting great leaders and skilled members, highlight the training and development initiatives available to prepare teams for working virtually, and describe an approach for evaluating virtual team effectiveness. Our goal is to help managers understand the complexities surrounding the building, development, and performance assessment of virtual teams.

KNOWLEDGE, SKILLS, AND ABILITIES

As any basketball coach knows, building a winning team starts with recruiting talented players. Good coaches identify the skill set required for each position. Building a winning virtual team also begins with selecting members who have the knowledge, skills, and experience to collaborate effectively and accomplish the team's mission. Accordingly, we begin by identifying the KSAs that virtual team members and leaders need.

As a starting point, we reviewed the KSAs considered critical for members of face-to-face teams (Stevens and Campion, 1994) and then reviewed research studies in the fields of information technology, computer-mediated communication, and group dynamics that focused on virtual teams. To confirm our insights from the scientific literature, we conducted interviews with twenty-five virtual team managers, facilitators, and consultants. What emerged was a set of KSAs we believe are important for leading and participating in virtual teams. The KSAs we describe form the basis for selecting virtual team participants and creating training programs to strengthen virtual team performance.

We grouped the KSAs into three categories: individual team member KSAs, team KSAs, and team leader KSAs. Many of the KSAs needed to perform effectively in the virtual environment mirror those needed for success with face-to-face teams. However, the virtual team's reliance on electronic communication and the challenges of working in the global environment dictate that additional individual, team, and leadership KSAs are required to produce a winning record. The KSAs outlined here provide a starting point for managers concerned with selecting, training, and evaluating their virtual team members.

Individual KSAs

The unique challenges of working virtually require that team members develop mastery around self-management, virtual communication, cultural sensitivity, trust building, and competence in using information technology. The ideal virtual team member will be a self-starter, capable of selecting the appropriate communications medium to match the message, sensitive to the nuances of communicating across cultures, insightful about strategies for engendering electronic trust, and eager to embrace new technologies that facilitate team collaboration.

Self-Management KSAs. Building on our basketball example, at the first scrimmage, the coach describes the drills for the day and blows the whistle, and the players hustle to their positions. Similarly, in face-to-face teams, the leader reviews the agenda, and the team springs into action. However, in the virtual environment, much work can be accomplished serially as well as simultaneously. For instance, product development efforts can "follow the sun" as team members hand off their latest development efforts to their virtual colleagues working in different time zones around the world. In essence, the virtual team never rests. Virtual team members may also work in relative isolation. Often they lack the prodding of the coach's whistle or the leader's calling the meeting to order, and they rarely see their teammates at work. Working on a virtual team often requires members to be their own coaches and leaders, setting personal agendas and motivating themselves to take appropriate action. Accordingly, a skill set critical for virtual team membership includes abilities to behave proactively and manage themselves.

Proactivity skills in the context of virtual teams may include identifying required behaviors, seeking out relevant information, taking the initiative to contact team members, overcoming time and distance barriers, and staying the course without managerial intervention (Bateman and Crant, 1993). Closely related to proactivity is self-regulation, defined as "those processes that enable an individual to guide his/her goal-directed activities over time and across changing circumstances" (Karoly, 1993). Self-regulation also requires effective time management skills. A virtual team member must balance the demands of the local unit with obligations to virtual teammates who may be located across many time zones. Proactivity, self-regulation, and time management are desirable KSAs for all team members, but they are critical KSAs for virtual team members.

Communications KSAs. Communication in virtual teams has two challenges: sending information so that the message is heard and gathering feedback. Sending information virtually requires the special ability to select the transmission medium most appropriate for the message content. Sharing routine information may merely require e-mail or depositing a document in a shared work space. Solving a complex problem requires a richer communication medium such as a teleconference. And resolving what appears to be a stalemate requires an even richer medium afforded by a videoconference, where both the content and emotion of the message can be shared with the help of physical images.

Seeking feedback presents another special communication challenge to virtual team members. In face-to-face meetings, members receive feedback from shared information, facial expressions, body language, and many other subtle signals. In virtual teams, feedback based on visual cues may be hard to interpret or nonexistent. Similarly, not receiving any kind of communication from virtual teammates might signal that a member is being sanctioned and excluded or simply that a computer system is temporarily down. Virtual team members must learn to interpret the signals sent by their teammates, sometimes going off-line for one-on-one conversations and exchanges to clarify misunderstandings or overcome language and cultural barriers. Communications skills such as using the appropriate communications media to transmit information and interpreting feedback represent important KSAs for virtual team members.

Cultural Sensitivity and Awareness KSAs. A technology manager we interviewed commented, "Among the biggest challenges to virtual team effectiveness are the cultural differences among team members." This manager shared the story of a virtual team whose one Asian member, because of his cultural heritage, avoided open conflict with others. When he disagreed with his virtual teammates, he remained silent so others in the controversy could save face. Over time, others on the team learned to interpret their Asian colleague's silence as respectful deference. Team members politely prodded him to identify potential conflicts. In this instance, the KSA of cultural awareness and sensitivity was critical to shared understanding and virtual team effectiveness.

Trust KSAs. In face-to-face groups, trust among teammates develops based on perceived similarities, acts of benevolence, and demonstrations of integrity (Mayer, Davis, and Schoorman, 1995). Because virtual team members cannot easily observe their colleagues' efforts, they must often go on faith for some period of time while waiting for a tangible contribution from others to the team's mission. Lengthy intervals between communications, slow responses to teammates' questions, and failure to follow up on previous promises can all engender mistrust. In virtual teams, trust is created based on responsiveness and dependability. Mutual trust is maintained among virtual team members through demonstrated commitment to the team's mission by active and frequent participation—what some researchers call swift trust (Jarvenpaa, Knoll, and Leidner, 1998). Accordingly, virtual team members must understand that their trustworthiness will be assessed based on their behavior, not on their good intentions.

Comfort with Technology and Technological Change KSAs. What sets virtual teams apart from face-to-face teams is their use of information technology to link members situated in distant locations. Each virtual team member must be well versed and fully comfortable with the wide range of information technologies available to the team, including collaboration software packages, videoconferencing, and other communication media necessary for the team to work at full capacity (Staples, Hulland, and Higgins, 1999).

Technologically confident and competent team members form the foundation for building a winning virtual team. Equally important is the openness of team members to learn to use new technologies to their full potential. One consultant we interviewed reported that successful virtual teaming demands that team members be willing to change their mind-set about the use of technology to collaborate in new ways. He noted that for many individuals, virtual teaming represents a paradigm shift that requires individual flexibility, adaptability, and openness to new experiences.

Team-Level KSAs

Referring back to our basketball example, team KSAs deal with how the entire team collaborates to win games. A basketball team that is capable of making a smooth transition from offense to defense or to set up a play that leaves their best outside shooter in position to take an uncontested shot has developed team-level skills and competencies. Similarly, virtual teams must develop KSAs to capitalize fully on the strengths of individual members. Team KSAs deal with how virtual teams establish goals, agree on norms, solve problems, resolve conflicts, balance relationship and task activities, develop a learning orientation, and periodically renew themselves. Virtual teams that master these important KSAs surrounding group process and decision making are expected to develop real synergy where the team achieves at a level far greater than the sum of its individual members' contributions.

Establishing Virtual Team Goals and Defining Team Roles. Establishing clear goals and well-defined member roles are fundamental team-level KSAs for building a winning virtual team. Our technology manager interviewees stressed the value of a preliminary face-to-face meeting and a series of team-building exercises for establishing team goals. Interviewees also emphasized the importance of establishing agreement on team timetables and individual areas of responsibility and accountability prior to working virtually. When team members agree on the team's mission, goals, milestones, and deliverables, potential misunderstandings and conflicts when the team begins working virtually are minimized. Therefore, a critical team-level KSA is the ability of virtual teams to reach consensus around goals and roles.

Establishing Team Norms KSAs. Winning virtual teams develop a code of conduct and a set of norms that guide team interactions. Norms revolve around the use of specific modes of communication, acceptable response times, document archiving in shared work spaces, and establishing task priorities among other issues. Virtual team norms help team members communicate easily and collaborate effectively. For example, one virtual team developed norms to set priorities and avoid information overload. Team members agreed on coding electronic messages as AR (action required), IAR (immediate action required), or FYI (for your information—general information). In another virtual team, members developed norms governing communications, such as "I will log on once a day" and "I will be honest with my comments." The ability to establish norms governing team interaction was widely viewed as critical to team effectiveness.

Team Problem-Solving KSAs. An important KSA for virtual teams is the ability to solve complex problems. Research suggests that consensus is more difficult to reach with virtual teams, particularly those teams working on complex nontechnical issues (Hollingshead and McGrath, 1995). Consensus involves give and take, bargaining, and negotiation to arrive at a team output on which all team members can agree. These interactions typically require substantial team interaction, which is more difficult in the virtual environment. Virtual teams have difficulty duplicating the give and take found in face-to-face conversations because of response delays, slow typing, sequencing problems, and technical constraints embedded in some types of communication technologies used to solve problems. In addition, the absence of nonverbal cues that help regulate face-to-face conversation flow, like turn taking, providing instant feedback, and articulating hidden meanings, reduces the richness of communication and the speed of problem solving. Accordingly, teams must develop creative mechanisms for overcoming communications and problem-solving barriers imposed by working virtually. Some teams have used innovative technologies that facilitate brainstorming, ranking options, and using electronic discussion forums to reach agreements. Other teams combine computer technology and videoconferencing to resolve complex problems in real time. The critical factor is that virtual teams build the capacity to attack complex problems.

Team Conflict Management KSAs. Resolving conflict in virtual teams is more difficult than for face-to-face-teams. Because virtual members have only limited opportunities to observe the body language and hear the tone of voice or observe other team members' facial expressions, many virtual team conflicts may go undetected for long periods. How can virtual team members surface conflicts? Or as one virtual team consultant asked, "How do you read a virtual team as you would a face-to-face team?" Virtual teams need to develop early warning systems that alert team members to potential conflict.

One particular kind of conflict reported in virtual teams is the tendency for one or more members to free-ride or coast at the expense of teammates. Virtual team members who fail to keep their commitments, stop communicating, or disappear leave other team members in limbo or require others to compensate for the free rider's poor performance, usually leading to intense conflict. In one virtual team we studied, long lags between transmissions were seen as a signal of potential free riding and conflict. The team leader assumed the responsibility for off-line contact with members who were not communicating regularly, probing for potential conflicts and acting as a mediator when needed. Other virtual teams participated in virtual team conflict resolution training programs that sensitized team members to potential conflicts and provided opportunities to practice team conflict-resolution skills. The goal of this training was to build team-level conflict-resolution competencies in advance to be deployed as needed.

Balancing Relationship and Task Team KSAs. Virtual teams tend to be more task oriented and exchange less socioemotional information, slowing the development of relational links among team members. Most virtual teams do not have a virtual water cooler around which members informally exchange information. Because relational links are positively related to several team performance dimensions, including creativity and satisfaction, they may be key to maintaining winning virtual teams (Chidambaram, 1996). An important virtual team KSA is to balance energy devoted to task and relationship building. Teams must take advantage of opportunities to interact and build social ties in their virtual space. For one team, the completion of a difficult assignment was celebrated with cake and ice cream at each team member's work site. For other teams, professional or corporate conferences provided the occasion for face-to-face meetings and an opportunity to rebuild social capital. In virtual teams, all task and no relationship building leads to dull teams. A critical KSA is the capacity to strike a balance, overcoming barriers of time and distance and finding creative ways to build social bonds.

Many virtual teams meet face-to-face as needed to strengthen social bonds. One virtual team member reported that when her team goes too long without interacting in person, communications become terse and "snippy." These symptoms mean that the team needs to get together and reconnect. Beyond solidifying social ties, the face-to-face meetings provide an opportunity to reaffirm goals, clarify roles, and share learning experiences, all important KSAs for maintaining virtual teams.

Team Learning KSAs. A requisite KSA for winning virtual teams is the creation of a learning orientation. Because virtual teams can tap the knowledge and expertise of specialists around the organization and around the world, it is critical that they establish mechanisms to share information, learn from each other, build on each other's work, and provide candid and constructive feedback to teammates.

Traditionally, specialists have been trained to deliver finished products. In virtual teams, colleagues must be willing to share "half-baked" ideas, knowing that they will not have the chance to explain or defend themselves as they might in face-to-face teams. Working in a virtual community requires what one executive called "a huge cultural shift and psychological change from hoarding information to sharing information." The important virtual team KSA is the capacity to create a safe, secure team environment that enables and encourages easy collaboration. A strong learning orientation requires team members to experiment with different approaches for rapid information sharing, archiving best practices, and maintaining communities of practice (Robey, Khoo, and Powers, 2000). Winning virtual teams periodically assess their effectiveness, make necessary adjustments, and continuously improve their capacity for learning.

KSAs for Virtual Team Leaders

Effective leadership is the last critical component needed to build a winning virtual team. As one corporate executive noted, "The number one key success factor for virtual teams is strong leadership." Another executive emphasized, "It takes a huge effort to manage a virtual team and do it well." Given the complexities of virtual teamwork, what are the critical leadership KSAs?

We would expect that all of the KSAs required to lead a face-to-face team represent necessary but not sufficient competencies for leading a virtual team. Among other important responsibilities, leaders of all teams must be able to play a major role in defining the group's mission; setting high expectations; shaping the group's culture; coaching, counseling, and motivating team members; facilitating meetings; mediating conflicts; evaluating performance; and recognizing individual and group achievements. However, leading a virtual group frequently requires novel ways to enact these important KSAs.

The first requirement for a virtual team leader is to serve as a role model for team members. Virtual team leaders must consistently use the collaboration software, demonstrate a willingness to share information openly, choose the appropriate media for communication, and adhere to norms regarding promptness of responding to others. In other words, the virtual team leader must model the special skills and strategies needed for virtual collaboration. As one virtual team leader noted, "You have to demonstrate to your team that you get it."

When working virtually, and in many cases serially, it is easy to lose focus. The virtual team leader must help members maintain a line of sight to the ultimate objectives (Kimball and Eunice, 1999). A virtual team leader, particularly when working with a transglobal team, must continuously remind team members of their responsibilities. One virtual team leader stated, "My job is to remind my virtual team members who does what, by when." Another virtual team leader described a large part of his role as "managing by walking around in virtual space."

Team leaders often find themselves in the role of virtual coaches. For some team members, coaching takes the form of instructing team members on how to use new technology. In other instances, virtual team leaders may coach members off-line on the importance of tact and diplomacy in their electronic communications with colleagues. And as one team leader mentioned, "I do a lot of virtual hand-holding," helping to ensure physically isolated team members that their contributions are valued.

Another challenge for virtual team leaders is to provide virtual pats on the back for outstanding contributors. Rewarding excellence on virtual teams requires a special sensitivity to cultural differences in preferences for recognition. Moreover, some of the exuberance of group celebrations may be lost when team members are separated by thousands of miles. Developing creative ways to recognize and reward individual and team accomplishments virtually ranks high as an important skill needed by virtual team leaders.

SELECTING VIRTUAL TEAM LEADERS AND MEMBERS

In our interviews, we learned that organizations often underestimate the importance of careful selection when establishing virtual teams. The prevailing sentiment in many organizations appears to be that individuals with the technical skills for the team task are assumed capable of working collaboratively on virtual teams. Little consideration is given to the special challenges and the necessary KSAs associated with virtual teamwork. For example, the importance of cross-cultural sensitivity for working successfully on global virtual teams may be underestimated. Similarly, the special skills needed to confront the lack of participation by some virtual teammates may not be appreciated until a project is hopelessly behind schedule. Clearly, the costs of poor selection decisions in the creation of virtual teams may exceed the time and expense required to develop a systematic selection process. Accordingly, when virtual teaming is a key part of an organization's strategy, much more attention must be given to selecting virtual team leaders and members.

Experts advise managers to choose team members carefully and give each member a good reason for being on the team (Cascio, 2000). The goal, as with any other selection plan, should be to identify among current or potential employees those who possess the necessary combination of KSAs for leading and working on virtual teams. The starting point for developing sophisticated selection procedures is the identification of critical KSAs that team leaders and members must possess to accomplish the team's mission. As with colocated teams, members may be selected based on technical expertise and experience relative to the task demands. In addition, selection criteria may include a second set of attributes relative to teamwork, which include a variety of interpersonal, communication, and group process skills. More important, organizations should also consider a third set of selection criteria focusing specifically on the unique knowledge, skills, and experience necessary to function in a virtual team environment. The relationship among these three sets of KSAs is shown in Figure 5.1.

Tradition offers organizations several strategies for making selection decisions for virtual team members. Starting with the selection principle that the best predictor of future behavior is past behavior under similar circumstances, selection of virtual team leaders and members might begin with an examination of previous virtual team experiences. Perhaps the most efficient strategy for collecting this information is the modification of company application materials for hiring new employees and work history documents for current employees.

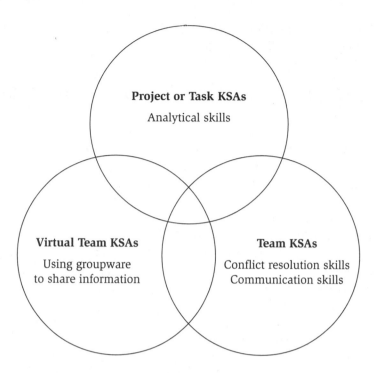

Figure 5.1 KSAs for Projects and Tasks, Teams, and Virtual Teams.

A typical application form includes a section on work history. Questions could be added to determine specific virtual team experience. Applicants could also be asked to report on their familiarity and skill with collaborative tools such as Lotus Notes, IP-Team, NexPrize, LiveLink, and other group software packages for managing projects, archiving documents, brainstorming, and building consensus in the context of virtual teams. Similarly, application materials could include sections where candidates report on special training they received related to leading and working virtually. Candidates with previous experience should already have a realistic preview of the many challenges associated with virtual teams. Similarly, for internal candidates, virtual team experiences and special training for working virtually should be part of an employee's personnel records and useful for selection decisions.

Application materials and work histories provide valuable information about a candidate's experiences and training related to virtual teams. However, these documents say little about the quality of employee contributions to virtual team effectiveness. Accordingly, archival data could provide additional information for making virtual team selection decisions. For both external and internal candidates, performance reviews, records of previous virtual team accomplishments, and references from former virtual team leaders (where available) should provide relevant information about the quality of virtual team contributions. In the case of internal candidates, evaluations by former colocated and virtual teammates would be valuable to the selection process. Application materials and work histories describing experience working virtually coupled with archival data of virtual team contributions should increase the accuracy of selection decisions.

Personality testing represents a second general strategy for selecting virtual team leaders and members. Personality testing may be valuable when considering internal and external applicants who lack previous experience with virtual teams. As our discussion of KSAs indicated, personality characteristics identified as important for virtual team success might include the ability to set personal goals, take initiative, and work autonomously. A second set of personality dimensions clusters around emotional control, tolerance for ambiguity, and openness to new experience. A third cluster might include important communications skills such as listening empathetically and cross-cultural sensitivity.

With respect to assessment of the personality attributes, a number of existing personality indexes exist. Obvious candidates include assessments of emotional intelligence (Goleman, 1995), proactivity (Bateman and Crant, 1993), action-state orientation (Kuhl, 1994), and the "big five" personality dimensions. For example, the NEO Personality Inventory (Costa and McCrae, 1992) measures such personality traits as assertiveness, independence of judgment, trust, cooperativeness, purposeful behavior, and dependability. These are characteristics hypothesized to be important to the effective functioning of virtual teams.

Most personality scales have high face validity, and many of them can be administered on-line with real-time scoring. The on-line format seems particularly well suited for selecting individuals who will spend a significant proportion of their time on-line. Organizations that decide to include personality inventories as part of their overall selection strategies will need to conduct systematic validation studies for the assessment of specific traits to establish their predictive validities in the virtual context.

Perhaps the most frequently used selection tool is the interview. Almost all organizations interview external and internal applicants for new positions, transfers, and promotion to new positions. Regarding the use of interviews for selecting virtual team leaders and members, organizations face a number of decisions, including the choice of interviewers, the nature and format of the interview process, and the use of face-to-face interviewing or videoconferencing to conduct the interview.

High-level executives who are focused on accomplishing important organizational projects usually take responsibility for appointing virtual team leaders. Virtual team leaders, in consultation with various stakeholders such as department heads and regional managers, then play a major role in selecting virtual team members. Selection under these circumstances is more likely to take into account technical expertise and regional or country representation rather than important skills for working virtually. For the selection of both virtual team leaders and members, organizations may have to educate these various stakeholders involved in commissioning and assembling virtual teams so that they have a better appreciation of the KSAs needed to lead and work virtually. When a virtual team has already worked together for some time, it is quite common for its members to participate in the selection of new team members. Given advances in videoconferencing technology, virtual team members can easily carry out the interview process virtually.

Among the many approaches to the selection interview, two strategies seem especially well suited for selecting virtual team leaders and members: the experience-based interview and the situational interview (Heneman, Heneman, and Judge, 1997). For individuals with previous experience working virtually, interview questions could probe how candidates coped with issues common to virtual teams. For example, a candidate for a virtual team leadership role could be asked to describe a virtual team project where team members might have underused available technology and explain how he or she resolved the problem. Similarly, candidates for a virtual team could be asked to recall a situation where a virtual team member failed to post important documents to the team's virtual work space and explain how they managed this unresponsive team member.

The situational interview approach does not require candidates to have actual experience working with virtual teams. Hypothetical problems are posed, and candidates are asked to explain how they might respond. Both the experience-based interview and the situational interview formats are excellent tools for identifying candidates with leadership qualities and team process skills important for virtual team effectiveness.

It has been well documented that interviewers form impressions and base evaluations on non-job-related factors such as a candidate's physical appearance. Conducting interviews with distantly situated candidates by telephone, videoconference, or e-mail might actually offset common selection errors such as stereotyping and similar-to-me effects and increase the accuracy of selection decisions. One study demonstrated that interviews conducted over the telephone were more accurate than those conducted face-to-face (Strauss, 1998).

Interviews are designed to learn how candidates have previously responded or how they might respond to job-relevant situations in the future. Simulations assess how candidates actually respond in situations they will likely face on the job. Accordingly, they represent a potentially excellent tool for selecting future virtual team leaders and members. Exercises can be created that capture many of the challenges associated with virtual work. For example, candidates might be asked to plan, organize, and complete a short project with virtual teammates. They would be required to communicate using virtual team software to complete their virtual task. The simulation creators could build a variety of obstacles into the experience that must be overcome, such as cross-cultural misunderstandings, technological breakdowns, and mistrustful teammates. Candidates for virtual team leadership positions might encounter situations requiring clarification of team goals, negotiation of tight deadlines, or the need to go off-line to coach or counsel individual team members.

CD-ROM technology should make it relatively easy and cost-efficient to create realistic simulations. How candidates respond in the simulation would provide valuable information on a variety of important KSAs, including skills in communicating virtually, organizing work, emergent leadership, and managing conflict on virtual teams. Use of simulations to select among internal candidates has the added benefit of providing specific feedback to each participant. Development of virtual team simulation materials used for selection can also serve as excellent training vehicles.

In our experience, organizations have yet to develop comprehensive strategies for selecting individuals for roles as virtual team leaders or members. Most of the effort to date has been directed to training and development rather than selection. However, a combination of good selection decisions and comprehensive training for working virtually is certain to be more effective than either approach in isolation.

TRAINING THE VIRTUAL TEAM

Organizations recognize the importance of providing virtual teams with the training they need to perform at full capacity. We discovered a range of programs designed to help virtual teams master communications technology, respond to challenges encountered at different stages in the virtual team life cycle, and collaborate across cultures.

Technology Training

Since virtual teams communicate predominantly by means of information technology, it is imperative that virtual team members be well versed in a variety of electronic communication media. Research has shown that virtual team members who are comfortable with technology are more likely to use it (Davis, Bagozzi, and Warshaw, 1989). Therefore, training for virtual teams frequently focuses on the mastery of communications tools technologies such as Webcasting, meeting managers, white boards, electronic bulletin boards, and other programs to facilitate information sharing (Solomon, 2001). Training new virtual team members in these technologies can reduce many communications problems. Similarly, training in the matching of technology tool and team tasks helps team members understand which technology is most appropriate for, say, mass distribution of noncontroversial documents and which technology is most appropriate when visual cues are critical for developing solutions.

With the growing popularity of virtual teams, there has been a corresponding proliferation of software packages to facilitate distributed team management. Many of the programs are complex, requiring substantial training. Software programs mentioned by our interviewees include IP-Team, DOME (Distributed Object Modeling Environment), HP CoCreate, WebX, and LiveLink. These technology software tools have advanced features designed to support effective virtual collaboration. Virtual teams often need coaching to exploit the full potential of these software programs.

Training in Group Processes

The challenges facing virtual teams change over the life cycle of the virtual team. To prepare virtual team members for the complex problems that await them at the various stages of their team's development, a number of training options are available. A growing repository of CD- or Web-based training modules exists to help new teams establish a charter, clarify team goals, and solidify team norms. As teams develop, additional training modules focus on process-related issues such as conducting an effective virtual team meeting, problem solving, and decision making. For example, eTeaming, a virtual team consulting organization based in Boston, has developed a series of computer-based training modules, such as "Challenges and Best Practices," "Building Trust and Relationships," and "Working Virtually in a Matrix Organization." Each module contains prework exercises that team members complete prior to the team's kickoff, application-based exercises to be completed during the team's operation, and opportunities for assessment after the team's projects are complete.

Some training modules are flexible and can be modified or combined to match the training needs of each virtual team member. Moreover, the modules can be completed at the team member's convenience, providing that the person meets a team deadline for completing the package of modules. The entire team must complete other training modules in a specified sequence. Team members collectively work through the modules, comparing notes by teleconference or e-mail, and discussing lessons learned along the way about virtual team collaboration. The group training modules provide an opportunity for team members to build social capital and practice the kinds of skills that will be needed to collaborate effectively in the future.

Cross-Cultural Training

A major advantage of virtual teams is the opportunity for experts situated in many parts of the world to work collaboratively. Cross-cultural training expands team member awareness of differences in language, cultural norms, and values, which is frequently critical to virtual team success. Cross-cultural training is designed to help virtual teams overcome communications barriers.

Because the meaning of words and the context in which they are spoken differ in various cultures (Gibson and Zellmer-Bruhn, 2001), virtual team members need to develop high levels of precision in their communications. Some training programs point out how easily cross-cultural misunderstandings develop and how to avoid many communications problems through careful choice of words. Similarly, work habits and communication preferences differ across cultures. Whereas the U.S. culture places a premium on individual behavior, Asian cultures value teamwork, cooperation, and group harmony. Alerting global virtual team members to deeply ingrained cultural values goes a long way toward avoiding potential misunderstandings. Finally, cross-cultural training prepares virtual team members for religious differences that may influence virtual team performance. For example, team members in the United States come to appreciate that their teammates in Israel may not be available for virtual conferences on Friday afternoons or Saturdays as they observe the Sabbath.

Face-to-Face Versus Virtual Training

While most of the training we have described is conducted virtually, experts agree that some team member training is best accomplished face-to-face. At the early stages in a virtual team's life cycle, face-to-face team-building training helps virtual team members build trust in their colleagues. Establishing positive relationships with virtual team members through such team-building activities as outdoor adventures and group challenges is frequently recommended for launching a virtual team. In addition, should substantive problems arise or communications break down at any point in the team's life cycle, another face-to-face training intervention may be the only way to repair the team fabric.

Advanced Training Versus Just-in-Time

A rigorous training program on all dimensions of virtual team collaboration prepares virtual team members for the challenges they will soon encounter. Therefore, a front-end investment in training should help the virtual team hit the ground running. However, some organizations bypass extensive pretraining for virtual team assignments. They argue that the rationale for using virtual teams (keeping up with the speed of business and improving efficiency) precludes the delays necessary for formal training. Remarked one executive, "We don't have anything formal in place. People don't want to spend two or three days learning how to be a virtual team. They want to learn as they go."

We interviewed officials at an organization that strongly advocated this just-in-time approach to virtual team training. The company has developed elaborate training manuals for virtual team leaders and members that provide extensive guidance on the virtual team start-up process, including defining members' roles, identifying cultural issues, and resolving conflicts. Team leaders and team members consult the training manuals as needed. The urgency of the virtual team context usually provides added motivation to master the skills described in the training manuals as appropriate.

MEASURING VIRTUAL TEAM PERFORMANCE

The success of a sports team is typically a function of the number of wins the team accumulates during its season. Although this may be an important measure of team success in athletics, there are other performance dimensions that coaches are also concerned about, like improvement throughout the season, team morale, participation, and effort levels. When evaluating team performance in a nonsports setting, organizations also need to be concerned with both outcomes and process. This is particularly true when it comes to assessing the performance of virtual teams.

In our interviews with virtual team leaders and members and in our examination of what others have written about virtual teams, it became clear that what is true for performance measurement in face-to-face teams is also true for measurement in virtual teams. High-quality performance evaluation systems for face-to-face teams form the foundation for similar systems designed to evaluate virtual team performance.

Performance measures in both settings must be linked to the overall strategy of a firm as well as to the desired outcomes for the team. These measures must be linked to the issues raised in the first two sections of this chapter. Performance measures should act as criteria against which to assess selection validity as well as the value and effectiveness of virtual team training.

Issues of what, how, why, and when to measure performance are only marginally different between the face-to-face and virtual teams. But if the devil is in the details, we want to consider some of these possible differences.

In face-to-face settings, team members and leaders are able to observe a substantial portion of the performance of their colleagues and subordinates. Performance judgments can be made on the basis of work outcomes as well as attendance and perceptions of team members' effort, cooperation, and collaboration. Typically, judgments of performance in face-to-face teams occur among participants within similar organizational or national cultures. These conditions do not exist for most of the virtual teams we examined. Thus, some modifications in performance measures are appropriate for virtual teams. In particular, Sparrow and Daniels (1999) remind us that multidimensional performance measures for virtual teams should include individual performance but also wider contributions to team performance, adaptability to new and changing work arrangements, and the ability to acquire and share knowledge.

What to Measure in Virtual Teams

Typically, organizations design performance measurement systems to assess both team performance and individual member contributions to their team's performance. Some organizations focus performance measures on team outcomes because they are concerned that they not jeopardize team cohesiveness by focusing too much on individual performance. Most organizations, however, choose to assess both team outcomes and member contributions. In face-to-face teams, individual contributions may be more obvious than in a virtual setting. Thus, virtual team measures must provide for the explicit determination of individual contributions. In particular, virtual team leaders might want to consider selecting performance measures that sample from each of four performance criteria domains obtained by assessing team- and individual-level outcome and process measures.

For example, from the team outcome perspective, organizations assess typical team outcomes like the quality, quantity, creativity, cost, and timeliness of the team's deliverables. In the individual outcome domain, organizations assess the same outcomes at the individual level, but they may also assess the extent to which each individual team member meets personal deadlines or milestones that contributed to the overall performance of the team. Uniquely, leaders of virtual teams might wish to assess the contributions team members made to organizational knowledge or learning. The electronic archives that result from virtual team interactions can at once become part of a firm's knowledge repository and provide performance information as to the number and relative value of the contributions made by each virtual team member to this repository.

The outcomes assessed in both face-to-face and virtual teams are quite similar. However, since it is along process dimensions that virtual teams differ most from their face-to-face counterparts, it is along process dimensions where performance measures should differ for the two teams.

In the two remaining performance domains, criteria that assess team and individual process contributions, performance measures could be selected that might provide useful knowledge unique to the virtual team environment. In the individual process domain, firms might wish to assess the extent to which individuals were able to resolve conflicts with their virtual team members, member willingness to provide useful and timely information and assistance when requested, and the extent to which members "disappear" from the team at crucial moments. Social loafing in face-to-face teams can be problematic but relatively easy to identify and address. In a virtual environment, getting by on the backs of teammates may be far more difficult to identify and correct. Because observation in the virtual environment is limited, it might also be useful to assess attitudinal variables for team members such as individual satisfaction with the level of information sharing and collaboration.

Good indicators of virtual team process include the extent to which the team uses its members' expertise in appropriate ways, the level of conflict or cohesiveness present in the team as a whole, and the extent to which the team collectively adds value to the firm's repository of knowledge and learning.

How to Measure Virtual Performance

In seeking to measure virtual performance, managers must understand and appreciate that how virtual performance is measured will also be influenced to a large extent by why performance is being measured, what elements of performance are to be measured, who will be doing the measuring, and when those measurements might occur.

Given the dispersed nature of virtual teams, the traditional model of performance measurement and evaluation by the leader may be useful and appropriate, but it must be augmented by performance input from other sources. The leader's inability to observe most of a team member's means to performance ends suggests that additional sources of performance evaluation input are needed. With virtual teams, these sources could be self-evaluations, evaluations from other team members, and evaluations from the team's "customers" inside or outside the organization. In fact, the virtual environment seems ideal for the use of 360-degree performance measurement systems (self and other evaluations).

Virtual leaders need to be aware that self-ratings and the ratings of others in a virtual environment may differ from similar ratings obtained in a face-to-face team environment. For instance, Weisband and Atwater (1999) found that self-ratings were more often inflated and less accurate in virtual settings than in face-to-face settings. They suggested that the lack of feedback cues about individual team contributions in a virtual setting might lead to inflated self-perceptions of one's contributions to the team.

In a virtual team, rating biases stemming from friendships or liking (as opposed to actual team contributions) of team members were less evident in ratings of others' contributions as compared to similar ratings in face-to-face teams. Managers of virtual teams who actively participate in as well as monitor communications among their virtual team members reduce the likelihood that these biases will damage the validity of their performance measurement and evaluation. In addition, virtual team leaders who use 360-degree performance information also reduce these biases as they evaluate collective performance input.

Performance measures for any team must be multidimensional in nature. The preceding discussion has stressed the importance of evaluating both the outcome and the process components of virtual team performance. Assistance regarding which performance dimensions to evaluate is provided with Kaplan and Norton's Balanced Scorecard (1992, 1993, 1996a, 1996b), a model that can give top executives a more comprehensive view of performance in organizations and their strategic business units.

Kaplan and Norton argue that focusing on financial indicators of organizational success provides an incomplete picture of performance. In most cases, these indicators reflect historical performance rather than indicate the organization's potential for future success. These authors suggest that in addition to financial measures, three other performance areas be evaluated to maintain a balanced approach to assessing organizational performance: internal business processes, innovation, and customer satisfaction. The Balanced Scorecard is probably appropriate down to the level of strategic business unit, but the authors did not consider its appropriateness at team levels.

Meyer (1994) addressed some of these issues at the team level with what he described as a "dashboard" evaluation template designed to assess multiple dimensions of team performance. His suggested team outcome and process measures included measures of member satisfaction, appropriateness of team staffing levels, development status (extent to which the project has been completed and is on schedule), project costs to date, indicators of when the next important reviews must occur, product costs, and product quality in addition to financial indicators (margins, revenues).

For virtual teams, we suggest an adaptation of the dashboard, which, in the spirit of virtual distances, we call the cockpit. To develop such a system, Meyer proposed that teams and organizations be guided by four principles. First, a measurement system should help the team, rather than top management, gauge its progress. The system should provide a tool for telling a team when it must take corrective action. This will be particularly important for virtual teams where communication between team members and leaders may occur infrequently (assuming that the team has a formal leader, which it may not), and determination of progress milestones and corrective actions may rest with the virtual team.

Second, a team must take the lead role in designing its own measurement system, and this measurement system should be consistent with the company's strategy. Cascio (1999, pp. 10–11) notes that virtual team–based "measures should be linked to the strategic direction, business objectives, and customer requirements for the company." Much of the literature suggests that virtual teams should develop a charter, contract, mandate, or set of objectives that top managers, team leaders, and members agree on. Also included in this charter or contract would be information as to the number and timing of team performance reviews.

Myer notes that one major advantage of such a charter and of team member development of and agreement on team performance measures is that members from different functions, companies, and cultures create a common language that they will need to use to work as an effective team. Without a common language, teams would not be able to reach a common definition of goals or progress. This is clearly what is needed with a virtual team whose members are separated by time, place, and culture. The discussions on what should appear on the virtual team cockpit or on what basis the team should be held accountable help create this common bond.

Third, because a virtual team is responsible for a value delivery process that often cuts cross several functions (for example, product development, order fulfillment, or customer service), it must create measures to track processes. As indicated, the evaluation of processes was one of the most important functions of performance measures in the virtual environment.

Finally, teams should adopt only a handful of measures. If there are too many performance measures, team members may spend more time collecting and providing data than working on important team tasks. Meyer suggests that no team have more than fifteen measures. If it does, it should take a fresh look at the importance of each.

Many of the elements that appear in Meyer's dashboard would be fully appropriate for the assessment of virtual teams. Figures 5.2 and 5.3 are adapted from Meyer (1994) for use by virtual teams to evaluate and report team and team member performance. The multiple measures in each of the templates provide both outcome and process information, the latter being especially important for assessing the performance of virtual teams.

The template in Figure 5.2 provides for the evaluation of team-level outcome measures (product development status, customer satisfaction, program costs, product costs, new customers identified, and new revenues generated), as well as team-level process measures (team morale, system utilization, system availability, and archive contributions by team members). The team member template in Figure 5.3 also includes individual-level outcome and process members submitted by each team member (possibly) as part of a 360-degree performance measurement approach. Other team members and key team stakeholders could use the same type of template to provide their evaluations of each team member's performance.

Given the technology used in virtual teams, teams could design their own templates for team members, leaders, and key stakeholders to complete and review. Each virtual team member could complete a self-evaluation template (as in Figure 5.3) reflecting assessments of personal contributions on appropriate performance dimensions. Similarly, each team member and interested stakeholders could complete a template for each member of the team on the same performance dimensions. These same individuals could also use a team-based template (as in Figure 5.2), reflecting performance dimensions associated with team outcomes and processes. Finally, the team leader or other managers could complete both of these evaluation forms.

The timing of these evaluations could be varied. For instance, as is the case in most face-to-face teams, this information would be collected on a regular schedule: monthly, quarterly, annually, or at project completion. This would

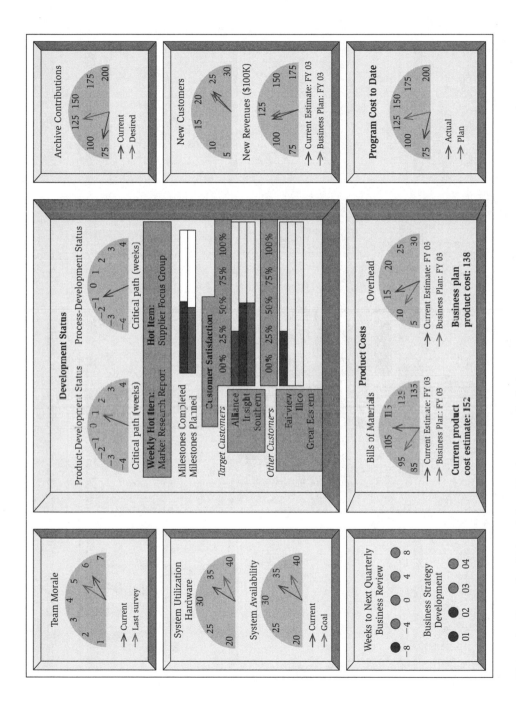

Figure 5.2 Example of Virtual Team Performance Cockpit.

Source: Adapted from Meyer (1994, p. 99).

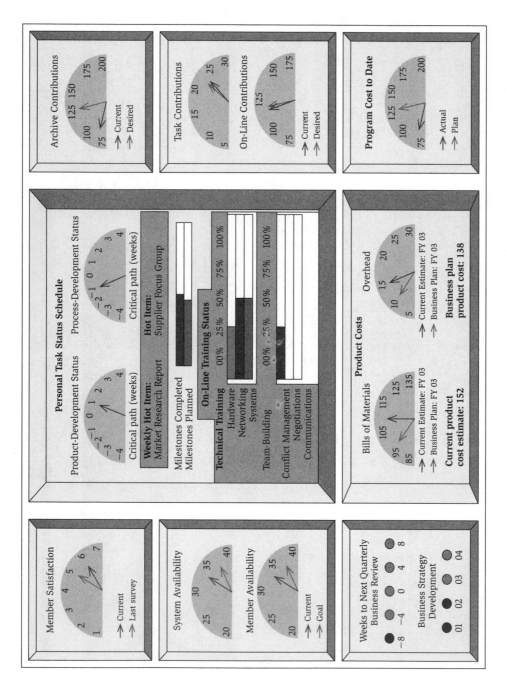

Figure 5.3 Example of Virtual Team Member Performance Cockpit.

Source: Adapted from Meyer (1994, p. 99).

provide the information for formal performance feedback by the team leader and of team performance by upper-level management.

The availability of Web-based technology suggests that all of this information could be collected and evaluated in real time. Anytime someone wanted to complete a self-, other, leader, or team evaluation, the resulting aggregation could be updated immediately so that the well-being of the virtual group and the relative performance levels of individual team members could be known instantaneously. As we have noted, the lack of personal contact between virtual team members and leaders means that leaders must keep a finger on the team's pulse in ways that are not needed for face-to-face teams. Real-time assessments with the various cockpit templates would afford this opportunity and allow for corrective action to be taken as quickly as necessary.

In addition to the team's developing the elements of its own cockpit templates, top management and team members should jointly define the circumstances under which top managers would review a team's performance and its measurement system. Two issues arise in this regard. First, measures should not be carved in stone. As a virtual team moves through its life cycle, certain measures will no longer provide useful information. Teams should regularly audit their performance measures to see if these measures are still useful given project stage and virtual team maturity.

Second, managers and team members should agree as to when certain measurement results are deemed to be out-of-bounds or suggesting potentially serious repercussions to the organization, thus triggering a formal review of the team's performance by top management. In the virtual environment, this prevents the team from undertaking actions that could threaten the viability of a project or unit or even the entire organization.

Finally, top managers should not assume that a performance cockpit developed for one team could be used as an identical cockpit for other teams. It is unlikely that top management can ever know what is best in terms of important measures for every team. One cockpit likely does not fit all. More important, building consensus around the cockpit indicators is an important step in virtual team development.

IMPLICATIONS FOR PRACTICE

As more organizations choose the virtual environment in which to operate, issues of virtual team member selection, training, and performance evaluation will become increasingly important to the success of these teams. The ideas offered here are grounded in both empirical research and practitioner anecdote. More research is needed if we are to determine the factors that allow organizations to build winning virtual teams. Until such time as sufficient research in this area has been completed, we offer the following summary points from this chapter.

- In building virtual teams, recognize the special knowledge, skills, and abilities needed to lead and work virtually: interpersonal and team skills requiring new forms of communication and information sharing, self-regulatory skills, and high levels of comfort with technology hardware and software for managing virtual tasks.

- Help virtual teams reach their full potential by carefully selecting team leaders and team members.

- Provide virtual teams with appropriate training at every stage of team development. This helps maximize virtual team effectiveness. Of particular importance are helping virtual teams build social capital, use technology effectively, overcome cultural differences, and build communities of practice.

- Create one or more team performance templates to focus virtual teams and their members on important team outcomes and, more important, team processes.

- Complement the performance templates with a 360-degree evaluation model to provide the developmental feedback for virtual teams and their members essential for continuous improvement.

- Use valid team performance measures as the bases for team recognition and reward. Careful development of team performance templates helps managers align virtual teams with strategic organizational objectives.

References

Bateman, T. S., and Crant, J. M. "The Proactive Component of Organizational Behavior." *Journal of Organizational Behavior,* 1993, *14,* 103–118.

Cascio, W. "Virtual Workplaces: Implications for Organizational Behavior." In C. Cooper and D. Rousseau (eds.), *Trends in Organizational Behavior.* New York: Wiley, 1999.

Cascio, W. "Managing a Virtual Workplace." *Academy of Management Executive,* 2000, *14,* 81–90.

Chidambaram, L. "Relational Development in Computer-Supported Groups." *MIS Quarterly,* 1996, *20,* 143–165.

Costa, P. T., Jr., and McCrae, R. R. *Revised NEO Personality Inventory (NEO-PI-R) and NEO Five Factor (NEO FFI) Inventory Professional Manual.* Odessa, Fla.: Psychological Assessment Resources, 1992.

Davis, F. D., Bagozzi, R. P., and Warshaw, P. R. "User Acceptance of Computer Technology: A Comparison of Two Theoretical Models." *Management Science,* 1989, *35,* 982–1003.

Gibson, C. B., and Zellmer-Bruhn, M. "Metaphor and Meaning: An Intercultural Analysis of the Concept of Teamwork." *Administrative Science Quarterly,* 2001, *46,* 274–303.

Goleman, D. *Emotional Intelligence.* New York: Bantam, 1995.

Heneman, H. G., III, Heneman, R. L., and Judge, T. A. *Staffing Organizations.* (2nd ed.) Middleton, Wis.: Irwin, 1997.

Hollingshead, A., and McGrath, J. "Computer-Assisted Groups: A Critical Review of the Empirical Research." In R. Guzzo and E. Salas (eds.), *Team Effectiveness and Decision-Making in Organizations.* San Francisco: Jossey-Bass, 1995.

Jarvenpaa, S. L., Knoll, K., and Leidner, D. E. "Is Anybody Out There? Antecedents of Trust in Global Virtual Teams." *Journal of Management Information Systems,* 1998, *14*(4), 29–64.

Kaplan, R., and Norton, D. "The Balanced Scorecard-Measures That Drive Performance." *Harvard Business Review,* Jan.–Feb. 1992, pp. 71–79.

Kaplan, R., and Norton, D. "Putting the Balanced Scorecard to Work." *Harvard Business Review,* Sept.–Oct. 1993, pp. 134–147.

Kaplan, R., and Norton, D. *The Balanced Scorecard.* Boston: Harvard Business School Press, 1996a.

Kaplan, R., and Norton, D. "Using the Balanced Scorecard as a Strategic Management System." *Harvard Business Review,* Jan.–Feb. 1996b, pp. 75–85.

Karoly, P. (1993). "Mechanisms of Self-Regulation: A Systems View." *Annual Review of Psychology,* 1993, *44,* 23–52.

Kimball, L., and Eunice, A. "The Virtual Team: Strategies to Optimize Performance." *Health Forum Journal,* 1999, *42,* 58–62.

Kristof, A. L., Brown, K. G., Sims, H. P., Jr., and Smith, K. A. "The Virtual Team: A Case Study and Inductive Model." In M. M. Beyerlein, D. A. Johnson, and S. T. Beyerlein (eds.), *Advances in Interdisciplinary Studies of Work Teams: Knowledge Work in Teams.* Greenwich, Conn.: JAI Press, 1995.

Kuhl, J. "A Theory of Action and State Orientations." In J. Kuhl and J. Beckmann (eds.), *Volition and Personality: Action Versus State Orientation.* Seattle: Hogrefe and Huber, 1994.

Lipnack, J., and Stamps, J. *Virtual Teams: Reaching Across Space, Time, and Organizations with Technology.* New York: Wiley, 1998.

Mayer, R. C., Davis, J. H., and Schoorman, F. D. "An Integrative Model of Organizational Trust." *Academy of Management Review,* 1995, *20,* 709–734.

Meyer, C. "How the Right Measures Help Teams Excel." *Harvard Business Review,* May–June 1994, pp. 95–103.

Robey, D., Khoo, H., and Powers, C. "Situated Learning in Cross-Functional Virtual Teams." *IEEE Transactions on Professional Communications*, 2000, *47*, 51–66.

Solomon, C. M. "Managing Virtual Teams." *Workforce*, 2001, *80*(6), 60–65.

Sparrow, P., and Daniels, K. "Human Resource Management and the Virtual Organization: Mapping the Future Research Issues." In C. Cooper and D. Rousseau (eds.), *Trends in Organizational Behavior.* New York: Wiley, 1999.

Staples, D. S., Hulland, J. S., and Higgins, C. A. "A Self-Efficacy Theory Explanation for the Management of Remote Workers in Virtual Organizations." *Organization Science*, 1999, *10*, 758–776.

Stevens, M. J., and Campion, M. A. "The Knowledge, Skill, and Ability Requirements for Teamwork: Implications for Human Resource Management." *Journal of Management*, 1994, *20*(2), 503–530.

Strauss, S. "Seeing Is Deceiving: Effects of Face-to-Face, Videoconferencing, and Telephone Media in Judgments of Job Interviews." Paper presented at the annual meeting of the Academy of Management, San Diego, 1998.

Weisband, S., and Atwater, L. "Evaluating Self and Others in Electronic and Face-to-Face Groups." *Journal of Applied Psychology*, 1999, *84*, 632–639.

Wellman, B., and others. "Computer Networks as Social Networks: Collaborative Work, Telework, and Virtual Community." *Annual Review of Sociology*, 1996, *22*, 213–238.

CHAPTER SIX

Pay Systems for Virtual Teams

Edward E. Lawler III

Rewards are an important element in any formal organization. In order to be effective, organizations must answer the fundamental question of why individuals should commit their time, effort, and ideas to it. Creating a good alignment between the way an organization rewards its members and the strategic agenda of the business in order to accomplish this is a major challenge. There is an infinite variety of approaches to rewarding individuals for their performance and membership in organizations. There is also a wide variety of approaches to organizing and managing complex organizations. In this chapter, the focus is on specifying the correct reward strategies for organizations that adopt virtual teams.

In examining the relationship between rewards system and virtual teams, four types of virtual teams are considered: parallel, production and service, project, and management. Each requires somewhat different processes and behaviors. Thus, it is necessary to consider how they should be rewarded separately. Each of these four types of teams can take the form of traditional face-to-face teams or virtual teams. When they are virtual, as a general rule they have somewhat different operating characteristics and as a result need different reward systems. The degree of virtuality (see Chapter One, this volume) needs to be taken into account in decisions about how the virtual teams are rewarded. A virtual team that rarely or never meets and has members from different organizations and countries is clearly different from one that meets occasionally and draws its membership from the employees of a single domestic company.

The traditional approach to designing work organizations calls for hierarchical decision making, simple repetitive jobs at the lowest level, and rewards based on carefully measured individual jobs and job performance. This "control approach" is losing ground to more involvement or high-performance approaches to management (Lawler, Mohrman, and Benson, 2001). One of the reasons for this is the growing use of teams. In a team-based organization, an emphasis on individuals and traditional controls simply does not fit. This is particularly true in the use of virtual teams, which lack traditional face-to-face supervisor relationships and often make the close monitoring of work output very difficult.

The advantages of the involvement approach are said to be greater organizational efficiency, including higher-quality products and services, greater speed, less absenteeism, less turnover, better decision making, better problem solving, and lower overhead costs—in short, greater organizational effectiveness (Lawler, 1996). In the case of teams, it can lead to more integration and higher levels of self-management.

Employee involvement approaches to organization design generally argue that three features of an organization should be moved to lower organization levels:

- Information about the performance of the organization
- Knowledge that enables employees to understand and contribute to organizational performance
- Power to make decisions that influence organizational direction and performance

Some approaches to involvement also consider how pay systems should be changed to fit a more involvement-oriented management approach (Lawler, 1996). They generally favor rewards based on group or organizational performance but do not describe in detail how pay should be designed to fit particular involvement practices. Others simply suggest paying everyone "fairly" in order to avoid such dysfunctional effects of paying for performance as competition, false reporting of performance, and conflict between superiors and subordinates.

Teams have emerged as a widely used vehicle for facilitating the movement of power, information, and knowledge to lower levels of an organization. Research suggests that organizations are increasing their use of teams and that they use a variety of teams (Lawler, Mohrman, and Benson, 2001). All types of teams, however, share at least one common attribute: in order to be effective, they require a supportive reward system (Mohrman, Cohen, and Mohrman, 1995; Wageman, 1995). Not surprisingly, traditional pay systems that emphasize individual jobs and performance are not a good fit.

In order for teams to be optimally effective, a reward system is needed that recognizes the required behavior and skills. The challenge is to create a fit between the characteristics of the reward system and the characteristics of the team. Because teams differ in their purposes, structure, and virtuality, no reward system design is likely to be universally effective. The key is to design a reward system that fits the characteristics of the team and the organizational context in which it operates. This is not a simple task. It requires an approach that chooses among the major pay system design options based on the outcomes they will produce when they are applied to a particular type of team in a specific environment.

Our consideration of the design choices will first look at the outcomes that pay can affect and then consider two major design decisions: how to determine base pay and how to pay for performance.

REWARD SYSTEM OBJECTIVES

A great deal of research shows that reward systems in general, and pay systems in particular, can affect individual and organizational behavior in important areas (Rynes and Gerhart, 2000). Unfortunately little of this research has dealt with virtual organizations, teams, and working relationships. Nevertheless, it gives a great deal of guidance with respect to how reward systems can affect virtual teams. The research on reward systems suggests that they influence a company's strategy implementation and overall effectiveness in six ways:

1. *Attracting and retaining employees.* Studies on job choice, career choice, and employee turnover clearly show that the types and level of rewards an organization offers influence the types of employees it attracts and retains. Overall, companies that offer the most rewards tend to attract and retain the most people. However, different types of rewards appeal to different types of people. For example, high levels of risk compensation may attract entrepreneurial personalities, while extensive security-oriented benefits generally attract those who like to avoid risk. Individual incentive plans attract people who want to operate on their own and control their own fate, and collective rewards are more likely to attract individuals who like shared responsibility and collective action.

2. *Motivating performance.* Reward systems can motivate performance when certain conditions exist. Employees must perceive that the organization ties important rewards in a timely fashion to effective performance. They also need to feel that they can influence the type of performance that drives pay. People have mental maps of what the world is like, and they use these maps to choose the behaviors that will lead to outcomes that satisfy their needs. Employees are inherently neither motivated nor unmotivated to perform effectively; their motivation

depends on the situation, how they perceive it, and what rewards they need and value. In general, an individual is motivated to behave in a certain way when he or she believes that behaving in that way will lead to attractive outcomes. This is often referred to as a line of sight. They also need to believe that they can behave in rewarded ways and that it is possible to perform at the desired level. These conditions have clear implications for pay systems. To be motivational, the systems must create a clear and achievable line of sight between a person's behavior and the receipt of amounts of pay that are important.

3. *Promoting skill and knowledge development.* Just as pay systems can motivate performance, they can encourage employees to learn and develop new skills. The same motivational principles apply: individuals focus on learning the skills a company rewards. Some organizations have implemented skill-based pay, a relatively new compensation approach, to capitalize on this point. With skill-based pay, they can strategically target the types of learning they want employees to acquire and as a result improve their ability to perform in strategically important ways. By contrast, many job-based systems tie increased pay and perquisites to higher-level jobs, thereby encouraging individuals to learn those skills that they feel will lead to a promotion.

4. *Shaping corporate culture.* A company's approach to developing, administering, and managing reward systems can influence many facets of an organization's culture. For example, reward systems can influence the degree to which employees view a company as a human resource–oriented culture, an entrepreneurial culture, an innovative culture, a competence-based culture, a team-based culture, an entitlement-based culture, and a participative culture. Reward systems shape culture precisely because they have such an important effect on employees' skills, motivation, satisfaction, and sense of what is important to the organization. The behaviors they promote become the dominant patterns of behavior in the organization and influence employees' perceptions and beliefs about what the company stands for, believes in, and values.

5. *Reinforcing and defining structure.* Pay systems can reinforce and define an organization's structure. Often this is not considered when pay systems are designed. Thus, their impact on structure is unintentional, but that does not mean the impact is minimal. Pay systems primarily affect the level of integration and differentiation in an organization. People tend to unite when they are rewarded in the same way and divide when they are treated differently. As noted in earlier chapters, virtual teams present a particular challenge when it comes to developing integration and cooperation. In the case of a team, they can cause the individuals in it to pull together or to compete with each other. They can also cause teams to compete with each other as well as to cooperate with each other, depending on whether the teams compete for rewards or share equally in a reward pool that is influenced by the performance of multiple teams. In addition, pay systems can help define a company's status

hierarchy and strongly influence the types of decision-making structures and processes that exist.

6. *Determining pay costs.* Reward systems often represent a significant cost factor; pay alone makes up more than half of many companies' operating costs. Therefore, system designers must focus on how high these costs should be and how they will vary with the organization's ability to pay. For example, a reasonable outcome of well-designed pay systems might be an increase in costs when the company has money to spend and a decrease in costs when it does not. Another objective might be to have lower overall reward-system costs than do competitors.

Overall, because reward systems affect so many critical features of an organization, they are a crucial determinant of strategy implementation and organizational effectiveness. In order for a strategy to be successfully implemented, the reward system needs to be aligned with it in at least two respects. First, it needs to reward those behaviors that the strategy calls for. Second, it needs to support the development of the organizational capabilities and core competencies that are needed in order to execute the strategy.

DESIGN OPTIONS

In designing an organization's reward system, dozens of design decisions need to be made. All of them are important, but two have a particularly important impact on the effectiveness of teams (Lawler, 2000). The first addresses whether the pay system is based on a job description approach or a skills and competency approach. This feature is a critical determinant of the capabilities of individuals, teams, and the total organization. The second is how, if at all, the organization chooses to pay for performance. This feature is, of course, a critical determinant of whether individuals are motivated to perform effectively. It also affects the structure and culture of the organization in important ways. We will focus on these design decisions in the remainder of this chapter.

Paying the Job or the Person

For decades, organizations have based their financial reward systems on the types of jobs people do. Indeed, with the exception of individual incentive pay, sales commissions, and merit salary increases, most organization take the approach of evaluating the job, not the person, to set a pay level. This approach assumes that job worth can be determined and that the person doing the job is worth only as much as the job itself. Job evaluation programs and salary surveys are used to determine how much other organizations pay for the same or similar work. Pay grades are created, often as many as forty, and jobs are placed in one of the grades based on the results of the job evaluation. This approach can assure an organization that its compensation costs are not dramatically out of line with those of competitors, and it gives a somewhat objective basis for pay rates.

The major alternative to job-based pay is to pay individuals for the skills or competencies (or both) they possess. Rather than reward people for scaling the corporate hierarchy or taking on additional job responsibilities, the company rewards them for increasing what they can do and what they know. This approach generates very different corporate cultures and employee skill development patterns than does a job-based approach. Skill-based pay can help to create a culture of concern for personal growth and development and a highly talented workforce. In factories that use this system, it typically means that many people can perform multiple tasks, resulting in a highly knowledgeable and flexible labor force.

One of the first skill-based pay plans in the United States was installed in a General Foods plant in Topeka, Kansas, over two decades ago (Lawler, 1978, 1986). The plant had skill-based pay from its inception. Its approach encouraged individuals to learn all of the tasks that their team was asked to perform. As individuals were certified as having learned the skill, anywhere from twenty-five to fifty cents was added to their hourly pay rate. Over time, most individuals reached the top pay rate; in effect, they almost doubled their pay from their entry wage rate. Skill certification was handled by a peer appraisal process, except in a few cases where technical experts were brought in to certify more complex skills.

The approach used in this plant is very similar to ones that are used in many manufacturing locations today. It is used most commonly in process technology operations such as chemical plants, oil refineries, and other situations where highly interdependent team behavior is needed. This pay-per-skill-learned approach typically is not used in union situations. In them, two, three, or four pay rates are established; over time, individuals progress from an entry wage to a fully skilled wage (often level two), and then some continue progressing to an expert level. This progression is based on their learning certain identified packages of skills, and in that respect, it is quite similar to the pay-per-skill-learned approach. But instead of pricing individual skills, it simply bundles them together, sometimes giving individuals choices about which sets of skills they learn in order to complete a package that will allow them to move up to the next higher pay rate. This approach is somewhat simpler to administer than the pay-per-skill approach because it involves fewer pay rates.

An alternative to traditional job-based pay plans that is used in some team situations is to establish a small number of very flexible, generic job descriptions. This approach reduces some of the dysfunctional features of a traditional job-based system but does not incent individuals to learn a specific mix of skills that can contribute to team effectiveness.

In most cases, skill-based pay tends to produce somewhat higher pay levels for individuals, but these costs usually are offset by greater workforce flexibility and performance (Jenkins, Ledford, Gupta, and Doty, 1992). Flexibility often leads to lower staffing levels and less absenteeism and turnover, both of which drop because employees appreciate the opportunity to use and be paid for a wide range of skills. Skill-based pay can be a challenge to administer. To date, for example, there are no well-developed systems for determining the worth of individual skills in the marketplace.

In general, skill-based pay seems to fit well in companies that want a flexible, relatively permanent workforce oriented toward learning, growth, and development. Many new team-based plants use this approach, as do plants that are moving toward high-involvement management methods. In addition, more companies are applying skill-based (often called competency-based) pay to knowledge workers, managers, and service employees where the strategy calls for high-performance teams or one-stop service and a high level of customer focus and satisfaction. Examples here include American Express, Frito-Lay, and Aid Association for Lutherans. The competency systems often give only very general definitions of what a competency is; these definitions tend to lack behavioral descriptions of the competency and as a result are difficult to use as a basis for determining pay (Spencer and Spencer, 1993). Typical competencies include leadership, teamwork, and business knowledge. The advantage of these generic competencies is that they do not need to be frequently revised and changed as organizations and teams change their structures and performance goals (Lawler, 2000).

Fit with Teams. Table 6.1 summarizes what has been said so far about job-based versus skill-based pay. The characteristics associated with skill-based pay seem to be a much better fit for most types of teams than are those associated

Table 6.1. Impact of Job- and Skill-Based Pay

	Job Based	Skill and Knowledge
Attraction	Provides good market data	Attracts learning-oriented and high-skill individuals
Motivation	No performance impact	Little performance impact
Skill development	Learn job-related and upward-mobility skills	Can motivate needed skill development
Culture	Bureaucratic, hierarchical	Learning, self-managing
Structure	Hierarchical, individual jobs and differentiation	Horizontal teams based
Cost	Good control for individuals' pay rates	Higher individual pay

with job-based pay. A key requirement for the effective operation of any kind of team is learning on the part of team members. They need to learn how to operate as team members; often they also need to develop new technical knowledge about the organization and its work processes and methods. The need to learn how to operate as a team may be particularly acute when the team is virtual and the individual team members need to work in a highly interdependent mode. This is often a new experience for many team members. Properly administered skill-based pay or competency-based pay can be a powerful tool for encouraging individuals to learn what is necessary in order to make teams effective.

A key issue in many types of teams is the management of lateral processes. This is often best facilitated by individuals on teams learning multiple steps in production and service processes, so that they can communicate with individuals who are before and after them in the process, and participate in lateral process management activities. Paying for skills also creates the possibility of varying individuals' pay by the amount of skill and knowledge that they can contribute to a team. Highly skilled individuals can be paid more, an important retention device, particularly in environments where knowledge and skill are important keys to team effectiveness and competitive advantage.

Types of Virtual Teams. That there is some variation among the skill needs of the different types of virtual teams points to the importance of using skill-based pay, as well as the kind of skill-based pay that is needed, which varies somewhat from one type of team to another. Parallel problem-solving teams such as quality circles and suggestion teams lend themselves to being virtual. They rely on individuals' contributing their ideas to various problem-solving activities and usually are only a part-time commitment. Being virtual allows team members to work together even though their regular jobs are dispersed from one another. Because the team activity is not a full-time commitment on the part of the people, investing heavily in learning additional skills is often not worthwhile, although some investment may be needed.

A few additional skills may be needed to aid the problem-solving and group process. This is particularly likely to be true with virtual teams when the team includes members from different countries and organizations and when they use new technologies. However, the skills that are needed are often learned by individuals without their being paid for learning them. Skill-based pay that encourages cross-training can sometimes be a significant aid to problem-solving teams, because it gives individuals a better overall understanding of the work process. This can contribute to a more integrated group and one that can communicate better, a big need when groups are virtual. It also can improve people's ability to problem solve, diagnose, and innovate in work system design. There remains the question, however, of whether it is worth investing in cross-training simply so that people can participate briefly in parallel teams.

The situation with respect to the advantages of skill-based pay is quite different when virtual teams are self-managing production and service teams. Here, individuals typically spend all their time in a single team. Virtual teams of this type can be used to coordinate work flows between functions and to manage a customer who wants products and services for several parts of a company. Depending on the kind of production or service process the individuals are in, the learning and development needed may involve cross-training team members so that individuals can understand the entire work process and better coordinate their work. This often is particularly important for virtual teams because coordination can be a challenge when individuals are not colocated. Knowledge of what someone else is doing can substitute for actually seeing them do it.

Alternatively, the development needs in a work team may involve developing particular kinds of management and technical expertise so that supervisors and staff support are not needed. Depth knowledge development is particularly important if the team is doing complex knowledge work and it is impossible for any one individual to learn all the knowledge necessary to address the issues that come up as a team does its work. A typical approach in this case is to identify a few individuals as depth experts in various areas and to reward them with extra pay for their depth expertise. In the absence of a skill-based pay system, there is often no way to reward this kind of depth knowledge. Many organizations for years have recognized this fact by putting in technical ladders, which reward individuals for becoming increasingly expert in a particular topic.

Project teams typically involve a specific work assignment that may take weeks, months, or even years to accomplish. Team members may or may not spend all their work time on a project team, but they are rarely on many teams simultaneously. Project teams often are made up of individuals from different parts of an organization or from different organizations, and as a result often have a diverse membership that operates virtually. Virtual project teams are a form of team where skill- and knowledge-based pay is a particularly good fit. A key success factor in knowledge work teams is the presence of some individuals who have knowledge of multiple functions. In virtual teams, there may be special skills that need to be learned so that the team can operate virtually. For example, virtual teams may need process facilitators, videoconferencing support, and cross-cultural and language expertise.

In job-based pay systems, it is hard to get individuals to learn multiple functions because there is usually no reward, and indeed, there may be a punishment for learning a second function, for example, marketing or engineering. When complex project work is involved, it is often impossible to find a person who has a good knowledge base in all of the functions that are required to make for a successful project. This does not mean that there cannot be a number of individuals who have mastery outside the single function, however. This is critical to allowing project teams to integrate their work and make good trade-offs among the demands of the different disciplines in developing a new product or service (Mohrman, Cohen, and Mohrman, 1995). It is especially critical in helping virtual project teams integrate because they often lack relationships among members and the chance to observe each other.

In order to encourage lateral career moves, an organization often has to do more than simply have a pay-per-skill approach. Often, lateral career tracks need to be developed so that individuals will be significantly rewarded for making cross-functional moves that do not necessarily involve moving to a higher level of responsibility or a higher pay grade. In the absence of such a structure, individuals typically run the risk of losing money by making a lateral move. This can come about because they do not move into a higher pay grade and they are in an area where they are not an expert, and thus are likely to lose out in the case of merit pay increases or bonuses that are based on performance. While they are learning a new function, they are at a disadvantage when competing for pay increases, because the other individuals in the area are already experts in the function.

If a virtual project team's work involves complex knowledge work, depth expertise in one or more areas is often critical to its success. Knowledge-based pay, which rewards people for developing deeper and deeper levels of expertise, as in a technical ladder, can be a helpful tool here. It not only rewards people for developing important knowledge; it helps to retain the technical experts in the organization by paying them more than they would be paid in many traditional job-based structures. The typical approach here involves defining multiple levels of technical expertise in disciplines such as engineering, accounting, finance, and human resources. Each level has a set of skill descriptors attached to it, and when individuals demonstrate that they have mastered the skill set at a new level, they are given a promotion and a pay increase, recognizing their additional skills and knowledge.

Management teams are a relatively new form of teams. Little research has been done on them, and they are quite rare. The idea of multiple individuals acting in concert to jointly manage either individuals or teams is not widely accepted. It is clear, however, that in order for management teams to operate effectively, the individual managers need a set of skills that are not normally present in most managers. They need to learn how to coordinate their behavior, act together, distribute work among themselves, and avoid being played against each other by the individuals who work for them. When management teams operate in a virtual mode, even more new skills are needed. They need to learn how to operate in a virtual environment and how to coordinate their actions and present an integrated position to the groups or individuals they are managing. The skills needed are even greater if the management team crosses functional, business unit, and national boundaries. Thus, it is particularly important that management have a reward system that encourages them to develop their skills as virtual team members.

Prevalence of Rewards for Skills. Given the positive fit between skill- and knowledge-based pay and teams, it is not surprising that the research evidence on the use of this approach to pay shows that it is most frequently used in team environments (Lawler, Mohrman and Benson, 2001). This is particularly true with respect to production and service teams. They make more use of skill- or knowledge-based pay than any other kind of team structure. There is less knowledge available on how much skill-based pay is used in conjunction with project, parallel, and management teams. A good guess is that project teams in particular tend to stimulate its adoption and the abandonment of job-based systems. Because of the newness of virtual teams, there is no evidence of how they compare to traditional teams when it comes to the use of skill-based pay, but our analysis suggests that they have a greater need for it. The simple fact is that operating in virtual mode requires more skills. It is also clear that the more virtual a team is, the more it requires individuals to learn new skills.

As more and more organizations move toward being team based overall, the pressure to change to skill- and knowledge-based pay is likely to grow. This is particularly likely to be true in the case of virtual teams. They need all the help they can get when it comes to integration and knowledge about how they and the organization should work.

Table 6.2 summarizes what has been said about the applicability of skill- and knowledge-based pay to virtual teams. As can be seen, slightly different forms of pay for skills fit each of these types of virtual teams. Thus, the challenge is

Table 6.2. Virtual Teams and Skill-Based Pay

Type of Team	Skill-Based Pay
Parallel	May be used to encourage cross-training and virtual team skills.
Production and service	Use to motivate cross-training, virtual self-management skills, and some depth skills and to retain most skilled team members.
Project	Use to motivate development of depth expertise and cross-functional knowledge and virtual team operating skills.
Management	Use to motivate the development of depth expertise, cross-functional knowledge and career tracks, and virtual management team skills.

to design skill- and knowledge-based pay systems that fit the type of team that is the focal point of the design process.

Performance-Based Pay

The most important strategic decision a company must make about its reward system concerns whether and how pay will be based on performance. Although paying for performance is the most common approach in the United States, it is not the only approach that can be or is used. One alternative is seniority-based pay, frequently used by government agencies in the United States and in other parts of the world. In the past, many Japanese companies have based pay on seniority, although they often gave bonuses tied to corporate performance.

Most U.S.-based businesses say they reward individual performance through a merit system, but creating an effective merit pay system is easier said than done (Kerr, 1975; Heneman, 1992). In fact, some observers have concluded that many organizations would be better off if they did not try to relate pay to performance and relied on other factors to motivate performance (Kohn, 1993). The main reason is that companies find it difficult to specify the types of performance they desire and to determine whether employees have demonstrated them. A second reason is the fear that it will reduce intrinsic motivation. Despite the attention this fear receives, the research evidence does not support the view that it is a serious problem (Cameron and Pierce, 1997).

Organizations face a number of options with respect to how they relate pay to performance. They must determine what kinds of rewards they will give (possibilities include stock and cash), how often they will give them (ranging from time periods of a few minutes to many years), and whether performance will be measured at the individual, group, or organizational level. Finally, they must determine what kinds of performance will be rewarded. For example, managers might be rewarded for sales increases, productivity volumes, cost-reduction ideas, the ability to develop subordinates, and so on. Teams can be rewarded for quality and productivity, and also for safety, cost reductions, and helping other teams.

Rewarding some behaviors and not others has a major effect on performance, so a company must pay close attention to its strategic plan in deciding what to reward. Once it develops a strategic plan, it can define key performance objectives and design reward systems to motivate the appropriate performance (Lawler, 2000). In the process, pay system designers need to consider the importance of choices such as short-term versus long-term performance, risk taking versus risk aversion, individual performance versus team performance, team performance versus total corporate performance, cash versus stock, and return on investment maximization versus sales growth. An organization can make effective pay decisions, such as whether to use stock options and what to reward, only after it has carefully considered whether it supports the desired behaviors.

Three general points about relating pay to performance bear mentioning here. First, bonus plans generally do a better job of motivating employees than do pay raises and salary increase plans (Zingheim and Schuster, 2000). With them, an individual's pay can vary substantially from time period to time period, while a raise usually becomes an annuity and as a result does little to relate current pay levels to current performance.

Second, objective performance measures are better motivators than subjective measures. In general, employees assign higher credibility to objective measures, such as sales volume or units produced (Lawler, 1990; Rynes and Gerhart, 2000). They therefore often accept the validity of these measures but not the validity of a boss's rating. Thus, an organization that ties rewards to objective measures typically can create a much more credible link between pay and performance than can one that bases pay on subjective, nonverifiable measures, such as a supervisor's rating.

Third, group and organizational plans generally work best in creating integration and the kind of teamwork that virtual teams may need (Schuster and Zingheim, 1992; Zingheim and Schuster, 1997). Under these plans, it is usually to everyone's advantage that each person works effectively because all share in the financial results of higher performance. When people feel they can benefit from another's actions, they are likely to support and encourage good performance by others (Wageman, 1995). This is not true under individual plans, which tend to produce differentiation and competition. On the other hand, group and organizational bonus plans separate individual behavior from rewards and as a result have more difficulty establishing a clear line of sight from individual performance to the reward.

In individualistic countries such as the United States, there continues to be a strong demand for individual pay for performance (DeMatteo, Rush, Sundstrom, and Eby, 1997). However, when the reward system formally recognizes individual performance, it reduces the pressure on the team to appraise and deal with poor performers. Indeed, a forced distribution rating system for performance appraisal creates a situation where it is in the best interests of individuals to have some poor performers on their teams. Thus, in face-to-face work teams, they are much less likely to encourage and support performance improvement on the part of poor performers than when there is a collective pay situation in which poor performers hurt everyone's opportunity to earn a bonus. The same is likely to be true in a virtual team, although in a virtual team, it may be more difficult for individuals to deal with poor performance because of the lack of face-to-face contact. One possibility is the use of electronic messages, but these may be easier to ignore than face-to-face communication.

Table 6.3 elaborates the consequences of different pay-for-performance approaches. As can be seen, they have quite different impacts. In reviewing the

Table 6.3. Impact of Pay for Performance

	Individual Merit	Team Incentives	Organization Plans
Attraction	Good for high performers	Good if team does well	Good if organization performs well
Motivation	Good line of sight	Moderate line of sight	Weak line of sight
Skill development	Encourages learning skills that lead to rewarded performance	Encourages team skills	Encourages learning about business
Culture	Performance oriented, job focused	Team focused	Business involvement
Structure	Individual accountability	Team integration	Organizationwide integration
Cost	High if significant merit awards given	High if significant rewards given	Possible self-funding from profit improvements

right combinations of them for different kinds of teams, we will look separately at parallel, work, project, and management virtual teams.

Parallel Teams. Because virtual parallel teams do not represent a fundamental change in the structure of organizations, they have the fewest implications for performance-based pay. Some argue that no pay-for-performance-system changes need to be made in order to support parallel team operation regardless of whether they are virtual or face-to-face. However, there is some evidence that rewards can and should be used to motivate effective problem solving in parallel teams, although research has not been done on virtual parallel teams.

Advocates of participative management have suggested for a long time that gain-sharing plans that use a bonus to share cost savings with all employees (such as the Scanlon plan) fit extremely well with the use of problem-solving teams (Lawler, 1986). There is a history of combining suggestion groups with the type of cost-saving bonuses that are part of gainsharing plans, and the research shows very positive results. Virtually every review of these plans argues that bonuses improve the economic performance of the organization because they encourage the generation and adoption of new practices and designs (Lawler, 1990). There is good reason to believe that the results would be the same in the case of virtual parallel teams. Perhaps even more than face-to-face, they need to be motivated and the organization needs a reason to adopt their improvement ideas. Virtual teams may not have the opportunity to use personal contact in order to influence each other and the rest of the organization. In some cases, they may not even have the chance to observe the impact of their improvements directly. Thus, it may be even more important to have bonuses when virtual teams are used.

Profit sharing, stock option, and stock ownership plans that cover all employees also can be somewhat supportive of problem-solving groups. They distribute financial rewards that may be somewhat related to the effectiveness of the problem-solving groups and the implementation of their ideas. Their major weakness is line of sight, and thus in many instances (for example, in large organizations), they do not have a significant impact on the effectiveness of the problem-solving groups.

The alternative to gain sharing and profit sharing is to give bonuses, stock, or other valued rewards to teams for their suggestions. This system can help clarify the rewards that are available to parallel teams and create a relatively strong line of sight. A number of organizations have used this approach with parallel teams, which in most respects is simply a group version of the classic individual-suggestion-program approach. An estimated savings amount is calculated, and individuals who contribute to the idea are given a percentage of the estimated savings. It closely ties the development of the idea to the financial bonus. It poses a number of risks, however.

Often the estimated savings are not realized. Thus, individuals are rewarded even when the company does not gain. Furthermore, individuals may feel they are not rewarded fairly because they get only a small percentage of the savings. There are almost always issues of who should be included among the recipients of the bonus. Finally, most useful suggestions have to be accepted and implemented by many people. The classic suggestion program does not reward people for accepting and then developing the suggestion. Thus, they may not have the motivation that is needed to produce gains. Quite the opposite is true with gain-sharing plans, where no one gains unless an idea is successfully implemented. In this respect, a gain-sharing plan does a better job of clarifying what the desired outcomes are than does a bonus plan that rewards only the team.

Ironically, the situation where team reward plans are most needed is where it is particularly difficult to use one. When virtual parallel teams involve members from different organizations and countries, motivating the team can be very difficult because there are no rewards for their performing well as virtual team members. However, it can also be difficult to create a reward plan for these teams because of national differences in laws and culture and the need for several organizations to change their reward practice.

What clearly is incompatible with virtual parallel suggestion teams is the use of individual suggestion systems that reward individuals. They are in direct conflict with the idea of team ideas. They reward the wrong kind of behavior and compete directly with group suggestion and problem-solving approaches. In cases where they have been used, individuals have been known to claim ownership of ideas that were developed as part of the group problem-solving process. In some cases, they have submitted them through individual suggestion reward programs in order to try to get a personal bonus for an idea that was actually a product of a problem-solving group. Also, with this system in place, individuals are much less willing to share their ideas and thoughts in a group setting than they are where only collective rewards for groups developing a suggestion are offered.

A number of organizations use a recognition approach in order to reward teams for their successes. Unfortunately, there is basically no research evidence to indicate how effective recognition rewards are in this application. The variety of recognition vehicles used is enormous. Some companies emphasize appearances before senior executives, while others give symbols that in some cases involve significant outlays of money (such as clocks or televisions). Although little research has been done on recognition programs, an educated guess is that they can be powerful if they are used astutely. The key is to give them when groups accomplish something significant and to deliver a reward that the group values.

Determining what a group values can be a challenge. Obviously, there are cultural differences in how much various types of recognition rewards are valued. These can be a particularly important issue if the virtual team is international or multicompany. For example, there may be enormous differences within a group as to the value of a trip to a ball game or a chance to present an idea to the CEO. It also may be difficult for virtual teams to experience some types of rewards as a team if they are geographically dispersed. With the exception of the issue of how much recognition rewards are valued, most of the other considerations with recognition programs are the same as those involved in giving financial rewards for producing an idea.

Production Teams and Service Teams. Perhaps the most common way to reward the members of work teams of any kind is to appraise their individual performance and then give them a merit pay increase or bonus based on the result (Lawler and Cohen, 1992). Instead of rewarding the team as a whole, organizations simply add a dimension to the performance appraisal of individuals that focuses on their effectiveness as team members. This usually counts toward their overall appraisal and determines the amount of pay increase or bonus they get. In essence, it continues the historical individual pay-for-performance practices of most organizations but adapts it slightly to a team-based environment.

Assessing individuals creates a conflict in direction that can be self-canceling with respect to effective team behavior. It asks individuals to compete for a given amount of money but changes the basis of the competition from individual performance to performance as a team member. In other words, individuals end up competing with other team members to be the most helpful, cooperative, and best team member. This fails to change the performance focus from the individual to the team and does little to get individuals to focus on how effectively the team is performing. Thus, it makes sense to use this only when work teams are loosely interdependent and need a minimum of highly interdependent behavior in order to be effective. It is likely to be a particularly dysfunctional practice in the case of virtual teams because it does not strongly address a key issue for them: integration. It also may not help to clarify the objectives of the team, and it may be particularly difficult for a supervisor to rate the performance of individual virtual team members because they cannot easily observe the work behavior of each individual. In some cases, they may be able to do electronic monitoring, but this can produce misleading information and often is not available. Finally, team members have the best information but may not be willing or able to provide good evaluations. This may be particularly true when teams are multinational because in some cultures, peer evaluation is considered inappropriate.

The most powerful way to motivate team performance is to establish objectives and metrics for successful team performance and link rewards to team success (Mohrman, Mohrman, and Lawler, 1992). This approach is especially appropriate for virtual teams because it integrates teams and clarifies their outcomes. In order for team performance pay to work, there must be clear and explicit objectives, accepted measures, and good feedback about team performance (Abosch and Reidy, 1996). Team performance appraisals provide opportunities for teams to conduct self-appraisals and obtain customer evaluations. These data can be used to assist managers in the determination of team ratings.

There are three ways of directly rewarding performance at the team level. First, rewards can be tied to team performance through the use of a merit pay system that bases salary increases or bonuses on team performance appraisal. Second, special awards can be provided to teams in order to recognize outstanding performance. Third, a gain-sharing or profit-sharing plan can be used. It can be structured to pay all teams the same bonus or bonuses that are funded by the overall plan but adjusted to reflect the performance of particular teams. All of these are more difficult to install when teams are multinational and multicompany. The first two of these are probably the most practical in the case of multinational and multicompany virtual teams because they do not require as much change in the typical company's pay system.

Frequently, managers are uncomfortable with giving the same size reward to all team members, so they differentially reward individuals. This is potentially a counterproductive action. Providing different rewards to individual team members can undermine cooperation and collective effort. Furthermore, if there is high interdependence among team members, particularly in a virtual team where performance is much less likely to be easily observable and, in some cases, understandable, often it is not possible to measure individual performance accurately; as a result, the rewards are not based on valid measures of performance.

If the work of team members is not highly interdependent, it may make sense to combine team and individual merit pay (DeMatteo, Rush, Sundstrom, and Eby, 1997). A bonus pool can be created based on team performance, with the amount divided among members based on measures of individual performance. For this not to be divisive, it is critical that the manager solicit input from team members about the relative contributions of individual members. A mature work team may be able to use a peer evaluation system to differentiate individual rewards based on individual contributions to the team's performance. It is possible to have teams do appraisals of individuals in which they divide a pool of money that originally was generated by the effectiveness of the team. This in effect rewards individuals for being cooperative in producing the bonus pool but still recognizes individual performance. It is more effective if team members assess team performance before they assess individual performance, because team performance sets the framework for individual performance. This approach has been successfully used with face-to-face teams, but there are no reports of its use with virtual teams.

The second way of linking pay to team performance is through the use of special award or recognition programs. In contrast to appraisals with goals- and formula-driven approaches, they reward exceptional performance after it has occurred. In order to be effective, special awards should be used only to recognize truly special team achievements. Because work teams perform ongoing and repeated work to produce products or services, performance that meets the requirements of customers should happen regularly, but extraordinary performance is likely to be rare. Therefore, special rewards often are best used to supplement and not to substitute for other team pay-for-performance systems. Special awards can be motivating and enhance team cohesiveness. There is a certain pride that comes from being associated with a successful team, and public recognition can solidify it. They are relatively easy to establish because they do not require changes in the basic pay system and thus may be particularly useful when virtual teams are multinational or multifunctional.

Gain sharing, profit sharing, and stock plans are the third major approach that can be used to provide rewards for team performance. Gain sharing requires the work unit that is covered by it to be relatively autonomous and responsible for a measurable output. These plans typically give the same amount of reward to all teams in a particular work unit or location. They suffer from a poor line of sight but can be effective and may be the best choice if the work of virtual teams is highly interdependent and all the members are in the same organization (McAdams and Hawk, 1994). Gain sharing clearly provides the best line of sight and has been widely used to support and reward face-to-face production teams in Weyerhaeuser, Monsanto, 3M, and a host of other corporations that use production teams in factories whose process technologies create interdependent work. They should be effective with virtual teams as long as their members are in the same organizational unit. If the work is not interdependent, then each team can be rewarded from a common bonus pool for its performance.

In choosing among the different approaches to rewarding virtual work teams, the critical issue is the degree of integration and differentiation of the team with respect to the rest of the organization. If the team is not highly autonomous, then providing rewards at the team level may be counterproductive. When there are critical interdependencies between a team and other parts of the organization that need to be accounted for, rewarding a team for its own performance may push differentiation too far. When a work team develops its way of doing things and members become close, members may become myopic in their understanding of the needs of the broader organization, and suboptimization can be the result. The use of a gain-sharing or profit-sharing plan that rewards team members based on the performance of the larger organizational unit can serve to integrate the team into the rest of the organization and act as an offset to the strong cohesiveness that tends to develop in a work team.

In general, an organization composed of work teams needs to make sure its pay-for-performance systems motivate the right kinds of team performance. This often is best done through a mix of team-level and organizational-level pay-for-performance systems (Zingheim and Schuster, 1997). The more that work teams stand alone as performing units, the more rewards should be focused at the team level. The greater the interdependencies between work teams and functional groups and among different work teams, the more that pay-for-performance systems should operate at the organizational level. Organization-level rewards also are appropriate for multicompany teams, but they can be supplemented by team plans.

Project Teams. Project teams, whether virtual or face-to-face, present a particularly interesting challenge for reward systems. They often require a reward system that is specifically designed to support them. Traditional pay-for-performance systems focus on individuals and tend to measure and reward performance on an annual schedule. Both of these practices are inconsistent with motivating project teams. The obvious first choice for motivating a project team is a reward system that establishes metrics for successful group performance and sets rewards tied to the accomplishments of the group. It also is desirable to have the rewards distributed at the time the team completes its project. Thus, one popular and effective approach to rewarding project teams is to give spot bonus awards to them when they complete their projects. In the case of virtual teams, this can clarify their goals, motivate them to perform, and cause them to integrate their behavior.

Rewarding a project team's performance may be difficult if, as is often true, the membership of the team changes during projects. It may not make sense to reward everyone equally when some individuals are there for 10 percent of the team's activities, while others may be there for 100 percent of the activities. Unequal rewards are a possibility, but it can be difficult to determine how large they should be because amount of time spent may not be a good measure of someone's contribution to a project.

When virtual team members come from different organizations, it may be particularly important to reward team performance. Because they lack many of the integrating influences that single-organization teams have, a team bonus plan can satisfy a very important need. It is probably best used as a supplement to each organization's reward system so that team members are motivated to make their project team succeed in ways that benefit their organization.

One alternative or complement to rewarding project group performance at the end of each project is to rely on a gain-sharing plan, profit sharing, or stock ownership system that covers a total organizational unit. This may be a preferred alternative to rewarding individual teams when, in fact, the teams' activities have a major impact on the effectiveness of the unit and it is difficult to measure the effectiveness of the team. It also may be a preferred alternative if project teams are in existence for short periods of time and, as a result, the timely measurement and rewarding of the performance of individual teams is difficult. It clearly makes the most sense when organizations want their project team employees to have a long-term organizationwide focus. It is not as desirable when the objective is to clarify the desired outcomes of the project or integrate the team.

Sometimes it is necessary and desirable to focus on individual performance in a project team environment. The best approach is to measure the contributions of individuals to the team's effectiveness at the completion of each project. Individual ratings can be modified by the success of the overall project. This approach should be used with some caution in the case of virtual teams because it is likely to weaken the integrative impact of the reward system. Of course, this can be reduced by using peer group measures of how team oriented individuals are.

In many cases, it is desirable to use peer ratings, as well as customer satisfaction ratings. Peer ratings are particularly critical because in most project teams, peers are in the best position to assess the contribution of team members. This is likely to be true whether the team is virtual or face-to-face, but perhaps it is more important in the case of face-to-face teams. Over the course of a year, individuals may accumulate a number of ratings that reflect their contributions to each project on which they worked. Performance-pay treatment then becomes a derivative of how effectively they performed on each of the projects on which they participated. Alternatively, spot bonuses can be paid at the end of each project.

Management Teams. Many of the same issues that arise when project teams are paid for performance also arise when management teams are paid for their performance. A major difference exists, however, because management teams, like work teams, are usually permanent teams, so spot bonuses and one-time awards are less relevant. They also often are not as highly interdependent as project teams, and this means that a greater possibility exists for rewarding individual performance. Like project and production teams, they can be rewarded as stand-alone entities based on performance appraisals and measures of team performance, or they can be rewarded based on a larger, organizationwide gain-sharing, profit-sharing, or stock-based plan. The choice among these is essentially one of the degree to which line of sight and motivation are important versus the degree to which integration of the total work unit is important.

Pay-for-performance plans that focus on an individual team's performance tend to separate the team from the rest of the organization but integrate it, an important consideration in the case of virtual teams. In the case of management teams, however, too much integration may be a problem because it can give the management team a different goal orientation than the teams or individuals who report to that management team. If integration within the management team is necessary in order to integrate relatively unrelated operations, business units, organizations, or companies, then it may make sense to measure and reward the management team as a team. But if it is integration between the management team and the people who report to them that is critical and the success of the units they are supervising depends on this integration, then rewarding the management team separately does not make sense. Instead, they should be included in either a corporatewide or business unit–wide plan that treats them the same as it treats the teams or individuals who report to them.

Unfortunately, there is no automatic right approach to rewarding virtual management teams for performance. There is little research on virtual management teams, so all we can do is make suggestions based on what is known about teams and rewards. What clearly is right is considering the degree to which the team itself needs to be integrated and how integrated the team needs to be with other parts of the organization or organizations. This understanding then should be used to determine whether the team is rewarded separately or as part of an integrated unit that may include the part of the organization that reports to the team or the total organization.

The Particulars of Pay for Performance. Table 6.4 summarizes what has been said so far about the fit between rewards for performance and four different

Table 6.4. Teams and Pay for Performance

Type of Virtual Team	Pay for Performance
Parallel	Gain sharing or other business unit plan to reward savings; possible recognition rewards for teams
Production and service	Team bonus if team is independent or business unit bonus if teams are interdependent
Project	Possible one-time bonus (or more often), based on project performance assessment; profit sharing and stock plans; possible peer assessment
Management	Possible team bonuses; profit sharing and stock-based plans

types of virtual teams. It clearly makes the point that one size does not fit all types of teams. Key to all the approaches shown is the measurement of performance and interdependence. Valid measures of performance need to be available, and the reward system needs to reinforce the key interdependencies among individuals and among teams; otherwise, the reward system may reward the wrong kind of performance, and do more damage than good.

IMPLICATIONS FOR PRACTICE

That the traditional approaches to pay do not fit a team-based work environment is hardly surprising, given that the pay systems in most organizations were designed to support and reward individual behavior. Virtual teams require pay practices that are focused on collective behavior. As long as reward systems remain focused on individual performance, they are at best neutral and in most cases counterproductive to creating effective face-to-face and virtual teams. Unfortunately, there is no easy answer to the question of what kind of reward system designs fits best in a team-based environment. The best answer seems to be that it all depends on the kind of team and the technology and strategy of the organization.

Two general approaches to pay seem to fit best with virtual teams: an emphasis on paying the individual instead of the job and pay-for-performance approaches that focus on collective performance more than individual performance. Taken together, these two generic approaches can encourage individuals to learn the right skills to make virtual teams effective and can motivate the right type of performance focus on the part of individual teams and organizations.

Following are recommendations for practice:

- Skill-based pay that encourages cross-training can improve problem solving and integration in virtual parallel teams.

- Skill-based pay for cross-training, management, and technical expertise is useful in virtual production, service, project, and management teams.

- Identifying a few individuals as depth experts (for example, in facilitation, technology, or cross-cultural skills) and rewarding them with extra pay for their expertise is an effective means of motivating skill acquisition for virtual teams.

- Rewarding for lateral career moves is particularly important in virtual teams to encourage members to gain this expertise and retain them when they do.

- Team-level objectives, metrics, and bonuses for performance are particularly helpful for motivating virtual teams charged with problem solving and innovation (examples are parallel or project teams).

- Individual rewards for performance in virtual production or service teams are a poor choice because they fail to focus the team on collective performance.

- If virtual team members are not highly interdependent, it may make more sense to combine individual and team-level rewards rather than using only team rewards.

- If interdependencies exist across virtual teams in an organization, a mix of team- and organizational-level rewards is likely to be effective because it encourages integration across teams.

- For virtual management teams, the key is whether integration is needed more within the team or between the team and the unit; if the latter is the case, the team should be rewarded for organizational performance.

References

Abosch, K. S., and Reidy, D. B. "Supporting Teams Through Rewards Systems." *American Compensation Association Journal,* 1996, 5(4), 72–81.

Cameron, J., and Pierce, W. D. "Rewards, Interest and Performance." *American Compensation Association Journal,* 1997, 6(4), 6–16.

DeMatteo, J. S., Rush, M. C., Sundstrom, E., and Eby, L. T. "Factors Related to the Successful Implementation of Team-Based Rewards." *American Compensation Association Journal,* 1997, 6(4), 16–28.

Heneman, R. L. *Merit Pay.* Reading, Mass.: Addison-Wesley, 1992.

Jenkins, G. D., Jr., Ledford, G. E., Jr., Gupta, N., and Doty, D. H. *Skill-Based Pay: Practices, Pay-Offs, Pitfalls, and Prescriptions.* Scottsdale, Ariz.: American Compensation Association, 1992.

Kerr, S. "On the Folly of Rewarding A, While Hoping for B." *Academy of Management Journal,* 1975, *18,* 769–783.

Kohn, A. *Punished by Rewards.* Boston: Houghton Mifflin, 1993.

Lawler, E. E. "The New Plant Revolution." *Organizational Dynamics,* 1978, *6*(3), 2–12.

Lawler, E. E. *High-Involvement Management.* San Francisco: Jossey-Bass, 1986.

Lawler, E. E. *Strategic Pay.* San Francisco: Jossey-Bass, 1990.

Lawler, E. E. *From the Ground Up: Six Principles for Creating New Logic Organizations.* San Francisco: Jossey-Bass, 1996.

Lawler, E. E. *Rewarding Excellence: Pay Strategies for the New Economy.* San Francisco: Jossey-Bass, 2000.

Lawler, E. E., and Cohen, S. G. "Designing Pay Systems for Teams." *American Compensation Association Journal,* 1992, *1*(1), 6–19.

Lawler, E. E., Mohrman, S. A., and Benson, G. S. *Organizing for High Performance: The CEO Report on Employee Involvement, TQM, Reengineering, and Knowledge Management in Fortune 1000 Companies.* San Francisco: Jossey-Bass, 2001.

McAdams, J. L., and Hawk, E. J. *Organizational Performance and Rewards: 663 Experiences in Making the Link.* Scottsdale, Ariz.: Consortium for Alternate Reward Strategies Research, American Compensation Association, 1994.

Mohrman, A. M., Mohrman, S. A., and Lawler, E. E. *The Performance Management of Teams: Performance Measurement, Evaluation and Incentives.* Boston: Harvard Business School Press, 1992.

Mohrman, S. A., Cohen, S. G., and Mohrman, A. M. *Designing Team-Based Organizations: New Forms for Knowledge Work.* San Francisco: Jossey-Bass, 1995.

Rynes, S. L., and Gerhart, B. *Compensation in Organization.* San Francisco: Jossey-Bass, 2000.

Schuster, J. R., and Zingheim, P. K. *The New Pay.* San Francisco: New Lexington Press, 1992.

Spencer, L. M., and Spencer, S. M. *Competence at Work.* New York: Wiley, 1993.

Wageman, R. "Interdependence and Group Effectiveness." *Administrative Science Quarterly,* 1995, *40,* 145–180.

Zingheim, P. K., and Schuster, J. R. "Best Practices for Small-Team Pay." *American Compensation Association Journal,* 1997, *6*(1), 40–49.

Zingheim, P. K., and Schuster, J. R. *Pay People Right! Breakthrough Reward Strategies to Create Great Companies.* San Francisco: Jossey-Bass, 2000.

CHAPTER SEVEN

Meeting the Performance Challenge

*Calculating Return on
Investment for Virtual Teams*

Alec R. Levenson, Susan G. Cohen

When does it make sense to operate virtually versus face-to-face (FTF)? Answering this question requires knowing what the costs and benefits of virtual teams are, that is, their return on investment (ROI). It also requires understanding how virtual teams' objectives relate to the company's strategy.

At its core, ROI is a straightforward concept that is evaluated by measuring the benefits relative to the costs. Yet as with most other things in life, the devil is in the details: calculating ROI in practice can be quite difficult. Despite this difficulty, or perhaps because of it, there is clear demand for tools to carry out the task. Although ROI and related valuation concepts have long been applied to capital spending decisions, their use for teams is much more the exception than the rule.

This chapter presents a framework for applying ROI in the virtual team context. ROI is typically calculated by comparing the benefits relative to the costs of one approach versus another and can be done as a forecast or retrospectively. This chapter examines how to calculate ROI for virtual compared to FTF teams to determine the value of activities that have already occurred.

THE COMPARISON SCENARIO

What should the comparison scenario be when considering ROI for virtual teams? Do we want to know the ROI from working in a virtual team versus a FTF team? Do we want to know the ROI from work performed by a virtual team versus the work not happening at all? Are we looking to forecast what the expected ROI is as a resource allocation tool, or do we want to use ROI in a backward-looking sense to evaluate the worth of work already done for performance management and other purposes? These are not idle questions because the elements needed to determine ROI can differ significantly from one case to another.

Forward-Looking Versus Backward-Looking ROI

For forward-looking ROI, alternatives representing best case, worse case, and most likely outcome scenarios should be considered for appropriate contingency planning. This means forecasting the different outcomes that are likely to occur, determining the costs and benefits that would occur in each case, and calculating a different ROI estimate for each scenario.

The details of how to conduct such forward-looking ROI are no different for virtual teams than they are for FTF teams and are covered in detail elsewhere (Levenson, forthcoming). We focus attention here on backward-looking, or retrospective, ROI: calculations that ask what value was derived from a team's activities after they have already happened. That still leaves the question of looking at virtual team relative to FTF team ROI or at virtual team ROI as a stand-alone concept. That distinction frames our discussion in the chapter.

Choosing Between Virtual and FTF Interaction

In many cases, operating FTF is not a viable option. Teams are put together with geographically dispersed members for a good reason, and it is either impractical or infeasible to colocate everyone while the work is being done. The continued move toward globally organized work is one of the underlying trends that has helped to foster the rapid spread of virtual teaming. When team members are located on different continents, bringing them together for extended FTF work is either extremely expensive or it means that they cannot perform their other nonteam-related responsibilities while away from their home base of operations, or both.

Although operating FTF may be impractical except in rare circumstances for such teams, it turns out that operating virtually can be quite inefficient because of the difficulties of using electronically mediated communication and the current state of capabilities offered by technology. This is one of the reasons that kickoff FTF time is so critical for virtual team success (Duarte and Snyder, 1999). What emerges is not an either-or choice of doing the work entirely virtually or entirely FTF, but instead a continuum of choices over how much of the work on a given team will be done virtually versus FTF. In this sense, asking what the ROI is of operating virtually versus FTF is quite relevant, even for teams that are geographically dispersed across multiple continents. We discuss two such examples of teams with members from the United States and Europe that occasionally met FTF. In those cases, managers balanced the coordination benefits of meeting FTF versus the travel costs.

When geographically dispersed team members reside in the same country, operating FTF is more of a viable option that should be considered carefully rather than haphazardly. We discuss one such example. In this case, all of the members were located in the United States, but the locations ranged from one side of the country to the other.

Of course, ROI is useful only as an aid to decision making, not a substitute for it. The best-calculated ROI numbers mean little unless interpreted in the context of the firm's strategic objectives and resource allocation decisions over a range of possibilities. It is for this reason that the ROI from operating more virtually versus more FTF may be the wrong focus in some settings. In these cases, knowing the ROI from the team's activities relative to doing nothing at all may be the most pressing concern. We take up this issue as well as we discuss the case examples. But first, we consider ROI in the virtual versus FTF context.

IDENTIFYING BENEFITS AND COSTS

In order to calculate ROI, all of the most relevant costs and benefits have to be identified and quantified. To examine the benefits and costs of operating virtually versus FTF, we break them into three groups: objective business outcomes, subjective business outcomes, and design, input, and process aspects. All of these have the potential to influence a virtual team's compared to a FTF team's ROI. We discuss first how to sort through each element's importance and then how to prioritize which elements to focus on when conducting the ROI calculation with examples from each case.

Before launching into the discussion, it is important to put this in the context of the larger volume and the costs and benefits of virtual teaming covered in the other chapters in this book. Our discussion here is focused on the costs and benefits that we think are best suited for considering virtual team ROI, not all virtual team costs and benefits broadly defined. (These are partly research based, though in the interest of maintaining a practitioner focus, we have not cited the research on which it is based. Where the empirical evidence is either nonexistent or inconclusive, our statements are based on sound reasoning.)

Regardless, the research on virtual teams is emergent and ongoing. More important, which costs and benefits to consider for an ROI calculation depend heavily on the team's context, charter, and stakeholders. As such, only some of the potential costs and benefits highlighted here likely should be considered for the ROI for any particular team.

Objective Business Outcomes

In order to make the task of calculating ROI manageable, we start by considering the team outcomes that are easiest to link to the bottom line. These outcomes, described in Table 7.1, are cycle time, timeliness, and productivity; quality; and customer satisfaction. All can be (and typically are) measured objectively.

Regardless of the type of team (work team, parallel team, management team, or something else), improving at least one of these outcomes is always an objective:

- *Cycle time, timeliness, and productivity.* Virtual teams often have more difficulty coordinating their work when communicating electronically because of efficiency losses. Thus, productivity may suffer when not working FTF. One exception is when key work can be done asynchronously on a globally distributed team; in this case, the asynchronous parts of the work can be done around the clock, with members in different time zones handing off the work to each other at the end of the local workday.

- *Quality.* There may be a trade-off between productivity and quality when operating virtually. The same lack of proximity that causes productivity to suffer simultaneously might allow for better quality. This is because key team roles can be filled with the people best suited for playing those roles regardless of where they are located. The drawback is that coordination difficulties might lead the team to compromise on the quality of the output. Both the positive and negative impacts of virtuality on quality need to be considered when calculating ROI.

Table 7.1. Objective Business Outcomes

	Potential Benefits from Operating Virtually	Potential Costs from Operating Virtually
Cycle time, timeliness, and productivity	If globally distributed and work can be done asynchronously, then team can work around the clock	May be harder to coordinate and accomplish team's objectives when not FTF
Quality	Geographical dispersion means can include the best experts wherever they are located	Will team settle for second-best outcome because work is too difficult to coordinate?
Customer satisfaction	Geographical dispersion allows closeness to multiple customers	Coordination problems can lead to lower customer satisfaction

• *Customer satisfaction.* Similar to quality, customer satisfaction in the virtual setting may be higher because of the ability to staff the team with the best talent. In addition, the geographical dispersion of virtual teams means that key team members can be chosen for their proximity to important customers and other stakeholders. But coordination difficulties have the potential to negate some or all of the benefits in terms of customer satisfaction. For proper ROI analysis, both the positive and negative impacts of virtuality on customer satisfaction need to be factored in.

Regardless of the organizational context, no one would argue about the importance of considering each of the outcomes in Table 7.1 when calculating ROI for a virtual team. However, the same cannot be said for other types of outcomes that typically are associated with teams and might be considered candidates for inclusion in team ROI. The basic problem, as discussed by Levenson (forthcoming), is that traditional ROI calculations focus on benefits as measured by changes in net income or cash flow. Thus, other benefits with an indirect impact on the bottom line that do not generate a direct improvement in cash flow may be too subjective to measure for those who like clean and simple ROI calculations. Thus, if the objective is a very conservative ROI calculation, perhaps only the outcomes in Table 7.1 should be considered.

Subjective Business Outcomes

A fairly strong argument can be made that there are additional potential benefits and costs of a virtual team beyond those in Table 7.1. Table 7.2 describes the leading candidates: creativity and innovation, organizational learning and diffusion of best practices, and the attitudes and longevity of the team members. The literature on teams (Cohen and Bailey, 1997) clearly demonstrates that each of these is an important team outcome that has the ability to have a significant impact on the bottom line.

The fact that the outcomes in Table 7.2 are more difficult to measure objectively than the outcomes in Table 7.1 does not diminish their importance. It does, however, influence the extent to which they can and should be included in ROI. We start here with a discussion of the potential costs and benefits associated with each of these in the virtual team context and then take up the issue of whether and how to include them in ROI later. These outcomes are:

• *Creativity and innovation.* One of the most powerful benefits of teams in general is their ability to foster better creativity and innovation through cross-functional collaboration than is possible otherwise. Similar to the impact on quality, the ability to include the best role players, regardless of where they are located, gives a virtual team a clear potential to produce new ideas that can transform the company to the benefit of the bottom line. Stacked up against this

Table 7.2. Subjective Business Outcomes

	Potential Benefits from Operating Virtually	*Potential Costs from Operating Virtually*
Creativity and innovation	Geographical dispersion means the ability to include the best experts wherever they are located; multifunction input may be easier to obtain	Creativity may suffer when team members have to figure out how to collaborate in unfamiliar setting
Organizational learning and diffusion of best practices	More functions and stakeholders possible, so greater diffusion of learnings from the team's work The interpersonal networks that are developed can increase the capacity for learning from future activities, not just the current team's work Greater use of electronic communication, which is the first step in knowledge management	Knowledge management systems often are not well developed, so teams may spend more time struggling with technology than using it productively
Attitudes and longevity	Sometimes allows teams to avoid forced relocation away from home, which increases employee satisfaction Increases understanding of how to work with people across distances and develop relationships that are mediated electronically The relationships developed can be applied to later projects, assuming the extra effort is taken to build the relationships initially	Lack of traditional forum for building relationships informally means they may never get formed Virtual team responsibilities may be treated more as add-on than FTF team responsibilities

potential is the drawback that creative teamwork is traditionally done FTF. Thus, the virtual team that benefits from including the best available talent often faces an unfamiliar learning curve when collaborating electronically.

• *Organizational learning and diffusion of best practices.* These include improved learning about changes in the market for the company's products and how best to execute the intermediate processes necessary to create those products. Having geographically dispersed members means that the key role players needed can be included on the virtual team. Perhaps more important is the way that virtuality forces the members to interact with each other. Knowledge management is foremost about developing the capacity to share knowledge wherever it is needed throughout the organization. The main failing of knowledge management efforts is their inability to develop ways to communicate relevant information effectively across time and space. Because virtual teams rely on electronic and asynchronous communication much more than FTF teams do, they are forced to try to solve those knowledge management problems in order to get their work done. Thus, they have the potential to be much more successful at knowledge management.

A large countervailing force is the fact that existing knowledge management systems often are not well developed or used, so a virtual team may spend more time struggling with technology than using it productively. On the upside, the geographically dispersed interpersonal networks and relationships that are forged through working on a virtual team can increase organizational learning at least through the knowledge that the team members use subsequently in other tasks, whether done FTF or mediated electronically.

• *Attitudes and longevity.* One of the more important benefits of working virtually is the potential to increase commitment and loyalty fostered among team members who otherwise might be forced to relocate to achieve the team's objectives. The relationships developed also can be applied to later projects, assuming the extra effort is taken to build the relationships. The problem here is that the traditional forums for building relationships informally in an FTF context means that those relationships may never get formed. Even when the team members run into difficulties in forming good relationships while working on a given virtual team, the lessons learned might increase their capacity to be successful in future virtual teaming or other electronically mediated collaboration situations (thereby increasing the organizational capacity to develop such networks). On the downside, virtual team responsibilities may be more likely treated as add-ons to one's "regular" job than FTF team responsibilities.

Design, Input, and Process Aspects of Virtual Team ROI

In addition to the outcomes listed in Tables 7.1 and 7.2, other sources of ROI (or lack thereof) include a number of design and process characteristics that distinguish virtual from FTF teams (see Table 7.3):

Table 7.3. Design, Input, and Process Issues

	Potential Benefits from Operating Virtually	*Potential Costs from Operating Virtually*
Travel and face-to-face meetings	Reduce FTF costs by operating virtually	May underestimate travel needed for effective performance
Technology	If managed properly, working virtually can encourage greater and more effective use of technology, driven by necessity	If advanced planning is minimal, expenses may be underestimated
Training and coaching	If new ways of training and coaching virtually are developed, they can be deployed at low cost in other settings	Traditional ways of training FTF more expensive to use and less efficient in virtual context
Leadership	Often able to choose the best person regardless of location	Leadership effectiveness may be hindered by lack of proximity to other team members
Communication and decision making	May have more efficient use of electronic forms of communication	Some types of communication and decision making may be harder to facilitate in the virtual context
Career development	More opportunities to participate in critical tasks, gain relevant experience	"Out of sight, out of mind" might limit career advancement
Personnel and salary costs	FTF meeting time may be more focused, more efficiently used	May be less efficient use of time, so total time costs may be greater
		Possible exception: global teams where work can be done asynchronously around the clock
Administrative and other support costs	More points of contact with different support functions in the organization that may be spread out	FTF interaction by leader may be crucial when dealing with administrative and information technology support personnel

- *Travel and FTF meetings.* One of the potential benefits of operating virtually is lower travel expenses. This can be a source of major cost savings for teams with geographically distributed members. However, managers often underestimate the amount of travel needed for maximal effectiveness.
- *Technology.* If managed properly, working virtually can encourage greater and more effective use of technology. The fact that members have to use technology to communicate pushes them to consider using technology in ways that might otherwise be ignored by team members who have little to no spare time for learning new systems. Necessity is the mother of invention here, or, at least in this case, learning. Yet technology training often is treated as an afterthought, if done at all, so the expenses in learning new technologies are frequently underestimated, which can cause budget overruns.
- *Training and coaching.* Traditional ways of training FTF are more expensive to use or less efficient if not adapted properly to the virtual context. On the upside, if new ways of training and coaching virtually can be developed, they can be replicated at low cost.
- *Leadership.* Constructing a virtual team enables the selection of the best team leader (whether chosen by the team's supervisors or self-selected by the team) regardless of location. Yet remote leadership poses a number of problems for effective teamwork. This can be of particular concern if the leader is remote and a large portion of the rest of the team members are colocated.
- *Communication and decision making.* There can be both positive and negative contributions from operating virtually. In some cases, communication and decision making may be best done in person; in other cases, virtuality might improve effectiveness. When electronic communication is preferred (such as distributing a memo by e-mail), such options are available to FTF teams as well. Here we are talking about the ways that communication and decision making differ for FTF and virtual teams.
- *Career development.* Having the opportunity to participate in virtual teams should provide more opportunities to participate in critical organizational tasks. The experience gained could promote career development. Yet if the experience is gained by working with those who are not directly responsible for deciding on a person's advancement, then the "out of sight, out of mind" nature of this kind of virtual teaming might negate the positives gained from the work experience.
- *Personnel and salary costs.* There may be less efficient use of time overall in virtual teams, so the total personnel time costs may be greater than if the work were done FTF. One possible exception is for global virtual teams, where the work can be done asynchronously around the clock. Note that this is a subtle distinction, however. When calculating the personnel costs, what should be included is the total time put into the project. If the total time is the same for a global virtual team yet that team accomplishes key tasks in less calendar time

because of asynchronous work done continuously over multiple time zones, then the team has faster cycle time but no savings in personnel costs. In reality, though, if such a team is able to meet key deliverable deadlines in faster calendar time, it likely can accomplish more tasks in the course of a year than a colocated team with the same number of members. In this sense, their productivity is higher, which is the same thing as saying the personnel costs per unit of output are lower. Because FTF meetings happen less often, the time a virtual team spends in FTF meetings may be much more efficiently used than the typical FTF meeting for a colocated team.

• *Administrative and other support costs.* A virtual team has more points of contact with different support functions that may be geographically dispersed within an organization, which increases the team's ability to access such resources. But if the team is not colocated with the key resources needed to support it, it may have difficulty getting appropriate and timely responses from support personnel. This can be an issue particularly when the team leader is remotely located away from support functions that are centrally located.

CALCULATING ROI FOR VIRTUAL TEAMS

The basic definition of ROI is straightforward: $ROI = B/C$, where B is the benefit and C is the cost. There are a number of critical challenges involved in calculating ROI: coming up with monetary values for things that are difficult to quantify, forecasting ROI ahead of time, creating a confidence interval for the precision of the ROI estimate, and making the link back to the firm's strategy. Our discussion here builds on the framework used by Levenson (forthcoming) to calculate ROI for teams in general.

Only costs and benefits that are significant, meaning they account for a large enough fraction of the total costs and benefits of the team's work, should be included in the ROI calculation. The precise threshold to use depends on the team's context, but as a guide, Levenson (forthcoming) suggests considering only costs and benefits that account for at least 5 percent of the total. In addition, how easy it is to figure out the magnitude and likelihood of realizing the costs and benefits of a particular virtual team outcome or process should be considered. If the likely magnitude is quite small, then it may not make sense to include that outcome or process in calculating ROI.

There are two ways to consider ROI for virtual teams. What is the ROI in a vacuum, that is, what is the virtual team's ROI relative to doing nothing at all? What is the virtual team's ROI relative to what a FTF team could accomplish? In both cases, it is necessary to identify the true costs and benefits of the virtual team. Where the approaches differ is the baselines used for valuing those costs and benefits. One way to make the difference clear is to separate out the

ROI for a team into two components and express it in net present value (NPV) terms:

$$NPV = NPV_{ftf} + NPV_{vt} = (B_{ftf} - C_{ftf}) + (B_{vt} - C_{vt}),$$

where NPV_{ftf} is the NPV (ROI expressed as a difference instead of a ratio) from doing the team's tasks in an FTF (colocated) setting and NPV_{vt} is the additional value (positive or negative) from conducting the team's activities in a virtual setting. In cases where it is impractical to think about operating FTF, this is equivalent to saying that NPV_{ftf} cannot be calculated, which reduces the NPV to being equivalent to calculating NPV_{vt}.

CASE EXAMPLES

We apply our ROI framework to three virtual teams that we studied: a scenario planning team for a consumer durables manufacturing company, a new product development team comprising members from a consortium of large vehicle manufacturers, and a team charged with integrating the purchasing departments and processes from two companies that had recently merged. We discuss the first case in detail and then briefly discuss the other two. We have changed certain identifying information to protect the anonymity of each company.

Scenario Planning Team

This virtual team is charged with doing scenario planning for a consumer durables manufacturing company. The company has expanded globally in recent years, but the United States still accounts for a majority of sales. That fact and the need to design products that satisfy local cultural preferences mean that scenario planning for U.S. product development is partially segmented from product development efforts targeted at other regions of the globe.

The products produced by the company have fairly long research, development, and production cycles; this is not an industry where new variations within a product line are rolled out every year. Thus, scenario planning for how customer needs and tastes will evolve takes place over a five- to ten-year horizon. This particular team was charged with developing scenarios of how consumer lifestyles and preferences would evolve over that horizon in the United States.

The seven team members were drawn from a number of functions representing key stakeholders in the product development life cycle. In terms of geographical dispersion, five of the members were located at corporate headquarters in a central part of the United States more than eight hundred miles away from either coast. The team leader and the seventh member were located on opposite coasts of the United States, three thousand miles apart from each other. In addition, the team employed a consulting company to help in the scenario planning process; the consultant assigned to work with the team also resided far from both company headquarters and the two remote team members.

Objective Business Outcomes. Table 7.4 lists the objective business outcomes for this team:

• *Cycle time, timeliness, and productivity.* The team divided its work into two distinct parts. The creative brainstorming was done almost exclusively FTF at headquarters at regular intervals; the meetings held in the interim were conducted by telephone and were used primarily for process checks and setup for the FTF meetings. Thus, the team minimized the inefficiencies inherent in telephone meetings by deferring much of the key work for the FTF meetings. The virtual meeting inefficiencies resulted in relatively minor cost increases relative to doing all the work FTF.

Table 7.4. Objective Business Outcomes for Consumer Durables Scenario Planning Team

	Benefits from Operating Virtually	Costs from Operating Virtually
Cycle time, timeliness, and productivity		✓ Meeting and telephone conference inefficiencies resulting in possible lost productivity
Quality	✓✓ Customer surrogates in workshops rated scenarios helpful. Not clear that the outcome had anything to do with operating virtually	
Customer satisfaction and implementation success	✓✓ Team design with multiple stakeholders means more likely that new product development ideas generated from scenario planning would be implemented	✓ Less informal stakeholder contact by remote leader resulting in lower probability of implementing the ideas generated

Note: ✓ = Small Impact;
✓✓ = Medium Impact;
✓✓✓ = Large Impact. For this and the following tables, we made these evaluations of likely economic impact based on data from interviews of team members and stakeholders. Thus, they represent a subjective assessment of the impact of each cost and benefit on the bottom line.

- *Quality.* The stakeholders and other "consumers" of the scenarios created by the team seemed happy with the team's output. However, it was not clear that the quality of the scenarios would have been much different had the team been located FTF. Quality might have suffered had colocation been required for all team members because the remote members, including the leader, could not have participated. Yet the team's choice to do the key creative work FTF meant that the vast majority of the work, including the planning and process time done over the telephone, could have been done FTF with about four to eight additional FTF meetings at headquarters. This would have significantly increased the travel costs, but not materially affected the remote members' ability to meet their other responsibilities.

- *Customer satisfaction and implementation success.* A key metric for this team is whether the scenarios ultimately are integrated into each business unit's product planning and development process. Therefore, it was quite important that the remote members took part because they represented key stakeholders and internal customers for the team, one of which would have had no representation otherwise for a major business unit accounting for an entire product line for the company. This was a key benefit of the team's composition, which required geographical dispersion. On the downside, the fact that the leader was remote meant that other key stakeholders had less informal contact with him, which decreased implementation success.

Subjective Business Outcomes. Table 7.5 details the following subjective business outcomes for the scenario planning team:

- *Creativity and innovation.* The team clearly benefited from greater cross-functional representation enabled by the ability to tap members from geographically dispersed locations. The remote members also were able to bring perspectives on the marketplace that were not immediately apparent to the team members residing at headquarters, away from the population centers on the two coasts of the country. These team members from different functional and marketplace perspectives engaged in a dialogue that stimulated creativity in their scenarios.

- *Organizational learning and diffusion of best practices, attitudes, and longevity.* These were among the most highly rated benefits that arose from the team's work and took multiple forms. First, traditional team-related benefits from having cross-functional members work together were evident here. Thus, working on the team greatly increased the chances for successful future collaboration among the members on other projects. Second, there was significant learning about how to operate virtually. There was almost unanimous agreement that if the team had to do a similar task virtually again, they would be much more efficient with structuring the virtual versus FTF work. These

Table 7.5. Subjective Business Outcomes for Consumer Durables Scenario Planning Team

	Benefits from Operating Virtually	Costs from Operating Virtually
Creativity and innovation	✓ Team dispersion enabled greater inputs and creativity beyond benefits created by cross-functional composition of team Greater marketplace adaptability	✓✓ Team reserved all creative brainstorming work for FTF meetings
Organizational learning and diffusion of best practices	✓✓✓ General managers could include more functions and stakeholders on team Wanted better organizational learning and potential diffusion of ideas New relationships among team members suggest greater productivity on future projects	✓ Multiple failed attempts with different knowledge management systems
Attitudes and longevity	✓✓ The two remote members appreciated not having to relocate Positive benefit in terms of working together in future	

Note: ✓ = Small Impact;
✓✓ = Medium Impact;
✓✓✓ = Large Impact.

individual learnings positioned the team members as internal experts who could consult on virtual teaming efforts within the company, albeit informally.

Design, Input, and Process Issues. Table 7.6 contains the remaining ROI issues for the scenario planning team. Key highlights include:

- *Technology.* This was much more of an impediment to than facilitator of team effectiveness.

Table 7.6. Design, Input, and Process Issues for Scenario Planning Team

	Benefits from Operating Virtually	Costs from Operating Virtually
Travel and face-to-face meetings		✓ Geographical dispersion: extra trips
Technology		✓✓ Design of a Web-based system that was not used due to team member resistance and lack of training
Training and coaching		✓✓ Additional costs for "on-the-road" team building, in part a response to the geographical dispersion of team
Leadership		✓✓ Distant leadership created some inefficiencies; informal style of leader conflicted with needed added planning to overcome virtuality weaknesses
Communication and decision making		✓✓ Not everyone informed about decisions made at main corporate site
Career development	✓ Knowledge and skills increased for team members working with those from other functions located elsewhere; additional learning for members due to geographical dispersion from contact with outside designers and customers	
Personnel and salary costs	✓ FTF meeting time more focused, more efficiently used	✓✓ Extra time costs of inefficient distant leadership
Administrative and other support costs		✓ Added administrative costs created by distant leadership

Note: ✓ = Small Impact;
   ✓✓ = Medium Impact;
   ✓✓✓ = Large Impact.

- *Training and coaching.* The team incurred significant up-front costs by taking a trip to evaluate potential consulting partners to employ in the scenario planning work. This greatly increased out-of-pocket costs for travel and the implicit costs of team member time. But it helped build a strong foundation of shared understanding and common language among the members, which had a positive impact on the subjective business outcomes (see Table 7.5).

- *Leadership; communication and decision making.* In addition to the issues of coordination and lack of access to headquarters-based stakeholders issues created by the remote leadership, there was an additional cost as well: inefficiencies created by an informal leadership style. The team leader and company culture were used to consensus building through open conversation, something that is hard to achieve in a virtual setting. This tendency toward informal leadership styles needs to be counteracted by explicit planning to create the conditions needed to facilitate such interactions in a virtual setting, something this team did not do.

Determining ROI. Having detailed all the possible costs and benefits to be considered for this team, the next step is to determine what to consider for the team's ROI calculation by asking these questions:

- What was the ROI to operating as virtually as the team did? Should they have tried to do more work virtually? More work FTF?
- Taking the degree of virtuality as given, what was the ROI from the team's efforts relative to what the organization would have achieved otherwise?

Taking the second question first, the team's output was clearly important in the company's long-run strategic product planning process. Senior management was committed to scenario planning as a way to ensure that they properly considered different states of the world that could have a fundamental impact on the very survival of the company in a competitive environment. Thus, as long as the team's scenarios raised top management's awareness of the possibilities and helped them make better-informed decisions, then the upside potential benefits from the team's efforts were extremely large. However, those benefits would be realized only many years later, long after the team completed its work, and they would be realized only in a diffuse way as they interacted with other inputs in the research, development, production, and marketing processes. Thus, assigning monetary values to the team's output based on expected changes to the bottom line was not feasible without resorting to wild guesswork.

What about the other potential benefits from the team operating the way it did? Tables 7.4 through 7.6 list a number of other benefits that the team indicated were potentially significant (those with two or three check marks), including greater implementation success, marketplace adaptability, more cross-functional and better organizational learning, and better attitudes on the part of the remote members. In the cases of implementation success and marketplace adaptability, these also were best assigned monetary values by the team's supervisors. The positive impacts on learning and member attitudes should not be minimized. But from an ROI standpoint, it is quite difficult to draw a direct link from these to the bottom line.

In such cases there is a natural inclination to abandon ROI because it is too difficult to calculate the direct monetary benefits. Levenson (forthcoming) suggests an alternative approach: take the issue directly to the stakeholders. The question to ask is, "How much would you be willing to pay for the output [the scenarios] that the team produced and the ancillary benefits [better learning and attitudes]?" If the answer exceeds the costs, then the team produced positive ROI (an ROI ratio that is greater than one and positive net present value).

When working with this team, we did not attempt to ask this question of the stakeholders, but that does not diminish the importance of the communication exercise. Instead of forcing the stakeholders to reveal their valuation of the team's output, a tricky political situation in most cases, the team could produce complete cost estimates and give those to the stakeholders as input for calculating ROI. The stakeholders would then have all the information needed to decide how to reward the team based on the cost measures and their own subjective evaluation of the benefits. They would also be well positioned to use that information when making future resource allocation decisions in related scenario planning and virtual teaming situations. In other words, the stakeholders would be able to reap all the benefits that calculating ROI is supposed to produce without forcing the team to produce questionable estimates of the monetary value of the scenarios' benefit to the organization, something better left to the stakeholders themselves.

Take Advantage of Existing Data to Assign Monetary Values. There are other possibilities for assigning monetary value to the benefits. An organization that culturally puts a high value on learning may already have in place initiatives explicitly designed to achieve improved cross-functional collaboration and learning. If the team members were able to compare the expected future learnings from their scenario planning with the efforts that the other learning initiatives hoped to achieve, they might be able to assign a monetary value based on the budgetary dollars being spent on the latter initiatives.

Similarly, drawing a link between improved attitudes and future turnover and advancement is difficult but not impossible to do. It is not cost-effective for the team members to conduct an entire study of such links within the organization simply to assign a monetary value to those benefits and the ROI derived from working on the scenario planning project. But organizations often already have such estimates available from prior efforts. Where available, the team members can use those results to project what the bottom-line value to the organization of increased commitment and loyalty will be in terms of reduced turnover and internal promotion.

In this case, though, no such separate estimates were available that could have allowed the team members to assign monetary values to the improved learning and attitudes. Thus, we are left with only those benefits best valued by the team's supervisors. In cases like this where the stakeholders are best suited to value the team's output because of high degrees of subjectivity, the team's role in helping to calculate ROI may lie solely in producing cost estimates. This is still an important and challenging task because the team members are best suited to determine how much implicit resources were spent in terms of their own time and the unbudgeted time of other departments and support staff. Of course, they may feel inclined to misreport the costs, overestimating in cases where there is pressure to show that the project was worthless and underestimating in cases where their own rewards depend on demonstrating positive ROI. But these incentive problems exist in all ROI calculations.

The subjective nature of virtual team ROI is one reason that those accustomed to thinking about ROI only in terms of impacts on net cash flow might shy away from the methodology we describe here. Yet such critics cannot hide behind the supposed objectivity of cash flow estimates. It is widely acknowledged that managers frequently manipulate budgetary revenue and cost numbers to meet cash flow and profit performance goals. Indeed, such behaviors have contributed to the downfall of entire companies such as Enron, Global Crossing, and WorldCom. All ROI estimates, whether based on traditional cash flow measures or the newer approach we use here, must be viewed as inherently subjective and susceptible to manipulation.

The ROI from Operating More or Less Virtually. Going back to the ROI options available to the scenario planning team, the team itself was much better positioned to answer the first set of questions: What was the ROI to the team's functioning as virtually as it did, as opposed to more virtually or more FTF? This is a much more manageable task because it appeared that the benefits from the team's efforts—the scenarios—likely would have been the same under alternative degrees of virtual work. The team members indicated that the quality of the scenarios would not have differed had they been colocated. The main difference in their eyes was that they would have been able to meet the project deadlines without as much time and effort needed. Thus, their time would have been used more effectively.

Of course, the downside to doing more of the work FTF would have been greater travel costs, which counteract the implicit cost savings from less time spent on the project. Thus, it is impossible to say ahead of time how the ROI from operating more FTF compared to the ROI from doing the work the way the team did. Consider again the different components of ROI that can be calculated for questions such as these, expressed in NPV terms:

$$NPV = NPV_{ftf} + NPV_{vt} = (B_{ftf} - C_{ftf}) + (B_{vt} - C_{vt}).$$

Asking whether the team would have had greater ROI in a strictly FTF collaboration setting is equivalent to asking whether NPV_{vt} is greater or less than zero, that is, whether the additional marginal benefit from operating virtually exceeds the additional marginal costs ($B_{vt} > C_{vt}$). But we already stipulated that in this case, the additional benefit to operating virtually was zero ($B_{vt} = 0$) because the team believed that the quality of the scenarios would have been no different.

What about the other potential benefits from operating virtually? Because the team had (and exercised) the option to operate more FTF when it seemed critical to do so, the positive outcomes listed under the first column in Tables 7.5 and 7.6 were not really benefits from operating virtually. Rather, they represented benefits from putting together a geographically distributed team that had the option to vary the degree to which it operated virtually. Thus, determining whether the gain in NPV terms from operating virtually was positive comes down to evaluating whether the net change in costs from operating virtually is less than zero ($0 > C_{vt}$). If it is, then the team realized positive marginal ROI.

So which costs should be included in that calculation? Again, we consider only those that could be attributed to the team with a degree of certainty and were large enough to account for a significant fraction of the costs incurred by the team. In Tables 7.4 through 7.6, these include the extra travel costs incurred from operating FTF (including the on-the-road team building), the money wasted on Web technologies that were never used effectively, and remote leadership and meeting inefficiency problems. The last, however, arguably should be excluded from inclusion as additional marginal costs from operating virtually in this case. Why? Because we are comparing the degree of virtual operation the team used with the alternative of even more FTF collaboration with the same geographically dispersed members.

Shifting the work that was done virtually to being done entirely FTF (while maintaining the same membership) would have necessitated more travel time by the remote members. So the savings in time to make decisions because of virtual meeting and remote leadership inefficiencies would have been counteracted by increased time for travel to the FTF meetings. Although these offsetting effects may not have been precisely equal, our sense is that they were close enough not to warrant figuring out which one might have marginally exceeded the other. We are thus left with the extra money spent on travel costs that would have occurred with the extra FTF meetings weighed against the money that would have been saved on the wasted Web technologies. If the former exceeds the latter, then the team exhibited positive marginal ROI from operating with the degree of virtuality that they did.

Thus, in this case, we are able to reduce the ROI calculation for choosing to operate more or less virtually into a simple comparison of two different out-of-pocket cost estimates. But by now, the danger in taking that simple inequality at face value should be clear. What if it turns out that the estimated additional costs were a negative $5,000, that is, the saved travel costs from operating less FTF exceeded the wasted Web technology costs by that amount? Is this a clear win for their choices? From a performance management standpoint, the answer is probably yes. But from a strategic planning standpoint, we do not have enough information to answer that question.

Suppose the entire costs incurred by the team amounted to $100,000 in out-of-pocket costs and $200,000 in implicit time costs for the team members and others who provided services that supported their work. We could express the marginal ROI from operating virtually in this case as the marginal cost savings over the total project costs: 5,000/300,000 = 1.67 percent. This is a very low ROI under normal circumstances that would compare ROI to a hurdle rate that all capital spending projects must exceed in order to justify the cost of capital (that is, cash).

Note, though, that this is a very conservative ROI estimate. In particular, all of the potential benefits that we deemed too difficult to assign monetary values to are implicitly assumed to be zero. Thus, even when asking what the ROI from a team's past actions was (backward-looking ROI), we still have to wrestle with issues of forecasting future events. In this case, the two leading issues are organizational learning and better team member attitudes. The conservative worst-case scenario approach might assume zero future bottom-line value from the team's efforts on these points, but more optimistic scenarios would do otherwise.

Consider again the benefits from increased organizational learning. Suppose the team forecast that the insights on virtual teaming gleaned from their work on the scenario planning project meant that they expected future virtual teaming efforts would run more smoothly (for example, in terms of more efficient meeting times and better use of Web technologies). Because this organization has been moving to do more and more virtual teaming out of perceived necessity, there is a generally recognized need to improve virtual teaming skills throughout the company. One way to value the monetary benefits from the potential learnings would be to compare them to the insights that would be gained from hiring an outside consultant to facilitate a workshop or series of learnings on virtual teaming. The potential money saved from not having to hire someone from outside could be used to value the organizational learning produced by the team's work.

Similarly, external estimates of the link between improved attitudes and reduced turnover and recruitment costs could be used to assign monetary values to the benefit the team's work generated as a result of increased loyalty and commitment on the part of the remote members. Suppose that the team goes through these exercises and arrives at potential benefits of $25,000 for organizational learning and $10,000 for improved attitudes. They also recognize that the chances of each of these occurring differ significantly.

Let us assume that in talking to the human resource department, the team discovered that hiring an outside facilitator to give a workshop on virtual teaming was slated as likely to occur in the next fiscal year. They then assign a 50 percent probability of realizing the $25,000 cost savings from not hiring that facilitator. This probability reflects both the uncertainty over whether the facilitator would have been hired to begin with and their belief that the facilitator would have produced a workshop format better suited for disseminating the virtual team collaboration learnings than they designed on their own.

In contrast, the team assigns only a 10 percent probability of achieving the expected $10,000 cost savings from improved attitudes. This reflects the fact that the remote team members were not likely to quit had they been forced to do more traveling to do all the team's work FTF.

Putting these together with the earlier cost estimates, we get a very different picture of the team's ROI from operating virtually. One way to combine the different estimates is to do a probability-weighted ROI calculation. Assuming that the team estimates a 100 percent chance of achieving the originally estimated $5,000 cost savings, we have

$$\text{Probability weighted NPV} = \$5,000 + (\$25,000) \times (.50) + (\$10,000) \times (.10) = \$18,500.$$

This yields an ROI of 6.17 percent, much higher than the estimated 1.67 percent from the cash flow cost savings estimate that considered only travel and Web technology costs.

Viewed yet another way, the ROI when including the organizational learning and improved attitudes benefits can seem even higher. The advantage of the probability-weighted ROI is that it averages expected future benefits over different scenarios that may or may not occur (which is reflected in the estimated probabilities). The disadvantage is that in many ways, it reflects a state of the world that will never occur. For example, if the organizational learning benefit is realized, then the bottom-line boost to the organization will be the full $25,000, not the 50 percent smaller value used when calculating the NPV ($12,500).

One way to account for these different scenarios that makes the link between the estimated probabilities and the ROI calculations more transparent is by using a reporting format like Table 7.7. In the final row, we have applied the reasonable assumption that the probability of achieving both the organizational learning and improved attitudes benefits is lower than the chance of achieving either benefit on its own.

The numbers in Table 7.7 underscore why ROI, even when carefully calculated, at best is an aid to careful decision making, not a substitute for it.

Table 7.7. Range of Expected Benefits from the Scenario Planning Team's Work

Factors Included in ROI Calculation	Chance of Achieving the Results	Estimated NPV and ROI, Conditional on the Results Being Achieved
Travel and Web technology costs only	100 percent	$5,000 NPV, 1.67 percent ROI
Travel and Web costs plus organizational learning	50 percent	$30,000 NPV, 10 percent ROI
Travel and Web costs plus improved attitudes	10 percent	$15,000 NPV, 5 percent ROI
Travel and Web costs, organizational learning, and improved attitudes	5 percent	$40,000 NPV, 13.3 percent ROI

Table 7.7 has four different ROI estimates, all of them reasonable under different scenarios of how events will unfold after the team finishes its work, ranging from 1.67 to 13.3 percent. In addition, there is the probability-weighted ROI estimate of 6.17 percent. There is no particular reason, without further information on the firm's strategy and budget allocation decisions, to rule out any of these estimates. Instead, the entire range of ROI estimates is best presented to the team's stakeholders in its entirety.

Large Vehicle Production Alliance R&D Team

The second case is a consortium of large vehicle manufacturers from the United States and Europe that used a virtual team to design the next-generation vehicle. Dividing production process into discrete parts and subcontracting the separate pieces out to different manufacturers is nothing new. But having the design team from the different companies convene virtually is. This enabled the company that was taking charge of the consortium much greater flexibility in choosing the best subcontractors for the project, regardless of geographical location of their lead R&D personnel.

The two biggest concerns facing the consortium were whether the virtual team members could work effectively together and whether the consortium could convince potential customers that this new approach to design would produce a vehicle as reliable as what their competitors were offering. Because the scope and volume of production are determined jointly with key large customers in this industry, the commitment of customers to purchase a new vehicle is crucial to its financial success.

Table 7.8 details the objective business outcomes for this team. The subjective business outcomes are in Table 7.9 and the design, input, and process issues

Table 7.8. Objective Business Outcomes for the Vehicle R&D Team

	Benefits from Operating Virtually	Costs from Operating Virtually
Cycle time, timeliness, and productivity	✓✓ Productivity benefits from implementing the best of the cost savings ideas from each partner	✓✓ Coordination difficulties due to geographical dispersion add time and costs to development effort
	Time zone differences allow for around-the-clock work and lowered cycle time	
	Productivity increased by decreased coordination costs	
Customer satisfaction	✓✓✓ Customers sufficiently satisfied to award contract	

Note: ✓ = Small Impact;
   ✓✓ = Medium Impact;
   ✓✓✓ = Large Impact.

in Table 7.10. Unlike the case of the scenario planning team, it is very straightforward to determine whether the design team produced large enough ROI for the consortium. Although the team experienced a number of technical difficulties associated with virtual teaming that impeded their effectiveness, they delivered a design good enough to win a large number of orders for the new vehicle. Thus, the ROI to the consortium from using the virtual team was very high.

One reason that the ROI calculation does not necessarily need to go any further in this case is that the virtual team's charge was delivering a design that would win enough initial orders to make their efforts worthwhile. Yet the ROI from virtual teaming in this case goes deeper because of the learnings subsequently applied during the vehicle production process.

One of the more interesting benefits was the insights gained into the effective use of new technologies for vehicle design. Because of the enormous costs in creating and testing a prototype production process, it is much more economical if manufacturers can do a complete markup of the finished vehicle electronically before starting to produce a prototype. Working out design flaws electronically provides the potential for enormous cost savings from avoiding errors that traditionally are discovered only after millions of dollars of costs have been incurred.

In this case, the team used a cutting-edge design tool to do a complete electronic markup of the vehicle. Although this created additional computer

Table 7.9. Subjective Business Outcomes for the Vehicle R&D Team

	Benefits from Operating Virtually	*Costs from Operating Virtually*
Creativity and innovation	✓✓✓ Specialized expertise of each partner applied to development effort, for example, metal composites expertise	
Organizational learning and diffusion of best practices	✓✓✓ Best practices diffused in terms of what was developed and the processes and technology used	
Attitudes and longevity	✓✓ Ability to remain at home and work on project builds employee satisfaction Apply learnings and the relationships developed to future projects	

Note: ✓ = Small Impact;
✓✓ = Medium Impact;
✓✓✓ = Large Impact.

security costs, those were more than offset by the reduced relocation costs incurred during the design phase. More interesting, use of the technology changed the dynamic between team members that is typical on new product development teams: the use of virtual technologies to resolve design disagreements made them less personal and more task based. This enabled more objective decision making, which reduced the cost of conflict and allowed the team to focus much more effectively on the goal of producing the best product to fit both customer needs and business and technology constraints.

Postmerger Integration Team

Our third case comes from a team charged with identifying efficiency gains from integrating the purchasing departments from two companies that had recently merged. The merging companies had headquarters in Europe (a non-native-English-speaking country) and the United States. The team was equally balanced with representatives from both countries.

Table 7.10. Design, Input, and Process Issues for the Vehicle R&D Team

	Benefits from *Operating Virtually*	*Costs from* *Operating Virtually*
Travel and face-to-face meetings	✓✓✓ Extremely large colocation costs if FTF; limited to key personnel for specific time periods Avoid large travel costs for key personnel not colocated	✓✓ Still have travel costs for key FTF meetings, but virtual technology reduces the number needed
Technology	✓✓✓ Large investment in technological infrastructure Additional costs imposed by virtuality: features to integrate the work across organizational and national boundaries, greater technical support, firewall and security costs	
Training and coaching	✓✓ Training needed on common systems and processes; communications and information technology for collaborative work; team building and cultural awareness; working virtually Most of the training costs would have been incurred even if the development team from the different partner organizations was colocated; much more of a cross-organizational than virtual collaboration issue	
Communication and decision making	✓✓ Appropriate processes need to be negotiated among partners Organizational and cultural differences create communication mishaps One clear benefit of virtuality: use of virtual technologies to resolve design disagreements make them less personal and more task based, reducing the cost of conflict	
Administrative and other support		✓ Distributed model might require more administrative support

Note: ✓ = Small Impact;
 ✓✓ = Medium Impact;
 ✓✓✓ = Large Impact.

From the most basic bottom-line perspective, the team returned significant ROI, finding cost savings of $94 million (Table 7.11). On this score alone, the team produced more than enough benefits to justify their cost of working together. Yet from a performance management standpoint, the savings identified might have consisted only of low-hanging fruit, meaning that a more effective team might have identified even greater cost savings. Their high degree of inefficiency in terms of virtual team processes and rework suggests this may be the case (Tables 7.12 and 7.13).

Yet the team's inefficiencies around virtual team meeting practices provided a potential silver lining to the organization in terms of future benefits. One key benefit centered around developing cross-cultural norms about the use of e-mail, an area that caused enormous miscommunication and rework for the team.

Table 7.11. Objective Business Outcomes for the Postmerger Integration Team

	Benefits from Operating Virtually	Costs from Operating Virtually
Cycle time, timeliness, and productivity	✓✓✓ Achieved shared cost savings goal of $94 million (but may have been low-hanging fruit)	✓✓ Meeting inefficiencies Lack of follow-through between meetings created time delays
	The cost savings could likely have occurred without operating virtually, but close collaboration between partners driven by shared strategic focus	Limits to obtaining volume cost advantages created by decentralized purchasing decisions and lack of integrated system between partners
Quality	✓✓✓ Commodity experts from each partner organization work together virtually to develop best practices	✓✓ English-language fluency an issue, particularly at operational levels
Customer satisfaction	✓✓✓ Geographical dispersion enabled expertise to be located close to the customer base	

Note: ✓ = Small Impact;
  ✓✓ = Medium Impact;
  ✓✓✓ = Large Impact.

Table 7.12. Subjective Business Outcomes for the Postmerger Integration Team

	Benefits from Operating Virtually	Costs from Operating Virtually
Creativity and innovation	✓✓ Best expertise from both partner organizations applied to procurement issues	✓✓ Limited face-to-face time and the pressure to achieve quick savings limited creativity
Organizational learning and diffusion of best practices	✓✓ Substantial learning about the procurement processes in both organizations The relationships developed between counterparts (those from each organization working on the same commodity) could be applied to future commodity issues Greater use of e-mail and adoption of twenty-four hour response norms to facilitate virtual effort	✓✓ The lack of shared information technology systems and the need to develop a procurement knowledge management system limited diffusion of practices
Attitudes and longevity	✓✓ Relationships developed across national cultures and language barriers satisfying and important for future work together Avoided forced relocation away from home, increasing employee satisfaction and reducing turnover Voluntary temporary relocations to new country and culture satisfying for particular employees	✓ Communication and language barriers frustrating to employees Lack of follow-through invisible until the next meeting, creating time delays and rework; frustrating for employees Additional work created by merger, but no additional resources for team, creating employee dissatisfaction

Note: ✓ = Small Impact;
      ✓✓ = Medium Impact;
      ✓✓✓ = Large Impact.

Table 7.13. Design, Input, and Process Issues for the Postmerger Integration Team

	Benefits from Operating Virtually	Costs from Operating Virtually
Travel and face-to-face meetings	✓✓✓ Weekly videoconferencing meetings save travel costs	✓✓ Senior managers still travel to meet FTF with counterparts; no meeting minutes leads to rework
Technology	✓ Develop norms to use e-mail efficiently and effectively	✓ Need to develop integrated knowledge management system
Training and coaching	✓ Training helped team members deal with cultural differences and the merger	✓ Very limited language training Not enough team building
Leadership	✓✓ Effective coaching by leaders with cross-cultural skills	
Communication and decision making		✓ Lack of disciplined decision-making processes and tracking created rework
Career development	✓ Procurement knowledge and lateral skills increased by working with counterparts across organizations, job rotation	
Personnel and salary costs		✓ Extra time spent due to data confusion, lack of meeting minutes, lack of follow-through
Administrative and other support costs		✓✓✓ Requirement for substantial information technology support to develop knowledge management system (global procurement system)

Note: ✓ = Small Impact;
  ✓✓ = Medium Impact;
  ✓✓✓ = Large Impact.

A second benefit was the relationships forged between individuals on different continents who likely would work together on future projects.

Putting It All Together

ROI can be used to evaluate team performance in both a relative and absolute sense and to inform strategy and resource allocation decisions.

In an absolute sense, the vehicle design and merger integration teams provided significant ROI to their organizations. In contrast, it is too difficult to say for sure what the bottom-line impact of the scenario planning team was because of the diffuse nature of the impacts generated by their deliverables.

In a relative sense, it appears that the scenario planning and vehicle design teams provided higher ROI than the merger integration team. By this, we mean that the former teams' accomplishments probably came much closer to the maximum that could be achieved under ideal circumstances. The latter, in contrast, exhibited clear inefficiencies that inhibited optimal performance. Note that we reached this conclusion from the team members' qualitative assessment of their performance as a virtual team (detailed in the tables), not a numerical calculation of ROI. Trying to forecast what a team's ROI would be under ideal circumstances is difficult and time-consuming, making it impractical to do so in most cases.

The precision with which the ROI estimates need to be calculated for the vehicle design and merger integration teams is much less than for the scenario planning team. The contribution of the former teams' output to the company's bottom line is extremely high. Just as important, both teams' goals satisfied key strategic imperatives at the heart of their companies' ability to remain competitive. Had they failed, there would have been immediate negative consequences for the bottom line; having a rough estimate of the virtual teaming costs needed to achieve the substantial expected benefit was sufficient ROI calculation. The scenario planning team also was focused on a key strategic issue, but one with few immediate negative downside impacts on the bottom line. Hence, it was subject to much more budgetary scrutiny, creating the need for more precise ROI estimates.

IMPLICATIONS FOR PRACTICE

This chapter has highlighted a number of issues that are important when considering virtual team ROI. First, it is critical to recognize the distinction between forward-looking and retrospective ROI. Retrospective ROI is easier to calculate, yet it suffers a generalization problem: after the fact, it can be quite difficult to assess the extent to which a team was successful because of its own efforts versus random luck (that is, events and forces external to the team's control that evolved in a favorable way). This is why forward-looking ROI is more useful as a decision-making and resource allocation tool.

Second, asking what the ROI of a virtual team is requires an assessment of why the virtual team exists. In some cases, there are members who represent different geographically dispersed parts of the organization, parts that have to be represented among the core team members because of the information they possess and stakeholders involved. In other cases, there are people with particular expertise who would not work for the organization if they were forced to move to where the bulk of the other members live (consultants, independent contractors, telecommuters).

One way to recast the virtual team ROI question is to think about the hypothetical example of leaving out a team member with key business unit, divisional or functional knowledge, or links to stakeholders. What does excluding that person do to the ability to accomplish the team's goals, the ability to get the team's recommendations adopted, assuming the goals are accomplished, and the costs needed to achieve both of these? If the answer is that the work could never be accomplished, then asking the question of virtual versus FTF work ROI is not the right question. Instead, one would have to revert to stand-alone ROI and relate the issue back to the team's mission and the company's strategy.

We have the following recommendations for practitioners:

- Use forward-looking ROI for resource planning and strategic decision making.

- Use backward-looking ROI for performance management.

- Consider a range of different scenarios when forecasting ROI.

- Virtual team ROI can be calculated relative to doing nothing at all (ROI in a vacuum) or relative to doing more of the work FTF.

- Include all relevant costs and benefits, but only those large enough to account for a significant fraction of the total.

- Include both objective and subjective business outcomes whenever feasible.

- Do not ignore design, input, and process aspects of virtual team ROI, though they may be too hard to quantify in some cases.

References

Cohen, S. G., and Bailey, D. "What Makes Teams Work: Group Effectiveness Research from the Shop Floor to the Executive Suite." *Journal of Management*, 1997, *23*(3), 239–290.

Duarte, D., and Snyder, N. *Mastering Virtual Teams: Strategies, Tools, and Techniques That Succeed.* San Francisco: Jossey-Bass, 1999.

Levenson, A. "ROI and Strategy for Teams and Collaborative Work Systems." In M. Beyerlein and others (eds.), *The Collaborative Work Systems Fieldbook.* San Francisco: Jossey-Bass, forthcoming.

SUMMARY

The authors of the chapters in Part Two have highlighted a number of important factors related to the people and context involved in virtual teaming that link back to the design model set out in Chapter One. One is that selection, training, and performance management help to develop enabling conditions for virtual teams. For example, Blackburn, Furst, and Rosen highlight the importance of cultural awareness and sensitivity on the part of virtual team members. These skills are needed to create shared understanding across cultures, a key enabling condition we discussed in Part One. In a similar vein, they discuss the importance of individual member ability (and willingness) to trust. As examined by Gibson and Manuel in Chapter Four, this skill is complicated by the cultural differences and goes hand in hand with cultural awareness to create trust, the second enabling condition for virtual team effectiveness.

At the team level, skills related to norming are critical for establishing the optimal level of integration, our third key enabling condition for virtual team effectiveness. Equally important, Blackburn, Furst, and Rosen discuss the necessity of a learning orientation in virtual teams. This is a theme echoed at a more macrolevel in Chapter Three, in that knowledge management techniques serve both to integrate and improve innovation in global virtual teams. Finally, Blackburn, Furst, and Rosen also emphasize the importance of virtual team leader knowledge, skills, and abilities (KSAs). Many of these are described subsequently in the Chapter Eight. Worth noting here are the skills required for rewarding and motivating virtually, which Lawler also addresses in his chapter.

Beyond KSAs, Blackburn, Furst, and Rosen's ideas around selection and training also link back to our design model. We encourage the use of several of the assessment methods they recommend. These tools help assess skills such as cultural sensitivity and laterality that promote the enabling conditions of shared understanding, integration, and trust. In the area of training, their suggestions pertaining to technology, focusing on the importance of matching the technology to the task, are a key argument put forth by the authors in Part Four of this book.

A second key take-away from this part is that selection and training must be developed hand in hand with assessment and rewards systems that focus on particular skills and capabilities most pertinent in virtual teams. Both Lawler and Blackburn, Furst, and Rosen recommend explicit determination of individual contributions to virtual teams; the importance of multiple sources of leader, member, and customer evaluations of virtual teaming; and the alignment of the virtual teaming effort with the effectiveness of the firm. These techniques go a long way to helping to overcome the degree of difficulty that results from virtuality and degree of differences and help to achieve shared understanding and integration. Extending the points made by Blackburn, Furst, and Rosen regarding virtual competencies and performance, Lawler argues that such skills need to be reinforced with skill-based pay in teams. Rewarding cross-functional capabilities is most critical for increasing integration in virtual teams that may lack relationships among members and whose work is invisible to each other. The importance of cross-functional capabilities was also evident in Chapter Four as a key mechanism that establishes trust, particularly in the cross-cultural collaboration that often occurs in virtual teams. Although pay for performance is a potentially powerful tool for motivating virtual teams, Lawler argues that unless the KSAs required for virtual team effectiveness have been specified, performance-based rewards are extremely difficult to implement. Thus, a third key take-away from this part, repeated throughout the book, is that the level of integration and differentiation of the team with respect to the rest of the organization, and within the team itself, should be a critical factor in selecting how best to support virtual team efforts. Critical questions to ask are, "How much does this team need to interact with other teams within or outside this organization? Do team members need frequent (perhaps daily) contact to accomplish their work or can they operate fairly independently?" Answers to these questions help determine the specifications for the support systems.

In Chapter Seven, Levenson and Cohen reiterated this theme, emphasizing the importance of linking the people and context factors in designing virtual teams back to the strategy of firm. A key learning from their chapter is the danger of looking at possible benefits of virtual teams in a vacuum. They demonstrate that such calculations are insufficient for making key decisions that may have a significant impact on a firm's bottom line. Thus, a final take-away from Part Two is that firms must acknowledge that it is almost always more difficult to operate virtually, and they must carefully design the supportive context that virtual teams need to succeed. Equally important is the internal design of the team, the topic of Part Three.

PART THREE

CONSTRUCTING THE DESIGN

*Leadership, Knowledge Management,
and Information Sharing*

INTRODUCTION

All those assumptions about knowledge and the environment you are
operating in have huge design implications. What it means for teams is that it
determines what kind of teams you need. It determines the kind of
connections between teams and what kinds of problems you are going to
run into in getting teams to be effective.
—Conference attendee describing team design

How teams are designed can determine whether they succeed. The elements of team design important in face-to-face settings may be even more important for virtual collaboration given the complexity that must be managed. New designs also may be required as a result of the virtual team's reliance on technology-mediated communication. The chapters in Part Three address three facets of virtual team design: team leadership, social structure, and information sharing. Although these design elements are important for face-to-face teams as well, there are unique requirements of the virtual setting, and the chapter authors challenge us to think about how best to structure virtual teams. In contrast to Part Two, the focus here is on the team itself rather than the organizational systems that support teams.

Chapter Eight by Tyran, Tyran, and Shepherd examines emergent leadership in virtual teams, based on research with geographically dispersed executive M.B.A. teams. In the majority of the teams studied, leaders did emerge over the course of the semester. Those viewed as leaders took initiative, assigned tasks, coordinated efforts, and set performance standards. They carried out these leadership functions relying on e-mail to communicate. At our conference, a global project team leader described how carefully she thought about what and how she communicated electronically across cultures: "I'm reflecting on the e-mails, and I realize that over time, the exchanges that I initiated did become more than just information. It forced me as the leader to think about, given all the information that I exchange, why I chose the information and how I make my assumptions explicit to those in other cultures." She had recognized the importance of her electronic written communications to the success of her team.

Tyran, Tyran, and Shepherd suggest that the relationship between emergent leadership and performance may be contingent on the amount of trust on the team; if trust were average or low, emergent leadership led to high performance, but if trust were high, emergent leadership did not seem to matter for performance. Perhaps if trust is high, leadership functions are more likely to be shared by several members, with less reliance on any individual team member. One caveat must be made: the teams studied were not embedded in an organization. Emergent leadership may function quite differently when a team is part of an organization and someone ultimately has hierarchical authority.

Maznevski and Athanassiou in Chapter Nine examine the social structure of virtual teams using social capital and social network theory. Social capital is the value of the intangible resources found in relationships among people. Social network theory describes the pattern of relationships among people. The authors convincingly assert that the effectiveness of virtual team members as knowledge managers depends on the structure of the relationships established within and outside the team. They present a contingency model that recommends different configurations of social capital depending on task imperatives and outputs. For example, if a virtual team is charged with integrating systems postmerger (an integrating task), they recommend that team member networks should be tight, with most members linked to other members. In contrast, if a team is charged with changing an organization structure from functional to divisional (a differentiating task), they recommend that team member networks should be loose, with few linkages among members but strong links between team members and constituents in the organization.

The authors assert that it is easier to build strong ties in face-to-face relationships and recommend face-to-face meetings when strong ties are required. At our conference, this notion was challenged. Some argued that social capital could indeed be built through technology, as the following participant did:

> I would argue that there are some ways that technology can facilitate social capital and learning about each other, and that is through, for example, personal Web sites. As a personal example, I learned a lot about my husband before I ever started dating him because he has this fabulous Web site. I knew where he was from, his favorite songs, so I think you can learn a lot of things about people that you wouldn't necessarily learn in interaction, particularly if somebody is more of an introvert. If you're working with engineering teams, maybe there are people who are not socially adept, so you can learn more about them in that way.

Clearly, making connections through technology can help to build strong ties, but coinciding with the views of other scholars in this book, we would argue it does not replace face-to-face interaction.

Chapter Ten by Cramton and Orvis discusses information sharing in virtual teams. They identify several barriers to the sharing of task, social, and contextual information, such as the magnitude of the information-sharing task, the dispersion of team members, and the inability to anticipate what is important to share. They point out that contextual information is often not shared because people take their situations for granted and wrongly assume that remote partners have a similar situation. They highlight what leaders can do to encourage effective information sharing, such as establishing procedures for sharing the different types of information and creating communication norms.

The lack of sharing anything other than task information was discussed at our conference by a practitioner in a high-technology firm:

> I was thinking about how information is shared in our organization in virtual teams, and the only thing that really seems to get shared through technology and virtual teams is task information. Social information and contextual information are really never shared. I started to think about what kind of technology is out there to facilitate that type of information sharing, and I thought that the technology really doesn't support that very well. It does create this need not only for face-to-face but also carefully constructed face-to-face meetings.

It is ironic that designing virtual teams involves planning for face-to-face interaction to build social capital and ensure effective information exchange. The chapters in this part suggest that virtuality cannot fully substitute for face-to-face encounters.

CHAPTER EIGHT

Exploring Emerging Leadership in Virtual Teams

Kristi Lewis Tyran, Craig K. Tyran, Morgan Shepherd

In traditional teams involving face-to-face interaction, leadership has a strong influence on team performance and individual team members' satisfaction (Bass, 1990; Hackman, 1990b). Leaders can influence team behavior and performance in several ways. For instance, leaders often facilitate effective task distribution within a team. By assigning tasks to individuals with the skills, knowledge, and abilities to perform them best, a leader can greatly increase team effectiveness and efficiency (McGrath, 1984). In addition to task focused behaviors, leaders inspire others through communication of a vision for the team's work (Conger and Kanungo, 1988). Having clear goals and objectives is critical to effective team functioning, and leaders can facilitate team members' understanding of objectives (Hackman, 1990b). By providing motivation, guidance, and mediation, a leader can strengthen the interpersonal relationships within a team and thereby promote synergy and cohesiveness.

Given the importance of leadership to traditional teams, we would expect that leadership is also a critical factor for virtual teams. However, it is not yet clear how the conditions of the virtual team environment may influence leadership practice. Our exploration of the role of leadership in virtual teams is based on findings from an exploratory field study of thirteen teams.[1] The study was designed to help us explore four important questions:

- Do leaders emerge in virtual teams, and if so, when and why?
- What types of leadership behaviors do leaders of distributed teams exhibit? Specifically, are perceived trustworthiness and leadership style

183

relevant and important to team members when assessing team leadership?

- How are communication patterns related to the leadership of virtual teams?
- Can an emergent leader increase a virtual team's performance?

EMERGENCE OF LEADERS IN VIRTUAL TEAMS

One common challenge for virtual teams is that there are times when there is no designated leader or authority figure for the team. This situation may arise under a variety of circumstances; for example, a virtual team may comprise peers or members from different organizations. In such cases, the virtual team members are expected to organize and accomplish their tasks with minimal supervision. Such self-managed teams, whether they are traditional or virtual, have become increasingly popular in organizations (Manz and Sims, 1993). The members of self-managed teams are given extensive autonomy and responsibility for controlling, organizing, and managing their job tasks (Hackman, 1990b). When self-managed teams are used in organizations, they are often assumed to be self-leading, because leadership is assumed to be less important when all team members are equally responsible for performance outcomes.

Self-managed teams that meet in the traditional face-to-face environment sometimes struggle in their initial development stages, and recently there has been a focus on using leadership to increase the performance levels of these teams to help overcome some of the initial challenges associated with team interaction (Stewart and Manz, 1995). In such cases, the team leadership role may or may not be assigned to only one individual. Leadership may rotate among team members according to the task and relationship needs of the team (Katzenbach and Smith, 1993). Role rotation may work effectively when trust and group cohesion are high. Team members feel comfortable taking on the leader role when their skills and abilities are best used and yet feel equally comfortable relinquishing the leader role when another team member would better facilitate and coordinate the team's activities.

Leader rotation does not always operate effectively. In these situations, a single leader may emerge in response to inefficiencies in team coordination and cooperation (Hollander and Julian, 1969). An individual may emerge as a leader due to individual characteristics. Research on emergent leaders in traditional teams has found that these leaders share several common qualities and characteristics, including effective listening skills (Johnson and Bechler, 1998), high self-monitoring skills (Kolb, 1998), dominance, intelligence, confidence in their abilities (Smith and Foti, 1998), and whether the leader role is dominated by men or women (Kent and Moss, 1994). Leader emergence may also occur in response to characteristics of the team, such as a need for guidance and facilitation. A leader is said to emerge in a team when the team as a whole reaches a consensus that they perceive the emergent leader to be their leader (Bass, 1990).

In order to assess whether a leader emerged in any of the thirteen teams that participated in our study, we asked the individual participants to rank their team members with regard to leadership. We found agreement among team members that leaders emerged in nine of the thirteen virtual teams participating in our study. The fact that leaders emerged in the majority of teams suggests that it is not uncommon for leaders to emerge in virtual teams. Those viewed as leaders were perceived to be effective in taking the initiative, assigning tasks, coordinating team member efforts, and setting performance standards. Consider the following comments about the people who were considered to be the leaders of two of the teams in our study:

> She always plans ahead of time and gives the team directions and guidance to follow. She always reads the materials first and sends out her input so her team will know what to consider while writing up assignments. Even when she was not the assigned leader, she did not just wait for e-mails from teammates. She always contributes and her materials are always good and well thought out [Howard, speaking about Julie, team 4].

> She was proactive in taking the lead on assignments that needed a guide and was organized and disciplined about meeting deadlines and refining drafts [Larry, speaking about Nancy, team 12].

Research of traditional teams indicates that there are common characteristics and behaviors associated with effective leaders. However, not much is yet known about the leaders in virtual team environments. In an effort to learn more about the specific behaviors associated with the emergent virtual team leaders in our study, we asked the participants to provide their perceptions regarding the leaders of their teams.

BEHAVIORS OF VIRTUAL TEAM LEADERS

Team leadership involves many functions, most of which fall into the categories of addressing task needs and maintenance needs (Bass, 1990; Hackman and Walton, 1986). With respect to these functions, important qualities for a team leader to have are the abilities to monitor and mediate the team's interaction and to determine when and how to intercede (Barge, 1996). Effective team leaders also network with individuals inside and outside the team.

Another important skill is data splitting, defined as filtering through the information gathered by the team and determining what is important and what is not (Barge, 1996). Once a team leader has evaluated information about the team's performance and task, actions to improve performance are determined and taken. These actions may be designed to motivate individuals or coordinate with outside forces through networking to ensure adequate information and resources to accomplish tasks.

For traditional teams, trust in a leader's ability to facilitate team task and relationship interaction effectively has been found to be a critical factor in achieving the consensus necessary for a leader to emerge (Bass, 1990). In uncertain environments, team members trust a leader to have the experience, knowledge, and ability to guide them. In examining the importance of trust in teams and team leaders, we found it useful to categorize trust into three types (McAllister, 1995; Mayer, Davis, and Schoorman, 1995):

- Role performance trust, which concerns demonstrating competency with the tasks and behaviors necessary to accomplish team goals.

- Altruistic behavior, or demonstrating to team members that a leader will act for the good of the team even when it involves sacrificing self-interest (Kanungo and Mendonca, 1996). When an individual demonstrates this type of trust, often referred to as ethical integrity trust, it inspires others to trust that this person will do the right thing in most situations.

- Affective bond trust, which relates to a person's ability to form friendship bonds with individuals through the development of long-term relationships (McAllister, 1995).

We examined the perceptions regarding these three types of trust and found that the emergent leaders in our study were more likely to be rated higher with regard to these aspects of trust. In particular, leadership ranking was most strongly correlated with role performance trust. Leadership ranking was also significantly correlated with ethical integrity trust and affective bond trust. With regard to role performance trust, it appears that the leaders in our study gained the trust of their teammates through reliability, consistency, quality of work, initiative, and experience, as illustrated in the following comments:

> Reliable, consistent, clarifier of ideas, significant contributions, confident [Tony, speaking about George, team 7].

> This is the twelfth distance-learning course Bill has done, and he was able to provide valuable insight at the beginning of the course about how these teams work best—about communication, allocating workload between team members, and so forth [Josh, speaking about Bill, team 9].

> I used five criteria to identify the leader in our group: (1) quality of work delivered on time, (2) good communication skills, (3) ability to keep group focused on task, (4) ability to garner group support for project, and (5) ability to productively handle stress. Bill was the clear winner [Patty, speaking about Bill, team 9].

> Tom was first to take action and volunteer a plan for accomplishing assignments. He usually provided the most feedback and remained consistently on time with his contributions [Susan, speaking about Tom, team 5].

In addition to trust issues, leadership style has been found to play a role in team success. One well-known model of leadership is transformational leadership, which involves developing a strategic vision and then communicating that vision so that followers are motivated to work toward achieving the goals associated with it (Conger and Kanungo, 1998). Transformational leaders know their teammates and inspire and motivate to transform the members of the team to see the team's vision and the organization's vision as their own (Bass and Avolio, 1994). Transformational leadership style is highly related to perceived trustworthiness of a leader; team members see a leader as transformational when they trust that leader to act in their best interests (Bass, 1998). Research on transformational leadership in traditional teams has identified several techniques that transformational leaders use to motivate and inspire, including serving as a role model for ethical and moral conduct, communicating high expectations, stimulating followers to be creative and innovative, and providing a supportive climate through listening (Bass and Avolio, 1994).

In our study, we found evidence to suggest that a high leader ranking was also associated with traits of inspirational and transformational leadership, including behaviors of influencing through the use of values and ideals, inspirational motivation, intellectual stimulation, and individual consideration. Although almost all communication was conducted by e-mail, it seems that some of the emergent leaders were able to inspire and motivate using computer-mediated communication. Examples of team members commenting on these qualities include the following:

> Jane often took the lead on assignments. She would be the first to suggest ideas. It was a very motivating experience. We all had to keep up with her pace [John, speaking about Jane, team 11].

> He always had his work completed. He also made comments and suggestions for every module, which allowed everyone to benefit from his ideas. He is very opinionated but supportive. He proved to be a great leader [Ken, speaking about Greg, team 1].

> She was willing to do more to promote harmony and tried to be positive and encouraging [Howard, speaking about Julie, team 4].

She tried to be a consensus builder during the rare times the team was at odds on an issue in a case [George, speaking about Cindy, team 7].

COMMUNICATION AND LEADERSHIP IN VIRTUAL TEAMS

To date, little research has been conducted on the topic of emergent leadership and communication in virtual teams. However, by drawing on related research, it is possible to identify how communication may play a role in leadership and virtual team effectiveness. As with traditional teams, research on virtual teams has demonstrated the importance of effective communication and coordination within virtual teams (Lipnack and Stamps, 1997). One way to facilitate communication and coordination in a virtual team may be through the emergence of a leader. However, leadership may be somewhat more difficult to develop and enact in virtual teams, which may have a limited amount of face-to-face communication. Much of the electronic communication in virtual teams is text based (for example, e-mail). Although electronic communication helps to make virtual teams possible by enabling team members to communicate across distance and time, text-based electronic communication can present a challenge. For example, a recent survey of the research found that computer-mediated groups generally have lower communication efficiency than face-to-face groups because it often takes longer for computer-mediated groups to complete tasks. In addition, it can be more difficult to establish the meaning of information and establish feedback (DeSanctis and Monge, 1999).

Another aspect of electronic communication to consider is that the lack of visual and social cues, like body language and tone of voice, for text-based electronic communication may make it more difficult for team members to formulate impressions of their teammates (Walther, 1993). Because nonverbal communication can be an important source of information when assessing the trustworthiness of a new teammate, the use of text-based electronic communication may impede the development of trust in virtual teams. As several authors have noted, the importance of trust to virtual team effectiveness (Duarte and Snyder, 1999; Handy, 1995; Jarvenpaa, Knoll, and Leidner, 1998) and the ability of a team to develop trust in one another and a team leader in an environment of electronic communication may have important consequences for the performance of virtual teams.

The challenges of communication technology may or may not make it more difficult for a leader to emerge in virtual teams. The electronic communication channels that are associated with virtual team communication may offer an obstacle to some leaders since some commonly used electronic channels, such as e-mail, do not offer the visual and audio cues that exist in face-to-face communication. However, others may prefer the use of electronic communication channels. For example, some forms of electronic media, such as text-based conferencing and discussion groups, have been found to facilitate a more equal and fuller representation of team member inputs (Tyran, Dennis, Vogel, and Nunamaker, 1992). Unlike face-to-face conditions, where a vocal and assertive member can dominate the group, virtual teams that rely on electronic communication may be more likely to have emergent leaders who are skilled at facilitating and motivating through the written word rather than those who command the leadership role through a dominating vocal or physical presence. Thus, the characteristics of electronic media used in a virtual team setting may influence the type of leader who emerges. For instance, a virtual team that relies mostly on text-based interaction like e-mail or discussion groups may lead to the emergence of a leader who is able to lead through effective written communication skills.

In our study, we explored team communication through the use of communication logs and self-reported impressions of team member communication. Team members were free to communicate in whatever way that they wished: e-mail, electronic conferencing, telephone, face-to-face, or some other means. Despite the many options, the communication logs showed that e-mail was the preferred approach: virtually all of the communication by team members was conducted by e-mail. Only two interactions across all of the teams involved telephone contact. At no time did any team members meet face-to-face. Leaders who emerged communicated more on average, sending 13 percent more messages than their teammates. However, leaders were not always the ones who sent the most messages; over the period of the study, the emergent leader sent the most messages in six of the teams, but in two of the teams, the leaders sent the fewest messages.

With respect to communication issues, it appears that the quantity of messages sent was not the primary factor for emergent leadership in our study. When asked to comment on the person they viewed as the team leader, in no case did participants indicate that the leader was the person who sent the most e-mail messages. Instead, as indicated in the following comments, when communication issues were mentioned, the team leader was cited as being an effective communicator and able to lead the group through the use of text-based e-mail messages:

> His instructions were clear and concise, which allowed us to do our individual parts with less confusion [Josh, speaking about Bill, team 9].

> He helped us stay on track and did a good job if we started to get away from the point of the assignment [Sara, speaking about Brian, team 7].

> He was the glue that helped pull the team together for each assignment [Linda, speaking about Greg, team 5].

> He often contributed good thoughts and ideas, which facilitated the smooth interaction of the group [Theresa, speaking about Gary, team 8].

EMERGENT LEADERSHIP AND PERFORMANCE
IN VIRTUAL TEAMS

Traditional face-to-face team leaders can influence a team in a variety of ways. Team leaders assign tasks, clarify goals, motivate enthusiasm, set performance standards, and coordinate and facilitate achievement of objectives (Hackman, 1990a; Bass, 1990). The relationship between team leadership and team performance is not clear, however. The presence of a team leader is not always associated with higher performance; teams that have ineffective leaders may do worse than teams with no leader at all. Indeed, studies of traditional teams have found that some self-managed leaderless teams perform well.

In our study, we explored the relationship between leader emergence and performance. Team performance was assessed based on the quality of the nine assignments that each team turned in. When we first examined our data, there appeared to be no clear relationship regarding emergent leadership and performance. Although the highest-performing team had a strong leader and the lowest-performing team had no emergent leader, we found that the presence of an emergent leader was not necessarily related to team performance. Table 8.1 summarizes the team performance rankings: three of the six top-performing teams had no emergent leader, while six of the bottom seven teams did have an emergent leader. This suggests that the relationship between emergent leadership and performance is complex, perhaps involving other factors.

Trust among virtual team members has been shown to be significantly related to team performance: teams that have more trust in one another tend to perform better (Jarvenpaa and Leidner, 1999). This may be an important variable to take into consideration when evaluating the role of leadership on virtual team performance. In an effort to understand the contingencies that may be at play, we explored the relationship among trust, emergent leadership, and performance to see if any additional explanations could be found.

When we reexamined the findings after taking trust among team members into account, we found that the higher-performing teams either had an emergent leader who was highly trusted or the trust among team members was high. For example, the highest-performing team and the fourth-highest-performing team leaders were trusted highly with regard to role performance trust. Overall, both teams had a level of trust among the team members that was near the average for the teams in our study. We speculate that one reason these teams performed well was that they had a leader who was trusted to help the team get the job done. However, depending on the level of trust among teammates, a leader may not always be necessary. The third-highest-performing team did not have an emergent leader, but it did have the highest average level of role performance trust of all teams in our study. Its members may not have needed to

Table 8.1. Team Performance and Emergent Leadership

Team Number	Overall Performance (%)	Leader Emerged	Average Role Performance Trust
1	90.5	Yes	3.20
2	89.8	No	3.18
3	86.0	No	3.61
4	85.5	Yes	3.10
5	83.5	Yes	3.26
6	83.5	No	3.04
7	83.0	Yes	2.99
8	83.0	Yes	3.27
9	83.0	Yes	3.49
10	82.0	Yes	3.44
11	80.5	Yes	3.00
12	78.5	Yes	3.44
13	76.2	No	2.73

rely on a leader to be effective as a team because they may have trusted each other to perform well. The lowest-performing team had no emergent leader and the lowest average level of team role performance trust. It is possible that this team performed poorly because the members did not trust one another to perform well and there was no emergent leader to help them work together well. These results, although limited in their scope, provide some indication of how trust in the team and trust in a leader may interact with leader emergence to lead to higher performance. When trust in the team is high, leader emergence may or may not be a factor in performance levels. However, when trust in the team is low to average, an emergent leader seen as more trustworthy may have a more significant impact on team performance.

IMPLICATIONS FOR PRACTICE

We found that leaders do emerge in some virtual teams. Clearly, some teams saw one member as taking on the leader role. Leaders who emerged were generally perceived to be more trustworthy with regard to their ability to perform tasks, their integrity, and their ability to form friendly relationships. In particular, the ability to perform tasks effectively (role performance trust) was an especially common trait of emergent leaders in our study. In addition, the leaders appeared to have a transformational leadership style, as a number of the emergent leaders were described as having the ability to motivate and inspire others on the team. Although the emergent leaders communicated more on average than other team members did, the leaders were not simply those who communicated the most with the team. The quality of communication appeared to be important as well. In our study, almost all of the team communication was conducted by e-mail, and leaders were noted to be those who were effective at leading through this text-based communication channel. Finally, we found that virtual team performance was not clearly related to emergent leadership within the team. This relationship appears to be more complex, involving several characteristics of the team and emergent leader.

Our implications for practice to assist practitioners in designing and developing effective virtual teams using team leadership are as follows:

- Trust appears to be an important factor for leadership in virtual teams. When developing effective virtual teams and effective virtual team leaders:
  —Role performance trust was viewed as particularly important for the leaders in our study. Managers may be wise to select a leader who is strong in this area. Ethical integrity and affective bond trust are also important types of trust to look for in virtual team leaders.
  —We encourage managers to make efforts to facilitate effective leader emergence and trust development prior to beginning a project. One way to build trust may be to provide virtual team members a chance to get to know more about one another outside the virtual environment. If possible, it may be worthwhile to have virtual teams meet through initial face-to-face meetings that will help team members learn more about their teammates, assess their potential leadership qualities, and develop trust in others.
  —If face-to-face meetings are not feasible, then disseminating information about team members (for example, biographies, resumes, pictures, Web pages) may facilitate trust and social knowledge. This type of approach was used for the teams in our study and appeared to provide an effective way for team members to learn more about their teammates.
- Emphasize computer-mediated communication skills in virtual team leaders through training or selection. Communicating using technology means more than transfer of knowledge and information. The ability to inspire, motivate, mediate conflict, and develop interpersonal trust through a variety of communication media is critical in virtual team

leadership. If a virtual team will be communicating primarily through e-mail, then written communication skills, including the ability to write clearly and concisely and to motivate others through the written word, are especially critical.

- Virtual team leadership may be more critical during times of low to average trust among team members. If trust is low during any period of a virtual team's development, consider appointing a team leader who has the qualities discussed above. If trust among team members develops to high levels over time, then team leadership may become less important.

Note

1. The participants in the study were fifty-one students in a distance-learning executive M.B.A. program operated by a large public university in the United States, located throughout the United States and international locations. Almost all participants had over ten years of organizational work experience, and most were midlevel managers with several years of managerial leadership experience. No two participants in the study lived in the same city. The participants were randomly assigned to twelve distributed groups consisting of four members each, plus one group of three members. Due to the geographical dispersion of the team members in each team, none of the team members ever met one another face-to-face. The study was longitudinal in nature, with the teams studied over a period of fifteen weeks. So that each team member would have an opportunity to apply and demonstrate his or her traits as a team leader, each member of a team was assigned to serve as the "team coordinator" for two of the nine team assignments. The data collection included a series of nine self-reported communication behavior logs and a poststudy survey questionnaire. The communication logs tracked both the frequency and type of communication among participants. The poststudy survey questionnaire asked the study participants to rank their team members with regard to leadership provided to the team and to assess the leadership effectiveness of each team member. Also, the participants were asked to respond to a comprehensive set of survey questions regarding the trustworthiness and leadership style for each teammate.

    In the quotations throughout this chapter, team members are identified using pseudonyms to protect confidentiality.

References

Barge, J. K. "Leadership Skills and the Dialectics of Leadership in Group Decision Making." In R. Y. Hirokawa and M. S. Poole (eds.), *Communication and Group Decision Making.* (2nd ed.) Thousand Oaks, Calif.: Sage, 1996.

Bass, B. M. *Bass and Stogdill's Handbook of Leadership.* New York: Free Press, 1990.

Bass, B. M. *Transformational Leadership.* Mahwah, N.J.: Erlbaum, 1998.

Bass, B. M., and Avolio, B. *Improving Organizational Effectiveness Through Transformational Leadership.* Thousand Oaks, Calif.: Sage, 1994.

Conger, J., and Kanungo, R. *Charismatic Leadership in Organizations.* Thousand Oaks, Calif.: Sage, 1988.

DeSanctis, G., and Monge, P. "Introduction to Special Issue: Communication Processes for Virtual Organizations." *Organization Science,* 1999, *10*(6), 693–703.

Duarte, D. L., and Snyder, N. T. *Mastering Virtual Teams: Strategies, Tools and Techniques That Succeed.* San Francisco: Jossey-Bass, 1999.

Hackman, J. R. "Group Influences on Individuals in Organizations." In M. D. Dunnete (ed.), *Handbook of Industrial and Organizational Psychology.* Palo Alto, Calif.: Consulting Psychologists Press, 1990a.

Hackman, J. R. *Groups That Work (and Those That Don't).* San Francisco: Jossey-Bass, 1990b.

Hackman, J. R., and Walton, R. E. "Leading Groups in Organizations." In P. S. Goodman and others (eds.), *Designing Effective Work Groups.* San Francisco: Jossey-Bass, 1986.

Handy, C. "Trust and the Virtual Organization." *Harvard Business Review,* 1995, *73*(3), 40–50.

Hollander, E. P., and Julian, J. W. "Contemporary Trends in the Analysis of Leadership Processes." *Psychological Bulletin,* 1969, *71*, 387–397.

Jarvenpaa, S. L., Knoll, K., and Leidner, D. E. "Is Anybody Out There? Antecedents of Trust in Global Virtual Teams." *Journal of Management Information Systems,* 1998, *14*, 29–64.

Jarvenpaa, S. L., and Leidner, D. E. "Communication and Trust in Virtual Teams." *Organization Science,* 1999, *10*(6), 791–815. [http://www.ascusc.org/jcmc/vol3/issue4/jarvenpaa.html].

Johnson, S. D., and Bechler, C. "Examining the Relationship Between Listening Effectiveness and Leadership Emergence: Perceptions, Behaviors and Recall." *Small Group Research,* 1998, *29*(4), 452–471.

Kanungo, R. N., and Mendonca, M. *Ethical Dimensions of Leadership.* Thousand Oaks, Calif.: Sage, 1996.

Katzenbach, J. R., and Smith, D. K. "The Discipline of Teams." *Harvard Business Review,* Mar.–Apr. 1993, pp. 111–120.

Kent, R. L., and Moss, S. E. "Effects of Sex and Gender Role on Leader Emergence." *Academy of Management Journal,* 1994, *37*, 1335–1346.

Kolb, J. A. "The Relationship Between Self-Monitoring and Leadership in Student Project Groups." *Journal of Business Communication,* 1998, *35*(2), 264–282.

Lipnack, J., and Stamps, J. *Virtual Teams: Reaching Across Space, Time and Organizations with Technology.* New York: Wiley, 1997.

Manz, C. C., and Sims, H. P., Jr. *Business Without Bosses: How Self-Managing Teams Are Building High Performance Companies.* New York: Wiley, 1993.

Mayer, R. C., Davis, J. H., and Schoorman, F. D. "An Integrative Model of Organizational Trust." *Academy of Management Review,* 1995, *20,* 709–734.

McAllister, D. "Affect- and Cognition-Based Trust as Foundations for Interpersonal Cooperation in Organizations." *Academy of Management Journal,* 1995, *38,* 24–59.

McGrath, J. E. *Groups: Interaction and Performance.* Upper Saddle River, N.J.: Prentice Hall, 1984.

Smith, J. A., and Foti, R. J. "A Pattern Approach to the Study of Leader Emergence." *Leadership Quarterly,* 1998, *9*(2), 147–160.

Stewart, G. L., and Manz, C. C. "Leadership for Self-Managing Work Teams: A Typology and Integrative Model." *Human Relations,* 1995, *48*(7), 747–770.

Tyran, C. K., Dennis, A. R., Vogel, D. R., and Nunamaker, J. F. "The Application of Electronic Meeting Technology to Support Strategic Management." *MIS Quarterly,* 1992, *16*(3), 313–334.

Walther, J. B. "Impression Development in Computer-Mediated Interaction." *Western Journal of Communication,* 1993, *57,* 381–398.

CHAPTER NINE

Designing the Knowledge-Management Infrastructure for Virtual Teams

Building and Using Social Networks and Social Capital

Martha L. Maznevski, Nicholas A. Athanassiou

In today's business environment, where the descriptors "complex and dynamic" are increasingly gross understatements, virtual teams must be exceptional knowledge managers. Whatever their mandate, they need to scan the environment and gather the facts they need. They must combine facts and ideas to create new knowledge that will drive the organization in the right direction. And they need to transfer that new knowledge to others, in the organization or outside it, to execute the ideas. Research and development teams scan, gather, combine, and transfer knowledge when they develop a new process or product to meet a specific market need, and then they begin the journey of bringing it to market. Merger implementation teams manage these knowledge processes when they design systems and practices for the merged organizations. Global account teams of consulting firms do it when they develop and implement a strategy for serving a key client, and top management teams do it when they develop and implement a strategy for an organization as a whole.

The importance of knowledge management is well recognized (Davenport and Prusak, 1998; Prusak, 1997), and technology experts have developed sophisticated tools to help virtual teams (Lipnack and Stamps, 2001). There are dynamic search tools for scanning the environment or specific knowledge databases, filtering the information needed, directing it to the right person, and storing it in an organized way. Project networks for joint work allow virtual team members to combine and create knowledge by accessing and working on the same documents and other files and attending synchronous or asynchronous meetings on-line. Virtual teams can transfer their output to other members of the organization through e-mail; Web sites with audio, video, and other features; or videoconferences. The technology part of the knowledge-management infrastructure has advanced rapidly in the past decade, with innovations appearing ever more quickly in recent years.

Organizations and virtual teams, however, are not technological systems; they are sociotechnological systems, that is, social systems completely intertwined with technological systems (Giddens, 1984; Maznevski and Chudoba, 2000). No matter how advanced the technological infrastructure becomes, virtual teams will not be exceptional knowledge managers unless the social systems are given at least equal attention. Managers have made important strides on the technological side of the virtual team system and should turn their attention to new ways of thinking about the social side.

Designing the social system for the knowledge-management infrastructure in virtual teams is best approached through the lenses of social capital and social networks. Social capital is the set of assets embedded in relationships among people—in other words, in the social networks of the team—that the team members can use to get things done (Lin, 2001b). Individuals, teams, and organizations can all have social capital, but here we focus on the team's social capital. By drawing on and using various types of social capital, virtual team members select which sources to scan and gather information from, combine facts and ideas to generate new knowledge, and transfer this new knowledge to others (Nahapiet and Ghoshal, 1998). Social capital provides the social side of the knowledge-management sociotechnological infrastructure.

SOCIAL CAPITAL DRIVES KNOWLEDGE MANAGEMENT

Social capital is the value of the intangible resources lying in relationships among people, and it can be drawn on by those in the relationship to help them achieve something of value to them. Social capital, like its financial and human counterparts, must be invested in and maintained so that it can be continuously useful. Unlike other forms of capital, it exists only through a specific relationship between two people or groups. No single person can claim ownership over social capital, which disappears when the relationship on which it depends is severed. Because of friendships and obligations, social capital cannot be traded easily, and it enables the achievement of ends that would be costly or impossible without it (Lin, 2001a). Pairs of people, teams, organizations, and other groups can all have social capital; in this chapter, we focus on the virtual team's social capital.

In a virtual team, members are geographically dispersed, are often in different time zones, and may even be located in different countries with their unique cultural environments. The virtual team's task, from a social capital perspective, is shown in Figure 9.1. As the figure shows, social capital helps drive the virtual team's knowledge-management processes in four key ways. First, team members' knowledge is drawn from the organization, and second, from the external environment. The process of obtaining information is greatly facilitated with assets in the form of relationships. Team members hear about what is important from people they know, they are alerted to potentially useful knowledge and information, and they interpret the meaning of the information in part based on its origin. Perhaps more important, good relationships with the right people can help team members acquire knowledge and analysis that competitors cannot obtain. The fact that virtual team members are located in physically different places provides a potential advantage to these teams over colocated ones. By virtue of these different locations, virtual team members naturally tap into multiple sources of information and knowledge with their relationships, and this broad spectrum of knowledge can be leveraged on behalf of the team and the organization.

In a high-tech sales team in Northern Europe, for example, salespeople who almost never meet share information with each other over the Internet and mobile networks concerning large customers and competitors, as well as upcoming developments in their own company. They work with different parts of a relatively small group of large customers, see different facets of the same competitors, and talk with different contacts within their own company. As a team, they develop a much more comprehensive picture of their environment than a

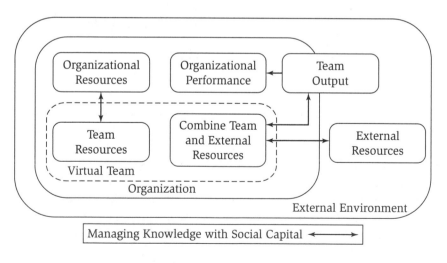

Figure 9.1 Social Capital and Virtual Team Knowledge Management.

colocated team would. Similarly, a strategic internal audit team in a global resources firm has members in each of the major plants and office buildings in the company. This team has a much better sense of the pulse of the company than they would if they were all stationed at headquarters.

The third role of social capital in virtual teams' knowledge management is within the team itself: virtual team members must combine their individual stocks of knowledge to accomplish their task. As we know from decades of research on teams, relationships among members dramatically affect how they combine knowledge (Athanassiou and Nigh, 1999; McGrath, 1984). With the right social capital, team members not only combine the knowledge in an additive way but also build and innovate synergistically. Virtual teams are at a disadvantage compared to colocated teams here. Because members are distributed in different physical locations, building and maintaining internal social capital is much more difficult for them. The virtual team managing a major customer account for a manufacturing hardware firm struggled with its task, and both the company and the customer were dissatisfied with the lack of responsiveness. The poor communication among team members and superficial relationships with the customer were certainly not resolved when the communication was limited to technological media.

The fourth role of social capital is in the output: virtual teams must execute their decisions. If the team output is an organizational change, such as a new management system for two merged companies, then it must be implemented within the organization. Team members' social capital with others in the organization, especially those with influence, facilitates the implementation process. If the team output is a service or product innovation, such as a new derivative instrument for financing acquisitions in developing countries, an approach to installing wide-scale information systems, or an innovative use of wireless technology, then the team must implement outside the organization. In this case, team members' social capital with clients, industry associations, marketing firms, and other external constituents plays a large role in the success of the execution. As with the two sources of social capital, virtual teams have a strong potential advantage over colocated teams with respect to their ability to implement decisions. Team members' distributed locations give them the potential to tap into a broader spectrum of clients, customers, and other external constituents with their social capital to achieve their goals.

In some ways, social capital is the relabeling of something we have known for years: that relationships play a key role in a team's success. The fact that relationships are more difficult to build virtually than they are face-to-face is why the field of studying virtual teams has arisen. However, the notion of social capital goes much further than the simple proclamation that relationships are important. The social capital perspectives help us to see that the role of relationships in the four key places previously outlined are all special cases of the same set of principles, with contingency factors determining how those principles apply in the different contexts. These basic principles are seen more tangibly in three tools necessary for designing the virtual team's knowledge management.

TOOLBOX FOR MANAGING KNOWLEDGE IN VIRTUAL TEAMS

Two tools, or specific ideas, are important to the ability to use social capital to enhance and facilitate knowledge management in virtual teams. Social networks are the structures that carry social capital, and two characteristics in particular are important to leveraging the social capital for knowledge management. The type of knowledge required by a team is related to the nature of the ideal social network configuration for the team, and tacit versus explicit is the most important distinction for applying social capital.

Social Networks: The Conduit of Social Capital

When someone new to an organization wants to find out the lines of authority and responsibility in its structure, the most frequent tool to use is a traditional organization chart. There, the organization is shown in the form of interlinked boxes with names and titles next to them. Typically, there is one box at the top with a few direct lines linking it to the second level of boxes. In turn, the second level of boxes is linked to others and so on until the organization unfolds beneath this one top box. This type of chart gives a picture of the organization neatly ordered in divisions, business units, departments, sections, and any other groupings in which the organization has been subdivided.

Yet when this same newcomer tries to connect these same boxes after asking the questions, "Whom do I go to to find out how our product development is conducted?" or "How do things get done to get new products developed and to market?" the picture she will draw is likely to be very different from that of the organization chart. This new picture will show the network of relationships that has evolved among the people in the boxes so that they can accomplish the goals of the particular activity such as new product development.

Small groups of the firm's managers and professionals with particular mandates that function as teams, virtual or otherwise, can also be seen in a similar manner. We can draw the relationships among members based on hierarchical considerations or as networks based on how things get done. To draw such a network we ask, "How extensively do you depend on each of the other team members in order to get your job done on the team?" Based on the answers, we draw the picture of dependencies among the team members.

Figure 9.2 shows three hypothetical teams with seven members each. Networks can be loosely or tightly knit. In other words, they can have different densities

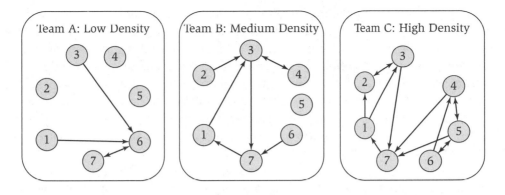

Figure 9.2 Social Network Configurations and Team Member Position Centrality.

(Wasserman and Faust, 1994). Team A is very loosely knit; it shows only three ties in terms of mutual work dependencies. In fact, its density is only .14 (three ties divided by twenty-one possible ties among team members). Team B is somewhat more compact because it shows six ties and has a density of .29. Team C is the most compact because it shows ten ties. This team's density of work dependency is .48. If everybody were to be connected to everybody else on a team, the density would be a perfect 1.

Although the density of the links among team members provides a sense of overall activity, other dimensions are important as well. For example, one can find the team members with positions of power in each team. In team A, three of its members depend on member 6 to get their job done. Thus, we know that member 6 is the person to go to if we want to get the other three influenced in a particular direction. Team B shows that member 3 is connected to the most people, followed by member 7. And in team C, member 7 has the most ties to others, followed by members 3 and 4. In social networks, being linked to many people is called centrality and is associated with power in the network (Wasserman and Faust, 1994). The more people a particular team member is linked to, the more central he or she is in the team's network.

More important perhaps, team member 7 on team C has a broker's position between two subsets of members. Team members 1, 2, and 3 are separated from team members 4, 5, and 6 by team member 7. Team member 7 is in a position to link a "structural hole" (Burt, 1992), or provide the missing link between team members 3 and 4 and, in fact, among any two members of the two subsets. Most managers know of these gatekeepers and the importance they play in organizations. This bridging role can be played by linking a team's members to knowledge that exists outside the team as well.

The strength of the ties matters too, and we distinguish between strong and weak ties. A link is stronger to the extent that it is closer in distance and it is relied on more extensively, usually characterized by deeper trust and commitment. In team C, member 7 links directly with member 1 but only indirectly with member 2 (through member 1). The relationship between members 7 and 1 is stronger than the relationship between members 7 and 2. Second, suppose member 3 depends heavily on member 7 to get her work done, and member 4 relies on member 7 only somewhat. The link between members 3 and 7 is therefore stronger than the link between members 4 and 7. Depending on circumstances, weak ties can be just as important as strong ties. For example, we know that in a job search, successful contacts are more likely to come from weaker ties than from stronger ones (Burt, 1992; Granovetter, 1973; Hall, 1992).

In all of this discussion about network analysis, we have focused on understanding the relative network positions and relational roles among pairs of team members. Clearly, this is a different approach to analysis of team dynamics from the study of individual team member characteristics, which is the more traditional approach (Borgatti, Jones, and Everett, 1998), or the study of aggregates of team-level indicators. In fact, the methods are complementary because they capture different aspects of the team's workings. The types of people staffing the teams—their predispositions, values, experiences, and personalities—matter just as much as the relationships they develop among themselves in order to achieve team objectives.

The within-team social network of a virtual professional services global account team, shown in Figure 9.3, has many characteristics that would not be seen if it were examined as a single homogeneous entity rather than a network. Although the overall density is moderate, there are distinct subsets of the team

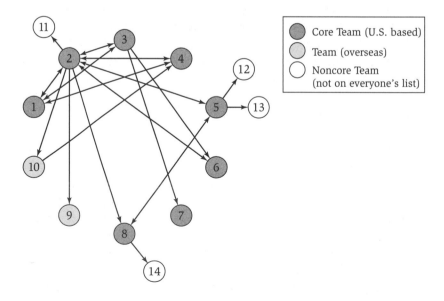

Figure 9.3 Team Advice Network That Leads to Social Capital.

with high densities and others with low densities. Knowledge flows within the subgroups are higher than knowledge flows across subgroups. In this team, the different subgroups coincide with the different subtasks of the group (different types of expertise to apply to the client's problems), and the network is appropriate. If the subgroup configuration did not coincide with subtasks, knowledge flows and management would be compromised.

In this network, member 2 is clearly the most central member: he talks with more people than does any other single member of the team. In this team, though, member 1 is the formal leader of the team, not member 2. This lack of correspondence between the formal and informal structures led to a great deal of conflict within the team. The formal leader would try to articulate team decisions based on her understanding of the team's state of knowledge, assuming her knowledge was complete. She was acting based on incomplete knowledge, though, and lost credibility with the team.

Member 8 fills a structural hole to member 14, or is the gatekeeper for member 14. In this team, member 11 provides important expertise related to a specialized consulting field. Without member 8, who happens to be the only team member located at the same office as member 14, this expertise would be lost to the team.

Finally, the pattern of strong ties is important to the understanding of the team. The strongest ties are among members 1 through 4, who are located at the same office, speak with each other frequently, and socialize together outside work. Relatively close ties exist in some other pairs as well. In only one situation is there a very close tie between a pair who are not colocated; these members (members 7 and 8) went through their initial staff analyst years together in the same office and maintain a close friendship.

The four important network ideas addressed here—density, centrality, structural holes, and strength of ties—capture some of the most important aspects of social networks, particularly with respect to knowledge management.

Tacit and Explicit Knowledge: The Cargo of Social Capital

If relationships lead to the creation of social capital that the virtual team can use to achieve its objectives, then we must recognize that the most valuable capital accessed through these relationships is knowledge.

Every aspect of knowledge accumulated over time has two complementary dimensions: the tacit and the explicit (Figure 9.4). The tacit dimension of knowledge, which cannot be articulated, is accumulated by persons over time. It defines and gives meaning to its complementary explicit dimension, a concept or skill that can be articulated, documented, and communicated (Polanyi, 1962). In other words, a person instinctively knows the tacit dimension of knowledge only by relying on his awareness of it because he can actually sense its corresponding explicit knowledge complement.

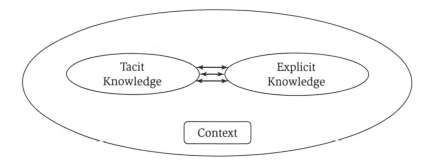

Figure 9.4 Complementary Dimensions of Tacit and Explicit Knowledge.

For example, it takes time for someone to learn how to ride a bicycle, and even then it is impossible for the rider to explain how he or she can harness the laws of physics to stay on balance. Thus, we know more than we can tell. Similarly, each of us is aware of numerous situations where concepts that we communicate with words verbally or in print are misunderstood by others. They are misunderstood because we as originators use words to explain how we understand deeper concepts while the receiver uses his or her own understanding of these words to give them meaning. Only if the originator's and receiver's understandings are totally shared is a similar meaning given to the explicit words by both the originator and receiver.

In a strict sense, tacit knowledge is inherently nontransferable; it would become explicit once it was transformed so that it could be transferred. So how can the bearer of tacit knowledge transfer it to someone else? First, the bearer must have credibility with the receiver. For the receiver, a communication that appears meaningless in the beginning in fact has a meaning that can be discovered by reaching a shared understanding of the explicit component of knowledge with the originator. Until this shared understanding can be achieved, the receiver must accept the originator's meaning because the originator can communicate only the knowledge that the receiver recognizes (the concept or skill described by words and actions) without the corresponding tacit knowledge that gives meaning to these details.

Thus, virtual team members need to establish mutual credibility and invest time to share each other's views of the team's distributed activities as represented by explicit knowledge or information in order to achieve this shared understanding. Another way to understand this is that tacit knowledge and skills may be taught through imitative learning and through trial-and-error performances critiqued by the experienced mentor rather than through knowledge fully conveyed by communication of words and actions alone. This is the second aspect of knowledge transfer that virtual teams need to understand and implement. Virtual team members must find ways to achieve credibility among each other and, for the tacit aspects of their tasks, to meet face-to-face (Nohria and Eccles, 1992). Furthermore, knowledge takes meaning from the situation, that is, the context, in which it is generated (Stewart, 2002).

Tacit knowledge gives meaning to explicit knowledge (explicit knowledge is codifiable as information in manuals, specification sheets, reports, memoranda, and data files). Tacit knowledge is not transferable; however, through face-to-face interactions, in the appropriate context, the "receiver" of the "carrier's" tacit knowledge achieves shared understanding of the explicit knowledge that is given meaning by this tacit knowledge that can't be articulated by either party. One acquires tacit knowledge from experience. One derives meaning from tacit knowledge depending on the context within which this knowledge is created or acquired. Thus, team-level tacit knowledge is created from shared contextual embeddedness, healthy and relevant relationships (social capital), and individual members who can enable exchange (intellectual capital).

Face-to-face interactions will benefit from taking place in the context within which the knowledge is created (see Figure 9.4). In the case of virtual teams that span a multinational corporation's many locations, such meetings may have to take place in both the knowledge originator's and the receiver's environments.

There is much evidence that the imitative learning needed to achieve a common understanding of tacit elements of knowledge is most effectively achieved through face-to-face interaction. Rich, multidimensional, robust relationships can be developed only through face-to-face interaction because it allows all senses into the process and is the only way to capture the entire bandwidth of human interaction. Such face-to-face interaction is necessary for problem-solving tasks (McKenney, Zack, and Doherty, 1992) because it is suitable for transmission of rich information. Also, face-to-face interaction is more effective than other communication media in conditions of ambiguity and uncertainty.

TOOLS IN HAND, READY TO DESIGN

The social network configurations and the distinction between tacit and explicit knowledge provide the tools for designing a strong knowledge-management infrastructure for a virtual team. The next step is to identify the network that best supports social capital for a specific virtual team.

Table 9.1 shows configurations for six knowledge-intensive team tasks, based on contingencies of task strategy and task output location. The configurations differ on three characteristics. First, the internal network of the team is either dense, with most people connected to most other people on the team, or loose, with fewer ties among members. Second, the external network of the team (within the organization or external to it) is either targeted to

Table 9.1. Configurations of Social Capital for Virtual Team Tasks

Task Imperative	Output Focused Inside the Organization	Output Focused Outside the Organization	Process Focus
Integrating	Examples: Integrating systems postmerger; consolidating research and development groups	Examples: Integrating multiple services for single client strategy; new product development	
	Tight networks among team members; most members have high centrality. Team members' organizational networks are targeted toward specific knowledge needs. Strong tacit knowledge links between team members and constituents in the organization.	Tight networks among team members; most members have high centrality. Team members' external networks are targeted toward specific knowledge needs. Strong tacit knowledge links between team members and external constituents.	
Differentiating	Examples: Changing organizational structure from function to product or geographical divisions	Examples: Adapting product to different markets; coordinating public relations campaigns in different locations	Combination and compromise: weak ties among team members.
	Loose networks among team members; few members have high centrality. Team members' organizational networks are targeted toward specific knowledge needs. Strong tacit knowledge links between team members and constituents in the organization.	Loose networks among team members; few members have high centrality. Team members' external networks are targeted toward specific knowledge needs. Strong tacit knowledge links between team members and constituents outside the organization.	Creation and collaboration: strong ties among team members.
Learning	Example: Identifying best practices and transferring to other units	Example: Benchmarking other organizations	
	Tight networks among team members for transferring tacit knowledge; loose networks for transferring explicit knowledge. Team members' organizational networks are broad and diffuse. Strong tacit knowledge links between team members and constituents in the organization; at least weak links with external constituents.	Tight networks among team members for transferring tacit knowledge; loose networks for transferring explicit knowledge. Team members' external networks are broad and diffuse. Strong tacit knowledge links between team members and constituents external to the organization; at least weak links with internal constituents.	

Note: For all three task imperatives, if the process focus is on combination and compromise, weak ties among members tend to be more effective; if the process focus is on creation and collaboration, strong ties among members tend to be more effective.

specific knowledge sources or broad and diffuse. If it is targeted, the role of gatekeepers, or those filling structural holes, is particularly important, and the team must pay attention to the configuration of the networks beyond the gate- keepers. If the network is broad and diffuse, then it will be composed of many weak ties that can be leveraged as multiple sensors into the environment. Third, ties to people in the external network are either especially strong or can be weak. Which configuration is the appropriate one for a team depends on the nature of the team's task with respect to three main characteristics: the target of the team output, the strategic nature of the task, and the process requirements of the task.

Team-Output Location

The first contingency variable is the target location of the team's output. Is the team making decisions about something that will be implemented within the organization or external to it? If the team is designing a change in perfor- mance evaluation systems, selecting and installing a new information manage- ment system, or integrating administration and support units after a merger, the team members need a tacit understanding of the systems and people involved in the change. The team will get the knowledge it needs and will be able to transfer the knowledge it builds only if its members have strong links with key constituents within the organization. If the team is developing a new product, designing a client strategy, or coordinating a marketing effort to all buyers in a specific industry, its members need a tacit understanding of the external con stituent. The knowledge needed will come from strong links with customers or clients or others in the targeted industry or market. These strong links will also facilitate knowledge transfer when the team executes its decisions.

Task Strategy

There are many ways of categorizing tasks, but the dimensions that most affect the configuration of social capital are integrating, differentiating, and learning. For some tasks, the imperative is integrating—for example, developing a global product or service, merging two organizations after the financial deal is closed, or designing a global knowledge database for the firm. In all these tasks, the team is charged with developing a single solution to a specific challenge or a single system for a particular target. Members of a virtual team with an inte- grating task bring different knowledge to the team, which itself must be integrated. The team's internal network must be dense, that is, each member must be linked to multiple other members, for the integration to be effective. Such a network is characterized by extensive internal social capital. To develop a solution that meets the needs of the target group, whether the target is others within the organization or customers or clients external to the organization, the team's external (outside the team) network must be targeted toward those spe- cific organizational or external stakeholders. This team must have its internal network tightly linked with that of the external constituencies and will have developed extensive external social capital. Virtual teams with members located close to the target groups are ideally suited for this type of activity.

For other tasks, the imperative is differentiating—for example, customizing a product to different markets, implementing a human resource management system in different locations, or marketing a new specialty industrial product to different industries. For these tasks, the team must coordinate customization and execution so firm resources are used most efficiently and there is consistency across the organization, but the emphasis is on adapting the decisions differently for different locations or targets. In this case, the team's internal network does not need to be dense, that is, members do not need to be linked to most other members; they can be loose, with each member linked to at least one other member on the team. As for the case of integrating tasks, the network external to the team, either within the organization or external to it, must be targeted toward the specific organizational or external stakeholders who will be affected by the team's decisions. Here too the team must have extensive external social capital, and once again, the virtual team's geographically dispersed members who are close to the target locations will offer a distinct advantage.

A third important strategic imperative is learning. Identifying and transferring best practices and benchmarking with other organizations are two examples of learning tasks, and these tasks require very different social capital configurations. Whether the internal network is dense or loose is less important than whether it is strong: whether there are few or many ties among members, the ties need to be strong ones reinforced by concurrent types of relationship (Brass, 1992), such as friendship, task advice, and relationship advice, if the learning imperative concerns tacit knowledge. The ties can be weak (of only one type of relationship, such as task advice) if the learning imperative involves explicit knowledge. External to the team, rather than being targeted toward specific constituents, the network should be broad and diffuse, with the team filling as many structural holes wherever possible. This learning configuration allows the team to access knowledge from the widest possible spectrum of sources and see multiple avenues for diffusing the information it learns. Once again, the virtual team can be a better learner if its members are located in geographical locations most appropriate to absorb needed knowledge. This is why Japanese automotive companies have branches of their design studios located in California and why European high-tech firms locate some of their research and development personnel in Silicon Valley.

Process Focus

A final contingency is the type of process the team is expected to engage in. Does the team need to combine ideas in an additive way and make compromises by negotiating give and take, or does it need to collaborate and create, combining ideas in a synergistic way and building new knowledge? For the former situation, such as selecting a global information technology vendor or coordinating the relationship between a large multibranched firm and its local advertisers, the ties among team members can be weak. For the latter situation, ties among team members must be strong. Combining and compromising can be done at the level of explicit knowledge, and weak ties are sufficient for these processes. Creating and collaborating require the transfer and development of tacit knowledge, which is possible only when ties among members are strong and multilayered.

Combining Configurations

The configurations are not mutually exclusive: a team can have the configuration that satisfies the requirements for more than one task. In fact, the more the team's social capital goes beyond a single task requirement, the more flexible its configuration will be. For example, if the team has a moderately dense network overall internally, it may have subsets of very dense and very loose networks, and it can obtain knowledge for tasks requiring both tight and loose networks. Alternatively, the same set of people in the virtual team can have a tight configuration for one task and a loose one for another. The social network among them forms differently depending on the task, just as its hierarchically defined linkages may not reflect the actual team configuration. If a team has loose networks overall, it will be able to gather and combine information as needed for the differentiated tasks, but it will not be effective in integrating tasks until it develops a denser internal network. Strong networks, such as the internal networks needed for creating and collaborating, can also combine and compromise; however, weak networks that can combine and compromise cannot also create and collaborate.

Furthermore, the configurations can be combined for more complex tasks. If the team's task is both internal and external (for example, selecting an acquisition target) or has multiple strategic imperatives (for example, designing a product that will be customized to suit different markets and developing targeted marketing strategies), then the virtual team's social capital should incorporate the configurations from both (or multiple) contingencies. This can be accomplished simply by adding up the requirements. For example, if the task requires targeted knowledge networks in the organization and outside it, then both networks should be developed. Note that because it is the team that is building social capital for the task, different people can focus on building networks to satisfy different aspects of the task requirement. If the team is to develop a particular type of knowledge expertise (an organizational need-targeted network in an organization with strong links to experts) to serve sophisticated client needs (external need-targeted network with strong links to clients), then some people on the team can focus on building a deep network within the organization while others do so with clients.

IMPLICATIONS FOR PRACTICE

The tools and configurations demonstrate that a social capital perspective to managing knowledge in virtual teams goes far beyond the advice to build a lot of relationships. For a virtual team, the single greatest challenge is building relationships. Advice specifying which relationships are more important for specific situations can help the team's efforts enormously. In this section, we provide some insights concerning how a virtual team should go about building and maintaining the types of social networks that best support the social capital it needs.

These insights begin with the fact that it is easier to build strong ties in face-to-face relationships. When people meet face-to-face, they experience each others' contexts, and a conversation is more likely to include a broader range of task-related and other topics than is a work conversation on the telephone or an e-mail exchange. Strong ties, or links that are based on multiple types of relationships between the same people, are therefore more likely to form in face-to-face interactions.

Where a configuration demands strong ties, the virtual team members need to meet face-to-face with the other people in the network. Some configurations need strong ties in the external network—within either the organization or the environment—but do not need strong ties among team members. In these cases, virtual teams are at a strong advantage over colocated teams because members of the team are already located in multiple environments and can build these networks face-to-face with their local stakeholders.

Other configurations require strong ties in the team's own internal network. In these cases, the team's performance will not meet expectations unless the team meets face-to-face on a regular basis. Team members need to develop multiple types of relationships among each other and interact with each other in multiple contexts. However, as we know from previous research, this does not mean the team needs to be together often or even for prolonged periods of time (Maznevski and Chudoba, 2000). Most important, the team should meet with a regular rhythm, such as every three to four months, for two to three days at a time. The meeting location should rotate through the different team members' home locations so that team members can learn tacit knowledge about those contexts from each other. These meetings should be planned to give team members multiple opportunities to build relationships and share tacit knowledge. This way, the deep relationships and shared knowledge can be leveraged and built on when the team is not face-to-face.

Because establishing credibility and face-to-face interactions involve establishing relationships, it is clear that building social capital through the virtual team network is a key prerequisite to knowledge transfer for virtual teams. This is no different from what traditional teams have to do. Yet virtual teams have to recognize that many traditional teams establish their routines to achieve these levels of credibility by a process that is not explicitly designed simply because they are colocated. Even much dreaded and seemingly aimless routine meetings help to achieve this end. Therefore, for virtual team members to achieve the same ability to share understanding of each others' tacit understanding of important knowledge, they must create explicit routines that will allow this to happen. In a sense, the biggest challenge to a successful virtual team is to create the team-level tacit knowledge of how to share each other's knowledge (Winter, 1987).

The configuration can also help determine the types of technology needed to support the team. If a team's internal network must be dense, then work-sharing software is important. Synchronous and asynchronous meeting capability, shared work space with the ability for everyone to work on the same documents, on-line white boards, and so on all facilitate the development and maintenance of dense networks. If the internal network can be loose, though, simple use of e-mail programs, with one team member coordinating the flow, are often sufficient. If the team needs to tap into the organizational knowledge in a targeted way, access to knowledge-management technology, such as human resource systems, Employee Relation Programs (ERPs), and data warehousing, are important tools, and working on the organization's intranet is sufficient. However, if the team members need to connect with targeted people in the external environment, issues of firewalls and compatibility with external systems become important. If the team members need broad and diffuse networks for learning, then access to news services and search technologies is critical externally, and data warehousing is an important internal tool.

Throughout this chapter, we have developed suggestions on how virtual teams can manage their knowledge flows. These can be summarized as follows:

- Virtual teams are sociotechnological systems. They must manage both technology and relationships to facilitate knowledge flows.
- Virtual teams should build high-quality social capital, or intangible resources lying in relationships among people.
- Virtual teams use social capital to draw knowledge from the organization, and the external environment, combine knowledge within the team and produce an outcome, and execute the decision within or outside the organization. On all but the third process, virtual teams can leverage their distributed locations to outperform colocated teams.
- Virtual teams should see themselves as a social network, or configuration of relationships of social capital, with various types of ties and relationships among members and between members and others.
- Virtual team members must build social capital with quantity, transferability, flexibility built on trust, and power.

- Explicit knowledge can be carried over weak ties, but transfer of tacit knowledge requires stronger ties.

- An effective virtual team must identify and build the precise network that best supports its specific knowledge-intensive tasks. The three most important task contingencies are focus of the output knowledge (internal or external), task imperative (integrating, differentiating, or learning), and process focus (combination and compromise, or creation and collaboration). The ideal density of social networks, scope of the networks, and strength of ties are all associated with particular task configurations.

- Strong ties must be built and maintained face-to-face; this is most effectively done in a rhythm of face-to-face meetings interspersed with virtual teamwork.

- Technology choices should be made to support the ideal configuration, not necessarily applying the same types of technology to every team.

References

Athanassiou, N., and Nigh, D. "The Impact of Company Internationalization on Top Management Team Advice Networks: A Tacit Knowledge Perspective." *Strategic Management Journal,* 1999, *19*(1), 83–92.

Borgatti, S. P., Jones, C., and Everett, M. "Network Measures of Social Capital." *Connections,* 1998, *21*(2), 27–36.

Brass, D. J. (ed.). *Power in Organizations: A Social Network Perspective.* Greenwich, Conn.: JAI Press, 1992.

Burt, R. S. *Structural Holes: The Social Structure of Competition.* Cambridge, Mass.: Harvard University Press, 1992.

Davenport, T. H., and Prusak, L. *Working Knowledge: How Organizations Manage What They Know.* Cambridge, Mass.: Harvard University Press, 1998.

Giddens, A. *The Constitution of Society.* Berkeley: University of California Press, 1984.

Granovetter, M. S. "The Strength of Weak Ties." *American Journal of Sociology,* 1973, *78,* 1360–1380.

Hall, R. "The Strategic Analysis of Intangible Resources." *Strategic Management Journal,* 1992, *13*(2), 135–144.

Lin, N. "Building a Network Theory of Social Capital." In N. Lin, K. Cook, and R. S. Burt (eds.), *Social Capital: Theory and Research.* New York: Aldine de Gruyter, 2001a.

Lin, N. *Social Capital: A Theory of Social Structure and Action.* Cambridge: Cambridge University Press, 2001b.

Lipnack, J., and Stamps, J. *Virtual Teams: Reaching Across Space, Time, and Organizations with Technology.* (2nd ed.) New York: Wiley, 2001.

Maznevski, M. L., and Chudoba, K. M. "Bridging Space over Time: Global Virtual Team Dynamics and Effectiveness." *Organization Science,* 2000, *11*(5), 473–492.

McGrath, J. E. *Groups: Interaction and Performance.* Upper Saddle River, N.J.: Prentice Hall, 1984.

McKenney, J. L., Zack, M. H., and Doherty, V. S. "Complementary Communication Media: A Comparison of Electronic Media and Face-to-Face Communication in a Programming Team." In N. Nohria and R. G. Eccles (eds.), *Networks and Organizations.* Boston: Harvard Business School Press, 1992.

Nahapiet, J., and Ghoshal, S. "Social Capital, Intellectual Capital, and the Organizational Advantage." *Academy of Management Review,* 1998, *23*(2), 267–284.

Nohria, N., and Eccles, R. G. "Face-to-Face: Making Network Organizations Work." In N. Nohria and R. G. Eccles (eds.), *Networks and Organizations: Structure, Form, and Action.* Boston: Harvard Business School Press, 1992.

Polanyi, M. *Personal Knowledge.* (2nd ed.) Chicago: University of Chicago Press, 1962.

Prusak, L. *Knowledge in Organizations.* Boston: Butterworth-Heinemann, 1997.

Stewart, T. A. "The Case Against Knowledge Management." *Business 2.0,* 2002, *3,* 80–83.

Wasserman, S., and Faust, K. *Social Network Analysis: Methods and Applications.* Cambridge: Cambridge University Press, 1994.

Winter, S. G. "Knowledge and Competence as Strategic Assets." In D. J. Teece (ed.), *The Competitive Challenge: Strategies for Industrial Innovation and Renewal.* Cambridge, Mass.: Ballinger, 1987.

CHAPTER TEN

Overcoming Barriers to Information Sharing in Virtual Teams

Catherine Durnell Cramton, Kara L. Orvis

Teams are created in work settings in the hope of bringing to the task a pool of resources exceeding what any single individual could offer. The premise is that different members of the team offer unique information and expertise to the collaborative effort. As a result of the merging of these different sources of information, a better product is produced.

As a result of recent developments in telecommunications and information technology, organizations are experimenting with the design of teams. They are bringing together individuals with the right information and skills to work in virtual rather than face-to-face environments using mediating technologies such as e-mail and the telephone. The hope is to realize the traditional advantages of teamwork despite the limitations of space and time. But there are challenges. This chapter describes the impact of virtualness on the amount and the distribution of information that teams must manage and how this hampers the essential information-sharing process. We describe the consequences for virtual teams of failures in the information-sharing process and suggest ways to avoid these problems. The role of the team leader in establishing effective information sharing in virtual teams is emphasized.

INFORMATION IN VIRTUAL TEAMS

The following case offers a point of departure for exploring issues concerning the initial distribution and subsequent sharing of information in a virtual team:

214

Brendan, Mike, and Marta have been working as a team for four weeks to develop a new product for their company, Design Solutions. Brendan and Mike work in the New York office, and Marta works in the Madrid office. Marta's job is to put together written weekly updates on the team's progress and provide them to company headquarters in London on Monday afternoons. Authorization to continue work on the project depends on Marta's filing timely and convincing status reports. One Tuesday, Brendan and Mike notice that Marta has not yet circulated Monday's weekly status report. Mike writes Marta an e-mail on behalf of the two of them, inquiring whether anything is wrong and asking her to circulate the report. Two more days pass without any word from Marta. During this time, Brendan and Mike become irritated and worry about losing the project. They write e-mails back and forth discussing Marta's motivation and work ethic. On Friday, Brendan gets an e-mail from a colleague in London who mentions that he plans to contact the office in Spain "when they reopen on Monday." Eventually, Brendan and Mike learn that the Spanish office has been closed all week for the observance of *Semana Santa,* Holy Week. They also learn from Marta on her Monday return that headquarters had asked her to provide the project's status report by telephone a day early, before the office closed for the week. She had done this on Friday afternoon. Because her office was closed during the ensuing week, she did not have access to her e-mail and did not know about Brendan and Mike's inquiries. It never had occurred to Brendan and Mike that the Spanish office would close for an entire week, and it never occurred to Marta that the New York office would *not* close for the period.

Types of Information

The Design Solutions case points to three types of information that are relevant to the work of virtual teams: task, social, and contextual information. Task information is about the carrying out of the task at hand—for example, how to use a tool, what resources are available, when products or reports are due, alternative approaches to performing the task, the status of the work, and inputs from stakeholders. At Design Solutions, Brendan, Mark, and Marta had some common task information, such as the current status of their work, but there also was some uniquely held task-related information: the request to Marta from company headquarters to perform the reporting function differently than she had in the past.

Social information is information about individuals and their relationships with each other. This includes personal motives and goals, personality traits, where individuals grew up and were educated, their philosophical outlook, and their networks and alliances. People use social information to help them interpret the behavior of others. In the example, relevant social information might include Marta's personality characteristics and her reputation in the company. If Brendan and Mike had known about Marta's conscientious style and her reputation within the Spanish office for following through on projects, they may not have jumped to the conclusion that her silence meant that she had failed to carry out her responsibility.

A third type of information important for teams is contextual information: information about the milieu or environment that surrounds tasks, individuals, and groups. Examples include the degree of supervisor support a person receives, the available equipment, competing responsibilities, cultural norms, holiday schedules, office layout, and local rules, expectations, and regulations. In the case, contextual information includes the difference in customs between Spain and the United States in the observance of Holy Week.

Distribution of Information

In a team, task, social, and contextual information may be unshared (known only to an individual or a subset of the team) or shared (known to all team members). Figure 10.1 illustrates this point. The rows distinguish these three types of information, and the columns describe the distribution of the information. Effective teamwork depends on appropriate information sharing: identifying important pieces of unshared information and converting them into shared information when decisions have to be made, inferences are being drawn, or work is being coordinated.

This is not an easy task in any team, and it seems to be more difficult in virtual than face-to-face environments. A long stream of research concerning traditional teams that meet face-to-face has shown that team members tend to focus discussion on information that is already known in common by the members. They often fail to discover or give scant attention to information that is known to only an individual or a subset of the members (Stasser and Stewart, 1992; Stasser, Stewart, and Wittenbaum, 1995; Stasser and Titus, 1985, 1987). This phenomenon is known as the common knowledge effect or biased discussion.

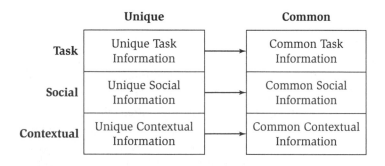

Figure 10.1 Types of Information Found in Group Collaboration.

Stasser and Titus (1985, 1987) developed a group task in which groups of four people were asked to evaluate the attributes of three candidates for an office and choose the best candidate. When each group member had a complete set of information, groups tended to settle on candidate A quickly. However, when information about the candidates was distributed among group members, groups often chose candidate B or C because they did not discover critical pieces of information known to individuals. Stasser and Stewart (1992) and Stasser, Stewart, and Wittenbaum (1995) developed a murder mystery task in which evidence would rule out two suspects and clearly implicate the third suspect if all clues were considered. They observed the same bias toward discussion of shared information.

According to Stasser and his colleagues, as the number of people who have a particular piece of information increases, so does the probability that it will be mentioned in the group's discussion. When it is mentioned, it probably will be salient to a larger proportion of the group because they have encountered it previously. Pieces of information known to only one or a few people compete at a disadvantage in the information pool with shared information. Moreover, when mentioned, this information may not be as salient to group members as shared information and fail to draw attention. Exacerbating conditions include information load (the total amount of information being considered), the proportion of shared versus unshared information (which affects people's ability to anticipate the existence of unshared information), and the use of technology-mediated communication (Hightower and Sayeed, 1995, 1996; Hollingshead, 1996; Stasser and Titus, 1987). These often are the conditions of virtual work, raising concern about the effectiveness of information sharing in such groups.

INFORMATION-SHARING CHALLENGES IN VIRTUAL TEAMS

There often is more information to be shared in virtual than traditional teams, and this information tends to be more dispersed. Moreover, virtual team members often fail to anticipate which pieces of information are important to share and how information sharing is affected by the use of technology-mediated communication.

More Information to Be Shared

One of the advantages of forming a virtual team is making use of knowledgeable team members even though they are dispersed across locations. This may result in a more diverse team than would be possible if membership was limited by physical colocation. Team members tend to be more diverse in terms of both the task information they hold and their personal backgrounds. In addition, because members are distributed across more than one location, there are likely to be more differences in their situations or context. For example, members cannot take for granted that they all observe the same holidays, use compatible versions of software, or experience the same types of pressures and demands on their time. Team members probably need to share more information about context—describe their situations to each other—in much greater detail than they would if they were working in the same location.

Consider the virtual team that was created by Whirlpool Corporation to develop a chlorofluorocarbon-free refrigerator. The team was composed of experts from the United States, Brazil, and Italy, named to the team because of the unique task-related information each member possessed. In addition to sharing task-related information, they had to gather and learn to interpret accurately a broad range of social, cultural, and contextual information about each other. Thus, to the extent that a virtual team incorporates more differences among members in task information, social background, and context than a colocated team, the team members will have to share a larger quantity of such information with each other in order to understand each other and work together successfully.

More Distributed Information

A second information-related challenge for virtual teams is that task, social, and contextual information is likely to be more distributed across locations than is the case in a colocated team. For example, in a virtual team composed of four members, there are four different local environments. Considerable communication is required of team members in order to make unique local information commonly known in the team. In comparison, colocated team members share the same local environment, and so the amount of task, social, and contextual information that must be communicated tends to be lower.

For example, it could be that the testing of components for Whirlpool's chlorofluorocarbon-free refrigerator is carried out in Italy. The results would be immediately available to the Italian team members. However, the results must also be communicated to the team members not on the scene: those in the United States and Brazil. The distributed nature of the task information introduces the possibility that it may be delayed, overlooked by the remote team members, or lost in transmission because of technical or human error. Managers, suppliers, clients, and other interested groups may communicate task-related information to whichever team member is on hand in their location. When just one member or a subset of a virtual team receives new information, they must determine whether fellow team members need to know the information and whether they already have it. If team members need the information and do not have it, then those who received it must remember to communicate it and be sure that the communication was successful. In the Design Solutions case, Marta's supervisor in London changed the plan for the weekly update. Neither he nor Marta realized the importance of sharing this uniquely held task information with the rest of the team. They did not anticipate that Brendan and Mark would not know about the Spanish holiday or that they would be concerned and irritated when they did not receive the weekly report. In a colocated situation, it is more likely that team members will be around when changes in requirements are made, so the information becomes commonly known.

There also is greater dispersion of social information in virtual than face-to-face teams. Working face-to-face, people are able to gather social information from interaction and observation. They absorb cues to a team member's meaning, mood, background, and priorities. One can detect accents, see credentials on the office wall, interpret tone of voice, observe how a person interacts with others, and hear stories. A team member may learn how to interpret his local partner's comments by chatting with her at the water cooler. However, he does not have the same opportunity to absorb social information about his remote partners. Social information easily becomes shared in a face-to-face setting relative to a virtual setting. In virtual teams, much social information is distributed across locations. One must be on location to hear accents, tones of voice, and stories and to see credentials and photographs on the wall.

Virtualness probably has a larger impact on the distribution of contextual information than task and social information. The working environments of members may differ in ways that their partners find difficult to anticipate. For example, a team member in one location may be under pressure to finish a job because of the press of another task. Yet his teammates in a different location may be struggling with an equipment breakdown that hampers their efforts. While such contextual factors affect the behavior of these members with the team, they are invisible to the other team members. Unless team members go to extra effort to explain their situations to remote partners, their behavior may be misinterpreted. By contrast, colocated team members share the same environment, tools, and materials. Information about the context of work is easily known in common in this team.

DIFFICULTY ANTICIPATING INFORMATION-SHARING NEEDS

To make matters more challenging, Cramton (2001, 2002) has described how virtual team members have difficulty anticipating which aspects of their local situation might differ from the situations of remote partners. People tend to take their local situations for granted and assume that remote partners' situations are similar. Consequently, they do not describe critical aspects of their local context to their virtual partners. As we have seen, Marta took the closing of businesses during Holy Week for granted, having no reason to guess that holidays were different in the United States than in Spain. Meanwhile, Brendan and Mike assumed that Marta was in the office during the week because they were. Such differences in contextual information might include the availability of equipment, holidays and customs, conflicting demands on one's time, travel requirements, or whether measurements are made in centimeters or inches. Because of the difficulty of anticipating what differences might exist, virtual team members have a tendency not to provide important information about their own situation or to ask the right questions in order to identify critical information about the situations of their remote partners.

Impact of Technology-Mediated Communication

A defining characteristic of virtual teams is that they use technology-mediated communication much more than face-to-face interaction in order to communicate (Maznevski and Chudoba, 2000). Members of virtual teams may meet face-to-face periodically, but most of their collaboration typically is carried out through the use of technologies such as e-mail, telephone, electronic chat, fax, and videoconferencing.

Technology tends to have an impact on the speed and ease of information sharing and the availability of cues. Communication through text-based media such as e-mail and electronic chat tends to be more laborious than verbal conversation (Graetz and others, 1998). As a consequence, people often opt not to type out details that they would communicate verbally. For example, Straus (1996) found that groups communicating through text-based electronic media exchanged an average of 740 words, whereas those communicating verbally and face-to-face exchanged an average of 1,702 words. The details, qualifications, and social rituals that are left out of such messages can be important to group performance and viability.

For example, a partner in a small firm specializing in the design of performance appraisal systems sent a six-paragraph e-mail to his three partners concerning the firm's new association with a larger consulting company. Among other suggestions, he proposed that the partners be highlighted as subject matter experts on the consulting company's Web page. One of the three partners, Jim, responded with an e-mail consisting of two words, "Good plan." However, when Jim's photograph appeared on the consulting company's Web page, Jim was outraged and blamed the consulting company for overstepping itself. He had approved of the overall approach outlined in his partner's e-mail but apparently did not read or respond carefully to the details. His short, quickly written e-mail gave no sign of his reservations.

Technology-mediated communication also restricts the transmission of cues to the meaning of messages. Individual media differ in the range of cues they transmit, but none provides as much information as face-to-face interaction. For example, technologies that rely on the written word, such as e-mail and electronic chat, lack paralinguistic cues such as vocal pitch, loudness, rhythm, and hesitations. Research has shown that messages are understood more accurately when such cues are available (Apple and Hecht, 1982; Chawla and Krauss, 1994). If Jim had reviewed the proposed plan in a face-to-face meeting, others might have noticed him looking at his watch and heard his distracted tone of voice when he said, "Good plan."

Furthermore, Cramton (2001, 2002) has observed that virtual team members can overlook the parts of messages that senders consider to be most important. This is because paraverbal and verbal cues signal not only meaning but importance. In other words, such cues help people signal which parts of a message are most salient to them. When communicating through technology, people often are not successful in directing their readers' attention. In the case of the performance appraisal system design firm, the plan to highlight the partners on the larger consulting company's Web page did not stand out to Jim in the six-paragraph e-mail.

Problems of confirmation exacerbate the problem. Technology-mediated communication can reduce the ease with which people confirm that a message has been received. When information is conveyed face-to-face, receivers of messages can signal their understanding through what researchers call back-channel communication: head nods, brief verbalizations such as "yeah" and "m-hmmm," smiles, and the like. However, these signaling activities tend to be more laborious for people who are communicating electronically. It takes time and effort to write e-mails that say in effect, "I received your e-mail, and this is what I took as the key point. Is that what you intended?" Observed one member of a virtual project team, "With so much information going back and forth, it was difficult for my teammates to absorb every detail. Because I couldn't see if the receiver was paying attention, I didn't know if my message had to be repeated. Yet it is time-consuming to let the sender know my perception of the message."

Cramton (2001, 2002) identified three additional technology-related information-sharing problems in virtual teams. She described how information sharing in virtual teams is hampered by human-computer interface mistakes and technology failures. Important messages fail to reach team members because e-mails are addressed incorrectly or lost in transit. For example, in one virtual team, a team member communicated with the others through a listserv. Unbeknown to the team members, the address recorded in the listserv for one of the team members was outdated. The address was still active, but the team member no longer checked it and had no idea that this was the address registered with the listserv. When messages were sent by listserv to the team, this member never saw them because they landed in the unchecked mailbox. Because the messages were not returned as undelivered, the other team members assumed he was getting the information. Eventually, he missed several on-line meetings, stirring considerable pique among his team members, who thought he was knowingly slighting the team. Cramton demonstrated that virtual team members are not very good at detecting and correcting such failures.

In addition, virtual team members often differ in how often they can access their supporting technologies. Some people can access electronic mail and project databases twenty-four hours a day, seven days a week, while others have more limited periods of access. In addition, norms concerning how often people check for e-mail messages differ across cultures. When some team members access e-mail only once a day or every few days, whether by custom or constraint, this limits team coordination and slows the pace of work. As a result, members of virtual teams sometimes grow out of sync with each other. Subsets of the teams communicate frequently with each other, while other subsets are perceived to lag behind and delay the team's progress. If team members do not discuss their assumptions and technical constraints, they may unknowingly violate each other's expectations.

Finally, Cramton pointed out that silence can have multiple meanings in virtual teams and that partners often misinterpret the meaning of their partners' silence. A partner's silence can stem from technical failures, discomfort about airing conflict or sensitive matters in text, confusion about logistics, or travel. Silence may mean agreement, disagreement, or indifference. It can be interpreted as a response or as no response. For example, a scientist in the United States had discussed a possible joint project with a colleague from another country at a conference. As the time for formal planning neared, the scientist e-mailed the colleague to see if he still was interested. The e-mail came back undelivered, so the scientist re-sent it. Two weeks passed without a response. Wondering whether the silence meant that the remote colleague was uninterested, the scientist decided at the last minute to re-send the original message to be sure there was no technical problem. A reply came immediately: "You're right," he wrote. "I never got this message. We've been having some strange technical problems lately that have kept us unconnected. Regarding the project, I think this would be an exciting opportunity."

Even in meetings conducted face-to-face, it can be difficult to interpret the meaning of team members' silence. However, geographical dispersion and reliance on computer-mediated communication add new dimensions of uncertainty about the meaning of silence and complicate efforts to resolve uncertainty. A partner could be out of town or silenced by technical problems. He may not have received a message or may have focused on parts of it other than what was most important to the sender. There seems to be a tendency to fall silent rather than address sensitive issues because of the difficulty of communicating nuances through electronic media rather than face-to-face. In particular, uncertainty about the meaning of silence can make it difficult to know when a decision has been made in a virtual team. If some members do not respond to a query, their partners must either contact them again or make a guess about the meaning of their silence.

Inappropriate Attributions

Failures to share important task, social, and contextual information can have a detrimental impact on the attributions that virtual team members make about each other. Attribution is the process by which people make inferences about the causes of events. For example, when Marta failed to circulate the weekly report, Brendan and Mike made attributions about why they had not received it. Attributions can be dispositional or situational. In other words, an event can be explained as having been caused by the personality of an individual or by something about the situation. In the example at the beginning of the chapter, Mike and Brendan could explain Marta's failure to provide the report as being due to something within Marta (a poor work ethic) or something situational (the boss asking her to provide a verbal report). The attributions people make play an important role in determining their subsequent actions, feelings, and thoughts. When Mike and Brendan concluded that Marta did not circulate the weekly report because she was lazy, this attribution influenced their feelings about her negatively. Moreover, it would likely affect the way they worked with her in the future.

Cramton (2001) has suggested that members of virtual teams err on the side of dispositional attributions relative to members of colocated teams for two reasons: lack of situational information and the cognitive load presented by working under virtual conditions. Virtual team members often lack situational information because there tends to be a great deal of information to be shared, the information is distributed, it is difficult to anticipate what information needs to be shared, and the information-sharing process can be cumbersome. When remote partners do not have information about each other's situations because of these factors, they have less of a basis on which to make situational attributions. With situational information unavailable, people are likely to make personal attributions (Jones and Nisbett, 1972). Furthermore, if remote partners lack social information about each other, they will be unable to rule out inappropriate personal attributions. In the Design Solutions example, Mike and Brendan made a personal attribution concerning Marta's work ethic because they were unaware of events in Spain that were affecting her behavior. They also lacked social information about her reputation for conscientiousness that would have led them to question their personal attribution. Such attributions affect the communication, cooperation, and viability of a virtual team. In addition, people are less likely to try to modify a problematic situation if they perceive individuals as the cause of problems.

Concerning cognitive load, attribution research has shown that individuals who are working under a heavy cognitive load tend to make personal rather than situational attributions (Gilbert and Hixon, 1991; Gilbert and Osborne, 1989). This is because it generally requires less mental energy to attribute an event to someone's personality than to detect and analyze situational factors. Applying this point to virtual teams, Cramton (2001) has suggested that the sheer volume of relevant information, its distribution over locations, the mental energy required to analyze remote situations, and the time lags and technical challenges presented by mediated communication place a heavy cognitive load on virtual team members, resulting in a heightened tendency to fall back on dispositional attributions.

DYSFUNCTIONAL OUTCOMES

When virtual teams experience information-sharing and attribution problems, they risk dysfunctional outcomes such as poor decision quality, crumbling trust, fracturing of a team into in-groups and out-groups by location, and escalation of communication and coordination failures.

When decision-making groups dwell on shared information and fail to discover important unshared information, they make poorer-quality decisions (Dennis, 1996; Stasser and Titus, 1985). Because of the information-sharing challenges of virtual work, teams should be vigilant concerning this risk. Critical task information may be known in one location but not factored into overall decisions. There are several reasons that this can occur. First, the new information may not be communicated because those with the new information do not realize that remote partners need it and do not have it. Alternatively, communication attempts may fail because of human or technical error, and the failure may go unnoticed. Finally, communication may be successful, but those on the receiving end may not recognize and focus on the new information. It is particularly important for virtual team leaders to understand all the reasons that unique information can go unrecognized under virtual conditions and to implement procedures to offset this tendency.

Information-sharing failures also can affect trust in virtual teams. Such failures can be devastating to team trust when they occur early in the life of a virtual team. When technical systems and procedures are new, teams are particularly vulnerable to information-sharing errors. At the same time, team members may lack knowledge about and experience with each other. If failures occur and are blamed on remote partners as individuals, without insight into the challenges of information sharing under virtual conditions, trust can be damaged.

In addition, there seems to be a heightened tendency for virtual teams to fracture into in-groups and out-groups based on location because of information-sharing failures followed by inaccurate attributions and generalizations. In practice, virtual teams usually consist of clusters of individuals at various locations rather than scattered individuals. Cramton (2001) argued that there is a tendency for tensions to be felt as resentments between such clusters. She observed that when virtual teams experienced information-sharing problems that they did not understand, there was a tendency to blame problems on remote partners and then generalize these attributions to the entire subgroup of people in that location. For example, colocated subgroups were described by their virtual partners as "lackadaisical," "aggressive," and "having an inferiority complex."

Finally, negative personal attributions and the formation of in-groups and out-groups based on location tend to lead to the escalation of problems. Cramton observed that once such attributions had been made and in-groups and out-groups formed, people tended to withhold information from each other, further depleting their understanding of the situation and damaging decision making and coordination.

IMPLICATIONS FOR PRACTICE

Team leaders can make a difference in the handling of information in virtual teams and the conclusions that team members draw about each other and the task. According to Zaccaro and Burke (1998), a leader's role is to be a social problem solver. Leaders analyze the specific challenges at hand and generate and implement solutions. This chapter shows that information sharing and interpretation are critical challenges in virtual teams. Therefore, a key leadership function in distributed environments should be the facilitation and monitoring of information exchange and interpretation. Our five specific recommendations for leaders follow.

- *Establish procedures for information sharing within the virtual team.* It may be helpful for leaders to distinguish among task, social, and contextual information and to design procedures appropriate to each type of information. For example, task-related information may be best shared at a weekly dial-in conference call in which representatives at each location are guaranteed airtime. It probably is a good idea to designate a facilitator for such conference calls so that time is managed, focus is maintained, and new information is made salient to all.

Effective social information sharing may require other strategies. As is widely recommended, it is a good idea for a virtual team to meet face-to-face periodically. However, we recommend that the location of meetings be rotated so that all members visit all locations. This helps them absorb contextual information as well as social information. Weekly conference calls also can be used to facilitate the sharing of social information. We recommend that conference calls begin with a check-in period in which each participant says a few words about how he or she is. This can help people clear their minds in order to focus on the task and help others interpret what they say and gradually learn more about them.

Appropriate sharing of contextual information may be most challenging. People tend to take their own context for granted and have difficulty guessing how a remote context could be different. It is helpful for team members to visit the locations of their remote partners so they can calibrate their sense of how similar or different remote partners' situations are from one's own local situation. If such visits are not possible, it is good idea to have at least one influential person at each location stay familiar with remote locations through regular visits. It also is important for members of virtual teams to be alert to the dangers of assuming that remote situations are like the local situation. Rather than assuming, they should learn to make inquiries about contextual factors such as distances traveled, holidays, the nature of other people's jobs and responsibilities, the availability of equipment, practices for measurement, reporting, and communication.

Team leaders should consider designating subject matter experts to help manage task, social, and contextual information sharing. Stewart and Stasser (1995) found that groups recognized more unshared information when individuals had been assigned to serve as experts for particular domains of information. Group members learned to direct relevant new information to them and to consult these individuals when questions arose. The subject matter experts recognized new information when it surfaced and called it to the group's attention. Virtual team leaders might decide to designate subject matter experts for matters such as schedules or client feedback.

- *Provide resources.* It is the role of team leaders to negotiate for the resources that their teams need to be successful. Virtual teams often need resources of time, travel, and technology. A study conducted by Warkentin, Sayeed, and Hightower (1997) showed that when virtual teams were given a long time frame, they were able to exchange information as well as teams working face-to-face, despite the slower pace of the text-based communication media they were using. Team leaders may be able to facilitate performance by making sure that there is ample time for virtual teams to do their task.

Funds should be allocated for virtual team members to visit each others' locations and secure appropriate communication technologies. Graetz and his collaborators (1998) compared the experiences of groups using e-mail and text chat technologies to share information with those of groups working face-to-face or through teleconferencing. They found that groups using e-mail and text chat had a more difficult time with problem solving and coordination, shared less information, took more time to make a decision, and experienced more mental and temporal demands and frustration. However, telephone conferencing worked as well as face-to-face communication. Team leaders should consider investing in tools that allow the efficient use of voice-based communication, such as high-quality telephone conferencing, headsets for frequent callers, and tie-lines between locations. "Being able to call without worrying about costs is crucial," said one experienced virtual project team leader.

• *Create norms for communication.* Virtual team leaders should see themselves as norm setters. They should initiate the development of team communication norms and be sure that they are taught to new members and enforced. For example, they should see to it that clear understandings are established about how often virtual partners will check for and respond to messages and to what extent they will notify each other when they will be on holiday or out of the office for other reasons. People who suffer through unexpected silence on the part of a remote partner often draw inaccurate conclusions that linger even after communication resumes. Team members also should be encouraged to highlight important pieces of information or important parts of long messages sent by e-mail and other such technologies. Questions that need to be addressed by a remote partner should be placed and marked so they are instantly apparent.

Team leaders should educate team members about information-sharing pitfalls and the consequences of making assumptions about remote partners and locations. Norms should encourage people to seek out information when questions arise. Team members also should be taught to explain their own situation to remote partners; they should be proactive in sharing contextual information. Perhaps most important, team leaders should instill in their virtual teams a norm of giving the benefit of the doubt in ambiguous situations. It is quick and easy to leap to dispositional attributions about remote partners, but often inaccurate and destructive to collaboration. Situational causes should be routinely considered, even if information to support them is not immediately available. Virtual team leaders should model and teach this simple but powerful practice.

• *Build the virtual team's social identity.* People tend to be kinder in their attributions about others when they share a sense of identity with them (Pettigrew, 1979). Groups that have a strong sense of identity tend to be more cohesive with less emotional conflict and more satisfaction, which supports cooperation, coordination, and trust (Spears and Lea, 1992). Virtual team leaders should create a strategy to encourage the development of shared identity in their teams. Brandon and Pratt (1999) suggest emphasizing similarities among members such as similar educational backgrounds, shared goals, interdependence, and shared fate. They also propose that virtual team members develop symbols to represent their team—a name, logo, or letterhead, for example—and a group database containing members' discussions of team attributes, aspirations, norms, and procedures.

• *Monitor communication and intervene when problems arise.* Finally, team leaders should understand the maintenance of the information-sharing process in their teams to be a critical part of their job. They should keep tabs on the effectiveness of communication processes across locations and intervene when puzzles, misunderstandings, or problems arise.

References

Apple, W., and Hecht, K. "Speaking Emotionally: The Relation Between Verbal and Vocal Communication of Affect." *Journal of Personality and Social Psychology,* 1982, *37*(5), 715–727.

Brandon, D., and Pratt, M. "Managing Identity Development in On-Line Virtual Teams: A SIT/SCT Perspective." *Academy of Management Best Paper Proceedings,* 1999, pp. D1–6.

Chawla, P., and Krauss, R. M. "Gesture and Speech in Spontaneous and Rehearsed Narratives." *Journal of Experimental Social Psychology,* 1994, *30*(6), 580–601.

Cramton, C. D. "The Mutual Knowledge Problem and Its Consequences for Dispersed Collaboration." *Organization Science,* 2001, *12*(3), 346–371.

Cramton, C. D. "Finding Common Ground in Dispersed Collaboration." *Organizational Dynamics,* 2002, *30*(4), 356–367.

Dennis, A. "Information Exchange and Use in Small Group Decision Making." *Small Group Research,* 1996, *27*(4), 532–549.

Gilbert, D., and Hixon, J. "The Trouble with Thinking: Activation and Application of Stereotypic Beliefs." *Journal of Personality and Social Psychology,* 1991, *60*(4), 509–517.

Gilbert, D., and Osborne, R. "Thinking Backward: Some Curable and Incurable Consequences of Cognitive Busyness." *Journal of Personality and Social Psychology,* 1989, *57*(6), 940–949.

Graetz, K. A., and others. "Information Sharing in Face-to-Face, Teleconferencing, and Electronic Chat Teams." *Small Group Research,* 1998, *29*(6), 714–743.

Hightower, R., and Sayeed, L. "The Impact of Computer-Mediated Communication Systems on Biased Group Discussion." *Computers in Human Behavior,* 1995, *11*, 33–44.

Hightower, R., and Sayeed, L. "Effects of Communication Mode and Prediscussion Information Distribution Characteristics on Information Exchange in Groups." *Information Systems Research,* 1996, *7*(4), 451–464.

Hollingshead, A. "Information Suppression and Status Persistence in Group Decision Making: The Effects of Communication Media." *Human Communication Research,* 1996, *23*(2), 193–219.

Jones, E., and Nisbett, R. "The Actor and Observer: Divergent Perceptions of the Causes of Behavior." In E. Jones and others (eds.), *Attribution: Perceiving the Causes of Behavior.* Morristown, N.J.: General Learning Press, 1972.

Maznevski, M., and Chudoba, K. "Bridging Space over Time: Global Virtual Team Dynamics and Effectiveness." *Organization Science,* 2000, *11*(5), 473–492.

Pettigrew, T. "The Ultimate Attribution Error: Extending Allport's Cognitive Analysis of Prejudice." *Personality and Social Psychology Bulletin,* 1979, *5,* 461–476.

Spears, R., and Lea, M. "Social Influence and the Influence of the 'Social' in Computer-Mediated Communication." In L. Martin (ed.), *Contexts of Computer-Mediated Communication.* London: Harvester Wheatsheaf, 1992.

Stasser, G., and Stewart, D. "Discovery of Hidden Profiles by Decision-Making Groups: Solving a Problem Versus Making a Judgment." *Journal of Personality and Social Psychology,* 1992, *63,* 426–434.

Stasser, G., Stewart, D., and Wittenbaum, G. "Expert Roles and Information Exchange During Discussion: The Importance of Knowing Who Knows What." *Journal of Experimental Social Psychology,* 1995, *31,* 244–265.

Stasser, G., and Titus, W. "Pooling of Unshared Information in Group Decision Making: Biased Information Sampling During Discussion." *Journal of Personality and Social Psychology,* 1985, *48*(6), 1467–1478.

Stasser, G., and Titus, W. "Effects of Information Load and Percentage of Shared Information on the Dissemination of Unshared Information During Group Discussion." *Journal of Personality and Social Psychology,* 1987, *53,* 81–93.

Stewart, D. D., and Stasser, G. "Expert Role Assignment and Information Sampling During Collective Recall and Decision Making." *Journal of Personality and Social Psychology,* 1995, *69*(4), 619–628.

Straus, S. G. "Getting a Clue: The Effects of Communication Media and Information Distribution on Participation and Performance in Computer Mediated and Face to Face Groups." *Small Group Research,* 1996, *27,* 115–142.

Warkentin, M. E., Sayeed, L., and Hightower, R. "Virtual Teams Versus Face-to-Face Teams: An Exploratory Study of a Web-Based Conference System." *Decision Sciences,* 1997, *28,* 975–996.

Zaccaro, S. J., and Burke, C. S. "Teams Versus Crew Leadership: Differences and Similarities." Paper presented at the Thirteenth Annual Meeting of the Society for Industrial and Organizational Psychology, Dallas, 1998.

PART THREE

SUMMARY

The authors in the chapters in Part Three discussed key design elements for virtual teams: social structure, information sharing, and leadership. Four design principles for virtual team leaders emerge from these chapters:

- Build social capital to maximize intellectual capital.
- Develop social networks to support work-focused information exchange.
- Ensure effective information exchange.
- Lead the team more forcefully when trust is low.

Maznevski and Athanassiou demonstrate in Chapter Nine that social capital drives knowledge acquisition in virtual teams. Relationships between people who are geographically dispersed enable the acquisition of a broad spectrum of knowledge that can be leveraged on behalf of the team and organization. Relationships among members enable virtual teams to combine knowledge synergistically and creatively. In short, social capital builds intellectual capital. Relationships matter.

The social structure of a team determines the paths by which information is shared. The right paths depend on the virtual team task. The contingency model that Maznevski and Athanassiou proffer suggests that tight networks should be built for integrating tasks, loose networks for differentiating tasks, and a combination of tight and loose networks for learning tasks. External networks are key when the output is focused outside the organization. In Chapter Ten, Cramton and Orvis identify barriers to information sharing in virtual teams, and many of those barriers stem from the lack of relationships among virtual team members. The sharing of contextual and social information can determine the effectiveness of virtual collaboration, yet only task information tends to be shared. People who feel connected to one another and have a relationship are more likely to share contextual and social information with one another. Yet employees cannot be commanded to have relationships with one another.

Leaders can help teams determine appropriate procedures and paths for needed information exchange, however. They can help teams examine the types of tasks they need to perform and determine the communication links that should be put in place among team members and between team members and constituents in their organizations. They can help teams establish effective communication norms. They can also monitor to assess whether the needed communication occurs. They can help teams to develop a collective identity, encouraging shared knowledge of members' skills and personal attributes. Leaders can help to create the conditions for building relationships in virtual teams, even though they cannot command them. Relationships are likely to emerge from communicating and working together. By being explicit about the communication links required to perform the virtual team task successfully, the team leader helps the team to build the right relationships, increasing the team's social capital.

If a team is high in social capital, it likely has high levels of trust. As Gibson and Manuel discussed in Chapter Four, trust in a team is characterized by a shared psychological state of vulnerability based on mutual expectations. If team members have strong and multiple ties with one another, they are more likely to be open with one another and to trust the team. Tyran, Tyran, and Shepherd's finding in Chapter Eight that the higher-performing teams either had an emergent leader who was highly trusted or the trust among team members was high suggests a final design principle.

Perhaps strong virtual team leadership can function as a substitute for trust. If there is high social capital and trust on the team, then team members are likely to share leadership functions and exchange information that is required to perform their tasks. If there is low social capital and low trust, then a leader should be highly proactive in ensuring that the needed information exchange and collaboration occurs. Thus, a virtual team leader should assess the level of team trust. The leader can vary leadership style depending on the level of trust. If trust is low, the leader should take a strong stance in ensuring that the collective work gets done. Of course, Tyran, Tyran, and Shepherd's study was of emergent leadership, so their findings may not apply to preappointed leaders. In any case, virtual team leaders have a critical role in helping to build social capital and overcoming the barriers to effective information exchange. They are critical catalysts to developing the enabling conditions we discussed in Part One. Effective information exchange cannot occur in a virtual world without the use of information technology. We turn to this next.

PART FOUR

WIRING THAT CONNECTS

*Implementing Information
Technology*

PART FOUR

INTRODUCTION

There's a lot of technology to be had out there. How many of us know how to use it? You know, right now I've got a scanner that is an excellent paperweight on my desk at home because I haven't had the time to program it right.
—Practitioner at the conference commenting on the gap between availability and usability of technology

Information technology provides the infrastructure for virtual collaboration. Technological advances have led to the ubiquity of information technology tools, enabling anytime, anyplace work. But just because tools are available does not necessarily make them useful. The chapters in this part seek to help practitioners determine which tools are appropriate for their virtual teams' needs.

In Chapter Eleven, Riopelle and associates address three major questions: (1) What technologies are appropriate for teams operating in different contexts? (2) How does the nature of the tasks affect the choice and use of technology? (3) How does technology play a role in the development of virtual teams over time? They base their answers on a longitudinal study of six global virtual teams in five major corporations.

They point out that context is important for technology use in at least six ways: physical infrastructure, culture and language, accessibility of information, crossing time zones, team size, and maturity of the technology. For example, not all areas of the world have reliable electrical power or telephone connections, resulting in the inability of some members to participate fully and lost team productivity. Cultural and language differences affect preferences for technology use. For example, in one of their cases, an American manager preferred videoconferences as a medium to work out conflicts with his Japanese teammates directly, which ignored the Japanese cultural value for preservation of harmony in a group context. Organizational differences in technology infrastructures create incompatibilities and lack of accessibility to information that can be extremely frustrating for team members. Working across time zones not only extends workdays but may also limit the choice of communication technologies. As teams grow in size, technology limitations make some communication technologies inefficient and impractical. Things inevitably go wrong when technology is new, and unexpected problems can derail team functioning.

Riopelle and his coauthors present a typology of team tasks based on task complexity. They argue that if a task is very complex, requiring a great deal of information exchange and coordinated effort, then reciprocal communication and feedback will be essential for performance. Synchronous technologies such as audioconferencing or videoconferencing will be a superior choice for virtual teams to perform these highly complex tasks successfully. For less complex tasks such as idea generation, asynchronous media such as e-mail will be a better choice.

Examining teams in context as they develop over time provides a more complete understanding of the role that technology plays. The appropriate technology choice based solely on task may turn out to be the wrong choice for the team when context is taken into account. For example, the authors watched a sales team change from relying on face-to-face meetings and audioconferences to using a shared sales reporting database and asynchronous communication. Their initial choice reflected personal preferences rather than the nature of their task, but they modified it as the size of their team increased and they became more familiar with one another. In a couple of companies they studied, team members relied on e-mail to communicate with one another, even though their tasks called for more synchronous communication. One of the chapter authors at our conference had this to say: "What we saw in a lot of the teams that we studied is that they would start off with higher levels of technology, and that dropped off as they went on, until they got down to using the phone and e-mail as their primary tools. I'm not sure that is bad. I say this as someone who loves all these toys."

Based on their in-depth case analyses, these authors conclude that there is no simple prescription for choosing the right technology for a global virtual team. Instead, they provide a series of thought-provoking questions that allow team leaders and members to think through their technology options.

Chapter Twelve by King and Majchrzak looks closely at the match between the nature of a particular kind of work often performed by virtual teams and the team's choice of information technology tools. They focus on unstructured knowledge work, such as new product development, strategic planning, and organizational design.

King and Majchrzak review traditional features of collaborative technologies that attempt to support these characteristics and find them lacking. These limitations are primarily due to the fact that most technologies are designed to support either knowledge as objective, such as a focus on the information alone, or knowledge as action, with a focus on the process of information exchange, but not both. For example, knowledge repositories such as database programs treat bits of knowledge as objects and do not facilitate exchange. As such, they do not support spontaneity or transience of knowledge. In contrast, technologies such as electronic white boards have a knowledge-as-action focus, and although they do support spontaneity and transience, they do not do a good job of supporting knowledge encoding, sharing policies, or establishment of reuse priorities. Thus, the full spectrum of virtual team activities is left unsupported.

King and Majchrzak offer a number of recommendations for meeting the challenges of these limitations. They suggest that technologies be combined in order to address all of the characteristics of unstructured knowledge work. They emphasize four common themes: ensuring interoperability, balancing concerns of information security and sharing, creating and integrating search and retrieval processes, and implementing multimedia capture. These four strategies can go a long way toward helping virtual teams establish the appropriate technology support for the knowledge characteristics inherent in their tasks.

In Chapter Thirteen, Raven asserts that the choice of technology should take into consideration the structure of the virtual collaboration as well as the nature of the work. He is concerned with aligning tasks, structures, and technologies and suggests that the collaborative structure that is best aligned with unstructured knowledge work may not be a team but instead a community of practice (CoP).

He compares teams to CoPs along dimensions of mission, membership, leadership, task interdependence, structure, accountability, and resources and draws examples for his comparison from two cases: a new product design team from a four-company consortium and a knowledge management CoP from a newly merged organization. A team's mission is mandated, while a CoP's mission is emergent. Membership is designed in the team and is voluntary in a CoP. Leadership is explicitly defined for a team but emergent and dynamic in a CoP. A team's task is highly interdependent, while a CoP's task may not require interdependent effort. The structure for a team is designed based on the team's mission and interdependent work, while the CoP's structure is emergent. Teams generally are held accountable for accomplishing their work by external entities, while CoPs are accountable mostly to themselves. Finally, organizations typically provide teams with the resources they need to complete their work, while CoPs typically will have very limited resources provided by individual members.

The collaborative technologies available for virtual teams include groupware and knowledge repositories. Groupware enables communication between members of a team. Knowledge repositories store information for future use. Some products contain both functions. Raven concludes that groupware and knowledge repositories for virtual teams can be highly standardized and structured but must be flexible for communities of practice.

These three chapters introduce key issues in matching technology to task, structure, and stage of development to increase the effectiveness of virtual teams in dynamic environments.

CHAPTER ELEVEN

Context, Task, and the Evolution of Technology Use in Global Virtual Teams

Kenneth Riopelle, Julia C. Gluesing, Tara C. Alcordo,
Marietta L. Baba, David Britt, Willie McKether, Leslie Monplaisir,
Hilary Horn Ratner, Kimberly Harris Wagner

This chapter aims to help global virtual team (GVT) members understand that context and task complexity play a role in the use of technology over time in these teams and select the best technology for their team to use. We explore three basic questions:

- What technologies are appropriate for teams operating in different contexts?

- How does the nature of the tasks at hand have an impact on the choice and use of technology?

- How does technology play a role in the development of virtual teams over time?

We caution readers that there is no simple solution, no prescriptive "If *a*, then do *x*." A prescriptive approach will not work in most cases because the interactions among context, task, and technology issues are complex, and oversimplification can lead teams to make inappropriate choices. For example, what is appropriate with respect to videoconferencing in the early stages of task work

The research reported in this chapter was supported by a grant from the National Science Foundation's Innovation and Organizational Change Program and Wayne State University's Targets of Opportunity Program.

for one team may not be appropriate for another. Here we offer the insights we have learned from our research and some clear examples to explain the impact of context and task complexity on GVTs; highlight some patterns of technology use over time so teams can learn from them and chart their own course of development, making appropriate choices along the way; and conclude with a series of questions practitioners can ask themselves and their fellow team members to perform their own virtual technology assessment.

When it comes to virtual technologies for information sharing and collaboration, the old axiom, "One size fits all," does not apply. Rather, a more apt expression might be, "It depends." Good technology choices depend on uncovering the contextual and task issues a team is facing and learning to avoid the technology pitfalls that can derail a virtual team.

CASE PROFILES

This chapter is based on a longitudinal study of six GVTs in five major corporations.[1] The six teams span five industries (automotive, textile, telecommunications, computers, and consumer goods) and three functional areas (sales and marketing, information technology, and product development). The life cycles of the teams varied from two months to two years or more, and some teams are still ongoing. In a single GVT, there were members from as few as two to as many as twenty-three countries. This GVT case set provides the quotations and examples throughout this chapter and includes sufficient variety to demonstrate the complex interaction of context and team task and the effect of this interaction on the technology use in the GVTs over time.

The following case descriptions provide snapshots of the six GVT cases in our study, and Table 11.1 offers a summary profile of each team:

- Texaron Sales is an ongoing sales and marketing team that formed as an outgrowth of the company's increasing international sales in the textile industry. The team is composed of thirty-one members spanning twenty-two countries who adopted a sales technology application for the primary task of recording and tracking customer sales.
- Texaron Technology is an ongoing information technology team in the textile industry that formed for the strategic and operational task of standardizing and coordinating the company's information technology infrastructure as a result of overseas plant acquisitions and a domestic plant fire disaster, which temporarily forced production overseas. The team has twenty members spanning five countries, and members are divided into two subteams: one focusing on strategic managerial tasks and one performing operational activities. The

team meets quarterly in face-to-face meetings supplemented with audio- and videoconferencing, e-mail, and application-sharing technology.

• ASC NewBiz is an ongoing product and development team in the automotive components industry whose task is securing new business development with a key client, JapanCo, from proposal, through prototype development and testing, to production hand-off. The team is composed of seven members spanning two countries and uses audio- and videoconferencing, e-mail, and application-sharing technology.

• Ramtech was a two-month project task force team in the telecommunications industry whose challenge was to evaluate the viability of a specific software package for global implementation across the company and client network. The team had ten members spanning six countries. They began work with a one-week face-to-face immersion orientation and training, followed by six weeks of audioconferencing and e-mail communication, and concluded with working together face-to-face for one week to prepare the final report and present it to senior management.

• Celestial is an ongoing sales and marketing team in the consumer goods industry. The team was created as a result of a corporate reorganization to support global clients, and the team's task was to create a global sales and marketing strategy. Celestial is composed of twenty members spanning five countries. The team uses audio- and videoconferencing, e-mail, and application-sharing technology.

• HTM-TP8 was a two-year product development team in the computer industry tasked with fixing a flawed software system that was resulting in an inordinate number of customer complaints. Its six members, spanning two countries, used quarterly face to face meetings supplemented by weekly audioconference calls, fax, and e-mail.

THE IMPACT OF CONTEXT ON TECHNOLOGY

One of the most distinctive features of GVTs is context, defined as a way of life and work in a specific geographical area with its own set of business conditions, cultural assumptions, and unique history (see Chapter Sixteen, this volume). A major challenge for GVTs is to work across multiple contexts. Colocated teams, in contrast, take a single context for granted.

Contextual differences affect technology use and effectiveness in virtual teams in at least six ways: physical infrastructure, culture and language, accessibility of information, crossing time zones, team size, and maturity of the technology. The first step toward productive use of virtual technologies is developing an understanding of each team member's context. In this section, we explore

Table 11.1. Case Study Profiles

Profile	Ramtech	Celestial	HTM-TP8	Texaron Sales	Texaron Technology	ASC NewBiz
Industry	Telecommunications	Consumer goods	Computer	Textiles	Textiles	Automotive
Task	Global software rollout	Global product marketing	Global new product development	Sales reporting and coordination	Global information technology leadership	Product development
Number of members	10	20	6	31	17	7
Number of countries	6	5	2	22	4	2
Countries	Brazil, China, France, India, United Kingdom, United States	Argentina, Belgium, China, France, United States	France, United States	Argentina, Brazil, Brunei, Chile, China, Colombia, Ecuador, Hong Kong, India, Indonesia, Kuwait, Malaysia, Mexico, Peru, Philippines, Saudi Arabia, Singapore, South Korea, Taiwan, Thailand, United States, Venezuela	Japan, Germany, United Kingdom, United States	Japan, United States
Headquarters	United States	United States	France	United States	United States	United States
Number of time zones	14	12	8	10	14	9
Team duration	2 months	27 months, still ongoing	24 months	1 year, ongoing	7 years, ongoing	24 months

	3 months	15 months	7 months	5 months	5 months	3 months
Study duration						
Facilitator	Yes	Yes	Yes	No	Yes	No
Asynchronous technology						
E-mail	Used	Used	Used	Used	Used	Used
Voicemail	Used	Used	Used	Used	Used	Used
Fax	Used	Used	Used	Used	Unknown	Used
Express mail	Not used	Not used	Used	Used	Not used	Used
File sharing	Used	Used	Not used	Used	Used	Used
Web site	Used	Used	Not available	Not used	Not used	Not used
Synchronous technology						
Face-to-Face	Used	Used	Used	Used	Used	Used
Audio (phone)	Used	Used	Used	Used	Used	Used
Video	Not used	Used	Not used	Not used	Used	Used
Instant messaging	Not available	Not available	Not available	Unknown	Used	Not used
Application sharing	Not used	Used	Not available	Used	Used	Unknown

these six major ways that context has an impact on technology and ultimately a team's performance.

Physical Infrastructure

Context defines and determines the local physical infrastructure, that is, the basic utilities like power, telephone, and cable that make possible the communication technologies on which global virtual teams rely. Government policies and regulations, oversight, and economic development priorities determine the capacity, pricing, access, and standards of operation for information technology. Because each country establishes its own set of rules and standards, the variation in standards inevitably means incompatibility from country to country and a hurdle for GVT members to overcome. Two simple examples of infrastructure will illustrate how large an impact contextual differences in infrastructure can have on the ability of each GVT member to participate fully and equally in virtual collaboration: electrical power and the telephone.

Electrical Power. Not all geographical areas of the world are equal with respect to the reliability of electrical power. For GVTs, this means that individual team members may not be able to participate in or perform the work of the GVT to the same extent if their communication depends largely on electrical power sources with variable reliability. For example, for India and many other countries in Africa and Asia, hydroelectricity is a primary power source. During seasonal periods of drought, power is cycled on and off for hours or even days with little notice for long periods of the year. Sudden power losses mean loss of work and the time-consuming task of recreating it when it resumes. GVT team members living in other parts of the world may never experience such frequent outages and frustrations. Even if all members have identical equipment, the infrastructure of power, telephone, or cable may vary greatly and differentially affect an individual member's performance. In contrast, colocated teams generally would be affected by a loss of power at the same time and share in that condition equally with no explanation needed because the lights are out for all.

Differential power requirements even come into play when GVT members travel to another member's country for a face-to-face meeting. Travelers quickly learn that the electrical power requirements and outlets often do not match. A power conversion kit is an essential packing item for GVT members traveling to another member's country. However, even a plug conversion kit does not mean the power requirements are the same. France uses 220 volts, and the United States is standardized on 110 volts. An unaware HTM-TP8 member traveled from the United States to France and plugged in her laptop with a converter plug. It worked fine because the laptop's power supply automatically sensed the power difference and performed the power conversion, which was completely transparent to the team member. However, when the portable printer was plugged into the outlet using the plug adapter, a puff of smoke came out of the printer, and a burning smell quickly filled the room. The printer had been "fried" because it lacked an auto-sensing power unit to adjust to the difference in the power source. For the GVT team member, it meant loss of productivity and time, and for the company added cost to replace the printer. In contrast, colocated team members take for granted the electrical power supply, voltage, and plug outlet standards.

Telephone. As with electrical power, the context determines infrastructure. Telephone circuit reliability often varies by country, and the reliability may have a differential impact on GVT members' ability to use the telephone or to access the Internet to conduct their work. There are contextual differences in telephone cost and pricing structures as public and privately owned and operated telephone services set regulatory rates or tariffs for local and long-distance calls. A five-minute long-distance call may be several times more expensive or less expensive between callers simply by virtue of who initiated the call. Organizations can save money just by knowing who should call whom and when. In the United States, there is usually a fixed low rate for local calls no matter how long the caller stays on the line. This is not the case in many European countries, where charges are assessed by the minute and the rates are more expensive. Because of prohibitive costs, some team members may not be able to participate in audioconferences or engage in virtual collaboration using computers that require them to connect by telephone outside the office during nonstandard working hours—from home, for example. In colocated teams, these differences rarely surface because all are subject to the same regulatory rules and pricing within their context.

A good illustration of the impact of telephone infrastructure on technology use in a GVT can be found in the HTM-TP8 case. The HTM Company was headquartered in France, and the French government was the majority owner. The government also owns France Telecom, the telephone service provider, and GVT members were required by French law to use only France Telecom as their bridging service for audioconferencing. The service was sometimes difficult to reserve because of capacity limits, was not always convenient (because calling cards were required) for members who were not in their offices, and often varied in reliability. Team members complained that their calls were dropped in the middle of important discussions, and they had trouble reconnecting. Sometimes the rest of the team did not know a member was not present in the call or had missed large parts of the discussion until he or she was asked a direct question and did not respond. Comments also were sometimes out of sequence or did not relate to the content if members had been cut off. It always took the team a while to reorient their discussion after these technical difficulties occurred.

Culture and Language

Cultural differences regarding the role of technology in society and business affect preferences for technology use. Even if the infrastructure is in place and works reliably and people have access to it, communication technologies still may not be used by team members because differences in cultural norms and language lead to different media preferences and comfort levels with the technology. For example, consider cultural differences in expressing disagreements. In the ASC NewBiz case, a U.S. program manager thought it best to use e-mail for facts and figures but preferred videoconferences to work out the differences between the U.S. and Japanese team members in an open forum. This practice ignored the Japanese value for preservation of harmony in a group context and avoidance of open conflict. Videoconferences were actually the least preferred medium among Japanese team members for discussing and resolving disagreements. In contrast, another U.S. ASC project manager used one-on-one telephone calls with Japanese workers to air out disagreements in private conversations as a way to prevent potential embarrassment among team members and their bosses in videoconferences.

In another team, a U.S. member was wondering why it took his German counterpart so long to respond to e-mail and instant chat messages. He described the situation this way: "I fired off an e-mail message, and it took days for him to respond. In instant chat sessions, it just seemed like forever before I got a response back. I just couldn't figure it out." Later, during a debriefing discussion, clarification was offered. The German team member could speak English fairly well, but writing was considerably more difficult for him. To type in English meant he had to switch from the German keyboard layout on which he could type proficiently to an English keyboard, where many of the keys were in different places. He had to hunt and peck with two fingers to type a message. Furthermore, spelling and written sentence construction in English were a lot harder for him than just speaking, and he had no English spell checker. The U.S. team member had no idea his German counterpart needed more time to write in English and came to the inaccurate conclusion that his German counterpart was disinterested.

Often people using a second language in e-mail and chat need more time to respond or must simplify their vocabulary and sentence structure. The receiver, who is using his first language, may interpret the message incorrectly as an abrupt or rude response, as disinterest, or even as ignorance.

A Texaron Sales member stated how differences in language proficiency were a problem during audioconference calls involving the Americans, the British, and the German team members: "Language is a definite problem with virtual team meetings. Things get lost in the translation. U.S. speaks Southern American English, U.K. speaks British English, and the Germans try to listen and speak in a totally different language."

The lack of visual cues in an audioconference means that members cannot check for understanding and cannot know if everyone is following along in the agenda (that is, literally "on the same page") or even paying attention. This is especially disastrous during debates and discussion in conflict. The technology exacerbates a communication situation already made difficult by language barriers.

The ASC NewBiz case provides another example of the impact of culture and language on the use of collaboration technologies, even when the communication is primarily technical. The difficulties of effective communication using virtual technology in the light of the language difference between English and Japanese manifest themselves in a variety of ways. The ASC team used a specialized engineering software program to share files between Japan and the United States, but the software training manuals were written only in English; they were not available in Japanese. This meant that the Japanese engineers were required to do the additional, and tedious, work of translation before they could learn how to use a fundamental collaborative tool. Other difficulties arose when drawings given to JapanCo (ASC's client) needed to be done in kanji (Japanese text). Because the U.S. members could not produce the kanji text, they sent a file with English to the Japanese technical center. Their Japanese teammates transferred the file into their system, and that file was then transferred into the JapanCo system. Between transfers, sometimes text was inadvertently deleted and things would go amiss with the drawings, so the Japanese team members were sometimes put in an embarrassing situation when the file transfer contained errors and the drawings were not up to quality standards.

Accessibility of Information

Organizational differences in technical infrastructures can create incompatibilities that slow work or create varied access to technological resources among virtual team members, leading to frustration and delay. In the ASC NewBiz case, the engineering file-sharing system from Japan was slower and less reliable than in the United States, increasing the stress for Japanese team members because it took them more time to access the data needed to accomplish an identical task than it did their U.S. counterparts. Furthermore, there was a time when not every office had access to the file-sharing system for technical drawings, and some offices received their information by fax only.

In the Celestial case, the file-sharing system was also problematic. The system did not have a way to restrict access by suppliers who had relations with the firm's competitors. Consequently, the amount of information that could be posted for team sharing among team members was restricted for fear that a supplier would use the sales information with Celestial's competitor.

Other technology limits may arise in e-mail systems, especially in the broadcast of e-mail messages to groups of people simultaneously that can limit accessibility to data or restrict information sharing. E-mail distribution systems can limit the number of messages that can be broadcast to twenty-five or fewer recipients. Different local constraints, policies, or safeguards for e-mail can also be enacted as a result of previous technology failures or incidents. For example, e-mail file attachments with an extension of "exe" are commonly stripped off e-mail messages as they cross information technology security firewalls to prevent rogue viruses from damaging computer systems. Because of capacity or policy issues unique to the local context, small differences can lead to significant technology challenges for GVT members.

Crossing Time Zones

Working across multiple time zones creates a unique set of challenges for the use of collaborative technologies. Large time zone gaps often mean that many members of the team are required to work much earlier or later than the standard work hours. Consider a Celestial videoconference call among members in the U.S. Midwest, Hong Kong, and France. The U.S. facilitator needed to be in the office at 5:00 A.M. to participate in the call, not a convenient hour by anyone's expectations. When he arrived at work and went to the videoconference room, it was dark and the equipment was turned off, a situation the facilitator had not previously experienced because he had always done videoconferences during normal working hours, and a technician had already prepared the equipment. The meeting was scheduled to start in five minutes; he had no idea how to turn on all the equipment, and no one was in the office to call for help. He followed the power cords and began flipping switches. By the time he determined how to turn on the equipment, the meeting was already twenty minutes in progress. He knew how to operate the equipment but had never learned how to turn it on. Even experienced virtual team members can encounter unanticipated difficulties because time zone differences alter the availability or accessibility of services.

The ASC NewBiz case illustrates another typical example of the technical difficulties that can occur when teams work across time zones. One team member noted:

> The meeting was supposed to start at 4:00, but by the time we got dialed up and connected, it was 4:20. So that was a waste of time, and for the Japanese guys, 4:00 is 7:00 in the morning for them. And they usually don't come to work until 8:30, so they had to come in an hour and a half early and then sit around for twenty minutes while we tried to dial up. That was all a hassle. For us, it's staying late; nobody wants to stay late.

GVT work outside regular business hours may also mean that members are required to learn security settings and pass codes and be subject to building access and parking restrictions they would never need to know about if they were working during the normal workday. A final example makes this point clear. A GVT team scheduled a face-to-face meeting in a German corporate office, only to find that the meeting date fell on a German national holiday. The team had to get permission from the German Works Council to go to work and use the company's facility. The permission was granted only because no German workers would be attending the meeting and all the participants were non-Germans from other countries around the world.

Large time zone differences can lead team members to rely more on asynchronous communication technologies such as e-mail, voice mail, fax, shared drives, or even overnight express mail than they do on synchronous technologies such as telephone, audio- and videoconferences, instant chat, and text messaging. The overlap of normal business hours diminishes as the time zone gap increases among members. Consequently, the time available for convenient and available synchronous communication diminishes. In addition, key support personnel, from technicians to administrative support people, are often less likely to be available to troubleshoot technical issues, help the teams with meeting facilitation, or take meeting notes when off-hour work is conducted. Labor laws and union contracts governing working hours in local contexts and working conditions for overtime pay also need to be reviewed carefully to avoid grievances and noncompliance with bargained agreements.

Team Size

The size of the GVT has a direct impact on the choice, complexity, and cost of communication technology. For example, Microsoft's collaboration tool Net Meeting is widely used for synchronous communication because of its audio, video, application-sharing, and text chat capabilities. However, beyond a threshold of seven simultaneous users, the connection breaks down; a more complex and elaborate hierarchical branching structure for synchronous computer-mediated collaboration needs to be implemented to accommodate teams of eight or more people.

Office telephone conferencing systems often allow three-way calls to be established but do not allow a fourth person or more to be added to a group conversation. Consequently, more costly specialty telephone services are contracted to bridge multiple GVT members into an audioconference. Members dial a toll-free number and provide a personal identification number or conference reference number to gain admittance to a conference call, which will have a telephone operator confirm participation and announce late arrivals.

Team size can also make audioconferencing problematic, even with a good bridging service that has the capacity to handle large numbers of participants. When the Texaron Sales team attempted audioconferencing with thirty participants, they found that they could not effectively manage the turn taking or focus the discussion well enough to keep people engaged or productive, even when the team members were just exchanging information. Team members would lose interest or become distracted when listening was all they could do, especially when there were no visual or other physical cues to keep them involved. There are production blocking effects when only one person can talk at a time (Valacich, Dennis, and Connolly, 1994).

Technology Maturity

Global virtual teams, whether they are just starting up or are already well into their work, are often quick to adopt new technologies as they become available in the marketplace because they believe the technologies will help them get off to a good start or because they are desperately seeking any new tool they think may help them collaborate more effectively across distance and time. However, new technology that the team is not skilled enough to implement well or that is not mature enough to have the bugs worked out may completely derail a team at the fragile formation stage of their work when members are not comfortable enough with each other to overcome the obstacles the technology presents. The introduction of new technology can also shift the team's energy from enthusiasm and optimism to disappointment and pessimism if the technology does not meet expectations, and the team is forced to revert to a less-than-optimal, but previously tried-and-true, technology.

The Celestial GVT had this experience with the rollout of new corporate virtual space capabilities for team collaboration. The team embraced the technology when it was introduced, but the technology's lack of security functionality to wall off company-sensitive documents from vendors who worked with competitive firms led to a practice of not sharing to avoid problems, resulting in the abandonment of the file-sharing resource.

Even with familiar hardware and software tools, there are inevitable upgrades, patches, service packs, and new version releases that periodically reduce efficiency and effectiveness and cause performance dips as teams work to maintain commonality and compatibility for even the most technologically sophisticated and smoothly operating GVTs. For instance, when companies roll out new versions of software programs, they often adopt a phased approach, which means team members in different locations may have incompatible versions of the software they are using to collaborate.

Working Through the Challenges

GVT performance is directly related to team members' ability to anticipate, articulate, solve, and work through and around the challenges that contextual differences pose for the conduct of work mediated by virtual technologies. Unlike colocated teams working in a single context, the GVTs have added integrating and coordination challenges that can range from more obvious differences in time zones and working hours, to the finer nuances of file size limits on e-mail attachments, to less controllable or manageable differences in technology infrastructure that must be explicitly negotiated and managed. GVT team leaders and members can begin by taking the following key point into account when they make technology decisions.

- Context can have an impact on a team's performance in many ways, large and small. Before directly tackling the team's task, take the time to understand the differences in context among members.

THE RELATIONSHIP OF THE NATURE OF THE TASKS AND TECHNOLOGY

The second major question we are exploring in this chapter addresses the issue of the relationship of the tasks undertaken by virtual teams and the information technologies they use to help them accomplish these tasks. To facilitate the discussion about task work in teams, it is useful to group tasks into a typology according to their complexity (Cohen and Bailey, 1997; Bell and Kozlowski, 2002). As shown in Figure 11.1, we can place task complexity on a continuum of four major dimensions: work flow, task environment, external coupling, and internal coupling.

Task Complexity Characteristics	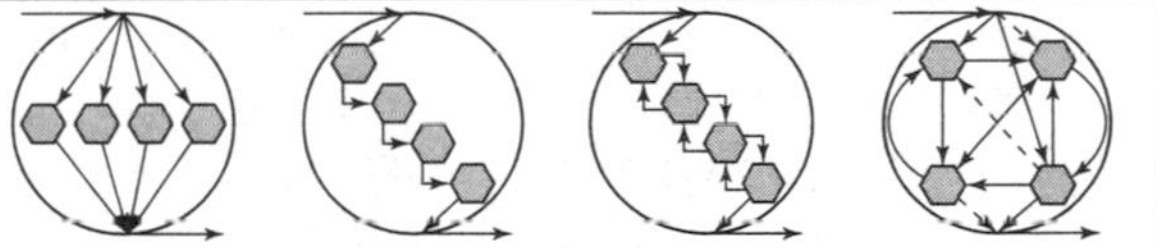			
Work flow interdependence	Pooled	Sequential	Reciprocal	Intensive
Task environment	Static	————————		Dynamic
External coupling	Loose	————————		Tight
Internal coupling	Weak	————————		Strong
Task complexity	**Low**	◄———————►		**High**

Figure 11.1 Task Complexity Typology.
Source: Bell and Kozlowski (2002, p. 20).

Work flow can be characterized by four arrangements according to how a team structures its activities (Van de Ven, Delbecq, and Koenig, 1976; Bell and Kozlowski, 2002):

- A *pooled or additive* structure in which work and activities are performed separately by all team members and then combined into a finished product
- A *sequential* structure in which work and activities flow unidirectionally from one member to the next
- A *reciprocal* structure with work and activities flowing back and forth between members over time
- An *intense* structure, the most interdependent, in which team members must diagnose, problem solve, or collaborate simultaneously as a team to accomplish their task

The task environment varies along a continuum from static to dynamic. A static environment is generally predictable and stable. It does not require much monitoring because it is unlikely to disrupt team tasks. A team's task environment can be quite dynamic, with many uncertainties that have to be monitored and new information that has to be digested very quickly. The failure of a team in a dynamic environment to detect a change in the environment can have a great effect on its ability to accomplish their task.

External coupling and internal coupling, the two remaining dimensions of task complexity, describe the team's relationships: the relationship between the team and its task environment and the relationship among the members in the team. A team's external coupling varies on a continuum from loose to tight depending on whether its activities are greatly affected by what goes on in its task environment, tightly coupled teams being the most affected. Internal coupling varies from weak to strong. Strong coupling means team members are highly interdependent in their tasks.

If we bring these four dimensions together, we can type teams according to the complexity of their tasks. Teams with low task complexity are generally in a static environment, loosely coupled to that environment, and have fairly low interdependence or internal coupling. These teams require only minimal information sharing or collaboration among team members, which usually means they have a pooled or sequential work flow. For example, a team with low complexity might be engaged in a fairly routine and predictable operation, such as fulfilling reporting requirements for a regulatory agency. As long as everyone is working independently on gathering their data and delivers their part of the report, the overall task can be completed smoothly, with little collaboration required among the team members. In a team with high task complexity, the environment is likely to be quite dynamic, the team will be tightly coupled to that environment, and the members will be highly interdependent with one another, requiring greater levels of information sharing and real-time collaboration. Teams with high-complexity tasks are usually characterized by reciprocal or intensive work flow arrangements. An example of this type of team might be a high-technology team in which product innovations and new competitors enter the marketplace daily, and the pace of work is rapid and highly interdependent.

The nature of the dominant task a GVT undertakes will set constraints on the team structure and process, including the use of information technology. The nature of team tasks creates demands that the team must resolve by structuring work flow arrangements appropriately (coordination, communication, and team processes) to meet the demands of the task, and by choosing information technologies that facilitate their work flow. The ability of a virtual team to operate effectively depends largely on the match between the task demands and the communication technology that the team uses (Straus and McGrath, 1994). If a task is very complex and requires a great deal of information exchange and coordinated effort, reciprocal communication and feedback are essential to performance, and synchronous technologies, such as videoconferencing or groupware, will be a superior choice for tasks requiring such a high level of collaboration. For less complex tasks that are essentially independent, such as idea generation, asynchronous communication media such as e-mail and Web-based discussion forums are often better choices.

Figure 11.2 indicates the placement of each of the teams in our study on the continuum of overall task complexity from low to high and on its four dimensions. The Texaron Sales team is the only one of the teams whose task can be characterized as low complexity. It used asynchronous technologies, a shared sales database and e-mail, as the primary information technologies to pool the work of the regional sales representatives and create a global sales picture. Sometimes they used express mail, another asynchronous technology, to send product samples to one another. Only in small regional groups did the team use a synchronous application sharing and chat technology to share information. An annual face-to-face meeting served the purpose of building camaraderie in the global sales team and providing education and training.

The other five teams had tasks that fell toward the high-complexity end of the continuum. Their task environments were dynamic and their work flows reciprocal or intensive, requiring team members to collaborate much more closely with one another to share information about and make sense of their fluctuating task environments. Team members needed to problem solve together so they could decide on appropriate action and move forward on their tasks.

Team Task Complexity	Dominant Work Flow	Task Environment	External Coupling	Internal Coupling
Texaron Sales Low X ___ High	Pooled-sequential	Static X ___ Dynamic	Loose X ___ Tight	Weak X ___ Strong
Texaron Technology Low X ___ High	Reciprocal-intensive	Static ___ X Dynamic	Loose ___ X ___ Tight	Weak X ___ Strong
Ramtech Low ___ X High	Reciprocal-intensive	Static ___ X Dynamic	Loose ___ X Tight	Weak ___ X Strong
HTM-TP8 Low ___ X High	Reciprocal-intensive	Static ___ X Dynamic	Loose ___ X Tight	Weak ___ X Strong
Celestial Low ___ X High	Reciprocal-intensive	Static ___ X Dynamic	Loose ___ X Tight	Weak ___ X Strong
ASC NewBiz Low ___ X High	Reciprocal-intensive	Static ___ X Dynamic	Loose ___ X Tight	Weak ___ X Strong

Figure 11.2 Illustration of Task Complexity Typology in Global Virtual Teams.

Texaron Technology, Ramtech, HTM-TP8, Celestial, and ASC NewBiz all relied on one or more synchronous communication technologies, such as audio- and videoconferencing, and application sharing, as well as face-to-face meetings, to work interdependently and in real time as often as possible.

Key Points

Research has shown a direct relationship between task complexity and the nature of a team's communication. Higher task complexity requires more synchronous, tightly coupled interaction than low task complexity, which leads to the need for technologies that can provide the team with opportunities for real-time collaboration. Some general rules of thumb can serve as initial guidelines to help teams match communication technology with their tasks. However, as we will discuss, teams need to consider more than these generalizations to make appropriate technology choices for their particular circumstances.

THE ROLE OF TECHNOLOGY IN THE DEVELOPMENT OF VIRTUAL TEAMS

A complete understanding of the role that technology plays in a global virtual team requires an understanding of how, as teams develop over time, technology needs also change and are affected by context as well as the nature of the task. In some cases, what might even appear to be an appropriate technology choice, if a team bases that choice on the nature of the team's task alone, may in fact turn out to be the wrong choice for the team when context is taken into account. It is not a simple "if x, then y" choice; it depends on the changing nature of the task in context. A closer examination of each of the six cases makes it clearer how technology changes as the nature of the task changes and how context exerts influence as teams develop over time. Many of the teams also used a cluster of technologies to respond to constraints imposed by their contexts.

Texaron Sales

International demand for textiles created overseas international outposts with a sales representative in each. When Texaron Sales was formed to respond to this demand, the team was small, and weekly audioconference calls between the overseas sales representatives and the company U.S. headquarters, along with quarterly, rotating face-to-face meetings, worked well to share sales data and help the remote sales representatives stay connected. Sales and marketing professionals, as an occupational cultural group, generally prefer face-to-face or personal contact to build relationships. This predisposition was partially responsible for the selection of telephone and face-to-face interaction for the team's communication, although an asynchronous medium would probably have suited the nature of their work flow arrangement better.

Over time, the number of Texaron sales representatives grew to the point that synchronous audioconference calls became impractical to schedule, and the cost of quarterly face-to-face meetings became prohibitively expensive. The synchronous technology of audioconference calls and face-to-face meetings had reached a limit for the growing team size and spreading geographical distribution. The environment had changed as well, with global customers wanting global accounting services. A shared sales database, which could be accessed asynchronously by each sales representative, addressed the needs of this larger, more dispersed sales team, as well as their customer reporting requirements. The new technology, which standardized the capturing and logging of sales information, provided clear advantages over previous practices. The technology served as an easy and convenient mechanism to stay in touch with each other despite the time zone differences, as well as a means to obtain the most up-to-date sales information and organize the group in a standard reporting format. Daily use of the sales reporting technology established a habit-forming practice quickly. A team member commented, "I think we're a little more intent on this technology than most other people in our company. There is nothing magic about us. It really has to do with the way we do business. If I'm doing business twelve hours away or if a sales team member is twelve hours away, I have to depend on this technology."

The sales reporting technology made a noticeable positive difference in managing sales through increased uniformity of sales reporting, updating accounts, and shaping the team's quarterly business review meetings, as well as providing additional value for their customers. A Texaron Sales team member explained:

> Before this sales technology, each person would do it differently. Now we have one standard process and one standard methodology that everybody uses. Before, it was very difficult to share all the information. What happens if the person was fired, promoted, or transferred out of the business? There's no paper trail. That paper trail has been a huge form of communication not just internally but to our customers as well.

The Texaron Sales team made an initial technology choice based on their culturally based work practices, a choice that may not have been ideally suited to their task but matched their preferred communication style and served their information needs for a time. When their task environment changed and team size made their initial choice no longer viable, they adopted an asynchronous technology that actually better matched the task and the team needs. They continued to satisfy their need for personal contact by meeting yearly in a large team meeting, face-to-face, and adopting synchronous collaborative technologies for smaller regional meetings.

Texaron Technology

International sales growth drove the company to make overseas plant acquisitions to meet production demands. This external condition, combined with a home plant fire, became a signal for management to have tighter internal coupling of plant production and scheduling flexibility to meet production quotas. It became readily apparent that the U.S. and overseas plants were based on completely different and incompatible computer infrastructures. Quarterly rotating face-to-face meetings were established among seventeen key management and operations personnel from Germany, Japan, the United Kingdom, and the United States to plan for standardizing and coordinating technological infrastructures for the global enterprise. Over time, task complexity and increasing demands necessitated that these face-to-face sessions be supplemented with more communication and work between quarterly meetings. This pressure for increased communication resulted in the creation of "technology rooms" at major sites that had the capability for synchronous audio- and videoconferencing and application sharing. A subteam at the operation level was formed to handle more of the technical day-to-day work as prescribed by the strategy committee members.

The Texaron Technology team is an example of a team that began work in a relatively static or stable task environment. However, increasing globalization, and the corresponding demand for collaboration across contexts, made it evident that weakly coupled coordination was no longer appropriate. The team also became more aware of how tightly coupled they were with their environment. They needed to work more interdependently in production scheduling to serve their clients and dampen the effects of disasters and economic crises in specific global contexts. This case is a classic example of a change in task complexity and a corresponding change in communication technologies to match.

Ramtech

The Ramtech case illustrates how a team can consciously structure communication and information technologies to match the complexity of their task. The team had only two months to evaluate the extent of management commitment to the implementation of a software product for work process management across the company's global plant network. Their primary business challenge stemmed from the fact that there was a very uneven buy-in among senior managers for the system, even though more than $200 million had been invested in it already. The team had to consider competitors and business partners who were way ahead in the development of similar work process management systems and a previous attempt to develop a coordinated system that had failed miserably, leaving them with unhappy customers whose orders had not been filled properly or on time.

The Ramtech team was also part of a formal task force process that limited their life cycle to two months and dictated a face-to-face meeting at the start and conclusion of their project, with distributed work to continue between meetings. The face-to-face meetings allowed the team members to develop their strategy and work flow process and to deliver the results of their project to senior managers. The team made the most of this prescribed structure by using different communication technologies for specific tasks along the way. The face-to-face start and finish allowed for the necessary sense making to develop an initial understanding of their challenge, how each could contribute to solving the problem, and finally to the formation of a solution.

At start-up, the team chose the forms of technology they would use for their virtual meetings and how they would use these technologies to accomplish their task. The team knew that what they really had to do was make sense of their dynamic environment and determine how best to position the work process management system within that environment. This sense-making task was highly intensive and interactive, requiring a kind of give and take and argument that could most easily be accomplished face-to-face or, if that was not possible, through telephone conferences. For this reason, much of the important work of interpreting and synthesizing was accomplished between face-to-face meetings through weekly telephone conversations. Between telephone calls, the team members gathered information in their local contexts about, for example, historical customer events, market forces, the positions of corporate managers, and costs. They chose e-mail to set the agenda for their audioconferences and then to reinforce responsibilities agreed on during these conferences. They also used a Web site as a document repository to facilitate sharing and access asynchronously. Because the company provided a reliable and uniform infrastructure for audioconferencing and e-mailing, there were no technological obstacles to overcome, and the corporate culture had instilled common work practices, including the norm of "any time, any place" with respect to communication. The team did not try any new technologies because they had no time to learn them. In sum, the team chose an appropriate mix of technologies to match specific tasks that a corporate context facilitated.

HTM-TP8

The HTM-TP8 team exhibited similar patterns in technology use to Ramtech except the duration of the team was two years instead of two months. HTM-TP8 was commissioned by senior managers as a special task force to tackle the troubled introduction of a new software product. Like Ramtech, they began their work together with a one-week face-to-face immersion period and followed that session with regular biweekly audioconference calls, supplemented by e-mail and fax, to communicate between quarterly face-to-face meetings. However, unlike Ramtech, whose audioconference discussions included open task conflict and problem resolution, conflicts that developed in the TP8 audioconferences were generally resolved in private one-on-one conversations. This pattern of technology use developed because the French team members preferred face-to-face meetings or private conversations for problem solving and resolution of sensitive issues. One French team member stated, "I'm for teleconferences when the subject is very precise and about the activities of the core team, with the condition that there be a face-to-face meeting every two or three months. I think that during a teleconference, it is possible to exchange information, but you can't exchange more than that. And only rarely can you decide based on nothing but words."

For the French team members, audioconferences were a means only for sharing information, which could have been done asynchronously just as well. The French members framed the audioconferences as the primary mechanism for maintaining the team members' attention and focus, rather than for problem solving or sense making. The HTM-TP8 team made slower progress than the Ramtech team partly because they did not have the same time pressure but also because they really worked collaboratively only during their face-to-face meetings once a quarter.

Other contextual issues affected the team's technology use over time as well. The audio bridge service used to establish the conference calls frequently failed, with members forced to dial back in, but there was no alternative because the company was mandated to use the state-controlled telephone system to conduct business. The frequent failure of the audioconferencing system may also have contributed to the restricted use of a rich synchronous medium to simple information-sharing tasks. Time zones were not an issue, however, because audioconferences could be scheduled during overlapping working hours (eight hours being the largest time zone gap) for the most part, and the U.S. team members in the Phoenix office were willing to participate outside normal working hours if necessary since they often arrived for work at 7:00 A.M.

Celestial

The development of the Celestial team began with a group of sales and marketing professionals who were colocated in Paris, the headquarters for their French client. The team members were used to a face-to-face situation in which rich collaboration had served them and their client well. When a new strategy and a merger of their customer with one of its competitors forced reorganization and the formation of the Celestial global team, new members in the United States, Asia, and South America were added to the team.

At the beginning of the newly merged global team, everyone had access to a full suite of virtual teaming technologies, including a number of new intranet and video technologies; for example, a Web-based team center was launched to provide a virtual work space, and a PC-based Web camera pilot was also conducted. Although some team members did experiment with and use the tools, they were not used frequently and stopped being cost-effective. Instead, the majority of the team relied heavily on standard technologies that had long been available in the corporate environment, such as e-mail, but preferred to collaborate face-to-face whenever possible. The nature of the team's task and factors in the team's context interacted to influence the team's technology use.

The Celestial team had a complex task created by the merger and the global strategy: they needed to examine and consolidate competing marketing projects in different parts of the company, resolve overlapping job roles, and develop and implement a global marketing plan. The team believed colocation was the only way to accomplish their task and made colocation a team philosophy in its team transition direction document. The team did not believe that even a supposedly rich medium like video technology could serve their need for collaboration, especially since the team had many personality issues to sort out, as well as complex task work to do. In one instance when they tried videoconferencing, team members in Paris and Taiwan had difficulty sharing effectively what was happening in their contexts. In fact, it had the opposite effect, creating an emotional situation that resulted in an explosion that could not be resolved without one-on-one telephone calls following the videoconference.

French culture played a role in the rejection of even the rich synchronous virtual technologies, although they may have been suited to the task. One corporate technology expert characterized the team's use of technology as "so French." France has lagged behind the rest of Europe in the implementation of Internet-based technologies partly because of the general cultural preference for face-to-face communication in which much of the meaning is taken from nonverbal cues (Evans, 1998).

Infrastructure issues also inhibited the use of virtual technologies, especially the virtual work space. The very technology that was meant to create sharing resulted instead in no sharing when senior managers sent out e-mail messages threatening punishment for not "locking down data." There were often difficulties in obtaining technical support for the technology as well, especially in remote sites. The team center had bugs in the system that discouraged even those team members who did try to use it. There was no standardized process for obtaining technical support and almost no support available in remote sites because the information technology experts assigned to the team did not have this assignment as part of their duties. NetMeeting, which the team did use occasionally, presented hurdles due to incompatible versions.

A change in the team's task after about six months of global collaboration led to a change in how the team used virtual technology, which actually produced a better match between task and technology than at start-up. The task became less complex, reducing the need for synchronous collaboration, when a drop in sales volume redirected the team's attention to regional sales. The team began to share information asynchronously in the team center, posting sales data and documents and conveying details about their local context.

ASC NewBiz

The ASC NewBiz team was launched to secure a contract for the manufacture of components for a vehicle that would be marketed in the Untied States, Japan, and Europe. The complexity of the task required strong interdependence between the U.S.-based team members and those located in Japan. Team members were familiar with videoconferencing technology and used it to collaborate. However, the pattern of technology use in the team reflects the constraints imposed by context and the counterintuitive solutions the team arrived at to address these constraints. If one considers task alone, it appears that videoconferencing would be the most appropriate choice for the team because the members were familiar with the technology and it facilitated the synchronous communication suited to the task. However, team members relied most heavily on e-mail to communicate with one another for two main reasons: the time zone difference and the language barrier. Because there was only a brief overlap at the end of the workday for the U.S. team members and the beginning of the next workday for their Japanese counterparts, e-mail was a more convenient way to share information and files and to ask questions that were not of an urgent nature. Moreover, given the language difference, sometimes even with complex issues, members preferred to broach a subject first through e-mail and then follow it up with a telephone call to ascertain understanding and discuss the matter. Alternatively, if a matter arose initially through a verbal exchange, especially if it was sensitive and might lead to conflict, a follow-up exchange would often occur through e-mail to verify understanding or pursue the matter. The design engineer for the NewBiz team summarized his e-mail use as follows:

> I'd always e-mail about the simple questions where I just needed a little detail, because I didn't want to take up time in a team meeting. The other thing I'd always e-mail was the complex ideas; for example, if I had a complex thought where I said, "Well if this and if that, but not this," I had to put it in e-mail because verbally we could never communicate because of the language barrier. But I can read in a foreign language and figure out finally what they're saying.

The reliability and capacity of e-mail had improved as well, to the point that team members had come to rely heavily on e-mail as the primary means of communication and file exchange in spite of the availability of other virtual technologies. Scheduled videoconferences were often cancelled due to holidays or other events. However, there were some tasks that could not be accomplished any other way. The occasional need to show members in the distant location a part or to put up a chart on the overhead for all to see made the videoconference the preferred way of meeting.

Key Points

It is not enough simply to match the complexity of a task with a particular type of technology. Although this matching is an important first step, the constraints imposed by context need to be considered to choose a suite of virtual technologies that will create conditions for effective virtual teams.

IMPLICATIONS FOR PRACTICE

There are no simple prescriptions for choosing the right technology for a global virtual team. However, to help practitioners choose a technology that will best fit their situation, considering both task and context, we offer in Table 11.2 a series of questions that help team members to think through the technology options available. Here, we provide a summary of best practices:

- Context has an impact on the reliability of the communication technologies on which members depend. Understand how the power, telephone, or cable services may affect an individual team member's participation in the team.

- Context develops local habits, which may differ significantly across members. Culturally derived work practices and language proficiency can affect technology preferences and its use.

- Security restrictions or circumstance may place constraints on team members' ability to share information.

- If a global virtual team spans more than six time zones, synchronous communication may be problematic.

- As teams grow in size, technology limitations may make some communication technologies impractical or inefficient.

- If technologies are new or still under development, allow sufficient time for unknowns.

- GVT teams need to match the degree of their task complexity to the appropriate asynchronous or synchronous technology, including face-to-face communication, to accomplish their work effectively.

- Asynchronous communication technologies are appropriate, and may even be the best choice, when tasks are low in complexity.

- Synchronous communication technologies are the most appropriate choice for complex tasks that require independent collaboration, such as sense making, problem solving, and decision making.

Table 11.2. Technology for Global Virtual Teams

Infrastructure

- Are there any large differences in local power, telephone, or cable infrastructures that will differentially affect a team member's performance? If so, who will be affected the most? How often? Are there predictable patterns of outages?
- What technology do members of the team have in common: e-mail, fax, file sharing, audioconferencing, videoconferencing, Internet access, or something else?
- What technology do members have access to outside the office?

Culture and Language

- How many different national and organizational cultures are represented on the team?
- What is the language proficiency of all team members?
- What are the local cultural, labor, or company rules about working at home or at the office on weekends or holidays?

Accessibility of Information

- Are there any special security restrictions or circumstances that might limit or exclude team members from accessing or sharing information (for example, suppliers, contract workers, managerial level)?

Time Zone Gap

- How many time zones do team members cross?
- If the number is greater than six, then what off-hour special logistical or technology access arrangements may team members need to make if they have to come to work earlier or stay later than usual? What can be done to ease the burden for people at the extremes of the time zone spread?

Team Size

- Given the size of the team, are there any special limits that might be exceeded (for example, distribution lists, file sizes, attachments, software or hardware licenses)?
- Are there any practical limitations, such as ability for everyone to participate, that also need to be considered?

Technology Maturity

- Given the communication technology that the team is planning to use, has the technology been thoroughly tested with other groups, or is this team among the first? If it is the first, can it afford the learning curve? What technical support is available to the team during normal business hours and off-hours if there are technical problems that need immediate resolution?

Task Complexity

- What is the degree of GVT task complexity? (See Figure 11.1.)
- Ask if the level of task complexity matches the technology the team is planning to use or is using already to accomplish its work?

(Continued)

Table 11.2. (Continued)

- In which direction are the four characteristics of task complexity moving along the continua? Will this shift the team's needs from asynchronous to synchronous technology as a medium for members to collaborate more in their work?
- Are there contextual constraints or preferences for technology that may make what would otherwise seem to be a good match between technology and task turn out to be an inappropriate choice for the team?

Note: Review these questions periodically, especially if there is a change in membership. Reprinted by permission of Sage Publications, Inc.

- Although sophisticated collaborative virtual technologies might be available, they may not be used because constraints imposed by context may have a greater influence on technology choices than task needs.
- Sometimes counterintuitive uses for technology turn out to be the best solution for a team.
- Face-to-face communication may be the best solution when task complexity and contextual complexity interact to create a formidable challenge to understanding and task completion. There is sometimes no alternative.

Note

1. See Chapter Sixteen, this volume, for a full description of the study and methods. Three of the cases we use in this chapter are provided detailed examples in that chapter to illustrate the development of teamwork over time. The three additional cases in this chapter are taken from the same study.

References

Bell, B. S., and Kozlowski, S.W.J. "A Typology of Virtual Teams: Implications for Effective Leadership." *Group and Organization Management*, 2002, *27*(1), 14–49.

Cohen, S. G., and Bailey, D. E. "What Makes Teams Work: Group Effectiveness Research from the Shop Floor to the Executive Suite." *Journal of Management*, 1997, *23*, 239–290.

Evans, D. S. "The Cultural Challenge of the Information Superhighway in France." *European Business Review*, 1998, *98*(1), 51–55.

Straus, S. G., and McGrath, J. E. "Does the Medium Matter? The Interaction of Task Type and Technology on Group Performance and Member Reactions." *Journal of Applied Psychology*, 1994, *79*, 87–97.

Valacich, J. S., Dennis, A. R., and Connolly, T. "Idea Generation in Computer-Based Groups: A New Ending to an Old Story." *Organizational Behavior and Human Decision Processes*, 1994, *57*, 448–467.

Van de Ven, A. H., Delbecq, A. L., and Koenig, R. "Determinants of Coordination Modes Within Organizations." *American Sociological Review*, 1976, *41*, 322–328.

Technology Alignment and Adaptation for Virtual Teams Involved in Unstructured Knowledge Work

Nelson King, Ann Majchrzak

Dozens of commercialized technology products exist to support collaboration in virtual teams. The first challenge that practitioners face is to understand how these technologies are related to the underlying work of these teams. This understanding can then serve as a filter for identifying candidate products. Key to this understanding is determining if teams are working in a routine manner or their activities involve distributed unstructured knowledge work, which is our focus. Such work is exemplified by teams tasked for new product development, strategic planning, business process reengineering, innovative problem solving, or organizational redesign, to mention a few.

This chapter shows through the use of a futuristic scenario that virtual teams involved in distributed unstructured knowledge work rely on a broad spectrum of technologies whose integration poses many challenges. It is more than making the technologies work together in a distributed computing environment. The nature of the work itself involves rapidly changing activities that often require different sets of technologies. The challenges can be overcome by understanding how distributed unstructured knowledge work unfolds and how the work interacts with technology. We focus more on understanding and overcoming the challenges of virtual teams than prescribing a set of products whose features become rapidly outdated.

We thank Cristina Gibson for her detailed suggestions for this chapter, as well as the comments of two anonymous reviewers to an earlier version of it.

A SCENARIO FOR DISTRIBUTED UNSTRUCTURED KNOWLEDGE WORK

Rapid advances in information technology make it possible to envision the future of virtual teams. Visualize the following scenario of a group of scientists, biologists, oceanographers, and biomedical engineers from different firms around the world. One is even sitting on a ship in the mid-Atlantic connected by satellite. A meeting is about to start, called by the chairman of a prominent biotech firm. Each of the participants has entered the virtual team Web site for this meeting, and their presence is indicated to the rest of the team. Although each participant is an employee of a different firm, they are all participating as part of a joint cooperative agreement among the firms. They take the opportunity before the meeting starts to review the on-line publications linked to the profiles of other team members. Just before the meeting starts, each member is notified of the updated agenda, which has just been placed in the team repository.

The chairman joins the meeting and explains that this team has been gathered to consider innovative products for combating multiple sclerosis. His idea was triggered by previous work that suggests that the phenomenon that makes ocean life buoyant in the water could be used in some way to identify drugs to combat this disease. Once the chairman is present, the audioconference is activated and a desktop camera broadcasts video of the chairman. A white board display is also activated. The meeting proceeds as follows:

> PETER [the chairman]: I'd like to start by describing an idea that I am drawing on the whiteboard. I remember a few years ago that something like this was done to deal with gravity issues on the International Space Station. Computer, can you find the notes of that meeting?

> COMPUTER: I'm sorry, Peter, but you haven't given me permission to search your personal space behind your corporate firewall.

> PETER: Okay; you now have permission. Computer, when you find something, make it available to the rest of the team.

> COMPUTER: According to my content-based search, there was a speech you gave in June 2004 in which astronauts were required to take various doses of the drug jifipin prior to take-off to test its effect on muscular breakdown in space.

> PETER: Not that exactly, but I think it occurred a little later than that.

> COMPUTER: Are you referring to . . .

> PETER: Yes, that's it. What happened?

> COMPUTER: The results were . . .

XIE: Are you suggesting that if we use a similar compound, this might relieve some of the symptoms of multiple sclerosis?

FRANCIS: It may be possible to draw parallels to the means in which fish stay buoyant in the water. Peter, I am marking up your sketch on the white board. We know that the following chemicals are involved, and we think they should work this way.

JORGE: I'm looking at my human genome database as we speak, and I'm finding some possible areas to examine. I have taken control of the video feed, so a DNA sequence should be visible on your screen. I think Patty might be able to help with this. I'll see if she is monitoring our DNA chatroom.

[The meeting continues and then wraps up.]

PETER: Let's summarize what has been discussed. Computer, can you list the alternatives that were suggested?

COMPUTER: According to transcripts of this audioconference, there were six alternatives, and two of these were discarded.

PETER: That matches my notes in entry 62. How about action items?

COMPUTER: I've created four action item entries: one for Xie and three for Jorge. There were also three issues left on the table, so the disposition of these items is unknown.

PETER: Okay. I'll turn these ideas over to all of you. Please take advantage of this virtual meeting capability, and report back to me in a month on your assessment.

Most of the technologies represented in this scenario exist today. Yet people continue to travel to meetings such as these—travel that narrows the number of participants, limits contribution to meetings, removes individuals from their home organization and desktop tools, and rarely incorporates active knowledge capture and search. In the next section, we describe key characteristics of unstructured knowledge work that makes the kind of sociotechnical support illustrated in this hypothetical scenario so difficult.

CHARACTERISTICS OF DISTRIBUTED UNSTRUCTURED KNOWLEDGE WORK IN VIRTUAL TEAMS

Teams engaged in new product development, research and development, strategic planning, software design, and organizational design are engaged in unstructured knowledge work. Teams in which the work involves different departments or organizations are engaged in distributed unstructured knowledge work (UKW). Such teams share several characteristics:

- Diverse computing environments (team members rarely use the same computing platform)
- Multiple domains of expertise (team members rarely share the same disciplinary knowledge)
- Spontaneity (knowledge develops unexpectedly)
- Transience (knowledge changes over time)
- Knowledge-sharing policies (how control is exercised)
- Encoding for sharing (preparing and labeling)
- Differences in knowledge reuse priorities between teams and the firm (immediate needs of each differ)

Diverse Computing Environment

When the team is distributed among various firms, technologies that make up one firm's communications and computing infrastructure are likely to be different from another firm's. Network protocols in one company may be configured differently from and incompatibly with another firm's network. Firewalls and security configurations may block communication with each other. Files for sharing may be stored on incompatible document management systems. Calendaring and e-mail products are often incompatible. Even computer technologies (CTs) from the same vendor may not be interoperable due to customization and configuration choices. Computing environments also can vary among locations within the same organization. Each department may have different document management and e-mail products. Some may insist on using Macintosh even if everyone else uses Windows operating systems. Some locations may be using older operating systems and office productivity software that is not compatible with newer versions. Variations in browser programming languages such as JavaScript can result in functionality being implemented in a slightly different manner between Netscape Navigator and Microsoft Internet Explorer.

The capacity and quality of a firm's infrastructure for communications also vary from firm to firm. These include intranet and extranet network capacity and traditional voice capabilities. Multipoint videoconferencing has high-bandwidth demands. The Internet cannot provide the necessary quality of service, and many firms limit traffic to the Internet due to the cost of Internet service providers. Private networks can be established among firms that provide the necessary bandwidth and quality of service; however, the cost of setting up these networks would be high, especially for short-lived projects like that described in the scenario. The cost of network bandwidth is likely to limit the use of virtual team tools that require high real-time bandwidth such as video- and audioconferencing. Audioconferencing conducted over a network may have too much jitter (missing data) and latency (delay) to maintain voice quality. Participants may sound as if they are on a cell phone with a poor connection. Desktop videoconferencing may not be possible in locations with insufficient bandwidth. Even if a network has sufficient bandwidth, jitter and latency may cause the picture to break up.

In addition to differences in infrastructure among firms, there are likely to be variations among team members in the formats and protocols for storing content in repositories that members of a virtual team use. Each member is likely to have knowledge in an electronic format best suited for his or her own use, limiting use by others. Suitability and efficiency of storing content influence their choices of how to organize their repositories.

Business units within a firm may also influence the choice of repository. Few firms have enterprisewide repositories suitable for all knowledge formats that exist within the firm. The existence of disparate repositories means that content varies in format and type of repository. The repositories that store content might be a document management tool, relational database, Lotus Notes database, or shared folder. These repositories have different mechanisms for access control and incorporating meta-data to encode each piece of knowledge. Someone looking for knowledge must know how to identify content (that is, how it is encoded) and how to work with the format of the content (that is, Word file or database record).

Products relying on communication and data protocols, such as for virtual meetings, are also a source of interoperability challenges. An example of interoperability is the group calendar feature of many virtual team products in which a member of the virtual team is enabled to schedule meetings based on the free time of other members. However, calendaring from a virtual team product is generally not integrated with the calendaring product used in a corporate infrastructure because the virtual team may cross organizational boundaries and the calendaring product selected by the team will be influenced by members familiar with other products. So a virtual team member who also has other responsibilities within a corporation must check at least two calendars. In addition, meeting times from one calendar have to be manually transferred to other calendars so that a member's free time is known. Standards for protocols do not ensure interoperability because vendors implement them in slightly different ways and products may require particular versions of a product to function properly (Central Intelligence Agency, 2000).

These variations in infrastructure and disparate repositories create complexities for virtual team support. Organizations providing support for virtual teams must have strong troubleshooting skills and experience in diverse computing environments. Testing in advance is also necessary because products from different vendors will be encountered in interfirm virtual teams. Sometimes it may be necessary to create and deploy a common computing environment across all of the firms involved in a virtual team so that interoperability around a core set of CTs is available.

Participation from Multiple Domains of Expertise

A second characteristic of UKW is that knowledge is distributed among multiple parties in a geographical, organizational, and disciplinary sense. A critical feature of knowledge work is that it requires the synthesis of multidisciplinary expertise and mutual learning in order to identify new solutions creatively (Dougherty, 1992). The resultant differences in education, background, experiences, and language make the team productive.

Multiple domains of knowledge also result in a multiplicity of interpretations; from these interpretations emerge new categories, constructs, and abstractions (Boland, Tenkasi, and Te'eni, 1994). One example from the new product development literature is the difficulty that engineering and marketing encounter to identify customer needs (Workman, 1995). What might be relevant to engineering may not be relevant to marketing. Even within engineering disciplines, there are multiple views of the same geometric representation of a product (King and Majchrzak, 1996).

In addition to a multiplicity of interpretations, multiple domains of knowledge result in a need to appreciate and reinterpret the underdeveloped context of each team member. Team members hold tacit knowledge unavailable to others, so context must be articulated for sharing to take place. Members from separate domains have their unique understandings and specialized knowledge base that must be employed while interacting and learning from each other to find new insights (Tenkasi and Boland, 1996). As a result, members of virtual teams need to better identify, discuss, and elaborate on their understanding of their own and others' context (Boland, Tenkasi, and Te'eni, 1994). However, representing context requires rich communication capabilities used during the process of constructing interpretations and exchanging those representations in dialogue with others (Boland, Tenkasi, and Te'eni, 1994; de Jong and others, 1998).

In addition to the ability to share interpretations, team members must eventually be able to integrate these different interpretations. Metaphors are often used to find a common language understandable to all domains (Majchrzak and others, 2000). The team will also need to develop its own vocabulary. For example, content can be located by entry number assigned by the repository rather than by the subject of the content (for example, "Entry 363" means "evaluation matrix for alternatives"). Groups involved in product innovation are also guided by visions that are often metaphorical and presented at a high level of abstraction (Leonard and Sensiper, 1998). These symbols have a specific interpretation to the team.

Including multiple domains of expertise results in virtual team technology that must allow an understanding to develop among members who share not only their different knowledge bases but also their different interpretations, context, and tacit knowledge and integrate them as well.

Spontaneity

A third characteristic of unstructured knowledge work is the spontaneity in which deviation from planned activities takes place. The first way in which spontaneity appears in UKW is the sequence of activities (Orr, 1996). Many tasks, such as design, have an iterative dimension (Thomas and Carroll, 1984). There are many situations for initiating a specific activity that deviates from the planned agenda (Markus, Majchrzak, and Gasser, 2001). This deviation can occur within a well-defined task. For example, Orr (1996) found that photocopier technicians often deviated from the stated process to get their job done. Deviation can also occur when broader tasks are ill defined or iterative in nature, such as product development. Many decisions made in organizations are made under ambiguity, causing the sequence of activities to unfold in unpredictable ways (Mintzberg, Raisinghani, and Theoret, 1976). For example, a team may discover an anomaly while reviewing detailed analysis. They may immediately begin brainstorming to identify the problem and then contemplate solutions. Once satisfied that a solution is possible, the team returns to continue discussing the analysis.

When the sequence of activities is spontaneous, the potential tools necessary to support the team will have to be used in an ad hoc manner. Work consists of trade-offs and deliberations, not procedures and decisions (Markus, Majchrzak, and Gasser, 2001; Pava, 1983). Different levels of collaboration are taking place so that "doing" and "talking" occur at the same time (Bardram, 1998). A discussion may begin verbally and move on to sketching when the speaker determines that the audience has not understood her oral description. When a technology embeds a structured process in carrying out a particular activity (Nunamaker, 1997), the spontaneous nature of activities means suspension of the process is needed so that another activity can take place (Lucas and Baroudi, 1994; Yap and Bjørn-Andersen, 1998). Ad hoc knowledge is transient and not known a priori. A design team may completely change its approach after seeing the results of stress analysis modeling. They might also choose to make a few minor adjustments but will not know until they see the results. CT developers should allow for improvisation and exceptions to standard procedures (Grudin, 1994). These people also have discretion over work methods, so no single tool is likely to be used exclusively for a particular activity (Markus, Majchrzak, and Gasser, 2001). Ease of use becomes critical because these tools are used infrequently, requiring just-in-time refresher training (Markus, Majchrzak, and Gasser, 2001).

In addition to an unpredictable sequence of activities and use of tools, participation by individuals is ad hoc. Participants in each step of the knowledge process are unknown in advance (Markus, Majchrzak, and Gasser, 2001). They may not be available due to other meetings or may choose not to attend based on the agenda but indicate they are available to attend when needed. Participants may also choose to make their contributions asynchronously.

The serendipity in this type of work suggests that technologies supporting virtual teams cannot impose a rigid sequence of activities on the work. Multiple paths and iterations must be easily added. In addition, the tools cannot be structured to assume the presence of any participant. For example, some work flow products allow roles rather than individuals to be assigned to a review or approval sequence. Anyone assigned a role can make the necessary approval so bottlenecks are minimized. Moreover, and paradoxically, technologies cannot be designed to assume they will even be used because knowledge workers have a whole range of approaches available to them that may use different combinations of tools. We encountered one CT that allowed scanned images to be placed in a repository. However, this feature was rarely used because fax machines were easier to use, especially when members of the team were away from their office.

Transience of Knowledge

Knowledge has a finite life. Results of a stress analysis test, for example, can invalidate some previous work or all of it. Even a small adjustment to a design means stress analysis must be redone. Once the stress analysis results are seen, they become obsolete as new designs are proposed. The design details have also changed with the adjustments. Hence, any effort to document intermediate results is subject to rapid obsolescence. When virtual teams are involved in unstructured knowledge work, transience of knowledge becomes an important productivity consideration. Majchrzak and others (2000) found that team members were less likely to capture their work when knowledge was transient. In such teams, knowledge changes over time as specific knowledge grows and is integrated with other knowledge (Markus, Majchrzak, and Gasser, 2001). Two characteristics of knowledge contribute to its transience.

The first characteristic is the relevance of the knowledge content compared with the cost of capture, encoding, and preservation. There is a cost to preserving content such as by taking the time to articulate rationale, transcribe videotapes, and update sketches. Thus, if the cost of capture is higher than the likely benefit of preservation, the knowledge becomes transient. The trade-off is illustrated with a product design example. A designer places a scanned image of her sketch in the team's document repository. A structural engineer points out a design flaw. Before she can make the change, a new design approach is suggested that requires a new sketch. Does the team annotate the original sketch to indicate the design flaw and the proposed remedy? The team members might if the original sketch has some utility in the future (for example, if the new idea has its own flaws). Do they take time to capture the change or work on the new idea?

There is also a cost to preserve content in such a way that it can be easily found later. Content must be categorized so others can find it. In order to find sketches by a key word search, key words such as *sketch 1* [of] *approach 1* [with] *structural flaw* [that has] *not been updated* might be necessary. Categorization is particularly difficult with transient knowledge because categories shift over time. For example, Majchrzak and others (2000) found that commonly used key words like *design* lost their value after several hundred entries were also called *design*. These costs of capture and categorization make the relevance-to-cost ratio particularly important to virtual teams. The relevance will change over time, and predicting key word usage in advance consumes valuable time with limited utility.

Knowledge may be transient not only because of its lack of relevance but because of the length of time that it needs to be preserved. Some knowledge that is captured may need to be preserved for substantial periods of time, such as in the defense sectors or for financial auditing and reporting. However, preservation of content may not be desired. For example, obsolete versions of a drawing without proper annotations in a design environment create confusion, especially when discovered by a new member to the team who is reviewing the earlier work. Yet prematurely discarding or not even capturing knowledge may be costly as team members search for lost content that had existed earlier.

The transience of knowledge therefore suggests that technology to support virtual teams cannot assume that preservation of knowledge is either appropriate or preferred. Thus, features that promote rapid capture, categorization, and discarding of knowledge are needed.

Knowledge Sharing

Once content has the potential for leaving the confines of a team or individual, control becomes necessary. A central issue underlying control is the fear of misuse, miscommunication, and misinterpretation. For example, given that corporate records can be used in court cases, some companies are afraid of capturing any knowledge related to product or service liability, because if they did not act on the knowledge, it can be used against them (the Explorer's problem for Ford is a case in point). There are also secondary issues. Knowledge contributors are often curious about who uses their knowledge so that new additions to a community of practice, such as an informal group of like-minded collaborators, can be identified.

These issues contribute to the need for features that control use of content. The purpose of capturing knowledge is to make it available to others. The technological implication is that knowing who is interested in content is as important as keeping it away from others. Simple access control methods are not enough. Creators of content need to be notified when someone has shown interest or used content. Knowledge creators want to provide necessary caveats and context to those who will use the information. For example, a virtual team wanted management to see only content suitable for them by using the key word *management review* (Majchrzak and others, 2000). However, the repository did not prevent management from looking elsewhere and incorrectly interpreting entries containing results from incomplete analyses.

Encoding for Sharing

When expertise is shared by passing information in a personalized exchange, whether face-to-face or by telephone or e-mail, cues and language are encoded so that the expert's content is put in an appropriate context. A designer may be unsure of a particular parameter and provides only a best guess to a trusted colleague. Information that is to be shared must be properly coded for the context of use.

Codification of context is difficult because it requires encapsulating content with sufficient context so that other members with different perspectives can make a proper interpretation. In one example of a virtual team, an entry in the team's repository contained analysis results showing the thermal effect overlaid on the structural strength of a design concept. Although this entry reflected collaboration among structural, materials, and thermal engineers, the interpretations of the results by each engineer were different: the materials engineer concluded that more cooling was necessary, while the thermal engineer concluded that stronger material was required (Majchrzak and others, 2000). Whose interpretation should be used to characterize the entry?

Assuming context and content are adequately codified, it may not be adequately categorized. Key word hierarchies coupled with text search capabilities made available by most repositories produce incomplete results. If search results are poor, team members have less incentive to search for content and classify entries with fewer key words (Majchrzak and others, 2000). They come to rely on alternative means of identification such as sorting entries by creation date. Recent entries can be located, but earlier work that might be applicable may be overlooked. Therefore, technologies that support virtual teams engaged in unstructured knowledge work must not expect participants to adhere to a predetermined categorization scheme or even to categorize their own entries. A team should have the option to develop its own categories that facilitate its own information exchange. In addition, technologies that search text and images within entries and documents need to be provided.

Differences in Sharing Knowledge Between Team and Firm

The final characteristic of virtual teams for unstructured knowledge work that should be considered for technological support is how much and which knowledge is sufficient for the team to use versus which knowledge should be made available to the firm for use by future teams (Markus, 2001). This expectation of whether reuse is by the team itself or individuals in the firm at large determines the type of encoding that is necessary. For example, if knowledge is to be used only by team members, context can remain tacit. Knowledge to be used outside the team requires much more significant codification.

How team members act on knowledge depends on whether the knowledge is held by the team or in a firm-level repository. When knowledge is generated and maintained by the team for its own use, members are likely to act on the shared content that represents this knowledge. Their membership on the team invites them to contribute from their personal knowledge base by making comments or adding information. In contrast, when knowledge is obtained or derived from a firmwide knowledge base, the team member is searching for knowledge rather than contributing knowledge. A team must be motivated to search a repository, for example, by being convinced of the quality or utility of knowledge in the repository or receiving incentives to do so. The expectation that knowledge in a firmwide setting in databases and repositories is ready to use when it becomes available presumes that individuals throughout the firm have a reason to act on the content.

Finally, the team's taxonomy may not be generalizable to a firmwide taxonomy. The team seeks to find a taxonomy to categorize content that reflects their work and facilitates communication with each other. When new ideas are being synthesized, there may be no suitable terms in a firm's taxonomy. There are also numerous differences in categorization schemes brought by members from different disciplines and different firms (Bowker and Star, 1999). A team taxonomy must reconcile these differences. The chasm between team and firm knowledge grows wider because the team taxonomy may depart from what exists and mapping is now required between them.

Therefore, technologies that support virtual teams engaged in unstructured knowledge work must reflect differences in team and firm knowledge reuse needs. When action is desired on an item in a knowledge base, allowable actions must be evident to team members. An entry allowing for multiple authors and notification when changes are made invites participation, while restricting use to read-only does not. Knowledge developed by a virtual team requires additional encoding to make it available to the firm.

Challenges Created by Unstructured Knowledge Work

The characteristics of UKW in the context of virtual teams discussed previously are grouped in Table 12.1 by their underlying characteristics. These characteristics are not mutually exclusive but grouped for the purpose of summarization. Technological challenges result primarily from interoperability issues related to information technology infrastructures and disparate repositories. Similarly, multiple domains of expertise pose user interface and repository integration challenges to contextualize knowledge according to the viewpoint of a user. Organizations are greatly affected by the nature of sharing, raising such issues as control, cost of encoding knowledge, and getting individuals and teams to interact with knowledge beyond their own interests. Finally, inherent in the knowledge management problem is the spontaneity and transience of the knowledge, which complicates decisions on what is shared and how it is shared.

To overcome these complexities, a wide range of functional requirements is suggested. We turn to how these needed functional requirements are currently being served.

Table 12.1. Characteristics of Unstructured Knowledge Work

Technological Challenge	Nature of Sharing	Nature of Knowledge
Diverse computing environment • Diverse information technology infrastructures • Disparate repositories Multiple domains of expertise • Multiple views and interpretations • Representing and appreciating individuals' tacit knowledge and context • Need to create common language and team context	Sharing requires control • Fear of misuse • Interest in its use • Permission Sharing requires encoding knowledge • Effort required to encode knowledge • Search limitations • Complexity of categorization Differences in sharing knowledge between team and firm • Expectation for reusing knowledge • Expectation for acting on shared content • Reconciling differences in taxonomies	Spontaneity • Ad hoc sequence of work activities • Ad hoc tool selection and adaptation • Ad hoc participation and serendipity Transience • Relevance changes over time • Longevity may be more or less important

TRADITIONAL FUNCTIONS OF TECHNOLOGIES SUPPORTING UNSTRUCTURED KNOWLEDGE WORK

The ideal set of technologies to support distributed unstructured knowledge work provides a virtual workplace and access to a firmwide knowledge base usable at the team level. The virtual workplace provides a repository that records the process of the group; electronic information sharing, such as through file sharing, e-mail, and electronic white boards; key words for each entry, such as for date and author; meta-information on the entries in the repository, such as context, conclusions, and glossaries of terms; and easy access and retrieval from the repository (Romano, Nunamaker, Briggs, and Vogel, 1998). In addition to the virtual workplace, there need to be facilities that allow access of knowledge throughout the firm by facilitating the access, creation, processing, storage, retrieval, distribution, and analysis of information across positional, physical, and temporal boundaries and allow the incorporation of members from other units and organizations with specific, otherwise difficult-to-obtain expertise (Lipnack and Stamps, 1997; Warkentin, Sayeed, and Hightower, 1997). There is no integrated package of these ideal technologies in current practice.

We argue that this is due to CT development that generally distinguishes between knowledge as object and knowledge as action (Blackler, 1993). Hansen, Nohria, and Tierney (1999) used a similar distinction when describing firms that emphasized the codification of knowledge (knowledge as object) versus firms emphasizing communication of knowledge (knowledge as action). These development viewpoints influence the features incorporated in a CT and result in a bifurcated view of virtual team support. Table 12.2 summarizes this argument in more detail.

Products That Treat Knowledge as Object

Knowledge that can be made explicit and stored in repositories so that it can later be retrieved and reused represents knowledge as object (Fahey and Prusak, 1998). The emphasis is on codifying knowledge. Many CTs that support knowledge management (KM) typically reinforce the paradigm of knowledge as object. Harris and Fenn (1999) of the Gartner Group identified ten functions needed to support KM: capture and store, search and retrieve, send critical information to individuals or groups, structure and navigate, share and collaborate, profile and personalize, synthesize, solve or recommend, integrate with existing business applications, and maintenance. The majority of these functions represent the knowledge-as-object view because of the emphasis on interacting with and managing a repository rather than on people and their interactions. Repositories for KM are typically described for use as integrated document management

Table 12.2. Technological Support of Knowledge as Object and Knowledge as Action

Characteristics of UKW	Knowledge as Object	Knowledge as Action
Diverse computing environment	Web-based portals increase interoperability of search and retrieval across disparate firm repositories	No agreement among market leaders on set of tools to provide; absence of integration with firm infrastructure (for example, hosted service)
Participation from multiple domains of expertise	Personalization features allow display of domains of interest	Tools (for example, discussion forum, chat, repository) are centered around team (or community of practice); members needing to draw on other domain resources must go outside and use other tools
Spontaneity of sequence, tools, and participation	Repositories target history of an activity, not activity as it progresses; document creation tools rather than collaboration; one-at-a-time rather than ad hoc authoring	Variety of synchronous and asynchronous features available for interaction; many features can be used in parallel (for example, chat while conference in progress)
Transience of knowledge	Emphasis on static content (for example, a document); create new version if knowledge changes	Synchronous tools (for example, conferencing and chat) allow high levels of transience through context; however, little support for rapid capture of frames and multimedia encoding or excerpting audio dialogue; repositories for later retrieval limited or nonexistent
Sharing requires control	Flexible access control to individual content objects across firm	Enrollment limited to team members; problematic when firmwide resources needed
Sharing requires encoding	Meta-data identify entry subject matter with few instances of contextual meta-data	Audio and visual channels encode dialogue, which allows sharing (but not encoding) context
Differences in sharing knowledge between team and firm	Support through the use of project areas within firmwide repositories	Virtual meeting products typically isolated from firm applications and repositories

(examples are FileNET, Documentum, OpenText) and more recently Web content management (for example, Interwoven, Vignette, BroadVision, Open Market, and ePrise). These tools strive for integration to the extent that all content—whether it be a scanned document, word processing file, or electronic form—is managed as discrete objects. These objects can then be submitted to a work flow tool such as an approval process. Similarly, Web pages consisting of multiple objects, including text and graphics, can be managed to ensure up-to-date content. These objects can then be approved for publication.

The knowledge-as-object view is based on captured content that is stored in a repository. There are products to enable the use of repositories. For example, portals are used to search and retrieve across disparate repositories. These portals and repositories are integrated with messaging products to send links identifying the location of content that is available for sharing. Repositories typically include facilities to structure content through use of meta-tags such as key words. Portals based on search technologies may also combine the structure of individual repositories to build an enterprisewide taxonomy that can be navigated by browsing.

Knowledge sharing in the knowledge-as-object view is content-centric. Objects need to be located from any repository and made available to others. Collaboration is focused on the object, such as allowing a threaded discussion regarding a particular document stored in a repository. For example, an author seeks comments on a rough draft of a report. A threaded discussion makes available all of the comments about this draft. Once objects are shared, it is possible to gather content from multiple sources for synthesizing, such as in data mining of structured knowledge objects. Results of the data mining may be encoded in a model to produce a solution or recommendation. Products also exist to profile and personalize unstructured objects that assist in aligning and grouping people into work and interest communities based on related objects. The numerous structures and data sources in a knowledge-as-object environment need to be kept current so products for electronic record management are employed.

Some functions from a knowledge-as-object view, shown in Table 12.2, address the characteristics of unstructured knowledge work identified previously. Portal products that can search and retrieve content across disparate repositories address the heterogeneity of computing environments. Portal personalization allows content to be presented in a structure familiar to a particular domain of expertise. Marketing has no interest in being updated on the latest engineering studies except perhaps for a particular new product project. Personalization allows end user choice just as in consumer portals such as Yahoo!

Once content is captured, its transient nature is managed through version control and record management products that allow for periodic review of content. Access control for governing the sharing of content across an enterprise is provided in most repository products. These repository products also facilitate the encoding of content meta-data such as identifying authors, subject, and key words for identification of content. However, content meta-data do not normally encode the content itself as in explaining how it is to be used. Several repositories also allow teams to set up their own project areas within an enterprise repository rather than having a separate repository.

Products That Treat Knowledge as Action

In contrast to the knowledge-as-object view, the knowledge-as-action view emphasizes communicating knowledge. Knowledge is no longer static content with a well-understood context, but is instead situated or acted on; the interpretation of the knowledge is solely dependent on how and who acts on it. This view recognizes that knowledge is often distributed among many different individuals and groups. Interpersonal communication is the essential means of knowledge formation and use. People can work together in a synchronous or asynchronous manner. CTs that facilitate knowledge as action focus on helping virtual team members communicate with each other across distance and time. In one study of virtual meeting products (Central Intelligence Agency, 2000), a set of functions was elicited for conducting virtual meetings:

- Chat, which provides a low-bandwidth communication channel for individuals or groups during meetings. The analogy is one of note passing.
- White board sharing, which is analogous to standing up and drawing on a white board in the meeting room.
- Application sharing, which is analogous to having others look over your shoulder at your desktop computer.
- File sharing, which is analogous to passing out hard-copy materials.
- Audio sharing, which is analogous to participating in a meeting by speaker phone.
- Video sharing, which provides a camera's view of a meeting.
- Awareness, which is a function that indicates in a virtual setting the presence of other participants.
- Scheduling and meeting creation, which is a function conducted in the past by secretaries although available electronically within a firm.
- Restricting attendance, which is analogous to inviting selected persons.
- Session management, which is concerned with enabling participants to use the various tools available. For example, only one user can draw on a white board at a time, requiring control of the white board to be switched among users.

Products with a knowledge-as-action view address different characteristics of unstructured knowledge work, as summarized in Table 12.2. Spontaneity is supported especially when an assortment of adaptable tools is available. Capturing of knowledge can support the transience of knowledge as dialogue takes place. An audiotape of an audioconference can be made with transcription as necessary. A videotape or screen capture can be made of any drawing on a white board. However, real-time recording does not address the determination of knowledge relevance.

Collaboration products often control content by limiting enrollment to team members. Team members recognize this barrier and feel free to interact because they know who can listen to them or read what they have written. The barrier is less clear when collaboration takes place when integrated with firmwide resources. Firmwide repositories often use groups rather than a list of individuals for access control. The same individuals may be involved but now are called virtual team X rather than listed individually. Furthermore, in order to promote sharing, access to content might be set to groups such as "all employees" or "anyone in engineering." Team members may be more inhibited when they realize that others outside the team can see what they have done in the present or sometime in the future.

The synchronous nature of virtual meetings allows context to be encoded by a person speaking and drawing. However, once content is captured, much of this context is lost unless an audio and visual excerpt is attached to an object. Finally, most virtual meeting products are isolated from enterprise repositories so that conveying team knowledge in a format for the enterprise is avoided.

WHAT'S WRONG WITH A BIFURCATED VIEW?

Each view emphasizes a different dimension of unstructured knowledge work. A knowledge-as-object view focuses on content. The lack of emphasis on collaboration in this view has not escaped notice. A recent *KM World* article pointed out that collaboration was being neglected in many KM initiatives (Matway and Andrews, 2000). Collaboration is limited in these technologies to making content available in an asynchronous manner. Technologies supporting the knowledge-as-action view place a focus on dialogue, primarily in synchronous activities. The robustness of repositories necessary for managing content and enterprise knowledge sharing is overlooked. We believe that by focusing on only one view rather than both, virtual teams are inadequately supported.

One consequence of a bifurcated view is that the full spectrum of virtual team activities is left partially supported. There is a need for flexible and adaptable tools to accommodate the spontaneous nature of knowledge as action. However, the availability of tools is constrained by a diverse computing environment. Some members of the team will inevitably have limited access to the range of tools available. For example, drawing on a white board might be refreshed only every few seconds due to limited bandwidth rather than multiple times per second of streaming video when bandwidth is abundant. The content available throughout the firm might not be available within a virtual meeting product because of the integration demands placed on the computing environment. The variety of actions that can be conducted by all members of the team is constrained by the availability of integrated tools that are easily integrated into a firm's computing environment.

A second consequence of a bifurcated view is that encoding of knowledge cannot keep pace with rapidly changing activities that are generating new knowledge and causing transience of existing knowledge. The traditional approach to supporting knowledge as object is storing content. Firms must integrate the search and retrieval process across disparate repositories. Integration of access control is the first step because each repository controls access differently. An index must be built that bridges differences in the way content is encoded. Furthermore, changes or additions of content must be recognized quickly if acting on knowledge is important. The master index will have to be updated as frequently as the expectations for timeliness in acting on knowledge. The notification mechanisms that can be employed for a small team are different from those used in a firmwide setting.

The capturing of content requires encoding to take place. Decisions must be made as to the extent of encoding, its format, and permissions allowed other parties in the firm. Once content is stored, its transience has to be managed. When access to team content is restricted to its own members, much of the project-specific context can be overlooked. However, some encoding is required, so there are practical limits to how much of the collaborative activities can be captured.

The capture of a white board sketch illustrates the challenges of encoding content. A team member sketches a part on the white board. A second member criticizes the shape and proceeds to refine the sketch. What should be captured? One point of capture could be the initial sketch. An audio clip of the criticism could be added to give context on why this sketch is transient and potentially obsolete. The second point of capture could be the refined sketch with an audio clip of the rationale for the change. A third member might find the two-dimensional sketch difficult to understand and proceeds to create a three-dimensional model. What screen captures should be preserved? How do you choose the meta-data terms for categorization?

The demands placed on technologies to support virtual teams in unstructured knowledge work from these two views are at odds. On the one hand, the spontaneity of a knowledge-as-action view demands flexible tools, integrated infrastructure, and fast retrieval of knowledge, with great demands placed on rapidly encoding incremental, highly contextualized knowledge. On the other hand, a knowledge-as-object view emphasizes broadly applicable knowledge and careful encoding for later retrieval.

IMPLICATIONS FOR PRACTICE

Our belief is that technologies currently supporting a bifurcated view will need to become combined if they are to support unstructured knowledge work in virtual teams. Table 12.3 lists functionalities required if both views are combined. Across this list, there are four common themes that must be addressed by practitioners using these tools, CT developers, and researchers of virtual teams:

- Ensuring interoperability
- Balancing concerns of information security with sharing
- Creating and integrating search and retrieval processes
- Implementing multimedia capture

Ensuring Interoperability

The opening scenario began with all members having sufficient bandwidth to use virtual team tools and communication channels and a computer able to index a repository quickly. For this scenario to be real, we will first need to see the telecommunications industry succeed at increasing available bandwidth. In addition, the various technologies to support unstructured knowledge work such as e-mail, repositories, and analysis tools will need to become integrated. The key to this integration will be a protocol for sharing directories. Today, each application requires a separate directory, with each controlling access to a resource such as an application or a set of documents stored in a repository. Firms are just beginning to deploy directory services, such as products based on the Lightweight Directory Access Protocol (LDAP), that can unify the administration of computing resources that depend on directories.

Balancing Concerns of Information Security with Sharing

Our scenario was based on technological support for the virtual team being hosted by Peter's firm. Outside experts were given permission to enter Peter's network and reach servers hosting the suite of virtual team technologies that would be needed. Peter felt the advantages of this interfirm collaboration outweighed the risks of letting outsiders into his network. However, he did not want to risk exposing information about his idea on the Internet and thus did

Table 12.3. Implications for Technologies Enabling Unstructured Knowledge Work

Characteristic of UKW	Implications for Enabling Technologies
Diverse computing environment	Low common denominator: browser, telephone, limited bandwidth applications Portals for knowledge map of disparate repositories and resources Firmwide search and retrieval across repositories
Participation from multiple domains of expertise	Allow personalization of portals and repositories Allow customized knowledge maps Create new communities of practice from overlapping domains Enable output of applications to be shared by virtual team Portals span both team (project) space and personal knowledge bases Autocapture of conferencing (audio transcripts, chat records, video of shared drawing spaces) of explicated tacit knowledge
Spontaneity of sequence, tools, and participation	Autotaxonomy generation (building of vocabulary and key words) Synchronous communication and conferencing Shared space (sketch pad and screen sharing) Annotation on shared space Adaptable tools available on demand with just-in-time training Ubiquitous connections Remote access Unified messaging (common access to telephone, e-mail, paging, voice mail, fax) Allow for suspension of one deliberation (and its tools) to engage in another deliberation (using different tools)
Transience of knowledge	Autocapture of conferencing (audio transcripts, chat records, video of shared drawing spaces) so relevance does not have to be assessed before capture Version control, content (records) management, link management Preserve external source of content by copying to repository For content that is not "owned" by a single individual, notify all interested parties when changes made or deletion proposed

Table 12.3. (*Continued*)

Characteristic of UKW	Implications for Enabling Technologies
Sharing requires control	Notify author based on others' interacting with content
	Access control list under author's control
	Mute audio and video channels
	Private chat areas
	Shut off autocapture
	Control exercised at individual document level (rather than folder)
	Usage log for tracking content
Sharing requires encoding	Autocapture of conferencing
	Autocategorization of created content by text mining
	Alternative retrieval methods (for example, browse, links)
	Referential links
	Support for human "content stewards" (that is, knowledge broker) to assist content creators in encoding in ways beyond own needs
Differences in sharing knowledge between members and firm	Publish to appropriate audiences availability of content
	Status indicators (for example, "draft," "need comments") on content
	Notify author when someone is interacting with content
	Expert profiling to identify sources for knowledge reuse in firm
	Support for human content stewards to determine what knowledge might have broader applicability beyond team
	Local taxonomies mapped to firm using thesaurus and synonym list

not host the virtual team on technologies provided by an Internet application service provider. Peter had given members of the virtual team permission to use his own firm's virtual team technologies. He had not given them permission to look at any of his repositories. When he wanted his own speeches searched from his private repository, he had to give specific permission to do so. An inter-firm virtual team poses these types of challenges to the security of a firm's digital knowledge.

The scenario introduces several information security implications. First, Peter's firm must allow outsiders into the corporate network. Specific resources must then be made available to them, such as Web servers hosting virtual team technologies. As a consequence, the firewall no longer provides an implicit means of access control to networked resources. Everyone on the network must also be given permission to specific resources. The scenario suggests that the change in permission should be self-administered. A virtual team should be able to allow an additional expert to participate without having to track down an administrator to make the changes. This means that an outsider would be given limited access to pass through a firewall and reach a particular resource, such as a document repository, on an ad hoc and transitory basis. Vendors have only recently recognized the need to provide directory-based resource provisioning (Hudgins, 2000). Directory-based resource provisioning unites the previously disparate functions of enterprise user administration, meta-directory, and Web authentication and access control, also referred to as extranet access management (MacDonald and Witty, 2001). Yet the greater challenge may be the change in organizational attitudes and practices toward the security of a firm's information resources.

The second implication is that specific content within a corporate information resource must now be protected with access control measures. Content must be explicitly assigned permission levels. For example, outsiders assigned to a virtual team may be given permission to use a portion of the document repository for the work of the virtual team. However, other parts of the repository should be off-limits to these outsiders. A burden is now imposed on a content creator unrelated to the virtual team to anticipate who might want to use a particular item. Moreover, sharing content requires control not only among virtual team members but also throughout the firm.

Creating and Integrating Search and Retrieval Processes

In our scenario, when the experts first logged on, they saw publication profiles of each other. Early in the meeting, the "computer" analyzed Peter's previous speeches to locate an idea he mentioned. Later in the meeting, Jorge searches the human genome database. These examples illustrate typical information retrieval tasks conducted by a virtual team that are currently quite difficult to do using existing technologies.

One difficulty in the search process has been identified by Kimbrough, Kirk, and Oliver (1995). They found that much research on information retrieval focuses on improving retrieval performance by creating context for key words and indexing terms using techniques such as latent semantic indexing or analysis of thesauri. Conventional search engines employ exhaustive search methods based on key words to generate a list of relevantly ranked documents (Hall, 1998). The presumption is that meta-data as key words can adequately characterize content even across multiple domains of knowledge and that the content creators have the ability and willingness to do so. Yet ongoing research in knowledge organization has indicated that this is unlikely to be true in the foreseeable future (Kapetanios and Norrie, 1998; Sigel, 2000). The challenges go beyond technical issues to include social and organizational issues (Budd, 2000; Fox and Marchionini, 1998). For example, Davis (1999) reported that loss of slack time to increase profitability limited encoding efforts for content that would normally be placed in a repository. To address this difficulty, text mining technologies have only recently appeared in firms. Text mining engines use search methods that combine lexical parsing and clustering techniques to extract phrases from the text and thereby uncover document content (Hall, 1998). The techniques may include semantic analysis to derive a sufficiently rich representation to capture the relationship between the objects or concepts described in the documents (Tan, 1999). The problem with both conventional and text mining technologies is that these methods are computationally expensive, requiring a substantial investment on the part of a firm.

Apparent from Table 12.3 is that portal products integrated with firmwide repositories are required. These portals allow users to have a personalized view of information resources and applications that are available to them across the firm. Portals on the Internet, such as Yahoo! allow a user to select subwindows that might include local weather, stock market reports, or the latest sports news. A portal user in a firm might wish to display a personal schedule, in-box, and the latest changes to a document repository. Portals and their embedded capability to search and retrieve across disparate repositories introduce two critical capabilities. First, with portals, content across disparate repositories and multiple domains of expertise can be brought together in one place. Second, portals allow personalization so that a knowledge map of individual and team interests can be constructed of relevant firm resources. However, deciding what content to put on the portal, how to categorize and encode the content, and how to facilitate this search process are issues ripe for piloting, prototyping, and experimentation.

Implementing Multimedia Capture

In our scenario, Peter's firm integrated digital recording technologies used in music videos to capture and encode multimedia formats. The experts wore microphones that identify the speaker, so transcription was based on voice recognition technology. All of the multimedia streams were synchronized using GPS clocks so that the order of speech could be preserved. There were separate streams from the audio or video dialogues, the shared screen for slide presentations, and the white board. A human knowledge broker tagged the deliberations and alternatives as they occurred, so that highlights of the meeting would be available for future reference; Peter decided that such overhead was necessary for this team to be effective. Freeze frames of the white board at the time a speaker finished his turn were generated with an audio clip of the speaker's explanation embedded in the deliberations. The freeze frame and the clip were then deposited, with encoded context and content, in the team repository for future reference. These technologies enabled multimedia capture in our scenario.

Although the reality of this scenario is within reach, there is much more that is understood about how to capture content than what content should be captured. The suitability of capturing multimedia is determined by what is needed, especially with respect to the relevance of content and its transient nature. Multimedia capture can support the activities of an ongoing virtual team by allowing previous decisions or problem-solving approaches to be revisited. Efforts are under way to allow for searching of multimedia images (Sullivan, 2000). However, capture for corporate memory might take a different form.

Knowledge capture of an engineering project as found in this scenario comes in many forms. Ribière and Matta (1998) suggest a categorization based on "profession" or domain memory, project definition memory, and project design rationale memory. Since the know-how of domain experts increases during the project, changes made in documents, tools, and methods must also be captured.

Knowledge capture has traditionally focused on documents. The Open Document Management API is an implemented specification for interoperable desktop application integration with document management systems. World Wide Web Distributed Authoring and Versioning is an implemented standard for distributed authoring and versioning functionality on Web browsers. However, virtual meetings generate multimedia content. Dialogue is captured in the form of audio or video recordings. Slide presentations and white board drawings are captured in a video format for future replay. How can hours of video be encoded into useful knowledge?

In addition to portals, autocapture products will play an increasing role in addressing spontaneity and transience of unstructured knowledge work, as indicated in Table 12.3. Audioconferences can be taped and transcribed automatically. Chat dialogues can be stored for future review. Videos of a team's shared space can be recorded and stored temporarily until selected frames or segments can be encoded. Voice recognition products allow searching for a spoken word and playing that portion of dialogue. Once the dialogue has been processed into text, autocategorization based on text mining technology can encode specific dialogues based on text patterns. For example, all dialogue related to action items and new ideas could be identified. Human content encoders could then look at these specific dialogues and further encode them according to a taxonomy.

Looking to the Future

Virtual teams involved in unstructured knowledge work create challenges that are only partially addressed by current CTs for supporting virtual teams. While combining the technologies that support both a knowledge-as-object and knowledge-as-action view is a first step, there are still gaps in what is necessary to support this type of work.

While flexibility and adaptability will be critical in products to ensure that technology is successfully used by a virtual team, future technologies will need to address how this type of work is actually done (Kanfer and others, 2000). Although we are enthusiastic about the technologies that are available, success of a virtual team is still wholly dependent on the sociotechnical savvy of team members to adapt the available technologies to their use. The next step in virtual team support is to understand unstructured knowledge work better, especially sharing and encoding knowledge. CTs will become fully supportive only if future development on enabling technologies strives to address the full spectrum of work required of virtual teams. A blend of disciplines will be required for such development: psychologists, human factors, organizational design, information systems, communications, computer-supported cooperative work, and engineering.

References

Bardram, J. "Designing for the Dynamics of Cooperative Work Activities." *Proceedings of the Association for Computing Machinery 1998 Conference on Computer-Supported Cooperative Work.* Seattle: Association of Computing Machinery, 1998.

Blackler, F. "Knowledge and the Theory of Organizations: Organizations as Activity Systems and the Reframing of Management." *Journal of Management Studies,* 1993, *30*(6), 863–885.

Boland, R. J., Tenkasi, R. V., and Te'eni, D. "Designing Information Technology to Support Distributed Cognition." *Organization Science,* 1994, *5*(3), 456–475.

Bowker, G. C., and Star, S. L. *Sorting Things Out.* Cambridge, Mass.: MIT Press, 1999.

Budd, M. "Overcoming the Obstacles to Meta Data Management." *Application Development Trends,* 2000, *7*(6), 65.

Central Intelligence Agency. *Interoperability Study—Assessing Four Major Collaborative Tools.* Washington, D.C.: Platinum Rail Project, Office of Advanced Analytic Tools, 2000.

Davis, J. G. "Knowledge Sharing and Management in Large, Multi-National Corporations." Paper presented at the Fourth Biennial Carnegie Bosch Institute Conference, San Francisco, 1999.

de Jong, T., and others. "Acquiring Knowledge in Science and Mathematics: The Use of Multiple Representations in Technology Based Learning Environments." In M. V. Someren, P. Reimann, H. Boshuizen, and T. de Jong (eds.), *Learning with Multiple Representations.* New York: Elsevier, 1998.

Dougherty, D. "Interpretive Barriers to Successful Product Innovation in Large Firms." *Organization Science,* 1992, *3*(2), 179–202.

Fahey, L., and Prusak, L. T. "The Eleven Deadliest Sins of Knowledge Management." *California Management Review,* 1998, *40*(3), 265–275.

Fox, E. A., and Marchionini, G. "Toward a Worldwide Digital Library." *Communications of the ACM,* 1998, *41*(4), 29–32.

Grudin, J. "Groupware and Social Dynamics: Eight Challenges for Developers." *Communications of the ACM,* 1994, *37*(1), 92–106.

Hall, C. "Text Mining Versus Conventional Search Engines." *Cutter Edge Newsletter* (email), September 29, 1998.

Hansen, M. T., Nohria, N., and Tierney, T. "What's Your Strategy for Managing Knowledge?" *Harvard Business Review,* 1999, *77*(2), 106–116.

Harris, K., and Fenn, J. *A Checklist of KM Technology Requirements.* Stamford, Conn.: Gartner Group, 1999.

Hudgins, C. *Directory-Based Resource Provisioning Systems.* Midvale, Utah: Burton Group, 2000.

Kanfer, A., and others. "Modeling Distributed Knowledge Processes in Next Generation Multidisciplinary Alliances." *Information Systems Frontiers,* 2000, *2*(3/4), 317–331.

Kapetanios, E., and Norrie, M. C. "Semantic Querying of Scientific Data Through a Context Meta-Data Database." *ERCIM News Online Edition,* October 1998. http://www.ercim.org/publication/Ercim_News/enw35/kapetanios.html

Kimbrough, S. O., Kirk, S. E., and Oliver, J. R. *On Relevance and Two Aspects of the Organizational Memory Problem.* Philadelphia: University of Pennsylvania Press, 1995.

King, N., and Majchrzak, A. "Concurrent Engineering Tools—Are the Human Issues Being Ignored? " *IEEE Transactions on Engineering Management,* 1996, *43*(2), 189–201.

Leonard, D., and Sensiper, S. "The Role of Tacit Knowledge in Group Innovation." *California Management Review,* 1998, *40*(3), 112–121.

Lipnack, J., and Stamps, J. *Virtual Teams.* New York: Wiley, 1997.

Lucas, H., and Baroudi, J. "The Role of Information Technology in Organizational Design." *Journal of Management Information Systems,* 1994, *10*(4), 9–23.

MacDonald, N., and Witty, R. *Toward E-Provisioning: Access360 and Critical Path Link Products.* Stamford, Conn.: Gartner Group, 2001.

Majchrzak, A., and others. "Technology Adaptation: The Case of a Computer-Supported Inter-Organizational Virtual Team." *MIS Quarterly,* 2000, *24*(4), 569–600.

Markus, M. L. "Toward a Theory of Knowledge Reuse: Types of Knowledge Reuse Situations and Factors in Reuse Success." *Journal of Management Information Systems,* 2001, *18*(1), 57–93.

Markus, M. L., Majchrzak, A., and Gasser, L. "A Design Theory for Systems That Support Emergent Knowledge Processes." *MIS Quarterly,* 2001 (under review).

Matway, L., and Andrews, L. "Collaboration: The Neglected Side of KM." *KM World,* 2000, *9,* 22.

Mintzberg, H., Raisinghani, D., and Theoret, A. "The Structure of 'Unstructured' Decision Processes. " *Administrative Science Quarterly,* 1976, *21,* 246–275.

Nunamaker, J. F., Jr. "Future Research in Group Support Systems: Needs, Some Questions and Possible Directions." *International Journal of Human Computer Studies*, 1997, *47*(3), 357–385.

Orr, J. E. *Talking About Machines*. Ithaca, N.Y.: Cornell University Press, 1996.

Pava, C. H. *Managing New Office Technology*. New York: Wiley, 1983.

Ribière, M., and Matta, N. "Guide for the Elaboration of a Corporate Memory in CE." Paper presented at the Fifth European Concurrent Engineering Conference, Erlangen-Nuremberg, Germany, 1998.

Romano, N. C., Nunamaker, J. F., Briggs, R. O., and Vogel, D. R. "Architecture, Design, and Development of an HTML/Javascript Group Support System." *Journal of the American Society for Information Science*, 1998, *7*(7), 649–667.

Sigel, A. "How Can User-Oriented Depth Analysis Be Constructively Guided?" In C. Beghtol, L. C. Howarth, and N. J. Williamson (eds.), *Dynamism and Stability in Knowledge Organization*. Würzburg: Ergon Verlag, 2000.

Sullivan, D. "Searching Inside of Images." *Search Engine Report* (online edition), Dec. 4, 2000. http://searchenginewatch.com/sereport/00/12-images.html

Tan, A.-H. "Text Mining: Promises and Challenges." Paper presented at the South East Asia Regional Computer Confederation, Singapore, 1999.

Tenkasi, R. V., and Boland, R. J. "Exploring Knowledge Diversity in Knowledge Intensive Firms: A New Role for Information Systems." *Journal of Organizational Change Management*, 1996, *9*(1), 79–91.

Thomas, J. C., and Carroll, J. M. "The Psychological Study of Design." In N. Cross (ed.), *Developments in Design Methodology*. New York: Wiley, 1984.

Warkentin, M. E., Sayeed, L., and Hightower, R. "Virtual Teams Versus Face-to-Face Teams: An Exploratory Study." *Decision Sciences*, 1997, *28*(4), 975–996.

Workman, J. P., Jr. "Engineering's Interactions with Marketing Groups in an Engineering-Driven Organization." *IEEE Transactions on Engineering Management*, 1995, *42*(2), 129–139.

Yap, A. Y., and Bjørn-Andersen, N. "Energizing the Nexus of Corporate Knowledge: A Portal Toward the Virtual Organization." Paper presented at the International Conference on Information Systems, Helsinki, Finland, 1998.

CHAPTER THIRTEEN

Team or Community of Practice

Aligning Tasks, Structures, and Technologies

Arjan Raven

The main enabler of the virtualization of teams and organizations is information technology. Through the use of phone, e-mail, fax, videoconferencing, and other communications technologies, individuals are able to bridge differences of time and space (Wiesenfeld, Raghuram, and Garud, 1998). However, evidence indicates that the use of technology is not yet very widespread. The set of technological tools that particular teams have access to is often limited, and the tools that are available are used in limited ways.

In addition to technological changes, perspectives on the roles of individuals in organizations have also changed in the past decade. Traditionally, employees were seen as information processors and decision makers. Individuals are no longer just processing information or making decisions, and they are not working in isolation (Mohrman, Cohen, and Mohrman, 1995). Recent views of work identify additional roles for people in organizations. Increasingly, work is seen as a social activity, where individuals are part of larger communities (Tyre and von Hippel, 1997). Instead of looking at individuals as just making decisions and processing information, a much richer understanding of their work and their need for support can be obtained by looking at workers as conversation makers and sense makers. From this perspective, workers become a part of a community, trying to interpret their work in its environment (Boland and Tenkasi, 1995). This change in the need and desire for collaborative work also creates a need for other tasks. Whereas workers traditionally engaged in activities that required the formulation and analysis of problems and the processing of large amounts of information, they are now expected to communicate, collaborate, create knowledge, and engage in dialogue and sense making. Increasingly, groups of people work collaboratively on novel problems. Because the tasks are not familiar, a viable work structure has to emerge as the work advances. This is where collaborative structures come to the fore. In order to increase the effectiveness of technology use, the technologies have to be aligned with the collaborative structures, which in turn have to be aligned with the tasks.

Collaborative structures (for example, work groups) can be categorized in a number of ways. Leadership style, size, characteristics of individuals who are members of the group, formality of the structure, and work processes are among the characteristics considered in collaborative structures. The diversity of technologies for the support of collaborative structures is impressive, and for each major category of tools, a number of competing products are available. For virtual collaboration by a work team, the obvious technologies that might support their interactions are communication tools such as telephone, fax, e-mail, and videoconferencing. But virtual teams, like face-to-face teams, can be supported in a variety of other ways, particularly through knowledge-management tools for the recording, sharing, and archiving of knowledge and experiences and for the management of documents. The challenges are in determining which collaborative structures are needed for a particular collaborative structure and what information technologies can support the tasks and structure of the collaboration.

This chapter investigates collaborative structures and places them on a continuum that ranges from a team to a community of practice, along a set of dimensions. Two cases, Design Team and Knowledge CoP (Community of Practice) are used to discuss the dimensions of collaborative structures and technology needs for each type of structure.

COLLABORATIVE STRUCTURES

Virtual work can be carried out using a variety of collaborative structures, including more informal organizations such as communities of practice. Many work groups are often neither a pure team nor a pure community of practice. Instead, they fall somewhere on a continuum between the two extremes.

Mohrman, Cohen, and Mohrman (1995) define teams as groups of individuals "who work together to produce products or deliver services for which they are mutually accountable. Team members share goals and are mutually held accountable for meeting them, they are interdependent in their accomplishment, and they affect the results through their interactions with one another" (p. 40).

The mission for a team is typically explicitly defined and based on business strategy. Members are officially assigned and are selected based on their knowledge or skills or as representatives of their organizational unit. The distinction between members and nonmembers tends to be clear. Leadership roles are usually clearly defined. The team structure is generally designed, formal, and stable. Members depend on each other for task completion. Accountability for goal accomplishment tends to be shared, and formal and social sanctions for nonperformance exist. Finally, time and resources are allocated by the organization of which the team is a part.

The concept of community of practice (CoP) was introduced by Lave and Wenger (1991) and popularized by Brown and Duguid (1991) and Wenger and Snyder (2000). Wenger and Snyder describe CoPs as

> groups of people informally bound together by shared expertise and passion for a joint enterprise. . . . Some communities of practice meet regularly. . . . Others are connected primarily by e-mail networks. A community of practice may or may not have an explicit agenda on a given week, and even if it does, it may not follow the agenda closely. Inevitably, however, people in communities of practice share their experiences and knowledge in free-flowing, creative ways that foster new approaches to problems [pp. 139–140].

The missions for CoPs are not mandated. Instead, they emerge from the community over time. Membership is voluntary, and members move in and out of the community with relative ease, especially at the periphery. The distinction between core and peripheral members is quite clear, and a CoP can have a large number of peripheral members. Leadership is emergent and dynamic and can be shared and rotated. The structure is informal and ad hoc and evolves with the life of the CoP. Interdependence between tasks is not required. Accountability focuses more on individuals than on the group, and the only sanctions for nonperformance are social in nature. Resources for CoPs are contributed by individual members. Membership in a CoP is typically on top of the existing work.

A review of the literature on teams and CoPs and the empirical investigation of the virtual collaborative efforts in the Center for Effective Organizations study (described in Chapter Three of this volume) identified the dimensions that characterize groups along the teams and CoPs continuum (see Figure 13.1).

Case Comparisons

Two collaboration cases, one more like a team and one more like a CoP, illustrate the different dimensions and the ways in which they define collaborative structures.[1] For each case, interviews were held with the majority of the participants in the collaboration.

The first case, referred to here as the Design Team, was a collaborative effort of four organizations in three large companies in the design of a very complex

Figure 13.1 Key Dimensions of Communities of Practice and Teams.

product. The design was for a small component in the larger product. The component was chosen because it required the input from multiple engineering disciplines. Design decisions in one area immediately affected design decisions in another, resulting in the need for careful coordination and collaboration among all the parties involved in the Design Team.

One of the objectives for the team was to show that virtual collaboration among the four organizations was possible. The success of the team in part determined whether the group of organizations would be awarded a much larger project. Because of this objective, there was a strong emphasis on the testing of technologies and the development of a work process. The team was highly virtual by design. The four organizations were very different and were situated in different geographical areas. The team members relied heavily on technologies for their interactions.

The second case, referred to here as KM CoP, concerned itself with the sharing of best practices around knowledge management within a manufacturing company. The corporation was the result of a merger between two large companies— one in the United States and one in a European country. The success of the merger depended on the ability to integrate the operations from both sides of the Atlantic. Members of the KM CoP believed that knowledge management was a key component of the integration and that the results of their collaboration could affect the entire organization. The number of members in the group varied over time, with a low of about twenty and a high of approximately fifty.

The collaboration was considered to be moderately virtual. Members were geographically dispersed, but electronic dependency was limited at the time of the study. Over the course of the study, the needs of the collaboration changed, and ultimately a decision was made for the structure to be more like a traditional team. The data presented in this chapter were collected when the collaboration was still a CoP.

Mission. The mission for a collaborative effort is the set of goals that are to be attained over the lifetime of the collaboration. The mission of a group can be mandated by management, or it can emerge from the collaborative effort itself. When the mission is mandated, a team structure is typically adopted. CoPs are more likely to define the mission internally. It is important to note that there are many variations on the continuum, and the mission may well necessitate a blending of the extremes.

The Design Team mission was mandated by management from the outset and subsequently adopted by the team members. Even the work process was predefined, albeit at a high level. Details of the process emerged as time passed and the work unfolded.

The mission for the KM CoP was a good example of the blending of extremes. With this collaboration, the mission was somewhat atypical for the structure, as it was closely aligned with the corporate strategy. However, it was not mandated. The CoP had emerged in response to a need identified by the corporate university and other groups and individuals in the corporation. The participants felt that knowledge management was of strategic importance for the company, that both partners in the merger could learn from each other, and that the sharing of best practices should be coordinated at the corporate level. The corporate university did not have the power or the resources to create a formal project around knowledge management. Instead, representatives from the corporate university created a CoP. As commented on by one participant: "It was a brainstorming process, and we collected several ideas and brought them together and created breakout sessions and worked on these ideas. Seven objectives were a result of this discussion during one afternoon with about thirty participants."

However, as may often be the case when CoPs form, the mission that was established may not work for everyone, and as it evolves some participants may become dissatisfied, as exemplified in the following quote: "The CoP has already met three times and we decided to focus on three or four areas. We decided on those in the second meeting, yet in our third meeting, we revisited the focus again. I had the feeling that we started again on the very beginning."

Another CoP participant commented, "One of the reasons we have not been effective is that the mission was not presented to newcomers, or reinforced with existing members. We didn't repeat the objectives at each meeting. That was a big mistake. We only took about fifteen minutes to introduce new members and should have spent about two hours."

Membership. The membership of a collaborative effort is the set of individuals who are part of the collaboration over its lifetime. Individuals can be voluntary members or part of the membership by design. In teams, the membership tends to be designed, whereas in CoPs, individuals tend to join because they are drawn to the community or because they are invited. Membership in both teams and CoPs tends to be fairly dynamic. A core of individuals tends to stay with the group for its lifetime, but a significant number of others temporarily join the group to make their contribution to the ongoing work. Turnover in membership can be extensive. This is particularly true for CoPs, where membership tends to be voluntary. In one of the KM CoP meetings, almost 50 percent of the participants had not attended any of the previous meetings.

In the KM CoP, membership was somewhat voluntary. Each business unit at the corporation was asked to select one or two individuals to participate in it. In the Design Team, members were selected for their expertise and as representatives of their company. Turnover within the Design Team appeared to be very limited.

Leadership. Leadership is both the act of determining and guiding the direction and those who provide this direction. Leadership in teams tends to be explicitly defined, whereas in CoPs, it is more emergent and dynamic.

Issues around leadership tend to center around how leadership should take place. For example, at Design Team, there was some discussion about the extent to which the leadership should be more or less participatory, but the general sentiment, confirmed in the following quotation, appeared to be that the leadership was proper: "Someone has to be in charge. Someone needs to apply authority. It is the appropriate thing to do. At times we have been directed. I haven't liked it personally, but it is the appropriate thing to do."

The need for "formal" leadership is often not the issue in CoPs. Rather, the question is whether a leader or a facilitator is needed. This was clearly demonstrated by the KM CoP: "We have a lack of moderation; if we had a strong moderator, that would facilitate the whole thing for us."

Facilitation is not always seen as the preferred solution. Another member discussing some problems within the CoP seemed to favor a leader over a facilitator: "The underlying cause of our ineffectiveness is that there is no real manager of the community."

Task Interdependence. Task interdependence is a measure of the extent to which participants in the collaboration depend on each other in their work. It assesses the need for coordination and interaction. Within a CoP, this dependence tends to be loose, whereas in a team, it can be very tight.

For the Design Team, task interdependence was very tight. Every design decision potentially affected other design decisions, and close coordination was necessary. One member of the team noted, "Each discipline gets together. If I need to do something, that will affect the other disciplines. We're there as a team. If I do whatever I want, then it may not be able to be manufactured."

In the KM CoP, on the other hand, the interdependence was loose or even absent. Although every member needed the CoP for her or his success, none of the individuals needed any of the other individuals in the group for their work. The focus of the CoP was on sharing best practices. Beyond that, the CoP did not have a collective project that would require coordination among the members.

Structure. The structure of a collaborative effort is the set of tasks and the sequence in which they have to be performed. It is the overall work process and specifies when and where interactions and coordination among participants in the collaboration are required. For teams, the structure is often designed, whereas for CoPs, it is more likely to be emergent. The structure of the work depends to a large extent on the mission and the task interdependence. Without a clear mission, it is hard to design the work processes.

For the Design Team, which had a clear mission and task, it was possible to create a general design of the work processes before the kickoff meeting. Details of the work emerged as time passed. For the KM CoP, the work structure was both undefined and changing. The flexibility and changing structure in a CoP, a primary function of this type of collaboration, can lead to frustration. Several members expressed a need to formalize the process.

Accountability. Accountability is the way in which the collaborative effort is evaluated. Teams generally have external entities by which they are held accountable, and any sanctions are formal in nature. CoPs, on the other hand, are accountable mostly to themselves, and sanctions generally are social rather than formal.

Members of the Design Team were held accountable by the team and their organization. Not all of the participating organizations evaluated the importance of the Design Team work in the same way. Assessment approaches also differed from organization to organization, causing comparison problems. A team member referred to a "state of turmoil" around performance evaluation because of system differences. Members of the KM CoP, in contrast, were evaluated only by their respective business units. Their contributions to the CoP were taken into consideration only if this was considered important to the business unit.

Resources. Resources are the funding, information technologies, materials, equipment, information, and access to people needed for a collaborative effort. Teams generally are provided with most of the resources they require for their work. CoPs typically have only very limited resources, which are provided by individual members.

For the Design Team, members were generally working full time on the design project. Some of the participating companies provided more support for their employees than others. Noted one member, "We can get instantaneous support to ensure that we are up and running, whereas at some of the other sites, they do not get that kind of response. That has caused a bit of a problem."

In the case of the KM CoP, the individual members contributed their own time, typically on top of their regular work, and their business units paid for the travel expenses.

When resource requirements for a task are high, a traditional team approach may be not be the best approach. It may instead be possible to use a team-CoP hybrid, starting with lower levels of resources and formalizing the structure as the potential benefits become clearer. A pure CoP may also be an option given that they are more risk taking when members are passionate about the task. It is also more likely that a CoP member will see the importance and potential benefits and will work on the task, even if it isn't officially part of his or her job description. A KM CoP member explained that the "CoPs are very new, and not every top manager is convinced that this is the way to do it. I have a small budget, but it is not necessary. If people are interested in this subject, they will participate."

ALIGNING STRUCTURES AND TECHNOLOGIES

Virtual work groups have many of the same characteristics as face to face teams and CoPs, but have an important additional component: their members are typically dispersed over a broad geographical area, spanning countries, and even continents, and cultures. As a result, they rely even more than colocated teams and communities do on collaborative technologies for their interactions.

For both virtual and colocated collaboration, knowledge—its creation, sharing, and application—is at the core of the work. The management of this knowledge provides a useful framework to explore the use of collaborative technologies. Hansen, Nohria, and Tierney (1999) identified two knowledge-management strategies. The first one, personalization, assumes that knowledge is highly dynamic and is stored in people's brains. A company following that strategy should support communication among people. The second strategy, codification, assumes that knowledge is static and can be removed from its context. This strategy suggests that knowledge should be codified and stored in systems.

Collaborative Technologies

The two strategies suggest two categories for support by information technologies: groupware and knowledge repositories. Groupware, also known as computer-supported collaborative work systems, consists of technologies that enable communication among members of a work group. The most widely used technology in this category is e-mail. The second category, knowledge repositories, is made up of systems that store knowledge for future use. Often such systems also contain functionality to search through the stored data and knowledge and to maintain the contents. A good example of a system that contains such capability is Lotus Notes. Many of the technologies are integrated to form products. For example, Intranets.Com provides the storage capability of a knowledge repository together with groupware functions such as e-mail.

Groupware. Research on groupware systems investigates a broad range of technologies and topics around information technology support for groups (VandenBosch and Ginzberg, 1997). Most of the technologies provide a general communication capability that can be applied to a large variety of tasks. Examples of technologies are e-mail, telephone conferencing, videoconferencing, remote presentation, instant messaging, chatrooms, and bulletin boards. Usage patterns for the technologies are determined by the groups and typically emerge over time. For instance, one of the teams that was studied had a clear expectation that e-mail would be responded to within twenty-four hours. Another group decided to minimize the use of videoconferencing. Many of the technologies become useful only once a critical mass of users adopt them.

Knowledge Repositories. Work in both face-to-face and virtual work structures depends on and leads to knowledge and information. In both the practitioner literature (Davenport and Prusak, 1998) and the academic literature (Walsh and Ungson, 1991), there is great interest in the ways in which knowledge and information can be preserved in organizations. The general academic area of research around this issue is usually referred to as *organizational memory*. Organizational memory research investigates how knowledge can be captured for future use (Huber, 1991), how information can be stored for decisions (Walsh and Ungson, 1991), and how knowledge can be stored for knowledge integration, organizational adaptation, goal attainment, and maintenance of the work group structure (Stein and Zwass, 1995). In collaborative work, all of these possible functions for organizational memory are important. Groups of people need to remember what their collective history is, they need to have access to knowledge and information from other teams and entities in the organization, and they need to be able to share their own knowledge and information with current and future groups and individuals.

Although people do much of the remembering and forgetting, there is an essential role for information systems in the creation and support of organizational memory. Clear examples can be found in consulting companies such as McKinsey and Co. (Bartlett, 1996) and KPMG (Alavi, 1997), where information systems are a key enabler for the retention of and access to knowledge.

Alignment Scenarios

In general, use of technology across the fourteen teams and CoPs that were studied was very limited. Most of the collaborations used only e-mail and the telephone. Design Team, somewhat of an exception, extensively used technologies. The KM CoP was more in line with the other collaborations and made very limited use of technologies.

Design Team. Design Team used both groupware and knowledge repository technologies extensively. In the groupware category, they used e-mail, the telephone, and a remote presentation tool that allowed individuals to share an application. Of the three technologies, e-mail and the remote presentation tool were most popular and rated as very useful. A team member said about remote presentation, "Typically, you don't communicate some things over the phone. But when you look at the screen and turn it and rotate it, you're seeing and communicating the same thing—looking at the same thing at the same time." The telephone was rated as only moderately useful in the Design Team, in part because of time zone differences that left very small windows for meetings.

The Design Team also used two specialized design tools that functioned as knowledge repositories and to some extent structured the work: CATIA, a computer-aided design system, and Metaphase, a product data management tool. CATIA was considered very useful, although an initial issue arose when the different companies were using different versions of the system. This was resolved through standardization on one version. Metaphase received more mixed evaluations, with ratings varying from "not useful" to "very useful." Some of the problems seemed to stem from the software itself: "The software glitches would not allow us to use the tool as it was designed to be used. We would get into it and could not get the information we needed. The software guys say that they know that the glitch is there, and it would have been fixed in a couple of months. It is like any other software: you get a bad taste when it doesn't work." However, at the companies where Metaphase had been used before, the evaluations of the tool were generally higher, so experience with the system seems to have played a role.

Although resources were available to acquire systems, support was not available at every company. Team members at some of the organizations made extensive use of the information technology support group at another organization that was represented in the team. "We were relying heavily on company people. They were stretched. We were finding that the software that was delivered to us was often not ready to be installed. There were bugs and glitches in the software."

One of the issues that had to be resolved was how the systems were to be connected across the participating organizations, which posed both technical and administrative issues: "There were a lot of connectivity problems we had to work out, and it took six weeks. We had to fill out paperwork and get cleared by security to provide access to the server down there. There were connectivity problems too. It took our information security people time to come down and figure out how to hook me up." But although there were some issues with the use of the technologies by the Design Team, nobody seemed to express a desire for other tools, for either communication or the storage of knowledge.

KM CoP. In the KM CoP, only three technologies were used: e-mail and telephone as groupware technologies and a project intranet as a knowledge repository. As a result of the limited resources and unclear leadership, technology use was very limited, although it was felt that it could be used to a much greater extent. In the use of the telephone, language tended to be a barrier: "Over the phone, some people may have more difficulties. It is basically like being taped. If you know that you are not good in English, then talking on the phone is hard."

The intranet was relatively new and was set up as a knowledge repository for the KM CoP. It seemed to be used mainly for the sharing of documents from face-to-face meetings. One of the problems was that it was hard to know when something new had been added to the site. One participant stated, "It would be nice to receive an e-mail whenever someone puts something new out there. It is a complex enough site that I may or may not stumble across it."

The limited use of technology was partly a result of the ambiguity about the mission of the KM CoP. Also, the CoP was less than two years old at the time of data collection, and it had not yet established patterns of behavior. Several members of the CoP had ideas for a more extensive use of technologies to increase interactions between the face-to-face meetings:

> I don't really understand the role in between meetings for the members or for ourselves if we are permanent members. Of course, you keep working on your own stuff and get ready for the next meeting, but is there anything else? What are the other channels of communication? I think that after I sent an e-mail with these questions, I received a couple of responses back and some requests that will require a little more communication, which I think is going to be good. But the starting point of how much you interact with the people other than when you are in the meeting, I don't know.

> There is not so much communication between the meetings. We need to intensify this. We need to have a meeting every three months. The intranet and Web site would be interesting for that and the most promising way to go.

> Yesterday I received an e-mail from the merger and acquisitions people with a general update on their latest things. I really enjoyed that. It would be good to have more of that in between the meetings. But everybody is so busy with daily work, and they are doing knowledge management as an add-on.

Given time, the use of technologies by the KM CoP may grow, especially given its decision to become more like a team. But the KM CoP was more typical of the technology use demonstrated by the other teams and CoPs in the study.

TECHNOLOGY USE

The use of groupware and knowledge repositories can be different for teams and CoPs. Extrapolating from these findings and from what is known about teams and CoPs, it is possible to draw some general conclusions concerning technology use (see Table 13.1).

Teams

Groupware is potentially very powerful in teams. In such structures, it is possible to select one product or suite of products that all members will use. Standardizing on a product (suite) has many advantages: the same functionality is available to all members; support can focus on one product; training can be mandated and needs to be developed and delivered for only one product; members can learn from each other about how to use the product; and sharing of data is easier. As a result, skill levels are developed to higher levels, and overall efficiency will be high. Knowledge repositories are important for teams, and several forms of such repositories were found in the teams that were studied. At the core of any such system is the structure of the knowledge (for example, the databases within Lotus Notes). For a traditional team, this structure will be relatively stable and can be mandated.

Communities of Practice

For CoPs, groupware is very appropriate, although it is used differently than in teams. In CoPs, there will be much less control over the products that are used,

Table 13.1. **Structures and Technologies**

Structure or System	Groupware	Knowledge Repository
Team	Systems can be standardized across all members. Training can be mandated and standardized.	Can be highly structured and standardized.
Community of practice	Should be flexible; different members may use different products. Different skill levels. Efficiency of use will differ across members.	Important for the preservation of knowledge, but should be flexible in structure. Different members may use different products.

and the technology skill levels are more likely to differ. Training resources will be limited, and this may make it more difficult to use the technologies efficiently and effectively. Knowledge repositories can be used for CoPs, but they are less pervasive and less structured than for teams. In CoPs, the structure of the knowledge cannot be designed. Rather, knowledge structures will emerge from the work and change as the community structure changes. In both instances, it is important for CoPs to take advantage of the flexibility of the technology to facilitate and extend the work of the collaboration. Despite the challenges in the implementation, collaborative technologies can provide essential support to CoPs. Through a careful analysis of the needs of the CoP, appropriate customization of the technologies, and training and support of the users, the use of technologies can lead to greater success of the collaboration.

IMPLICATIONS FOR PRACTICE

The findings in this chapter can be used for the assessment of existing teams or communities of practice and the design of new collaborative structures. For assessment, an existing work group can be categorized in terms of task resource intensiveness, its structure along the team-CoP dimension, and its information technology support as using groupware or knowledge repositories. For design of new collaborative structures, the findings can be used to think through issues associated with group structure and technology use prior to and during group formation.

The findings can help indicate possible challenges as well as potential solutions. For example, a mismatch in structure and information technology can occur in the type of system that is used or the way in which a particular technology is used (as when a knowledge repository is so rigidly structured that it cannot evolve with the changes in a CoP). An assessment of technology use can also identify new ways in which technologies can be applied.

Challenges can arise around the structure of the collaborative effort. A mismatch in task and collaborative structure suggests the need for changes in the structure along one or more of the dimensions. Typically, this means that a collaboration has to become more formal and has to act more like a team. The KM CoP ultimately decided that in order to fulfill the mission that had emerged from its work, it required much more extensive resources, clear leadership, and a structure that was designed rather than emergent. A first step in the change process was to seek executive support and recognition for the work of the CoP. New resources will mean more formal accountability and less flexibility in membership. In essence, the CoP is becoming a team, with both the responsibilities and benefits of a team. Noted one CoP participant, "It will change in a way that we will have a harder leadership in the future. We will have clear objectives, with targets, budgets, and timetables. We will have to work in a very formal way; it won't be informal. It will be more focused on business issues."

Most corporations have both teams and communities of practice in them, as well as hybrid forms that fall in between the extremes. Information technologies and technical support will have to be provided for all types of collaboration. While the basic infrastructure can be used for teams and CoPs, it is important to recognize that the systems will be used differently and that the implementation, training, and support have to be adapted to the needs of the collaboration. An approach for a community that is too rigid may doom the implementation of a new system, and at the same time economies of scale may be lost if technologies for a team are not sufficiently standardized.

This review of tasks, collaborative structures, and technologies in combination with the study results yields a number of insights that are relevant for the management of virtual collaborative work:

- Many work groups are not really teams, but are more like communities of practice or are a team-community hybrid. Decisions about a team versus CoP structure should be based on the nature of the collaborative task.
- In communities of practice, structure and leadership are typically emergent and dynamic. However, they can greatly benefit from clarity about the direction and facilitation of the group processes.
- Once a collaborative effort's mission becomes clearer, its need for resources and leadership is likely to increase. This may require a shift in collaborative structure.
- When the membership of a collaboration is highly dynamic, it is essential to reinforce the group's mission frequently.
- Technology use in virtual collaborations is limited. Collaborative efforts have to deal with users' lack of technology experience, limited training and support, user unfriendliness to technologies, and the cost of technologies. These issues are particularly true for CoPs because of the difficulty of mandating the use of a particular technology; resources tend to be nonexistent rather than limited, and technology implementation and support are provided by nonprofessionals.
- Technology support for virtual teams has to be evenly distributed across the participating organizations to avoid overstretching resources in any one organization.
- Support staff need to have an understanding of cross-organizational issues such as firewalls, data use policies, incompatible systems, and version management.

Note

1. The cases are derived from a study of virtual teams by the Center for Effective Organizations at the University of Southern California. The study of fourteen teams in seven companies was conducted between 1999 and 2001.

References

Alavi, M. *KPMG Peat Marwick U.S.: One Giant Brain.* Harvard Business School Case Study No. 9-397-108. Boston: Harvard Business School, 1997.

Bartlett, C. A. *McKinsey and Company: Managing Knowledge and Learning.* Harvard Business School Case Study No. 9-396-357. Boston: Harvard Business School, 1996.

Boland, R. J., Jr., and Tenkasi, R. V. "Perspective Making and Perspective Taking in Communities of Knowing." *Organization Science,* 1995, *6*(4), 350–372.

Brown, J. S., and Duguid, P. "Organizational Learning and Communities-of-Practice: Toward a Unified View of Working, Learning, and Innovation." *Organization Science,* 1991, *2*(1), 40–57.

Davenport, T. H., and Prusak, L. *Working Knowledge: How Organizations Manage What They Know.* Boston: Harvard Business School Press, 1998.

Hansen, M. T., Nohria, N., and Tierney, T. "What's Your Strategy for Managing Knowledge?" *Harvard Business Review,* Mar./Apr. 1999, pp. 106–116.

Huber, G. P. "Organizational Learning: The Contributing Processes and the Literatures." *Organization Science,* 1991, *2*(1), 88–115.

Lave, J., and Wenger, E. *Situated Learning: Legitimate Peripheral Participation.* Cambridge: Cambridge University Press, 1991.

Mohrman, S. A., Cohen, S. G., and Mohrman, A. M. *Designing Team-Based Organizations: New Forms for Knowledge Work.* San Francisco: Jossey-Bass, 1995.

Stein, E. W., and Zwass, V. "Actualizing Organizational Memory with Information Systems." *Information Systems Research,* 1995, *6*(2), 85–117.

Tyre, M. J., and von Hippel, E. "The Situated Nature of Adaptive Learning in Organizations." *Organization Science,* 1997, *8*(1), 71–81.

VandenBosch, B., and Ginzberg, M. J. "Lotus Notes and Collaboration: Plus ça Change . . ." *Journal of Management Information Systems,* 1997, *13*(3), 65–81.

Walsh, J. P., and Ungson, G. R. "Organizational Memory." *Academy of Management Review,* 1991, *16*(1), 57–91.

Wenger, E. C., and W. M. Snyder. "Communities of Practice: The Organizational Frontier." *Harvard Business Review,* Jan./Feb. 2000, pp. 139–145.

Wiesenfeld, B. M., Raghuram S., and Garud, R. (1998). "Communication Patterns as Determinants of Organizational Identification in a Virtual Organization." *Journal of Computer Mediated Communication,* 1999, *10,* 777–790.

SUMMARY

*When I look at communities of practice, I see many budding teams. You start
as a merging network, and suddenly there is a real task to do and teams
are formed. When I see creative work, there are times that are spent very
creatively, but there are other times that are spent in routine work. How much
leverage are we getting from this approach to trying to match the technology
to a specific task or specific structure, since it is so fluid?*
—Conference attendee questioning the approach of trying to match
technology to the task and work structure

Without information technology tools, virtual collaboration cannot occur.
Many commercial products exist to support various activities of virtual
teams. The chapters in Part Four provide guidelines for selecting the
appropriate technology tools. Three key questions emerge from the comparison
of these chapters: (1) What is the utility of trying to match technology to task
and structure? (2) Why is technology use so limited in the vast majority of virtual teams? (3) What can be done to facilitate effective technology use in virtual
teams?

Each of these chapters argues for aligning technology with tasks or group structure. King and Majchrzak focus on unstructured knowledge work. They assert
that most collaborative technology products rarely meet all the needs of the virtual team engaged in this type of work. Raven distinguishes between virtual teams
and communities of practice and recommends that these structural differences be
taken into account when technology choices are made. Riopelle and coauthors
also argue for matching task considerations with technology choice, adding that
context and team development may mitigate the initial premise.

Group structure is not static in modern organizations. Communities of practice may evolve into teams when organizations expect deliverables from them.
That is exactly what happened to the CoP that Raven studied. Teams dissolve
when their work is completed, yet team members may informally stay in touch
with one another based on common interests. In addition, virtual teams perform

a variety of tasks, and the nature of their work varies. Even teams whose primary focus is creative work, such as new product development teams, still perform some work that is routine. Usually organizations need to provide a technological infrastructure that can support a variety of tasks and collaborative forms. Thus, matching technology to a specific task or group structure has limited utility.

Nevertheless, the analyses provided by these chapters are still helpful for making technology choices. What is required is a broader view that considers task and collaboration structure in context. Riopelle and coauthors explicitly make this argument that simple prescriptions about choice of technology are not helpful. Instead, they provide a series of questions that allows practitioners to think through the technology options available and their implications for virtual teams. Clearly, if electrical power is shut off for several hours in a teammate's country, it does not matter which suite of products the team plans to use at that time. King and Majcharak recognize that most individual products are limited in their support for knowledge work, so they offer guiding principles so that the variety of tools that teams will use can be integrated with one another. For example, if tools are interoperable, teams can use different tools and still integrate their work. Raven states that most corporations have both teams and communities of practice in them and hybrid forms that fall between the extremes. He asserts that information technologies and technical support must be provided for all kinds of collaboration. Ultimately, the support that is provided may be more important for determining the efficacy of the information technology tools.

It is striking that the two large-scale studies of virtual teams represented in Chapters Eleven and Thirteen found little use of advanced information technology tools. Chapter Eleven is based on a longitudinal study of six global virtual teams from five major corporations spanning five industries and three functional areas. The complete data set in Chapter Thirteen is based on a study of fourteen virtual teams from seven companies spanning six industries and approximately ten functional areas (although the chapter comparisons are based on two virtual teams). The vast majority of teams studied relied on e-mail, telephone calls, and face-to-face meetings to do their work. Despite the plethora of tools available, virtual teams rely on the tried and true. Several people at our conference commented on the limited use of technology—for example:

> We have an information technology department that has the answer looking for the question, so we always have more than we need. Our virtual teams generally use less than what is available. As I get into it, I have also found that teams will tend to settle on audioconferences, global ones, because they are far less distracting than videoconferences and they can pick up on nuances and the voice if they know each other well enough [practitioner from a high-technology company].

Given all the tools that are currently available for virtual work, what limits their use? King and Majchrzak provide some hints, with their focus on the sociotechnical needs of virtual workers. They find that few commercial products adequately support the work requirements of virtual teams that are performing unstructured knowledge work. As a consequence, most stand-alone products would be inherently frustrating to users because they do not meet their full requirements. In addition, most products are not interoperable, and companies have not developed the sophistication with knowledge management that allows them to balance security needs with knowledge-sharing requirements or promote the search and retrieval of transient knowledge. They may not have the technological infrastructure, particularly on a global basis, to permit the multimedia capture of knowledge. However, these explanations cover just the technical half of the sociotechnical coin.

Riopelle and associates address the social side with its emphasis on context and team development. They point out many reasons that virtual teams may prefer e-mail and telephone to more sophisticated groupware. E-mail may be preferred to synchronous forms of communication even if it is not ideal for virtual team work. First, language fluency may be an issue. E-mail permits those for whom English is a second language to spend the time to construct messages. When multiple time zones are crossed, the ability to communicate asynchronously provides the least disruption to personal lives. When synchronous communication is required and meetings occur across multiple time zones, people are forced to work beyond their standard workdays, and teleconferencing may be the only viable communications medium. Most people would rather speak by telephone from their homes in the middle of the night than go into the office and operate videoconferencing equipment, although neither alternative is desirable. People often have personal, professional, and cultural preferences for meeting face-to-face or using the telephone. For example, Riopelle and associates describe two virtual teams where French culture played a role in the team's rejection of synchronous virtual technologies. In addition, new technologies may be difficult to learn. Teams may decide that they prefer to use a suboptimal technology rather than invest the time required to learn something new. Finally, as several other chapters in this book point out (for example, see Chapters Three and Nine), face-to-face meetings enable personal connections important for sense making and interpretive activities to be made, which are crucial for task accomplishment for virtual teams. Relying on tried-and-true technologies may not be a problem for most virtual teams.

What can be done to help facilitate the effective use of information technology tools? The tried-and-true tools can often be used more effectively, and a broader range of tools could be used if organizations provided needed support. First, as suggested by Blackburn and others in Part Two, organizations need to increase the training provided to technology users. The most successful training features an eclectic mix of resources that can be adapted to team members' skills and interests (Mankin, Cohen, and Bikson, 1996). The training should be provided from a user's perspective, covering how the tool can help users get their work done. Often technologically savvy users on virtual teams lead the way and can help others to use tools. These "on-the-job" gurus can help their teams embrace technology. As discussed in other chapters (see Chapter Ten), virtual teams should explicitly develop communication norms, including how they will use e-mail and other tools (for example, "We will respond to all e-mails within twenty-four hours"). Technology support must be provided, especially for teams using more sophisticated tools. Resources need to be made available so that problems, which will inevitably emerge (for example, compatibility issues or security concerns), are fixed quickly. They will derail virtual teams unless this support is provided. Help desks can be proactive, calling users to see if they need help with anything or stopping by to teach users how to use more advanced features of their systems (Mankin, Cohen, and Bikson, 1996). As we argued in Part One, the support that an organization provides can make the difference between effective and ineffective technology use. If information technology is the hard-wiring of virtual collaboration, then group processes and group development can be thought of as the flow of energy through this infrastructure. We turn to this in the last part of the book.

Reference

Mankin, D., Cohen, S. G., and Bikson, T. K. *Teams and Technology: Fulfilling the Promise of the New Organization.* Boston: Harvard Business School Press, 1996.

IT'S ALL ABOUT ACTION

Processes and Development

INTRODUCTION

Folks in our organization say, "Time is an awesome fact." That awesome fact is critical to strategy and the potential of virtual teams. On the one hand, there are promises that virtual teams are going to speed everything up, and it's going to happen instantaneously. On the other hand, all of these social and structural issues have a great deal to say about whether that time promise is kept or whether it's expanded exponentially so that it is stretched out to months and months and years and years. One of the critical pieces that's missing is the realization that allows us to put a value on time and to enter time explicitly into the equations of evaluation of virtual teams. If we can achieve the promise by paying attention to the interpersonal skills, familiarity, trust issues, the expertise, and the top management blessing, for example, then the team gets a much higher value.
—Virtual team facilitator for a major technology firm

Many organizations use virtual teams in order to gain process efficiencies for collaborative action. However, as the authors in this part caution, virtuality can complicate collaboration, and if effective processes are not developed, the team will be unable to realize its potential. The four chapters in Part Five address social influence processes, conflict management, attention and engagement, and developmental processes that must be managed in order to bring about key enabling conditions and outcomes.

Chapter Fourteen addresses the topic of influence and politics. Elron and Vigoda review potential tactics of social influence and suggest that in virtual teams, the manner, intensity, and circumstances in which they are used differ from their use in conventional teams. Examining interview transcripts representing ten members of virtual teams, they find that tactics often perceived as negative and dysfunctional, such as pressure, sanctions, and legitimating, are used much less in virtual teams in comparison to colocated teams. Those perceived as more socially acceptable and effective, including rationality, consultation, and assertiveness, are used more frequently. They argue that this is true because lower familiarity and intimacy serve as barriers to the less popular and less socially acceptable tactics. A practitioner at the virtual teams conference explained it like this:

> When you are virtual, there's potentially a higher risk to mistrust or there's more risk to behaving badly, whatever you define that as. So when you're virtual, how do you go ahead and establish those shared meanings and that level of intimacy when you don't have the opportunity to meet? Is there a higher risk to building trust because you don't want to trust anyone out of your sight? Maybe you essentially want to make everything very visible in the virtual setting.

Moving on from influence tactics, Elron and Vigoda address these issues as they discuss political processes in virtual teams. Defining politics as "influential activities and tactics engaged in by members to maximize their interests and goals," they find similar effects of virtuality. Members of virtual teams engaged in less political behavior due to less opportunity to interact informally, greater perceived risk in documented correspondence, and less hierarchy. Based on these findings, they delineate numerous best practices for managing influence and political processes in virtual teams.

In Chapter Fifteen, Griffith, Mannix, and Neale examine conflict by comparing more virtual teams with colocated teams in the same organization. Distinguishing among three types of conflict (task based, relationship based, and process based), they found that virtual teams experienced greater process-based conflict and that establishing trust was a critical factor in managing that conflict. Furthermore, both e-mail and face-to-face communication were key mechanisms for establishing that trust, as discussed in Part One. Griffith, Mannix, and Neale provide a number of conflict management strategies and techniques for improving the effectiveness of virtual teams through the effective use of functional conflict, such as building the capacity to identify conflict early.

In Chapter Sixteen, Gluesing and her colleagues examine how virtual teams with members dispersed over numerous geographical locations and time zones develop over time. Their focus is on how virtual teams can learn to identify and integrate the complexity that arises from the multiple contexts across which virtual teams must work. They define context as "a way of life and work in a specific geographical area with its own set of business conditions, cultural assumptions, and unique history." In this sense, their concept of context encompasses what we referred to in Chapter One as culture, combining elements of both organizational and national culture with the organizational infrastructure. The importance of considering context and developmental patterns continues to be a subject of much discussion among researchers and practitioners, as evidenced by this comment by a virtual team leader in the aerospace industry:

> Before you get on a team at our company, we go through a whole training process about the expectations of being on a team so that everyone speaks the

same language and knows the lingo of teams before getting on one. It's also very, very important to define your boundaries and conflict resolution up front because we've all been on teams where you hit that imaginary brick wall and then you get that curve where it goes down. Either the team makes it through that crisis, or you hit that brick wall and you disperse. Every team goes through a crisis, and at times, you need to go back to your foundation, your principles of why the team was created and how you are going to communicate and do the conflict resolution you need to get past that curve.

Gluesing and associates illustrate developmental sequences similar to that noted by this practitioner by examining three case study teams, describing patterns of change, growth, and progression toward greater maturity in the teams as team members interacted across multiple contexts. All three teams began with significant business challenges, but the pathways through development and maturation were different. Based on the three cases, the authors make a series of recommendations for virtual teams in three general categories: initial structure, enriching start-up, and facilitating integration. These learnings provide valuable best practices for virtual team effectiveness.

In Chapter Seventeen, Klein and Kleinhanns address the often conflicting priorities between time spent on virtual team activities and time spent on local (colocated) activities. They describe the deficit as a time gap that results in lack of mind-share (that is, concentrated attention focused on the task) and members' becoming distracted during meetings. This results in less effective collaboration. This phenomenon resonated with practitioners at the conference who participate on virtual teams. One commented, "I come out of a Fortune 50 company, a high-tech company. We had conference call technology in the early 1980s, and so we really got into it and really stumbled our way through. Eighty percent of the meetings that we went to were useless. There's this unbelievable focus only on information sharing, and people go off to Florida in their heads."

With situations like these in mind, Klein and Kleinhanns discuss numerous factors that impede full contribution to virtual teams under these circumstances, such as incompatible information technology, cultural misunderstandings, and difficulty crossing time zones. Furthermore, they argue that diversity of voices on the team can end up aggravating the time gap, leading many team members to complain about added hours required for virtual team activities.

They conclude with a set of tactics and techniques that team leaders can use to minimize the time gap and maximize team member mind-share. These strategies serve primarily to reduce the time required to accomplish the team's objectives or persuade team members to shift more of their attention to the team. Attesting to the value of such strategies, one of the practitioners at our conference stated:

One of the things that we eventually did in my company was that I got people to stop sharing information at meetings, and it became a thirty-minute meeting! It was crisp, with very clear facilitation goals for the meeting to get people involved, and it was focused on a particular problem or decision that had to be made, and we had to end up with some kind of an action item.

CHAPTER FOURTEEN

Influence and Political Processes in Virtual Teams

Efrat Elron, Eran Vigoda

The ways team members choose to influence each other and the political processes that take place within a team have important implications for the team's effectiveness. In this chapter, we investigate the ways both phenomena occur in teams where the dominant mode of communication is technology supported rather than face to face interactions. For example, consider the following dilemma faced by the members of an information systems group for two months, using conference calls, e-mails, and a face-to-face meeting at the end of the problem-solving process. The participants in the process come from four countries, and their specific goal was to reach a decision on the choice of a product that will be used as the database for the whole organization. As one of the group members explains:

> Even when you discuss things that are technological, it can have an emotional base. For many people, technology is like religion, and that is combined with what product people are most familiar with and what they feel most comfortable working on rather than just taking a neutral look at the advantages and disadvantages. The decision cannot be only rational, and many influence attempts take place at the meetings.

The authors' names appear in alphabetical order. Both authors contributed equally to this chapter.

It was situations like these, where both influence and politics play a part in reaching the final decision, that prompted us to address the topics in this chapter. We address several important questions: What kind of influence tactics are the most prevalent, and do they differ from the ones used in traditional teams? Which are found to be most effective in the eyes of team members? Are political processes, elsewhere termed organizational politics, minimized in virtual teams, or do they just assume different forms? What are the political results of the meeting of different cultures in these teams? And finally, what role does the organization in which the virtual team exists play in all this? Our discussion develops the idea of virtual organizational politics (VOP), which goes beyond conventional organizational politics. We expect our conclusions to aid managers and practitioners working with virtual teams to use their advantages more efficiently and recognize their potential weaknesses at work.

INFLUENCE AND POLITICS: A CASE EXAMPLE

Our suggestions regarding the ways influence and politics manifest themselves in virtual teams rely on the combination of the findings of our exploratory study and the adjustment of existing theories and empirical knowledge on influence and politics to the reality of these teams. Our study relied on ten semistructured interviews with members of virtual teams. Participants were Israeli employees of two international organizations from the high-tech sector. The headquarters of one organization is based in the United States and has several different locations there, a number of subsidiaries in Europe, and several locations within Israel. The second organization recently merged with a Canadian-based company. The merged organization has subsidiaries in the United States, Europe, and Asia.

Our interviewees were low- to middle-level managers who held a variety of positions in the companies. Seven participants were involved with one virtual team, and the others were members of two such teams. Members belonging to two teams were asked to concentrate on the dynamics occurring in the team that was most central to them in terms of investment of time and significance to their work. For most teams, interactions with all team members actively participating took place in the form of telephone conversations once or twice a week. Teams had face-to-face meetings between one and four times a year. One group, whose members were all in Israel but working in different locations, met approximately once a month. The total number of members in the teams described in the interviews ranged from three to twenty individuals. The teams' main tasks were varied; some existed mostly for the exchange of information and advice, and in others, the proportion of decision making was much higher. All teams consisted of people who were mostly from similar functional areas.

The main part of our interviews asked participants to describe and explain various influential behaviors and political processes relevant to their virtual teams and how they compared with their experiences in face-to-face teams. Significant parts of the interview were also dedicated to the understanding of the organizations the virtual teams were a part of, the defining characteristics of their cultures, and the forms of influence and politics prevalent in the teams' larger environment. At the end of each interview, participants were asked to fill out a short questionnaire in two parts. The first part specifically referred to perceptions of differences in frequency of the use of various influential behaviors between the participant's virtual team and his or her face-to-face work team. The second part asked about perceptions of organizational politics as apparent in the virtual team. Based on this evidence, an interesting image emerges of influence, political behavior, and power relations in situations where people do not interact face-to-face but use various other alternatives to perform their job tasks.

VIRTUAL TEAM INFLUENCE TACTICS

We have witnessed a rapid growth in studies that developed well-grounded models and theories of influence and politics in organizations (Bacharach and Lawler, 1980; Gandz and Murray, 1980; Ferris and Kacmar, 1992; Kipnis, Schmidt, and Wilkinson, 1980; Mintzberg, 1983; Pfeffer, 1992; Yukl and Falbe, 1990). These theories serve as the basis for this chapter. For our purposes, influence is defined as the intentional attempts to affect another to feel, think, or behave in a desired fashion. We influence someone to the extent our behavior has an effect, even if unintended, on that person. Our success in influencing people is one of the most important determinants of our effectiveness as members in organizations. Influence processes are important in teams as they determine how decisions are made, which strategies and policies are implemented successfully, how motivated the team members will be to achieve the team's goals, and how much cooperation and support will be a significant part of the ways members interact with each other.

There are many possible tactics of social influence, and the choice of specific tactics can depend on the social and physical context, the qualities and status of the individual or group we are trying to influence, the goal of our influence, our own dispositions, and the organizational atmosphere and culture in which the influence attempts take place. Each of these influence tactics has vivid meaning in interpersonal work-life contacts. Table 14.1 summarizes these tactics as they were identified in two seminal studies (Kipnis, Schmidt, and Wilkinson, 1980; Yukl and Falbe, 1990).

At first glance, most of the influence processes and tactics also seem applicable to interactions in virtual teams. Yet they are not all used in the same

Table 14.1. Influence Tactics

Rational persuasion	Using logical arguments and facts to persuade another that a desired result will occur
Inspirational appeals	Arousing enthusiasm by appealing to another's values, ideals, and aspirations or by increasing the other's self-confidence
Consultation	Asking for participation in decision making or planning a change when the other's support and assistance are desired; showing willingness to modify a proposal to deal with the other's concerns and suggestions
Ingratiation	Using praise, flattery, and friendly or helpful behavior to get the other in a good mood or to think favorably on you; acting humbly and making the other person feel important
Personal appeals	Appealing to the other's feelings of loyalty and friendship toward you when asking for something
Exchange	Offering an exchange of positive benefits or offering to make a personal sacrifice, indicating willingness to reciprocate at a later time, or promise of a share of the benefits if the other helps accomplish a task
Coalition	Using the assistance of others or noting their support to persuade the other to comply with the desired goal
Legitimating	Pointing out one's authority to make a request or verifying it is consistent with organizational policies, rules, practices, or traditions
Assertiveness	Demanding, ordering, and setting deadlines
Pressure	Seeking compliance by using demands, threats, frequent checking, or persistent reminders
Sanctions	Preventing or threatening to prevent benefits such as salary increases or job security
Upward appeal	Causing additional pressure to conformity by invoking the influence of higher levels in the organization, such as making a formal appeal to higher levels or obtaining their informal support
Blocking	Attempts to stop the other from carrying out some action by activities such as engaging in a work slowdown or threatening to stop working with someone

manner, at the same intensity, in the same situations, and with the same effectiveness as in conventional groups. For example, Latane and others (1995) suggested that physical space and distance affect social interactions and social influence. Their study was based on social impact theory, which states that physical immediacy and distance affect the effectiveness of influence efforts on the other person. In other words, different geographical location and greater physical distance between people result in less social impact and a lesser ability to influence others. Our own findings indicate that in virtual arenas, people will adjust their use of influence tactics to the physical distance, as well as the types of communication modes that go with it, the unique needs and conditions of the new cyberenvironment, and the differences in cultures.

When people are not seeing each other while engaged in a telephone conversation or in e-mail sessions, they miss valuable information in the others' reactions. One person we interviewed commented, "You only have the voice; you cannot see the body language. Someone says something, and it is not clear how to interpret it." Our related finding, reflected in each of the questionnaires, is that the limited interaction and the lower familiarity and intimacy that come with it serve in most teams as an objective gatekeeper to some of the less popular and less socially acceptable influence tactics (Yukl and Tracey, 1992). Tactics such as pressure, sanctions, and legitimating are used much less in virtual teams in comparison to face-to-face teams, while at the same time the use of rationality and consultation appear more often. Part of the explanation is that when facing our target of influence personally, we can use the checks and balances of face-to-face interactions, for example, by interpreting eye contact, gestures, or body language. Virtual teams do not allow such balances and force us to be more careful.

A potential positive side of teams that interact face-to-face and have a shared history is the creation of a more cohesive group with a strong obligation to group performance and a higher engagement in behavior and interaction patterns beneficial to the task (Jehn and Shah, 1997). Our research tells us, however, that the potential dark side of familiarity is the use of less pleasant and less rational efforts of influence, resulting many times in lowered effectiveness. As we will see, similar logic applies to the existence of politics in virtual teams.

VIRTUAL TEAM POLITICAL PROCESSES

Politics in organizations is best reflected by influential activities and tactics engaged in by members to maximize their interests and goals in the workplace. Most academics and practitioners agree that organizational politics is inherent in most, if not all, organizational processes and that it reflects the structure and dynamics of influence behavior and power relations inside organizations. Some definitions add that politics involves behavior not formally sanctioned by the organization (Ferris and others, 1996; Drory and Romm, 1988), given that politics is often associated with a variety of negative actions that are harmful and dangerous from the organizational point of view (Mintzberg, 1983; Ferris and King, 1991; Ferris and Kacmar, 1992; Parker, Dipboye, and Jackson, 1995). Studies that examined the effect of organizational politics on work outcomes concluded that organizations rife with internal politics usually evince low performance on various scales, from attitudes such as satisfaction and commitment to behaviors like citizenship and negligence (Maslyn and Fedor, 1998; Vigoda, 2000a). At the group level, the prevalence of politics has been shown to increase the level of detrimental conflicts in teams and to lower their performance (Elron, 2000). Hence, organizational politics needs to be studied in virtual teams due to its potential general negative impact on team members and the team as a whole. We define political behavior that exists in virtual teams as virtual organizational politics (VOP).

Overall, under the psychological distance created by the greater physical distance, individuals must face and obey different rules of the political game. Moreover, in most cases, it is harder to read the political map from a distance, and the meanings of political processes remain vaguer. One participant in our study described these differences:

> One of the most salient characteristics of political behavior inside or outside organizations is that it takes place in inner rooms, in hidden corners, and no one actually knows that it is there. You can't actually see it, but you eventually witness its results. You must be very careful in becoming engaged in such influential behaviors; therefore, virtual teams are a bad place to start practicing organizational politics. You can't see the people, you can't evaluate their power and secret weapons, and you have much less control over the entire process compared with face-to-face teams that are nearby. It is much more difficult to read and understand the political map when people are distributed all over the world.

Another interviewee had similar thoughts:

> I am not sure, but it seems that a more personal and face-to-face interaction invites more political maneuvers. When there is a higher level of anonymity, people become more careful with each other and try not to escalate situations that otherwise may easily become political. When such situations occur, we recommend taking them off-line, which means pushing them out of the relevant team dynamic.

Interpreting our interviewees' words, there is more risk involved in the meeting of others we do not know well. Risk and perceptions of risk are highly related to ambiguity and complexity of information. Because organizational politics is both ambiguous and complex, people tend to perceive their engagement in it as risky. In politics, some individuals gain advantages over others by simply gaining information and knowing better who stands in front of them. Learning the nature of the target person at whom you aim influential activities is a necessary precondition for every strategy of political confrontation. In other words, higher intimacy and familiarity provide reliable and trustworthy information that people need when they plan their moves, positions, and decisions in the group. VOP then is seen as an even riskier business than conventional politics mainly because of the lower levels of familiarity.

To know others' political tactics and the best ways to influence them, it is usually not enough to communicate from a distance, even if face-to-face meetings with other team members do occur once in a while. In support of this, studies have shown that e-mail is more effective in increasing the range, amount, and velocity of information and communication of unequivocal information (McKenney, Zack, and Doherty, 1992), whereas face-to-face communication is more effective in circumstances where levels of ambiguity and uncertainty are high and in socially sensitive and intellectually difficult situations (Nohria and Eccles, 1992). Because influence and political behavior are clearly defined among the most sensitive, ambiguous, and illusive organizational processes, they will be implemented more intensely by face-to-face meetings than by virtual conferencing. The application of political resources for manifesting ideas and obtaining goals in virtual teams carries much uncertainty and pervasiveness, which makes the entire process risky and at times even dangerous. In line with this interpretation, one participant argued:

> Usually people do not see politics as a positive phenomenon since it can sometimes and somehow harm them, especially in virtual teams. When you work with others in the same place, you get to know them faster, you quickly understand what behavior is considered appropriate and what isn't, and you let everyone else know the same rules. The risk of working in a multicultural virtual team is that they can whisper one to the other while we are not aware of it, until suddenly, out of nowhere, we get a phone call from one of them saying, "By the way, this guy should not be put in charge of the project since he never sticks to timetables." They know that we cannot verify such information since we do not hold their curriculum vitae or supervisor's evaluations, so we are more easily manipulated.

Another consequence of electronic media, especially e-mail, is that written words can indeed serve as documentation and evidence. People in teams that rely heavily on e-mail are therefore more careful with writing than speaking because of the permanency effect of the written word. Thus, political behavior takes on a more careful and covert form when documented.

An additional consequence of the difficulty of using electronic communication, combined with the lesser familiarity and closeness, is that virtual teams tend to be more task oriented and leave less space for the social aspects of a team's existence. Moreover, the electronic interfaces that virtual teams use are built and expected to operate on a more formal level, so much less informal transaction is conducted in virtual teams. Issues are discussed in order to find solutions for problems, and less time and space are available for lengthy or rich informal conversations to develop. As some of the participants testified, hardly any time is left for small talk or other social gestures among the virtual team members unless in one-on-one interactions. When two people want to talk to each other on a topic that is irrelevant to the task or the topic is of no interest to the other members, they are kindly requested to take their conversation offline, which means out of the general meeting (often held on the telephone). Because political behavior relies heavily on informal communication and transactions among individuals, virtual teams simply allow less political behavior from this perspective. Noted one participant, "Virtual teams are task oriented. You do not have enough chances to read and understand this politics, if it's there at all. In fact, I don't feel that I actually have enough opportunities to be exposed to such activities in my virtual team. We don't have that much time left for politics; we need to work."

Finally, it is interesting to note that to most of our participants, the virtual team they belonged to was less central than their formal role in the organization. This inherent characteristic of participation in most virtual teams means in practice that the team members spend most of their time interacting on a daily basis with their local environment and usually spend only a fraction of their workday immersed in the happenings of the virtual team (Klein and Barrett, 2001). In general, however, the more the team engaged in decision-making tasks rather than merely information sharing, the more central it became to its members, both formally and personally. The link of centrality to the tendency to engage in politics is direct. Although lower centrality could mean that people are more reluctant to invest time and energy in the team tasks, the lower investment also means less emotional involvement and vested interests and, in turn, less engagement in efforts to influence others and less interest in engaging in politics.

NATIONAL CULTURAL IMPACTS ON INFLUENCE AND POLITICS

Cultures are the deeply ingrained patterns of values, perceptions, assumptions, and norms shared by members of the same group (Schein, 1985). National culture is thought to be particularly potent, and its effects on individuals are perceived to be particularly resistant to change. Most studies on intercultural interactions conclude that they tend to be especially complex. The differences in the value priorities, goal preferences, and interpretive schema held by members of different cultures have the potential to increase misunderstandings, friction, and even conflicts. In the words of one of the team members, "I think it is a matter of associations. When I say something to someone from my own culture, immediately we have a hundred common words and associations that I don't need to explain. When I say the same thing to someone from a different culture, it takes a lot more effort."

In his review of the literature on cross-cultural interactions, Stening (1979) reports a variety of problems, such as disparities in attributions about causes and intentions of behaviors, communication gaps, stereotyping, ethnocentrism, and prejudice. There may be an added complexity in organizations because the differences in cultural values can be manifested in different attitudes toward organizational practices, such as motivational techniques and leadership styles (Erez, 1993; Erez and Earley, 1987; Hui, 1990). Moreover, the cultural differences that members bring to the organization imply that they are likely to have different assumptions about what a good team is or what constitutes an efficient organization (Gibson and Zellmer-Bruhn, 2001). These differences have implications for the cohesiveness and integration within organizations and organizational groups. Coordination and control can be difficult to achieve in culturally diverse organizations where individual differences of participants are enhanced by differences in their national cultures (Ghoshal and Westney, 1993). (It should be noted, however, that overall, the literature on group dynamics suggests that multicultural and heterogeneous work teams combine different knowledge bases that promote effectiveness and performance of teams and the organization; Eisenhardt and Bourgeois, 1988; Elron, 1997.) More specifically for the theme of this chapter, because virtual teams are mostly cross-cultural, it is interesting to search for variations in political behavior and influence tactics across members of multinational virtual groups and how these differences affect the functioning of the team.

Several studies on organizational politics have suggested that individuals from different nations are likely to perceive organizational politics differently, as well as react to it differently. Vigoda and Cohen (2002) found that Israelis and Britons react differently to the same levels of organizational politics in their work environment. An earlier study by Romm and Drory (1988) found significant differences in perceptions and exertions of organizational politics between Canadians and Israelis. Thus, what is seen as a negative political or influence tactic by one member of the group can seem neutral to another, and the results can be anywhere from a simple misunderstanding to severe negative emotions and dysfunctioning because influence and politics are such sensitive processes. When it comes to the actual meeting of these different cultures, it has been found that cultural boundaries and differences restrain people from using extremely aggressive influence and politics when they are contained in organizations (Elron, Shamir, and Ben-Ari, 1999). One of the explanations to the milder use is accountability. Many multicultural team participants try to be "on their best behavior" when in contact with members from other cultures because they feel that they are not only private individuals but also representatives of their country and culture. As a result, they tend to use tactics that are more acceptable socially.

Another explanation goes back to the notions of familiarity and risk. A multicultural team means different cultural norms and codes of behavior for different members, some directly related to the use of influence and politics. The difficulty in understanding the codes of another culture and the accompanying feeling of uncertainty increase the difficulty in achieving high levels of intimacy and familiarity, enhancing the risk effect. The differences in levels of understanding the language spoken in the team can have similar consequences. Some of the participants mentioned the role of language as a barrier for effective political processes to emerge. As one participant framed it:

> There is something more mild working in virtual teams. Since we are talking about multicultural groups, there is a diversity in levels of spoken or written English among all members. Although we understand each other pretty well, we sometimes do not express ourselves the same way as we do in Hebrew. We also sometimes do not get the bottom line or the accurate meaning between the lines as expressed by the other unless we have gotten to know him or her personally and relate the words with their face and personality. We therefore feel more limited with how strongly we can come on about things.

Less pleasant perceptions of the consequences of cultural differences also exist. More specific to the cultures involved in this study, Israelis perceived their foreign colleagues as separate cultural groups who behave differently from themselves when it comes to politics, mainly in the form of indirectness. Several participants argued that North American members used milder, gentler, and perhaps more sophisticated and covert influence tactics when compared to Israelis, who tend to be more direct and blunt. As a result, they partly adjusted their influence behaviors, which was perceived at times as an unwanted effort, especially when it was felt that the adjustment was made by representatives of one culture only:

> The North American members of our team are frequently indirect in their influential behavior. They will try very gently to convince you, and if you are not convinced, they will try once more, and another try, and another one, and so on and so forth, but all is done in a very civilized manner. We Israelis are different. We are more direct in our approach. We have less time to discuss everything all

over again. Explanations are given only once, and we expect the other side to understand it fast and either accept our position or reject it.

Our influential approach is more overt and direct, but this does not necessarily mean that we do not practice politics in our own way. Israeli politics, as distinct from American politics, is characterized by preparing the background in advance. Prior to the virtual team's meeting, an Israeli will talk with one or two more members to see how they can support his or her idea or position from another angle or something like this. This does not mean that an American will not engage in the same tactic, but she or he will be much more careful not to exceed accepted social norms. We, on the other hand, act differently, although we try to adjust ourselves to the team's codes of behavior. Still, we remain much more direct than others.

The consequence of the specific differences in directness is that team members from a more direct culture can sometimes perceive indirectness as political. An interviewee said that he knows who is more political among the Canadian members because "the person is never direct."

This is just one example of how differences in cultural behaviors can cause misperceptions that at times lead to misinterpretations of a person's political tendencies, which can result in rifts within the team. More generally, our findings suggest that in understanding cross-cultural contacts between members of specific cultures, we need to take into consideration that what may sometimes seem to be a relatively small difference on certain cultural dimensions may be magnified due to the contrast between the focal cultures. Because Israel is a Westernized country and Americanized in many respects, and members of all teams belonged to the same professional communities, had had a similar professional education, and had experience working with members of the other cultural group, the cultural differences that team members describe are surprisingly salient. Hence, to understand the true nature and the effects of these differences, we need to ask members of the culture not only about their values, habits, and practices but also about their culture in relation to the other culture.

Contrary to our expectations and to previous findings on face-to-face teams (Elron, 2000), no coalitions based on country of origin were reported. In fact, all participants reported that the use of stable coalitions in the virtual teams was nonexistent unless tense relationships existed in the larger environment.

ORGANIZATIONAL IMPACTS ON INFLUENCE AND POLITICS

The surrounding organizational culture is important as an external source of influence on team culture. It may affect the behavior of team members through its impact on the culture of the team itself and through its impact on the beliefs, norms, and values that individual members bring into the team. As Trice and

Beyer (1993, p. 2) noted, "Cultures provide organizational members with more or less articulated sets of ideas that help them individually and collectively to cope with . . . uncertainties and ambiguities." In our interviews, we found that one of the strongest effects on the norms of the virtual team regarding influence and politics is the culture of the organization it is embedded within. Moreover, in one of our organizations, the culture was so strong that the congruence between team and organizational values was considered crucial for the success of the team. In other words, team members observe the unwritten rule that their participation and behavior should cohere with the general cultural norms of the organizations. Consequently, there is a strong reflection of the organizational beliefs and ideology regarding how organizational members should behave with others and influence behaviors within the team. In other words, there is a direct relationship between the intensity of political processes in the organization and the intensity of these processes in the teams. Moreover, the effect on politics is also through the risk effect. Risk effect in the team is related to the risk effect in the organization: when members of the organization perceive the engagement in organizational politics as riskier, members of the team will have similar perceptions.

Both organizations in our study were knowledge organizations, and there is high esteem for rationality in all their processes and in the behaviors people display, as this participant noted:

> There is something called our company's values. These are the organization's values: you have to talk quietly, not have emotional outbursts, not interrupt somebody in the middle, come to meetings on time. You will never hear people shouting at each other. When I enter the building, the culture is very different from the outside world.

This rationality is then translated into the teams' processes:

> If you have eight people in the group and two are arguing between them in a telephone meeting for over two minutes, you simply stop it and tell them to take it off-line to sort out their disagreements and find a solution. The rest of the group doesn't need to waste time and be part of this.

In general, then, the specific cultures in our study contribute to rationality being the dominant mode of persuasion. This is not to say that this is the only influence behavior for the team. Participants from the merged organization indicated that beneath some of the rational decision-making processes existing in the Canadian organization, competition prevailed, resulting in pockets of high-level political activity. These activities have invaded the joint virtual team, with members blaming others for incompetencies behind their back through e-mail reports and telephone conversations to the central members of the Israeli part of the team. It is important to remember, however, that although the virtual teams are more or less the mirror image of their organizations in terms of politics, it is nevertheless a diluted image.

In addition to organizational culture, organizational structure also has an impact on influence and politics in virtual teams. As today's organizations restructure, layers of organizational hierarchies tend to be removed, resulting in flatter organizational structure. This flattening is strongly tied to the trend toward getting work done through teams rather than individuals. As the underlying assumption that fewer layers and teamwork enable better decision making strengthens, it has become the typical organizational structure of high-tech companies, manifested in the organizations that participated in our study. Their virtual teams are a reflection of this structure, characterized by a flat hierarchy, minimization of formal positions, and the movement of authority from the hands of selected individuals to those of the entire group. This has a direct effect on VOP by allowing all members of the team to be equally involved in decision-making processes and the sharing of power. This equality is strengthened through the use of e-mail, which easily allows all group members to participate in sharing information and the discussions that follow. Moreover, e-mail allows easy access to all members, even when they have higher formal positions.

As for the more specific issue of authority, all virtual teams that were globally dispersed in our study had nonautocratic leadership or no formal leadership at all. Usually the groups had a coordinator who was equal to all other members in terms of status, with only one group having a formal leader who had no power in terms of evaluating his team members' performance. Hence, the distribution of formal power and resources among team members is relatively equal, which leads to less diversity and more homogeneity among participants in terms of status. This leads to the minimization of political behavior aimed at powerful individuals (or, alternatively, at the least powerful ones).

Closely related to the low levels of formality (and also to the teams' moderate centrality) is the fact that team members in almost all groups were not dependent on their evaluations or reviews from the group leader or group members. This again resulted in less politics because it decreased both competition among group members and the need to engage in upward impression management:

> I think that traditional groups may face more internal politics than virtual groups do. Wherever the direct supervisor who provides a term review is also part of the team, politics will increase. In my team, for example, I do not provide the reviews. Instead, I am one of many others who give feedback, and the direct manager presents the integrated materials to the employee. On the other hand, people pay more attention to you if you are trying to practice organizational politics in your team.

The lack of formal hierarchy or centralized authority in most groups also increases the sense that a relatively high level of collaboration and spontaneous cooperation must be achieved to secure the group's goals and existence. Individuals mostly understand that beyond objective obstacles to acting politically, such influential behaviors in virtual teams may harm the mutual, integrative, and collective dynamics that constitute the core of the group. Perhaps this is another reason that individuals report less and milder political activity in virtual teams.

IMPLICATIONS FOR PRACTICE

The preliminary findings of our study explore some interesting prospects of politics and influential behavior in virtual teams. In general, these findings indicate that VOP may be significantly lower than operational politics in conventional teams. Members of virtual teams report lower intensities in the use of influence and political behaviors compared with similar activities of conventional face-to-face groups. In addition, the most dominant influence attempts used are rationality, consultation, and assertiveness, which are considered among the most socially acceptable tactics and also the most effective ones (Yukl and Tracey, 1992). The use of less acceptable tactics such as sanctions, exerting pressures and threats, and blocking information was denied by all our interviewees. Most participants agreed, however, that ingratiation, exchange, coalition, and even upward appeal may be relevant behind the scenes but not directly in overt team dynamics. In other words, politics does exist in virtual teams as it exists elsewhere; however, it is much more restrained and mild than politics in face-to-face groups and takes on a more rational form. Summarizing the explanations we found, we offer the following recommendations:

• *Minimize politics.* A consistent and general finding is that less socially acceptable influence tactics and high prevalence of organizational politics are clearly related to more negative attitudes and behaviors and to deficient performance at the individual, team, and organizational levels (Cropanzano, Howes, Grandey, and Toth, 1997; Ferris and Kacmar, 1992; Kacmar and Ferris, 1991; Parker, Dipboye, and Jackson, 1995; Vigoda, 2000a, 2000b). We find that this is also true for virtual teams. There are many difficulties in maintaining an effective virtual team. Establishing a strong team identity is harder, creating desirable group norms may take longer, control of social loafing may take more effort, and the lack of face-to-face social cues results in greater cultural and language barriers. Our study looks at a brighter side: less energy and emotional resources are needed to detect, prevent, and invest in political activities. Good logic presented in a rational manner is almost sufficient to run the group.

- *Conduct a limited number of critical face-to-face meetings.* It is the lack of close familiarity and intimacy that helps the more efficient and socially acceptable influence tactics thrive and prevent political games. It seems that two or three face-to-face meetings a year are the optimal number of meetings to keep team members from complete and problematic anonymity yet keep politics low.

- *Discuss cultural differences openly.* Cultural differences in the team restrain political activity but can also cause misperceptions of the meanings of actions members take. Efforts of understanding the differences in members' cultures have been shown to reduce political activity in teams significantly (Elron, 2000). These findings lead us to suggest that cultural differences in influence behaviors should be discussed openly, and a consensus on a comfortable range of such behaviors that are legitimate within the team needs to be reached.

- *Use flat structures.* The team structure is crucial in determining levels and type of politics. Insofar as the team structure is flatter and even without a manager (with one of the members appointed as the administrator of the team), employees will rely more heavily on rationality, reasoning, and perhaps assertiveness but not on other overt and more vigorous activities such as sanctions, blocking, coalitions, or upward appeals, which are more frequent in traditional teams. Therefore, managers should develop team structures that are as flat as possible and safeguard them, dividing responsibilities and authority equally among team members and allowing the teams to decide on its inner dynamics and procedures. Still, this should not interfere with managers' duty to define goals for virtual teams clearly as well as deadlines to meet these goals and stay in line with the organization's needs and vision.

- *Use an understanding of organizational culture to guide practice.* The political culture of the organization and the influence norms it holds have a strong impact on the intensity of political activity in the team. Because the typical virtual team has relatively low intensity of political activity, when political activity in a virtual team is high, check the organizational culture for signs of similar activity.

A general finding of our work is that organizational politics exists in virtual teams, although in a different manner and intensity compared with traditional work teams. Thus, although there may be a tendency to view the sometimes faceless virtual team members as task performers only, managers need to take into consideration that political activities do occur in virtual teams, even if in a milder or less intense manner. Important tactics for managing virtual organizations' virtual organizational politics can improve the effectiveness of the ever increasing virtual collaboration.

References

Bacharach, S. B., and Lawler, E. J. *Power and Politics in Organizations*. San Francisco: Jossey-Bass, 1980.

Cropanzano, R., Howes, J. C., Grandey, A. A., and Toth, P. "The Relationship of Organizational Politics and Support to Work Behaviors, Attitudes, and Stress." *Journal of Organizational Behavior*, 1997, *18*, 159–180.

Drory, A., and Romm, T. "Politics in Organizations and Its Perception Within the Organization." *Organization Studies*, 1988, *9*, 165–179.

Eisenhardt, K. M., and Bourgeois, L. J. "Politics of Strategic Decision Making in High Velocity Environments: Toward a Midrange Theory." *Academy of Management Journal*, 1988, *31*, 737–770.

Elron, E. "Top Management Teams Within Multinational Corporations: Effects of Cultural Heterogeneity." *Leadership Quarterly*, 1997, *8*, 393–412.

Elron, E. "Cultural Diversity and Political Processes in Multinational Top Management Teams." Paper presented at the Academy of Management Meeting, Toronto, 2000.

Elron, E., Shamir, B., and Ben-Ari, E. "Why Don't They Fight Each Other? Cultural Diversity and Operational Unity in Multinational Forces." *Armed Forces and Society*, 1999, *26*, 73–98.

Erez, M. "Toward a Model of Cross-Cultural Industrial and Organizational Psychology." In M. D. Dunnette and L. M. Hough (eds.), *Handbook of Industrial and Organizational Psychology*. Palo Alto, Calif.: Consulting Psychologists Press, 1993.

Erez, M., and Earley, P. C. "Comparative Analysis of Goal-Setting Strategies Across Cultures." *Journal of Applied Psychology*, 1987, *72*, 658–665.

Ferris, G. R., and Kacmar, K. M. "Perceptions of Organizational Politics." *Journal of Management*, 1992, *18*, 93–116.

Ferris, G. R., and King, T. R. "Politics in Human Resources Decisions: A Walk on the Dark Side." *Organizational Dynamics*, 1991, *20*, 59–71.

Ferris, G. R., and others. "Perceptions of Organizational Politics: Predisposition, Stress-Related Implications, and Outcomes." *Human Relations*, 1996, *49*(2), 233–266.

Gandz, J., and Murray, V. V. "The Experience of Workplace Politics." *Academy of Management Journal*, 1980, *23*, 237–251.

Ghoshal, S., and Westney, D. E. "Introduction and Overview." In S. Ghoshal and D. Eleanor Westney (eds.), *Organization Theory and the Multinational Corporation*. New York: St. Martin's Press, 1993.

Gibson, C. B., and Zellmer-Bruhn, M. "Metaphor and Meaning: An Intercultural Analysis of the Concept of Teamwork." *Administrative Science Quarterly*, 2001, *46*, 274–303.

Hui, C. H. "Work Attitudes, Leadership Styles, and Managerial Behaviors in Different Cultures." In R. W. Brislin (ed.), *Applied Cross-Cultural Psychology*. Thousand Oaks, Calif.: Sage, 1990.

Jehn, K. A., and Shah, P. P. "Interpersonal Relationships and Task Performance: An Examination of Mediating Processes in Friendship and Acquaintance Groups." *Journal of Personality and Social Psychology,* 1997, *72,* 775–790.

Kacmar, K. M., and Ferris, G. R. "Perceptions of Organizational Politics Scale (POPS): Development and Construct Validation." *Educational and Psychological Measurement,* 1991, *51,* 193–205.

Kipnis, D., Schmidt, S. M., and Wilkinson, I. "Intraorganizational Influence Tactics: Exploration in Getting One's Way." *Journal of Applied Psychology,* 1980, *65,* 440–452.

Klein, J., and Barrett, B. "One Foot in a Global Team, One Foot at the Local Site: Making Sense Out of Living in Two Worlds Simultaneously." In M. Beyerlein (ed.), *Advances in Interdisciplinary Studies of Work Teams.* Vol. 8: *Virtual Teams.* Greenwich, Conn.: JAI-Elsevier, 2001.

Latane, B., and others. "Distance Matters: Physical Space and Social Impact." *Personality and Social Psychology Bulletin,* 1995, *21,* 795–805.

Maslyn, J. M., and Fedor, D. B. "Perceptions of Politics: Does Measuring Different Foci Matter?" *Journal of Applied Psychology,* 1998, *84,* 645–653.

McKenney, J. L., Zack, M. H., and Doherty, V. S. "Complementary Communication Media: A Comparison of Electronic Mail and Face-to-Face Communication in a Programming Team." In N. Nohria and R. Eccles (eds.), *Networks and Organizations: Structure, Form, and Action.* Boston: Harvard Business School Press, 1992.

Mintzberg, H. *Power in and Around Organizations.* Upper Saddle River, N.J.: Prentice Hall, 1983.

Nohria, N., and Eccles, R. "Face-to-Face: Making Network Organizations Work." In N. Nohria and R. Eccles (eds.), *Networks and Organizations: Structure, Form, and Action.* Boston: Harvard Business School Press, 1992.

Parker, C. P., Dipboye, R. L., and Jackson, S. L. "Perceptions of Organizational Politics: An Investigation of Antecedents and Consequences." *Journal of Management,* 1995, *21,* 891–912.

Pfeffer, J. *Management with Power.* Boston: Harvard Business School Press, 1992.

Romm, T., and Drory, A. "Political Behavior in Organizations: A Cross-Cultural Comparison." *International Journal of Value Based Management,* 1988, *1,* 97–113.

Schein, E. H. *Organizational Culture and Leadership.* San Francisco: Jossey-Bass, 1985.

Stening, B. W. "Problems in Cross-Cultural Contact: A Literature Review." *International Journal of Intercultural Relations,* 1979, *3,* 269–313.

Trice, H. M., and Beyer, J. M. *The Cultures of Work Organizations.* Upper Saddle River, N.J.: Prentice Hall, 1993.

Vigoda, E. "Internal Politics in Public Administration Systems: An Empirical Examination of Its Relationship with Job Congruence, Organizational Citizenship Behavior and in Role Performances." *Public Personnel Management,* 2000a, *29,* 185–210.

Vigoda, E. "The Relationship Between Organizational Politics, Job Attitudes, and Work Outcomes: Exploration and Implications for the Public Sector." *Journal of Vocational Behavior,* 2000b, *57,* 326–347.

Vigoda, E., and Cohen, A. "Influence Tactics and Perceptions of Organizational Politics: A Longitudinal Study." *Journal of Business Research,* 2002, *55*(4), 311–324.

Yukl, G., and Falbe, C. M. "Influence Tactics in Upward, Downward, and Lateral Influence Attempts." *Journal of Applied Psychology,* 1990, *76,* 416–423.

Yukl, G., and Tracey, J. B. "Consequences of Influence Tactics Used with Subordinates, Peers, and the Boss." *Journal of Applied Psychology,* 1992, *77,* 525–535.

CHAPTER FIFTEEN

Conflict and Virtual Teams

Terri L. Griffith, Elizabeth A. Mannix, Margaret A. Neale

*Miscommunication and flaming e-mails between team members who were
geographically distributed were exchanged for weeks. The flames
eventually died down, but I don't know if the issue was ever resolved.*
—A virtual team member

Is conflict different within virtual teams? Are there unique communication skills for the perception and subsequent management of conflict in virtual teams? By their nature, teams that are virtual—members are not all in the same location—are likely to face challenges in their dynamics and in the perception and management of any ensuing conflict. The role of communication in conflict perception and management is critical not only because how a team communicates is a major factor that distinguishes more virtual teams from their less virtual counterparts, but also because skill in face-to-face communication and conflict management does not necessarily map on to skill in virtual communication and the (virtual) management of conflict.

While communication methods vary dramatically in virtual teams, communication technologies are part of the enabling force behind the existence of many virtual teams. Janine Kilty, director of worldwide human resources and vice president of health imaging at Eastman Kodak, reports that she sometimes spends an entire day in a single conference call. Kilty has found that such lengthy interactions without face-to-face contact have required that she learn how to communicate effectively using this medium and master the recognition of auditory rather than visual interaction cues. In general, members of

---

We thank Karen Jehn and Gregory Northcraft for their thoughtful advice during the development of this project and the people who made the project possible: Sai Allavarpu, Julie Harper, Nadine Lucas, Grace Tow, and the responding teams and managers.

distributed teams use synchronous and asynchronous communication technologies (such as telephone and e-mail), and the technology may vary depending on its ability to document the communication. *Media effects* is a phrase used to describe all the outcomes that result from the use of a particular communication medium. However, it is critical to keep in mind that few (if any) media effects are deterministic. Rather, the effects noted for a particular medium are generally a combination of the technological capabilities of the medium, combined with how well the medium is understood and how it is actually used in the group (DeSanctis, Poole, and Dickson, 2000).

Although media effects are a function of user experience as well as technological capabilities, use of electronic or computer-supported communication technologies, without face-to-face interaction, may alter the form or dynamics of conflict. For example, conflict may be hidden longer in more virtual teams than might be the case in more traditional settings. Nancy Chase, of QualityOnLine, notes that

> in a virtual team, when things go awry, they can do so for a longer period of time before they're noticed. . . . So the virtual team leader—any team member, but particularly the team leader—might want to be a little more vigilant to try to catch early warning signs that there's a problem with the team or the schedule. The problem is not usually intention or commitment to the team. It's usually some breakdown of communication. This is true in any group of people coming together; it's just exacerbated in a virtual environment [*Training Trends* (e-zine), 1999].

This is an example of one way that conflict dynamics may be altered in more virtual settings. It is also possible that the work environment of virtual teams may reduce some types of conflict. Articles about Verifone (written before it was acquired by Hewlett-Packard) describe how virtual teams were able to work around the clock without violating the personal time of any one team member (Pape, 1997). In addition, the use of asynchronous communication like e-mail may give team members time to think through a response rather than respond in the heat of the moment.

These anecdotal examples of conflict in virtual teams provide an interesting perspective from practitioners who are managing virtual teams. The rest of this chapter presents a more organized assessment of conflict across the variety of settings encountered by such teams and provides some key points to consider in the design and management of virtual teams in organizations.

VIRTUAL TEAMS IN MODERN ORGANIZATIONS

Managers should focus on three basic dimensions for identifying and understanding virtual teams: (1) members' relative locations, (2) percentage of time on the team task spent face-to-face, and (3) level of technological support. These dimensions are clearly related in practice. If a team's members are geographically distributed, we would expect to find that they would have high levels of technological support and would use electronic communication more frequently than more colocated groups. However, practice also suggests that even teams located in the same building may communicate largely by e-mail. In fact, in the organization described in this chapter, all teams spent an equal amount of time working face-to-face on the team task (approximately 13 percent). E-mail use did vary by whether all the members were colocated, but not to a great extent (34 percent of all task communication in colocated teams versus 45.76 percent in distributed teams).

The ideas we present on conflict take these possibilities into account. Some of the issues we raise are related to a reliance on electronic communication, others are more focused on the capabilities of the technology, and still others are more related to the outcomes of members' being physically separated. For clarity, we refer to more or less virtual teams, meaning teams with more or fewer of these technological and geographical characteristics.

THE ROLE OF CONFLICT IN TEAMS

Contrary to what may be popular belief, some level of conflict is necessary for the successful functioning of teams. However, conflict must be managed to be effective, and it is important to understand that not all conflict is the same. Broadly, conflict in teams is simply awareness by some or all of the members of differences, discrepancies, incompatible wishes, or irreconcilable desires (Boulding, 1963). There has been a debate in organizational research regarding whether disagreement within teams is advantageous (Eisenhardt and Zbaracki, 1992). One key to unlocking this complex relationship lies in the differentiation of conflict as relationship, task, or process focused (Jehn, 1995).

Relationship conflict (or affective conflict) is an awareness of interpersonal differences. It may include personality differences, hostility, and annoyance between individuals. Relationship conflict has a negative effect on individual and team performance and has also been found to negatively affect team member satisfaction and the likelihood the team will work together in the future (Jehn and Mannix, 2001). Team members with relationship conflict may be distracted from the task, work less cooperatively, or produce suboptimal products.

Task (or cognitive) conflict is an awareness of differences in viewpoints and opinions pertaining to the team's task. Task conflict may include disagreements about the task being performed—for example, disagreement regarding an organization's current hiring strategies or determining the information to include in an annual report. In contrast to relationship conflict, moderate levels of task conflict have been shown to be beneficial to team performance in various decision-making and team tasks. Teams performing complex cognitive tasks benefit from differences of opinion about the work being done (Jehn and Mannix, 2001). Task conflict improves decision quality as teams drop old patterns of interaction and adopt new perspectives. The synthesis that emerges from task conflict is generally superior to the individual perspectives themselves (Schwenk, 1990). Thus, the presence of task conflict, accompanied by its effective resolution, should improve team performance.

Process conflict includes disagreements regarding how to do the task or how to delegate resources (Jehn, 1997). Although it is the least examined of the three types of conflict, early work suggests that unresolved process conflict can be detrimental to team performance because it may focus attention on irrelevant topics or get in the way of the team's actually getting on to the task.

Recent research in this domain (Simons and Peterson, 2000) indicates that people often misperceive which of the forms of conflict they are experiencing. What is technically a conflict about the task, for example, may be taken personally and thus be experienced as relationship conflict. The comment, "I think you're wrong in focusing on the strategic plan when we're in the middle of a budget crisis," may be taken as a condemnation of the person rather than as a comment on the time and resource requirements of the situation. Misattribution may be more likely in newly formed or highly diverse teams, where a lack of deep knowledge of teammates may cause members to confuse one type of conflict with another (Gruenfeld, Mannix, Williams, and Neale, 1996). Thus, it is possible that by facilitating task conflict, a team may run considerable risk in also increasing the level of relationship or process conflict.

One factor that seems to break this cycle in teams is the existence of trust (Simons and Peterson, 2000). Teams characterized by trust in the form of competence, integrity, and benevolence face a lesser challenge (see Mayer, Davis, and Schoorman, 1995, and Chapter Four, this volume, for a discussion of the components of trust) in that they are more likely to be able to generate moderate levels of task conflict and avoid misinterpreting conflict. Furthermore, the sense of trust will make conflict, when it occurs, more easily resolved. Given trust, the task conflict noted above might be interpreted correctly as task conflict rather than a personal attack; the recipient may be more willing to trust that the colleague is focused on work rather than, for example, making points with the boss. These are tasks that traditional teams often find difficult to manage effectively, and there are special challenges that distributed teams face in identifying and managing conflict.

We believe that managing conflict successfully is a different process in more virtual versus more traditional teams. Past research and experience point to a variety of issues that make conflict management difficult in the best of circumstances. In the more complex and unfamiliar world of virtual teams, these hurdles are amplified. That said, there may also be attributes of virtual work that will make certain aspects of conflict easier to manage.

WHAT WE KNOW AND HOW WE KNOW IT

In our prior research (Griffith and Neale, 2001), we developed theoretical approaches for understanding differences and similarities across more traditional and more virtual teams. Here, we link these approaches to the experiences of over one hundred people involved in twenty-eight teams. In the following sections, we evaluate the dynamics and outcomes of conflict across both more and less virtual teams. Thirteen of the twenty-eight teams were colocated (all employed at the same company site). The other fifteen teams had at least one team member working away from the rest of the team, and some of these teams were spread across a variety of the company's locations. Our questions start with the most basic background issues of the construction of these teams and move toward the most complex regarding the perceptions and management of conflict.

The Organization

We partnered with a large software firm (which we will call SoftCo) to collect these data. We administered a Web-based survey to thirty-five teams representing employees from the company's three U.S. locations and a variety of European sites in exchange for help in developing and delivering training for virtual teams. Team members were e-mailed by a SoftCo executive asking for their help in return for a small gift (a company pen). Respondents were also told that the data collected would be used to improve training at the firm. The teams range in size from two to twenty-eight members. Fifty-seven percent of team members are male, with an average age of thirty-six. Forty-one cities are represented across the thirty-five sampled teams. Of these teams, twenty-eight provided data that we could use to evaluate conflict. The teams were all permanent, with reporting relationships to managers. Their areas of responsibility spanned most of the areas of the firm, including information systems, software engineering, human resources, and administrative functions such as purchasing.

Figure 15.1 plots these teams along the dimensions of percentage of time spent face-to-face on task, distribution (an aggregate measure taking into account the size of the group and the proportions working at the same location), and percentage of task communication done by e-mail. As can be seen in the figure, there were wide ranges on each of these measures: percentage of time spent face-to-face on task (0 to 68 percent), distribution (0 to 1.75, ranging from teams that were fully colocated to an eight-person team with seven locations), and percentage of task communication done by e-mail (10 to 57 percent). This range of teams is probably typical for many organizations. None of the teams was fully traditional (doing all their task work together) or purely virtual (where none of the members ever meet face-to-face).

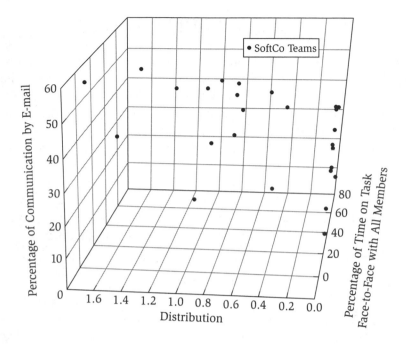

Figure 15.1 Range of Virtualness.

Given that the teams have some degree of control over their communication and meeting strategies, we will focus here on differences between teams that are colocated[1] and those that are distributed.

Questions and Answers

The field study provided an opportunity to address some of the basic questions of virtual teams and conflict and the possibility of rich insights given the team members' comments:

• *Do virtual teams experience more conflict than traditional teams?* We found that virtual teams had greater levels of process conflict than traditional teams, but only when also controlling for the effects of trust. We did not find differences in the levels of task or relationship conflict (see Figure 15.2). This result is consistent with some of our earlier work (Griffith and Meader, 2001) on investment clubs. There, we found that a focus on the process, but not task or social aspects, of team functioning was a positive predictor of portfolio value in more and less virtual clubs. Because more virtual teams have to manage greater complexity, attention to process can become a key to their success. A similar focus in less virtual teams, however, may get in the way of efficient and effective standard operating procedures.

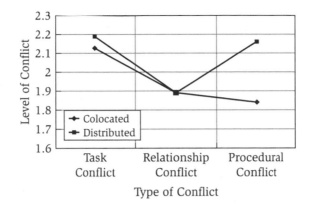

Figure 15.2 Levels of Conflict for Colocated and Distributed Teams.

Note: Level of conflict was measured on a scale of 1 to 5, with 1 meaning that no conflict was experienced and 5 that a lot of conflict was experienced.

The lack of differences in task and relationship conflict levels between virtual and traditional teams at SoftCo may be the outcome of the teams' structuring their work in a way that overcomes the challenges of distance. The data presented here are a single snapshot of the conflict and performance of these teams, and they may have already found solutions to problems initially encountered. Alternatively, the lack of differences may be an indication of adjustments in expectations. In the investment club study, Griffith and Meader (2001) argue that members of more virtual clubs may expect less emotional communication and may even self-select into such clubs to accommodate their preferences. Thus, even if relationship conflict occurs, it might not be recognized as such by team members. Alternatively, it may be recognized but not acknowledged as important. Unfortunately, we cannot tease apart these alternatives with our current survey measures. Future work that is more focused on observation over time may be able to disentangle these alternatives.

Earlier, we proposed that conflict is often the result of having to manage diverse perspectives. This leads us to the next question.

• *Are virtual teams more diverse than traditional teams?* Our expectation was that the answer would be yes. The cost of virtual teams is warranted when needed information is not available locally. Indeed, the more virtual teams at SoftCo were also more diverse in terms of the informational background of their members. This was measured by considering the educational level, functional area, and position in the firm. We also would have expected the more virtual teams to be more diverse in terms of the ethnicity and cultures represented. However, the firm was not comfortable with our requesting such information.

Such demographic or "social category" diversity has been found to lead to creativity and higher levels of performance on complex group tasks (Watson, Kumar, and Michaelsen, 1993; Williams and O'Reilly, 1998). However, demographic diversity has also been shown to increase relationship conflict and impede group functioning (Jehn, Northcraft, and Neale, 1999). Thus, the cumulative effect of different forms of diversity on virtual teams is an important topic but will have to be left for future study.

Conflict is the focus of our examination. Although structural issues such as diversity play a strong role, informational diversity was not related to increased levels of the three types of conflict in this firm. Furthermore, given the constraints placed on our access to team members, we could not address issues related to social category diversity. However, there are additional team dynamics that are also critical to our understanding of conflict in more and less virtual teams. As we noted, trust plays a role in our observation of conflict. In addition, identification with the team may vary from less to more virtual teams.

• *Do traditional team members identify themselves with the team more than members of virtual teams, and do they perceive greater trust within their teams?* This does not seem to be the case in this organization. Neither trust nor team identification is significantly related to the distribution of the team members. This may bode well for the management of more virtual teams, an indication that both trust and team identification can be high even in the more challenging virtual settings.

• *Does this mean that virtualness does not matter?* The relationships already noted seem to illustrate only minor differences between teams that work together and those that work apart: process conflict was higher in more virtual teams and information diversity was also greater, but not in a way that seemed to affect conflict. We do not believe that this is an indication that virtualness does not matter for team dynamics and outcomes; rather, we believe these results indicate a more complex set of relationships among team dynamics, the virtual environment, and conflict. We suggested that how the groups adjust their work structure or expectations may play a role in the results. We would like to examine this possibility in greater detail.

Technology effects are not deterministic. That is, teams adapt their structure, processes, and technology use to suit their needs (DeSanctis, Poole, and Dickson, 2000). Our assessment of whether more or less virtual teams have particular outcomes relies on these teams' acting in fixed ways. We doubt this is the case. Instead, we offer that these teams have more or less adapted to their situations. By consideration of additional and joint relationships, such as the role of trust and the perceived ability to notice conflict, we believe that differences in these teams can be identified and managerial implications drawn from the results.

• *What about performance?* We find that the distribution of team members does not seem to have an observable effect on performance. At SoftCo, teams with members who all work in the same location do not receive significantly higher managerial performance ratings than do teams with members distributed across locations. Process and relationship conflict, however, are related in expected ways to overall team performance. Our analyses show that regardless of virtualness, relationship and process conflict have significantly negative effects on performance as rated by the team's manager. Task conflict, however, does not seem to produce these effects.

The next step is to examine these effects from the perspective of virtualness. Earlier, we noted that teams that are more distributed have more process conflict and that this effect is clarified by controlling for trust. In fact, by knowing that a team has members who work apart and their level of trust, we can account for almost 50 percent of the team's process conflict. Additional analyses show these effects are not simply due to how the team communicates. Trust and distribution of the team members seem to be key to understanding performance. Apparently, we can manage trust independent of team colocation given our earlier result that trust is not tied to the distribution of the team members. However, process conflict, which is related to lower team performance, is positively related to the distribution of team members and negatively related to trust.

These effects can be seen in Figure 15.3. Teams whose members are more distributed but also have high levels of trust can expect to have lower levels of process conflict than teams whose members all work in the same location but with low levels of trust. Again, the powerful point in this issue is that trust is not a function of location. We can manage trust independently from the distribution of the team.

• *If trust is so important for the reduction of conflict, how can it be increased in more virtual teams?* At SoftCo, trust was higher the more the team communicated using e-mail and the more they worked together face-to-face. This is consistent

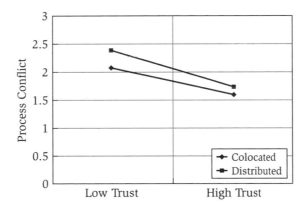

Figure 15.3 Process Conflict, Trust, and Distribution.

Note: Process conflict was measured on a scale of 1 to 5, with 1 meaning that no conflict was experienced and 5 that a lot of conflict was experienced.

with prior research on trust (Mayer, Davis, and Schoorman, 1995), suggesting that the relationship between behavior and trust is recursive: trusting behaviors are both antecedents and outcomes of trust. Teams need time together and communication to be able to develop trust.

These particular results are suggestive that this is "true" trust in this setting rather than the "swift" trust observed in some pure (members who never meet) virtual teams (Jarvenpaa and Leidner, 1999). Swift trust is differentiated from true trust in that swift trust can exist where there has been no opportunity to develop more traditional forms of trust (Meyerson, Weick, and Kramer, 1996). Both types of trust have been shown to have positive effects on team dynamics and performance.

With trust comes another opportunity: the ability to notice conflict. The psychological safety related to trust has been found to foster situations where openness and comfort in speaking up about difficult issues is possible (Edmondson, Bohmer, and Pisano, 2000). Conflict cannot be managed until team members are willing to address the issue or the conflict. Trust may make this necessary step in conflict management possible.

Our study provides additional insight to this perspective. We asked the team members the following question: "Sometimes it is easy to know when a conflict is occurring in a team; at other times conflict may be difficult to see. Thinking about this team, how often can you tell when there is a conflict?" Note that this is a question of their perceived ability to identify conflict, not a test of their ability to manage conflict. We also allowed the respondents to indicate that there was no conflict in their team. Figure 15.4 illustrates the results.

Trust and distribution account for 43 percent of the variance in team members' perceived abilities to notice conflict. It is also interesting to note that team

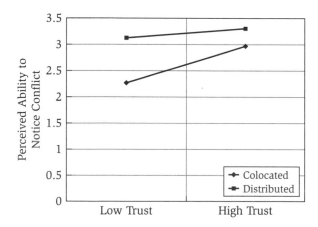

Figure 15.4 Perceived Ability to Notice Conflict, Trust, and Distribution.

Note: Perceived ability to notice conflict was measured on a scale of 1 to 5, with 1 meaning that the person was never able to perceive conflict and 5 that the person was always able to perceive conflict.

members' reported ability to notice conflict is not correlated with the perceived level of conflict in the team, suggesting that this is not just an indication of a conflict focus or of teams reaching a particular noticeable level of conflict.

These last results illustrate the importance of managing team dynamics. Use of e-mail, time spent with the full team working together, and the development of trust can all be managed explicitly. Teams can receive training that identifies the value of clear role responsibilities, the importance of following through on assigned tasks, and how to track members' completion of tasks. Trust is built as it is earned. In addition, the value of swift trust can be brought to the attention of more virtual teams. It is critical that trust be assumed (as is the case with swift trust) in the early stages, even before true trust has had a chance to form naturally. E-mail seems to have a unique role in the development of trust. Face-to-face communication, or the ability to work face-to-face with the whole team, did not seem to substitute for e-mail communication. E-mail may help to build trust among team members who use it more often, perhaps because e-mail allows such a quick response or because of its ability to document commitments.

We do have a paradox when we consider the statements of the team members regarding the signals that they used to identify conflict. While members of highly distributed teams report a greater ability to notice conflict, many of their comments regarding the signals that they used imply face-to-face interaction. We asked the respondents to think back to the last conflict they were aware of and then describe what made them notice the conflict in the team. Of the fifty-seven responses ("not applicable" was an optional answer), twenty-four could be identified as requiring face-to-face interaction. Many of the comments indicated visual clues: "flushing of a face," "clues in posture," "glancing at each other," and "body language." Other clues were more related to verbal communication: "pregnant silences," "team members tend to get quiet," "massive silence," "raised voices," and "derogatory comments." There was also a variety of ways conflict was perceived by e-mail: "flaming e-mails," "disconnect in the information/process," "receiving different messages regarding the same work," and "conflicting e-mails." It may be that more distributed teams are more focused on noticing conflict. They may work harder to sense the level of conflict in an effort to overcome the challenges of working apart, which is again an indication of how teams can adapt to the challenges of virtual work.

CONFLICT MANAGEMENT

There are basically five methods of conflict management:

- Avoidance, in which the issue is ignored, or more positively, left for a time when cooler minds can prevail
- Competition, in which one party tries to take all the gains

- Accommodation, in which one party tries to give all the gains to the others
- Compromise, in which the parties agree to split the difference
- Collaboration-integration, in which the parties find a solution where all can gain

Although there are times when each may be effective, avoidance and collaboration-integration seem to be the most prevalent choices in SoftCo's teams' management of conflict. The following examples from members of more virtual teams highlight the opportunities and challenges of these situations. This first set takes note of information sharing and strong communicative processes: "I approached my manager when I noticed tension between us, and we talked through what he was thinking and the fears he was having about me and my views of the department. We talked about some possible solutions to improve general team issues and seemed to work through the tension pretty well."

A project manager noticed conflict in an e-mail exchange regarding work assignments: "She called them separately, discussed what the issue was that each of them was facing, and also found out about their experience level and how they got along with each other. After talking separately, she did a conference call with both of the team members on-line and resolved the issues by assigning the tasks equally based on the experience. Both team members felt comfortable and satisfied."

Another respondent notes, "The entire team thrives on technical challenges. AOL Instant Messenger allows us to mitigate issues before they get out of hand."

The value of face-to-face communication was also noted: "When the entire department was approached regarding some unacceptable e-mails that were sent to certain individuals, our manager brought the group together and addressed it in a serious and formal manner without pointing any fingers and making anyone feel uncomfortable."

These examples were provided as responses to a request to tell us about the most successful case of conflict management they had recently observed. Many of these responses focused on getting issues out on the table and striving for a joint solution—a collaborative conflict management strategy. Although this is good advice for all teams, it may be even more crucial in virtual teams. Conflict must be identified before it can be addressed. Addressing conflict in more virtual settings may require a more explicit effort to make contact with the parties and perhaps a more explicit discussion (given the difficulty of conveying tacit ideas when not face-to-face). These increased costs may actually turn into benefits. A common problem in conflict management is that issues in dispute are not directly addressed. In the case of more virtual teams, when conflict management is in fact instigated, the process must be more explicit given likely communication restrictions. This more explicit communication may effectively avoid the common problem of misunderstandings found in less explicit communication.

We also asked respondents to describe the least successful case of conflict management that they had recently observed. These examples from some of the more virtual teams often fall into the category of conflict avoidance—for example, "Conflict is not currently being managed in this team. The team is choosing to use conflict avoidance as a method of conflict management. Some team members will confront others when or if they have an issue, but more often people keep the issues to themselves or push it under the rug."

In fact, of the twenty-nine examples of the least successful conflict management (from both more and less virtual teams), fifteen describe situations of conflict avoidance or lack of communication. One comment was especially telling: "We generally never have this problem, because those people just quit."

On a more positive note, team members seem to understand the challenges and the role that communication and trust play: "The tension in the team still exists. This issue made me realize even more some of the trust and communication issues we are having as a department."

The insights of the respondents are consistent with effective conflict management techniques. There is a focus on bringing the issues in conflict out into the open and working to solve problems in a way that integrates the parties' needs. However, it may be too early to celebrate the expertise of our respondents. Next, we consider additional questions and areas where this particular research may limit our ability to generalize.

OPEN QUESTIONS AND ISSUES

The respondents cannot tell us about conflicts they have not noticed. Only about half the respondents provided successful conflict management examples. Some stated that they had not been on the team long enough to notice conflict or that their team did not have any conflict at all. This may well be the case, or we may be seeing that not all respondents perceive conflict, and so miss the chance to manage their team's dynamics to the best degree possible.

Our study is based solely on the respondents' self-reports of conflict. We do not have measures over time or objective measures of the actual level of conflict in the teams. As we noted, misperception or misattributions of conflict are common in teams and inhibit teams' ability to manage their conflict effectively.

We have yet to assess the pattern of conflict in each of these teams. Relative levels of task, process, and relationship conflict play unique roles in team effectiveness (Jehn and Chatman, 2000). In addition, the time at which these types of conflict occur can be critical. Jehn and Mannix (2001) have demonstrated that higher group performance is associated with particular patterns of conflict. In their study of face-to-face teams, high-performing teams were characterized by low but increasing levels of process conflict, low levels of relationship conflict with a rise near the deadline, and moderate levels of task conflict at the midpoint of the interaction. To create this ideal conflict profile, team members had similar preestablished value systems, high levels of trust and respect, and open discussion norms around conflict during the middle stages of interaction. These patterns are currently being tested in a variety of teams, with different tasks and compositions. Whether these patterns will hold for virtual teams is uncertain, but certainly a topic for future research.

IMPLICATIONS FOR PRACTICE

The above discussion suggests three areas where practicing managers and their teams can improve their chances for success: the initial construction of more and less virtual teams, the role that awareness of conflict plays in virtual team function, and suggestions for the management of conflict, once it is noted. We believe that focusing on these key areas will provide a strong foundation for the support of virtual teams.

Initial Construction of Virtual Teams

We support experienced virtual team managers in arguing that it is important to get the structure and infrastructure of virtual teams right from the beginning. Explicit consideration of roles, trust, and communication processes should be addressed from the start. A face-to-face introductory meeting may be key. Chris Brennan of Lotus Institute and now IBM has worked for four years on the development of virtual teams. He believes that a facilitated face-to-face development session is important: "Our work suggests that the complication in a virtual team has to do with discipline and alignment. If you have 10 people located in 10 different places and they are not all sure that they know what they're doing, chaos breaks out. It is critical that they establish a relationship and trust each other" (Young, 1998).

Chris Newell, executive director of Lotus Institute, points to the importance of at least a one-day videoconference: "It's important to develop some level of trust and relationship before you can move into electronic communication." Although needs for trust may vary by type of project, Newell nevertheless recommends a statement of mission, norms, and agreements about how to operate and how to handle the technological aspects of the team's interactions. Such a guide might include rules about conflict management. For example, there could be an agreement to meet in person to address a conflict (Geber, 1995, p. 38). Janine Kilty of Eastman Kodak notes that overt conflicts often conceal underlying issues that hinge on matters of trust and respect. These should never be dealt with over the telephone or by e-mail, but must be handled face-to-face. Most virtual communities seem to have seen the value of such systems. A popular guide to the construction and management of such on-line communities advises that the community's "host" (moderator) point newcomers to electronic archives and that rules for behavior and the management of conflict be clear and developed before a community is opened (Rheingold, 1998).

The value of an infrastructure that can capture a team's history is echoed in comments by Susan Sowers, manager of Hewlett-Packard's corporate client computing group. She manages a virtual team of twenty-one people over three U.S. sites and notes that virtual teams need more formal communications, not fewer: "Cohesion can be broken when someone new joins. That's why it's particularly important to make sure that nearly all communications are kept in the shared database, so that a historical document of the group's work is available for the new person to peruse" (Geber, 1995).

A simple start to developing this infrastructure is to share communication capabilities and values. One way to resolve process conflict is by managing the complexity of the team's communication. At a minimum team members should know:

- Times it is reasonable to call (considering time zones)
- Days when calls are appropriate (considering cultural, family, or work schedule circumstances)
- Appropriate communication media and contact information (considering the form and urgency of the message)
- Documentation procedures, including uses of e-mail subject headings, file types, and urgency markers
- Meeting and contact schedules and milestones

As the team works together, there must also be time accorded for team assessment and maintenance. James Brault, director worldwide human resources for document imaging at Eastman Kodak, finds that group initiation and maintenance issues are too often ignored in virtual teams. Brault has written an extensive company guide, *How to Master Virtual Teams* (Brault, 1999), describing seven categories of skills and resources that must be present for virtual teams to work effectively:

- Clear direction, goals, and roles
- Appropriate and clear rewards and recognition
- Appropriate capability, skills, and training
- Established processes and norms
- Strong leadership
- Ability to use virtual technology fully
- Environmental mechanisms for face-to-face interaction

He argues that the team leader must be responsible for assessing the team and team members on each of these dimensions at the formation of the team and as the team works together. Taking on this assessment may set the stage for effective task conflict resolution and reduce the possibility of related process conflicts that might be misinterpreted as relationship conflict.

Awareness of Conflict

Conflict cannot be managed until it is noticed. This is an area in which virtual teams may be at an advantage if they develop a heightened awareness of communication through e-mail. Interestingly, the respondents from SoftCo's more virtual teams report a greater ability to notice conflict when it occurs. Perhaps in more virtual teams, when face-to-face communication does take place, this communication is less mundane, leading team members to pay more attention to the nuances of the communication. While conflict may go unnoticed, or at least take longer to be noticed in virtual teams, this does not have to be the case. The SoftCo respondents have developed approaches for noticing conflict through e-mail. To the extent that people can learn to notice conflict in face-to-face settings, we believe that there is at least equal opportunity for developing the necessary skills to identify conflict in more virtual settings.

It is possible that members of more virtual teams will be better able to focus on task and process conflict—positive types of conflict. Face-to-face communication is generally required to communicate tacit information. Relationship conflict, a negative type of conflict, may require tacit channels to communicate. Explicit forms of communication such as e-mail may be better suited to the communication of task and process conflict—possibly good news for more virtual teams.

Thus, we see two possible benefits for more virtual teams. First, if, as the results from SoftCo suggest, more virtual teams are more focused on noticing conflict, they may actually have a head start on conflict management. Their greater focus on noticing conflict gives them an initial lead over more traditional teams. The SoftCo data suggest that noticing conflict in more virtual settings is possible, and we would add that the likelihood of success will go up to the extent that teams make a conscious effort to identify conflict in its early stages. Second, it is possible that relationship conflict can be filtered out of computer-mediated communication. This could also be a boon to more virtual teams. Such benefits may serve to offset the very real challenge of greater process conflict overall given the more complex situations that virtual teams must manage.

The Conflict Management Process

Managing conflict is not trivial. The dynamics of working in a team are more complex than working alone, and virtual team dynamics are more complicated still. Research has shown that attention to process is key to the success of more virtual teams, and our study echoes those findings. Team performance is hurt by unresolved process conflict, and virtual teams are more likely to have process conflict. However, the SoftCo study suggests that this negative effect can be ameliorated by trust and increased communication, especially e-mail. In fact, Kodak's Brault suggests that "overcommunication" is the key, to communicate far beyond what you might in a more face-to-face setting. These effects can take conflict management from the stage of noticing conflict, through to understanding how to resolve the conflict itself. Virtual teams are not sentenced to increased conflict. Given appropriate resources, they can construct their environments so as to reduce unresolved process conflict and perhaps find ways to outperform their colocated counterparts by greater application of their diverse expertise.

Note

1. Included in the colocated group is one eight-member team with only one member off-site. This minor level of distribution seemed to fit more appropriately with the colocated, versus distributed, teams.

References

Boulding, K. *Conflict and Defense.* New York: HarperCollins, 1963.

Brault, J. "How to Master Virtual Teams." Unpublished manuscript, Eastman Kodak, 1999.

DeSanctis, G., Poole, M. S., and Dickson, G. W. "Teams and Technology: Interactions over Time." In M. A. Neale, E. A. Mannix, and T. L. Griffith (eds.), *Research on Managing Groups and Teams: Technology.* Stamford, Conn.: JAI Press, 2000.

Edmondson, A., Bohmer, R., and Pisano, G. "Collaborating to Learn: Effects of Organizational and Team Characteristics on Successful Adoption of New Medical Technology in Hospital-Based Surgical Teams." In M. A. Neale, E. A. Mannix, and T. L. Griffith (eds.), *Research on Managing Groups and Teams: Technology.* Stamford, Conn.: JAI Press, 2000.

Eisenhardt, K., and Zbaracki, M. "Strategic Decision Making." *Strategic Management Journal,* 1992, *13,* 17–37.

Geber, B. "Virtual Teams." *Training,* 1995, *32*(4), 36–40.

Griffith, T. L., and Meader, D. "Prelude to Virtual Groups: Leadership Roles and Technology Variety Within Investment Clubs." Unpublished manuscript, 2001.

Griffith, T. L., and Neale, M. A. "Information Processing in Traditional, Hybrid, and Virtual Teams: From Nascent Knowledge to Transactive Memory." In R. I. Sutton and B. M. Staw (eds.), *Research in Organizational Behavior.* Stamford, Conn.: JAI Press, 2001.

Gruenfeld, D. H., Mannix, E. A., Williams, K. Y., and Neale, M. A. "Group Composition and Decision Making: How Member Familiarity and Information

Distribution Affect Process and Performance." *Organizational Behavior and Human Decision Processes*, 1996, *67*(1), 1–15.

Jarvenpaa, S. L., and Leidner, D. E. "Communication and Trust in Global Virtual Teams." *Organization Science*, 1999, *10*, 791–815.

Jehn, K. A. "A Multimethod Examination of the Benefits and Detriments of Intragroup Conflict." *Administrative Science Quarterly*, 1995, *40*, 256–282.

Jehn, K. "A Qualitative Analysis of Conflict Types and Dimensions in Organizational Groups." *Administrative Science Quarterly*, 1997, *42*, 530–557.

Jehn, K. A., and Chatman, J. A. "The Influence of Proportional and Perceptual Conflict Composition on Team Performance." *International Journal of Conflict Management*, 2000, *11*(1), 56–73.

Jehn, K., and Mannix, E. "The Dynamic Nature of Conflict: A Longitudinal Study of Intragroup Conflict and Group Performance." *Academy of Management Journal*, 2001, *44*, 238–251.

Jehn, K. A., Northcraft, G. B., and Neale, M. A. "Why Differences Make a Difference: A Field Study of Diversity, Conflict, and Performance in Workgroups." *Administrative Science Quarterly*, 1999, *44*(4), 741–763.

Mayer, R. C., Davis, J. H., and Schoorman, F. D. "An Integrative Model of Organizational Trust." *Academy of Management Review*, 1995, *20*(3), 709–734.

Meyerson, D., Weick, K. E., and Kramer, R. M. "Swift Trust and Temporary Groups." In R. M. Kramer and T. R. Tyler (eds.), *Trust in Organizations: Frontiers of Theory and Research*. Thousand Oaks, Calif.: Sage, 1996.

Pape, W. R. "Group Insurance." *Inc.*, June 15, 1997, pp. 29–30.

Rheingold, H. "The Art of Hosting Good Conversations Online." [http://www.rheingold.com/texts/artonlinehost.html]. 1998.

Schwenk, C. "Conflict in Organizational Decision Making: An Exploratory Study of Its Effects in For-Profit and Not-For-Profit Organizations." *Management Science*, 1990, *36*, 436–448.

Simons, T. L., and Peterson, R. S. "Task Conflict and Relationship Conflict in Top Management Teams: The Pivotal Role of Intragroup Trust." *Journal of Applied Psychology*, 2000, *85*, 1–10.

Training Trends. "Quality Magazine." [http://www.qualitymag.com]. Aug. 1999.

Watson, W. E., Kumar, K., and Michaelsen, L. K. "Cultural Diversity's Impact on Interaction Process and Performance: Comparing Homogeneous and Diverse Task Groups." *Academy of Management Journal*, 1993, *36*(3), 590–602.

Williams, K. Y., and O'Reilly, C.A.I. "Demography and Diversity in Organizations: A Review of Forty Years of Research." In B. M. Staw and L. L. Cummings (eds.), *Research in Organizational Behavior*. Stamford, Conn.: JAI Press, 1998.

Young, R. "The Wide-Awake Club." *People Management,* Feb. 1998, pp. 46–49.

CHAPTER SIXTEEN

The Development of Global Virtual Teams

Julia C. Gluesing, Tara C. Alcordo, Marietta L. Baba, David Britt,
Kimberly Harris Wagner, Willie McKether, Leslie Monplaisir,
Hilary Horn Ratner, Kenneth Riopelle

Global virtual teams (GVTs) are those that span time zones and geographical boundaries. As the use of GVTs has increased, talk about this work now commonly occurs in corporate hallways, virtual conversations, and formal meetings. Listening to these conversations, it becomes readily apparent that members and leaders of GVTs are trying to figure out how to work in new ways and how to make global virtual work pay off for them personally and for their organizations. Much of the conversation among global team members consists of complaints: complaints about how long it takes to get things done, about how work gets disrupted by events out of the team members' control, about the difficulty of staying connected and aligned with team members for enough time to move forward on their tasks. Distance often equals delay (Fineholt, 2000), and team members complain they have to backtrack because agreements and decisions they thought they had made turn into disagreements. One team member said resignedly that "for every step forward, we seem to take two steps back, and it takes forever to get anything done." GVT members are frustrated when processes they have used in traditional colocated teams do not seem to work quite as well in their GVTs, and they are at a loss about what to do to improve their work together.

The research reported in this chapter was supported by a grant from the National Science Foundation's Innovation and Organizational Change Program and Wayne State University's Targets of Opportunity Program.

This chapter explores how GVTs develop over time based on data gathered through several years of ethnographic fieldwork in major corporations. We also offer action steps to GVT managers and members to help them "jump start" a new GVT, revitalize a stalled team, or help fast forward positive growth and development to increase the likelihood their teams will achieve their business objectives.

CONTEXT AND GLOBAL VIRTUAL TEAMS

The most distinctive feature of GVTs is context, which we define as a way of life and work in a specific geographical area with its own set of business conditions, cultural assumptions, and unique history. Most of what we know about team development comes from research on groups or teams that work in face-to-face situations sharing a single common work context. By common context, we mean that team members share the same physical, business, cultural, and historical environment, which forms the backdrop for their work. Even if team members come from diverse national cultures or are working together across organizational boundaries, such as functional (product development, manufacturing, sales) or professional boundaries (engineering, finance), their existing working conditions and business situation are shared. Team members are generally proficient native speakers of the team language and share meanings for the same words and symbols. They possess technical or professional expertise and communication skills, but are not usually trained in cross-cultural communication or about cultural differences. Sharing the same context also means that team members are subject to the same or similar environmental influences, ranging from organizational policies and resources to weather. Because they are working together within the same context, they take for granted implicit knowledge they acquire and share about how to interpret the world around them and act appropriately. For instance, a single context provides team members with a common and largely unspoken framework for how to communicate with managers, the expected work hours, the processes for obtaining resources, and even for what constitutes good work and rewards for that work. They also have the opportunity for frequent formal and informal interaction and for conversation about what is going on around them that allows them to develop shared meaning for events and a shared understanding about how to behave. It is a kind of ongoing, taken-for-granted, invisible sense making that keeps them aligned, even when the circumstances of their context change or pose new challenges.

In contrast, GVT members are scattered around the world, living and working in different contexts. Consequently, they cannot take for granted that other members share their contextual knowledge or that they have a common framework for working. Members of GVTs must work explicitly and vigilantly across multiple boundaries to identify and integrate the different contexts that can have varying relevance and impact on the team's task. For example, the context of a person working in Detroit on an automotive new product development team is very different from the context of another member of the same team working in Brazil or Germany. Different formal and informal rules dictate interaction in the workplace, there are different organizational policies and governmental regulations for human resources, and stability and efficiency of the economic and political environments vary greatly among these three locations. The differing circumstances can easily disrupt the process of team development because team members do not have the opportunity to engage serendipitously in sense making or learn about the context together just by being there. In fact, GVT team members typically are unaware of each other's contextual differences and changing circumstances because they are not in the habit of consciously considering context in their normal day-to-day colocated work. Context is taken for granted. In addition, GVTs usually have team members who are not native speakers of the same language, even if they all use a common language, such as English, to communicate in the team. Meanings for words are often different and dependent on local variations of the language. Because they are separated by time and distance as well, communication among team members is limited to relatively short episodes, most of them technologically mediated. The opportunities for misunderstanding are great. Teaming in a GVT also means that in addition to general and technical expertise, team members must be cross-culturally competent and open to different ways of working.

There is one final point about context we wish to make. Context is fixed to a geographical location with a way of life and work embedded in a cultural and historical tradition and is very slow to change. While team members bring with them to the GVT the assumptions and habitual behaviors they have learned in context, most of the experience and knowledge related to context is rooted in place and not easily transferable. A major challenge in GVT work is making multiple contexts explicit and then cocreating a new virtual context that is commonly shared.

Working across multiple contexts makes the development of GVTs significantly more challenging than in colocated teams because the complexity is significantly greater. The challenge is integration, which means the process of coordinating separate people into a balanced whole that produces behavior compatible with the complexity of the team's environment. It is difficult for GVTs to get started and easy for them to stall, or even to disintegrate, because multiple contexts make it difficult to develop the common knowledge that enables team members to maintain a shared view of their work and common expectations for their interactions in the pursuit of their tasks. Team members need to expend more time and energy to sustain the integration and development necessary for task achievement. The work of integration requires a high degree of vigilance and constant attention, which is especially difficult to accomplish when the team task is nonroutine, which is generally the case in GVTs (Earley and Gibson, 2002).

WHAT WE MEAN BY DEVELOPMENT

By development, we mean the patterns of change, growth, or progression of a team to a more mature state as team members interact across multiple contexts to achieve a task over time. The team development process itself consists of two major components: (1) the initial conditions at team formation and (2) the processes involved in early and ongoing development. Initial conditions and development processes can lead to (3) maturation, the desired result of successful development that teams seek to sustain to perform effectively. Figure 16.1 provides our definitions of initial conditions, processes, and maturation.

Since the early twentieth century, organizational researchers and practitioners alike have been interested in the development of small groups (those with three to thirty) or teams. It has been proposed that groups go through a series of phases, some linear in structure and some cyclical, and that successful development is essential to effective performance of work tasks. Early models emphasized the importance of balancing work tasks with effective management of relationships among team members. An example of this development process is the famous "forming, storming, norming, and performing" model (Tuckman, 1965) that is widely used in training programs.

More recent conceptions of team development have added the influence on team development of environmental factors outside the team (such as company reorganizations, mergers, or industry upheaval), as well as structure or the organizational dimensions of the team (for example, size of the team, meeting format and frequency) and the effect of time constraints (McCollom, 1990). Recent ideas about team development suggest that groups do not go through universal stages of development. Instead, there are many alternative pathways possible, depending on a combination of factors. For example, surges in development can be created by an impending deadline ("Uh-oh. We are running out of time. This is due next week!"), or teams can take action to adapt to environmental influences, such as adding or removing members to alter their skill sets to increase global capability (Gersick, 1988, 1989; McGrath, 1991; DeSanctis and Poole, 1994).

Many firms rely on GVTs to get to the market faster with better products and services. Yet development in GVTs is constrained by the complexity of working across multiple contexts, making it more difficult for team members to come up to speed and perform quickly. Ironically, GVTs may need more time than a colocated group to accomplish the same task (Fineholt, 2000),

Component	Definitions
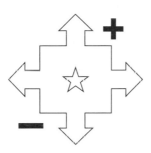 Team Formation	The initial conditions of a team at start-up. These conditions include members' individual characteristics and their social networks and the resources available to them (for example, information technology, budget, support people). Conditions also include the team structure and level in the hierarchy, as well as the nature of the team's task and how the team members and the organizations involved perceive it.
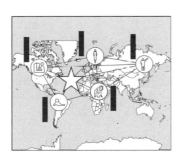 Development Processes	The processes in GVT development are composed of a series of actions and interactions that brings about an end or result. Processes can speed up or slow down a team's development and ability to accomplish its task. For example, how team members share information with one another about their work contexts can affect how quickly they are able to reach agreement.
 Team Maturation	Maturation is the state a team seeks to achieve and sustain in development. Maturation has these characteristics: a common task team members believe in and are committed to, collaborative interactions with one another and with important groups outside the team, and the ability to sustain a common task focus and collaboration across multiple contexts. In other words, the team successfully integrates people and contexts toward the achievement of a common task over time.

Figure 16.1 Development of Global Virtual Teams.

although the likelihood is that they will have less time. The challenge for international firms is to understand the developmental processes in GVTs and then to find ways to shorten the time it takes for a GVT to reach and sustain a level of performance that will deliver better and faster solutions in the global marketplace.

In this chapter, we share what we have learned about the multiple factors that interact to influence development in GVTs, and we strongly emphasize the important developmental processes that managers and team members can influence to speed the growth of these teams and increase their effectiveness.

CASE ILLUSTRATIONS

To investigate the processes involved in GVT development, we conducted a longitudinal study of six teams in five major corporations, using both qualitative and quantitative methods. We relied on multiple methods of data gathering: direct observation of face-to-face meetings and videoconferences of the full GVT or its subgroups; listening in (with permission) on audioconferences; interviewing individual team members (both face-to-face and virtually, using video and audio technology); collecting team documents (charters, presentations, surveys, reports); e-mail communication; and participating in social events. Interviews focused on the history of the team, the team's purpose, leadership, structure, communication patterns, use of technology, and changes in any of these dimensions that had taken place since the team's formation. GVTs were followed for varying periods of time. For teams of relatively short duration (say, two months), we followed the team over its entire life course. For teams that were ongoing, we tried to observe their start-up and follow them for a number of months. If an ongoing team had already been up and running for several months or more when we arrived, we followed their activities for three to seven months.

We have chosen three of these GVTs from our field research as case examples to provide a picture of their development from formation to maturation. The three cases are narrative descriptions that tell each team's story.

Ramtech Customer Processing Software Team

Ramtech is an American-based telecommunications corporation with manufacturing facilities all over the world. Long known for its technological prowess, Ramtech recently had come under attack by financial analysts and customers for being dominated by a technology-driven approach to its markets that was attentive to neither customer needs nor the increasingly global dimension of the business. A number of key customers were angry about what they perceived as a lack of responsiveness to their requests for a business-to-business e-commerce connection. One consequence of not responding rapidly to customer criticisms was a dramatic plunge in the value of Ramtech's stock during the late 1990s.

Top management was determined to address the problem through a broad-based effort to change Ramtech's culture, transforming it from a technology-driven to a customer-oriented company whose future leaders would be able to think and collaborate on a global scale. Toward this transformation objective, Ramtech created the Global Leadership Initiative (GLI). Senior executives hand-selected high-potential managers from all over the world to form interdisciplinary teams, and then trained and organized them to work collaboratively on a significant global business problem involving key customers.

One of the teams to participate in the GLI process was the customer processing software (CPS) team, which had ten members in six countries (the United States, Britain, Brazil, China, France, and India). There was also one American facilitator. This team's mission was to evaluate the extent of management commitment to the implementation of a SAP-based work management system and to facilitate buy-in to the system from top leadership around the globe. What the CPS team learned during the first colocated week was that Ramtech had already invested $200 million in the SAP software, but that resistance to changeover from a legacy system was being experienced across all levels of management, including senior leadership, even though resistance threatened the loss of customer business.

The CPS team was colocated for one week with other similar teams for immersion-level training through a detailed business simulation involving corporate strategy and culture change directed at achieving customer intimacy, and teaching skills in cross-cultural communication and collaboration. These sessions provided the team members with a common set of concepts, language, and experience with which to begin their task. Part of the colocated time was spent getting an orientation to the team's business problem and creating a plan for tackling it. The CPS team attempted to make sense of its mission by drawing together what members already knew about SAP software and existing efforts to make the changeover from legacy systems. This process involved various team members' telling stories from their experience and then collaborating to develop a summary that provided an open framework that could focus their work efforts, while still leaving room for discussion and debate. The CPS group established a participatory and collaborative interaction dynamic almost immediately. They worked through intense and open exchange without aggressive conflict, rotating their leadership, and remaining engaged and enthusiastic throughout the project. There were also plenty of opportunities for informal social interaction over meals, entertainment, and sightseeing.

After the first colocated week, members went back to their globally distributed jobs and spent about 10 percent of their time working on the CPS project. They met weekly by audioconference and also communicated by e-mail.

Virtually everyone participated in these sessions, with the exception of the Indian member, who was on detail in Mexico and had difficulty accessing a telephone line for the conference calls. There were three assigned roles for these conferences: minutes taker, logistics coordinator, and conference call facilitator. Follow-through was very good from week to week, and there was little social control needed or expressed. The members' work between these calls consisted of gathering data by conferring with selected individuals inside and outside the company with the objective of finding a way to make SAP work for the company globally. The CPS team addressed their challenge by seeking out information from trustworthy opinion leaders inside and outside the company (both managers and customers) and evaluating what they learned about the software to arrive at their own version of the truth.

Finally, when the group was only two weeks away from the final colocated week when they would make their presentation to management, a shift occurred in the group's orientation: from questioning whether SAP was the right system to questioning how they could support its implementation. Essentially, they agreed that SAP was not the best system given the need for flexible customer solutions. But Ramtech had already paid $200 million for the system, and to throw it out and start over would be too time-consuming, making a bad situation even worse, lengthening the time it would take for Ramtech to meet its customers' demands. They determined that Ramtech should implement SAP as quickly as possible.

The focus of the group now shifted to how they should present their conclusion and recommendations to the top management group. So committed was the team to its mission that members arrived two days early for their second colocated week at the project's conclusion in order to work on their presentation together with the help of their facilitator. When team members raised challenges to the decisions that they had made in a devil's advocate way, the decisions were reaffirmed with vigor. The team also volunteered to stay involved in the project throughout Phase I of their recommendations. The presentation was an unqualified success, and senior management authorized launch of the team's implementation plan.

Celestial Corporation's French Customer Team

The Celestial Corporation (CC) is a U.S.-based manufacturing and sales organization in the consumer goods industry with several major global customers. One key customer is French, with headquarters in Paris. For many years, CC had a French customer team in Paris (all French nationals) that maintained business relationships with its French customer's top management. In the late 1990s, CC initiated a major organizational restructuring to globalize its operations. One result was a decision to reconstitute the French customer team with additional talent and to give the new team a charter focused on the creation and execution of worldwide strategy for building business relationships with the French customer in countries around the world. An American senior manager was put in charge of the new French customer team, and he invited two other key Americans to join the team. One was a facilitator and the other an expert in a new marketing approach they referred to as product management.

Almost as soon as the new French customer team was reconstituted, the French customer announced its plan to merge with a major rival. This meant that two internal CC teams that served both the French customer and its rival needed to merge as well. Just after the two CC teams merged, however, it was announced that the customers' merger would be held up for some months by regulatory review within the European Union. This proved awkward for the French customer team, since its own merger suddenly had doubled the number of team members to twenty members spread over five countries (Belgium, France, the United States, China, and Argentina). It was unclear how to proceed given the fact that the two customer firms had not yet merged.

During this period of merger limbo, internal conflict broke out on the French customer team. Members of the CC team were anxious about their future, given the head count redundancy created by the merger, and wanted to know who would be staying on the team and who would be leaving. The American senior manager told the team members to get together with their functional counterparts and determine who would stay and who would go. Although the team members did work collaboratively to sort out their situation, this directive prompted even greater anxiety, as people in some functions were not sure how to make such decisions. There was criticism of the American senior manager; neither he nor the other two Americans had relocated to join the main body of the team in Paris but were trying to fulfill their roles through travel and virtual meetings while remaining in the United States and China (the product management expert was based in Hong Kong). The leadership role of the Americans was delegitimized by their absence, while the former French customer team leader (who was on site in Paris on a daily basis) continued to be viewed as the legitimate head of the team. This French leader also was critical of the Americans for their lack of French fluency because the French customer preferred speaking in French.

Given these tensions, it is not surprising that there was resistance to the American senior manager's idea of implementing product management in Paris. The French members of the CC team believed that the French customer was not interested in working as closely with CC as product management would require, but preferred a more arms-length way of dealing with suppliers. Realizing he could not implement product management in Paris under these conditions, the American senior manager (working through another American executive who had just joined the French customer company) devised an arrangement whereby the product management concept could be piloted at a French customer store in Asia. The recession in Asia made French customer managers in Asia eager to try new approaches, and the American executive felt he could keep the pilot fairly confidential from (that is, under the radar screen of) more resistant parties in Paris. This assumption proved to be wrong. CC middle managers stationed in China (who also were French nationals) began to feed bits of information about the pilot to their French CC team colleagues in Paris. Tensions mounted as the French CC team members in Paris worried about what was really going in China, a worry made more intense by uncertainty surrounding their own futures and their infrequent, sporadic communication.

Meanwhile, the former French customer team leader in Paris entered into an agreement with the French customer to launch a special project, *Nourriture Excellente,* touted as a French approach to product management that would be better than the American-inspired version in Asia. Arguments broke out between the French and American CC team members regarding what is "real product management" and which of the two projects had the greater potential for improving business results and being accepted by the customer. Each side tried to get the other side's project killed by their contacts within the customer organization. The American senior manager ordered the team to figure out how to link these two projects and gave them a deadline for reaching an agreement. A series of meetings ensued toward that objective. At one face-to-face meeting in Paris, the CC team seemed to have developed a plan for bringing the projects together. Two subgroups, one in Paris and one in Asia, then tried to implement the next steps that had been agreed on. A follow-up videoconference connecting Paris, Asia, and the United States, however, revealed that the French customer in Paris had rejected the linkage plan and that the French CC team members were no longer going to pursue the previously agreed-to arrangement to link the two competing projects.

This unexpected turn of events angered the CC team members in China, who demanded to know why they had not been involved in the discussions with the customer. Aggressive conflict broke out as each side blamed the other for the problem, bringing into the fight charges against individual personalities (for example, "You can't speak French," "I outrank you"). What became known as the videoconference from hell drew to a close as an American in China left the videoconference room in tears, determined to leave CC.

People remaining in the videoconference after the American left suddenly realized that something had gone terribly wrong—something that could damage their company and their own careers. The facilitator quickly made arrangements to talk with each individual privately and then try to get the group back together to resolve their differences. The facilitator conducted a form of shuttle diplomacy that enabled him to gain the viewpoints of each participant on an individual basis, which he then shared with the others. All of the anxieties and tensions that had been buried during the past several months emerged as a result of this process, and team members came to recognize the anxieties and pressures that were facing their colleagues. Chastened by their crisis and having internalized and become more sensitive to issues others were facing, the French and American groups came back together and began to work in earnest on a plan to connect their two competing projects. One symbol of their new shared understanding was the invention of a new term to designate both projects: *Produits Exemplaires,* a French phrase that joins key aspects of the two original projects.

Interestingly, business results for the French customer and the CC team had been strong throughout the conflict. After the merger was finalized, however, business results for both companies began a serious decline, largely as a result of problems experienced in the merger. The CC team turned its attention fully to the problem of boosting business results, a traditional area of work for everyone on the team in which all of the team members had excellent track records. They began to collaborate immediately, engaging in detailed discussions of core business issues, and using audioconferences and videoconferences to identify problems and create solutions that required cooperation across the team. For the first time, someone on the team suggested that they use the team Web site as a means to share ideas and coordinate their activity. The Web site had been in place from the beginning but had not been used as a team resource. The team also increased the amount of time they spent in face-to-face work, and two remote members, a new facilitator from the United States and the product management expert in Hong Kong, moved to Paris to integrate into the French context better. As the research was concluded, the CC team was in the process of working collaboratively to boost sales and profit margins.

HTM-TP8 Core Team

HTM is a computer hardware and software firm based in Paris. HTM formed the TP8 core team to remedy a crisis in customer satisfaction that erupted when a new software product was introduced to the marketplace. The team had a crisis on its hands with both customers and internally among three groups: software engineering, the customer service people in the field, and marketing staff. Each group blamed the other for customer dissatisfaction. Despite severe distrust across these three internal groups, the core team had to develop a new and better version of the product very quickly in order to reestablish customer satisfaction and confidence and ensure that the original market and profit goals would be met.

Company managers selected a leader for the team based on his product knowledge and expertise and his ability to work with a diverse team of people. Drawing on whom he thought would be the best from each functional area and geographical location, the leader pulled together five other individuals from France and the United States to work on the problem. Most of the team members had worked together before in some capacity or at least knew each other. All were used to working in a cross-cultural, cross-functional context. In fact, one of the criteria that the leader used to select the members of his team was each person's ability to work with unalike, or diverse, people. All members of the team were at high enough levels in the company to command resources and influence.

In addition to dealing with differences in values and work practices between the French and the Americans, the team had to address issues of autonomy and independence in the United States and strong customer relationships in the French organization, as well as distrust between engineering and marketing. The team also needed to increase the viability of a proprietary product when the market was moving to open systems. Beyond these contextual factors, there were budget cuts, reorganization of major corporate business units, downsizing, and increasing French control of a business that was previously American owned but was now French owned and being privatized by the French government. The American division was losing money faster than the European divisions, placing greater pressure on the Americans, who were responsible for engineering on the TP8 team. The environmental turbulence created a great deal of uncertainty for individual employees and tended to make some people behave in self-protective ways.

At start-up, the team members underwent a week-long face-to-face training that included company business strategy and the identification of key teaming processes they were expected to implement, as well as cross-cultural communication and team building. The members were housed together in a corporate training center where they ate and socialized together. Following their initial week of training, the TP8 team met every two weeks by audioconference and at least every quarter face-to-face, rotating these meetings between Paris, Boston, and Phoenix. They stayed in constant touch with one another through telephone, fax, and e-mail, which was often broadcast and not just one-to-one. English was the working language of the group, and all were sufficiently proficient in it to accomplish the work they needed to do. They also had as a member of the team a bilingual facilitator who contributed significantly to team members' interaction.

In the course of their two-year project, the team developed collaborative working relationships among all of its members, but it took several meetings and about six months for this process to occur, especially to overcome the distrust between engineering and marketing. The team members used a combination of processes to build a common definition of their situation. One key strategy was a focus on language as a primary success factor in their teaming process. Although they chose English as their working language, they did not want frustration or resentment to build among the French team members. They adopted the practices of using written materials in both languages to preserve a document's integrity, allowing side conversations in French, and stopping discussion frequently to check meaning and confirm understanding even though this took more time. At times, they employed translation. They also took advantage of a common product language to facilitate understanding.

The team accommodated differences in personality and cross-national, cross-occupational differences in work practices, values, and meaning by carefully structuring interaction, particularly with the help of the facilitator. For example, the team members negotiated a compromise loosely structured agenda format that was neither "the French way" nor "the American way." There were style differences that could have caused much conflict in the team, particularly between the representative from engineering, whose focus was on specifics, and the one from marketing, who often spoke in generalizations and used ambiguous language. Both people learned enough about each other's differences to accommodate them in structuring their interactions. The team also spent a considerable amount of time in their meetings clarifying meaning—not just discrepancies or misunderstandings that might occur as a result of the bilingual French-English language usage but also misunderstandings due to differences in occupational frameworks.

To negotiate the differences between marketing and engineering, the leader spent much time initially pushing the representatives to talk to one another. At one point, the leader had to force negotiation between marketing and engineering by putting the representatives in a room and telling them not to come out until they had resolved their differences and come to an agreement. This tactic required that the team spend six days in a face to face meeting instead of the three days that had been planned initially. The team leader also used a partnering process to facilitate a shared understanding. The TP8 team had a particularly critical customer situation in Italy on their hands when they began their work. At first, the team had difficulty coming to agreement about how to handle this customer. There was engineering-marketing conflict and France-U.S. conflict to resolve. The team leader facilitated the creation of a client task team that included both marketing and engineering representatives from Paris and Phoenix. The task team went to the client site in Italy to assess the situation and address the specific client problems. The partnering of representatives from both functions and both locations helped them to see and experience the situation together and to develop immediate solutions. Engineering lost the layers between development and customer needs, and marketing saw how hard the engineers worked to resolve the customer issues. In the face of a customer crisis outside the team, immediate and common to them both, the team members negotiated joint solutions to the issues, and their differences moved to the background.

Eventually, the team achieved an on-time delivery of the product with a level of stability and performance that was accepted internally by the various company stakeholders, as well as by the customers.

WHAT WE CAN LEARN FROM THESE STORIES

Table 16.1 and Figure 16.2 summarize the three case studies with a profile of each team's characteristics and development process from formation to maturation. In each case, all three teams began with significant business challenges; however, their pathways through development to maturation were different. The Ramtech and HTM teams hit the ground running and reached maturity without any significant disruptions in their development, although the HTM team took longer and their path went over more hills and valleys along the way. The CC team was moving along quite well until a corporate reorganization and a customer merger soon after created an impasse that took them quite a while to overcome. The team continued to backslide in their development until two crises forced the team to take actions to reintegrate, eventually putting them back on the path to further team development. Although the development pathways of the three teams are different, their stories provide important lessons about creating conditions for effective development in GVTs that are faced with working in the complexity of multiple contexts.

The discussion that follows highlights important patterns in the teams' development at formation, in ongoing development, and at maturation that provide learnings for managers and team members who find themselves either at the start of a new GVT or already trying to manage their development process. Our recommendations are summarized in Table 16.2.

Initial Structure

The three teams began their work together under different conditions. In the Ramtech CPS team and the HTM-TP8, senior managers helped to create favorable conditions for the teams by defining their tasks as strategic, critical to the companies' success, and urgent. In the Ramtech case, senior managers also tied the team's task to the career success of the team members. These actions helped to create buy-in and commitment of the team members to the task, which was especially critical since the members of both teams were assigned to work on these teams in addition to the duties of their regular jobs. This type of second or third job assignment is common in international businesses as managers try to make use of scarce talented resources who can tackle significant global business challenges. Because team members could readily see the importance of their team task for the company and to them individually, they could more easily commit to the task and to the team and give the extra effort and time it would take to achieve their business objectives.

In the CPS and TP8 cases, the Ramtech and HTM managers had also established general teaming processes (documented GLI and core team project management processes) that the teams should follow, and in the Ramtech case they time-bounded the task duration to eight weeks, which helped the teams by reducing the complexity that they had to manage at the start of their team

Table 16.1. Case Study Details

Profile	Ramtech	Celestial	HTM-TP8
Industry	Telecommunications	Consumer goods	Computer
Task	Global software rollout	Global product marketing	Global new product development
Number of members	Ten	Twenty	Six
Number of countries	Six	Five	Two
Countries	Brazil, China, France, India, United Kingdom, United States	Argentina, Belgium, China, France, United States	France, United States
Headquarters	United States	United States	France
Number of time zones	Fourteen	Twelve	Eight
Team duration	Two months	Twenty-seven months, still ongoing	Twenty-four months
Study duration	Three months	Fifteen months	Seven months
Facilitator	Yes	Yes	Yes
Development overview	Ramtech's member selection criteria, fixed short time frame, and high task visibility with one-week face-to-face immersion training provides formation jump-start for forceful initial team integration. This is followed by six weeks of frequent structured communication by audioconference calls, without major local or industry surprises, which sustained team integration. The project ends with a one-week face-to-face meeting for report preparation and presentation.	Existing Celestial domestic market team is functioning well until global reorganization assigns new outside noncolocated leader and other members to pursue controversial market strategy without any strong team re-formation processes. Team members engage in disintegrative practices until crises provide impetus for re-formation. Facilitator helps to rebuild team integration with new constructive integration practices. Team reintegrates with some colocation of members.	HTM-TP8 leader and member selection criteria, along with one-week face-to-face immersion training, provide formation jump-start for forceful initial team integration. Structured audioconference calls supplemented by fax and e-mail, combined with quarterly one-week face-to-face meetings rotated among three locations, provide sufficient team integration to complete objective successfully.

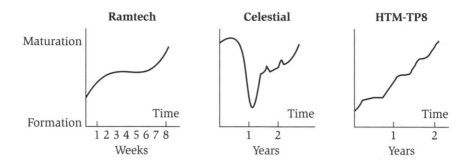

Figure 16.2 Case Study Profiles.

development. Specifying GLI and core team requirements saved the teams the time of trying to develop their own project management processes. The CPS team had the additional advantages of a project deadline and short project duration. The deadline provided just enough added pressure to focus their attention and increase their commitment because they knew the added demands placed on them would end in two months—something they could handle. The duration of only two months for the CPS team provided one additional advantage: there was less likelihood that events in the marketplace or in the company, such as mergers or reorganizations, would occur in such a short time frame and disrupt the team's development and progress on their task. Projects of longer duration are more vulnerable to disruption by external events.

In contrast, the Celestial French customer team began their work together as a global team under very difficult circumstances that slowed, and even set back, their development. Their complexity increased dramatically when they found themselves suddenly overnight in a global team, working across five countries and multiple contexts, when before they had been a primarily French team in a single context. They also had to cope with developing a new marketing strategy that was generally undefined, with sorting out their redundant membership, with competing projects, and with ambiguous leadership. These initial conditions meant that the team slowed down and almost came to a halt as team members spent their time on infighting or in limbo waiting for circumstances to sort themselves out.

Initial conditions in all three cases also were established in the selection of the people who would be the members and leaders of the teams. Ramtech's senior management selected a group of high-potential future leaders who were at the same organizational level in the company and had already proven themselves as professional experts who were competent in their disciplines and capable communicators who could share leadership as the demands of the task warranted. Senior managers of the HTM selected a person to lead the TP8 who was already a capable global manager adept at crossing cultures and

Table 16.2. Summary of Learnings

Initial Structure: Senior managers can structure a GVT at formation to create initial conditions advantageous to team development.

Key Learnings	Action Steps	Results
• A well-defined strategic and critical team task can speed team members' ability to work together and commit to their common task and increase the rate of team development.	• Define the team task as a high company priority. • Establish a fixed duration for the project or work and process guidelines.	• Increases team member commitment. • Establishes clear boundaries for time commitment and reduces complexity of the teaming process by clarifying expectations at formation, in ongoing development, and in reporting.
• Teams that begin their work with clear process guidelines have reduced initial complexity and can get off to a faster start. Teams that do not have guidelines can be slower to develop.	• Select a credible GVT leader based on professional expertise, experience, and cross-cultural competence. • Select team members who have professional expertise, experience, and cross-cultural competence.	• Matches skills to the task of integrating. • Team members start with the necessary skills to match the task and the interpersonal expertise to overcome differences and collaborate.
• People who come to the teaming process already possessing cross-cultural skills and who are respected professionals with command over resources can help teams speed development by balancing power and increasing collaboration from the start.	• Select team members who are at similar levels in the organizational hierarchy. • Select team members who previously have worked together well and have access to resources and organizational influence.	• Reduces initial complexity. • Helps balance power in the team. • Starts the members off with respect for one another, making trust more likely and speeding integration.
• Geographical distribution of team members can either speed up or slow down a team's development, because it affects the balance of power in a team.	• Select team members to avoid geographically based power imbalances. • Bring team members together face-to-face for dedicated work.	• Balances power to avoid clusters of people working together in one or two locations who may have a power base that can lead to power imbalance in the team (for example, near the customer or in corporate headquarters). • Orients members to the task, come to a common understanding of the business problem, and develop a plan of work.

(Continued)

Table 16.2. Summary of Learnings (*Continued*)

Start-up environment: Providing teams an enriched environment at start-up can speed development and help ensure that teams continue on the path to maturation.

Key Learnings	Action Steps	Results
• Facilitators who are skilled in global virtual teaming processes, such as cross-cultural communication and negotiation, can speed team development by helping the team integrate differences more quickly. • Storytelling is a valuable global virtual teaming process for sharing implicit knowledge across contexts because team members do not always recognize what knowledge or assumptions they hold and cannot easily express them, especially when there are cultural differences about what and how to communicate. • Establishing a clear team identity by means such as a logo or a slogan can help diverse team members stay connected when they are working apart. • Ongoing GVTs may need to slow down to speed up, spending some time in formation activities to ensure their continued development and to withstand environmental changes that can cause disintegration. • Early face-to-face time in which teams acquire key business concepts and learn new relational skills establishes a critical base helpful in maintaining and fostering development when later virtual work limits interaction.	• Provide immersion training when team members are together face-to-face at initial formation, especially if team members have never worked together before. • Assign a facilitator to the GVT who is cross-culturally competent and experienced and skilled in negotiation processes. • Provide a business simulation. • Establish a clear team identity, such as with a logo or slogan.	• Helps teams develop operating norms, identify skills and resources, create expectations for each other to provide a fast start with a clear direction and strengthens team relationships and collaboration skills. This training can include cross-cultural communication and culture-specific training if necessary, information about how the team task fits with business strategy, team process guidelines, and opportunities for team building and socializing. • Helps integrate multiple contexts by helping the team to monitor and adjust their processes and maintain common focus as conditions change and to avoid disintegrative processes. • Reduces time losses due to faulty processes. • Addresses both task and relationship skills needed in a GVT. • Can provide a time-compressed teaming experience in which members learn about the business and how they should collaborate, using GVT skills, to achieve a task. • Helps diverse team members stay connected when they are working apart. Team members can engage in this activity themselves as part of immersion training.

Table 16.2. (*Continued*)

Integration: To sustain development in GVTs, or even accelerate it, teams need to engage consistently and frequently in integration processes and avoid processes that can lead to disintegration.

Key Learnings	Action Steps	Results
• Frequent regular communication that uses communication technology matched to the team's needs is necessary to sustain and advance development in GVTs.	• Create opportunities for social interaction.	• Especially early in the team and regularly, either virtually or face-to-face, to allow team members to get to know each other personally and in relaxed informal settings. Socializing increases shared experiences, which more fully integrates the people in the team.
• Periodic face-to-face meetings are necessary for GVTs to maintain strong relationships, especially when they face significant challenges that can pull people apart or when they need to make progress on sensitive tasks that are too complex to resolve through restricted communication channels.	• Use storytelling.	• Allows for sharing knowledge when it is implicit, complex, embedded in context, and difficult to communicate.
	• Engage in round-robin sense making.	• Helps team members discover the knowledge they possess. Ask, "What do we know about . . . ," and allow each member to respond by telling a story to reveal his or her knowledge.
• Language differences can present barriers to integration even when English is the working language of the team and is spoken by all the team members; GVTs need to develop specific language processes to help the team remain integrated and continue on the development path.	• Check for understanding.	• Strengthens relationships, increases participation, and avoids costly misunderstandings. Frequently stop discussion to check that all understand in the same way, and clarify meanings if necessary.
• Extraordinary measures that force integration are often necessary in GVTs to counteract the impact of significant environmental challenges and keep the team from stalling in their development.	• Redefine the team task when conditions change.	• Maintains alignment of the team with corporate strategy or in the marketplace.
	• Surface differences in values and work practices.	• Helps with negotiation of a shared team working culture, usually with the help of a cross-cultural facilitator.
• To sustain development in rapidly changing complex contexts, GVTs need to establish open communication links with groups and people outside the team and engage in regular sense making, redefining their task if necessary.	• Negotiate a flexible agenda format.	• Accommodates cultural differences in communication style and work practices.

(Continued)

Table 16.2. Summary of Learnings (*Continued*)

Integration: To sustain development in GVTs, or even accelerate it, teams need to engage consistently and frequently in integration processes and avoid processes that can lead to disintegration.

Key Learnings	Action Steps	Results
• Significant rapid changes in the context, such as mergers or a business crisis, are a signal that teams should be mindful of disintegrative processes (for example, secret operations, infrequent communication, and unresolved conflict) to stop them before they disrupt team development. Virtual technology may be inadequate for communication in these instances.	• Initiate travel by a team member to another location.	• Helps the team member understand and appreciate firsthand the other's context and business situation, especially when information is implicit and complex.
	• Hold regularly scheduled face-to-face meetings in different locations.	• Rotating the meeting site among key global locations allows time together for complex problem solving and to balance power and increase team member knowledge of contexts.
	• Engage in frequent scheduled communication.	• Helps ensure efficient, consistent, and reliable communication that updates team members on each other's progress and incorporates new information. Use audioconferences with assigned roles for facilitation and logistics to make sure minutes are taken and the call runs smoothly.
	• Consider relocating team members.	• Helps resolve complex problems and difficulty in understanding when nothing else works. Useful even if colocation is only temporary.
	• Pair conflicting team members with one another.	• Partnering to work together to resolve a problem or urgent task fosters greater understanding and appreciation of each other's expertise and perspectives.
	• Allow different languages to be used in the team.	• Keeps nonnative speakers of the dominant language from working at a disadvantage and helps maintain power balance.
	• Create a metaphor to talk about a task.	• Helps team members discover commonality and integrate competing ideas or strategies.

Table 16.2. (*Continued*)

Integration: To sustain development in GVTs, or even accelerate it, teams need to engage consistently and frequently in integration processes and avoid processes that can lead to disintegration.

Key Learnings	Action Steps	Results
	• Use technical language.	• Establishes a common frame of meaning and reduces miscommunication.
	• Allow different team members to take a leadership role.	• Matches members' skills with the task to be accomplished at different points in time in accordance with changing conditions.
	• Consider using shuttle diplomacy.	• Allows frustrations and anxiety to be surfaced in a safe way and provides feedback that leads to broader understanding of each other's perspectives and contexts. Usually a facilitator, or sometimes a team leader, holds a series of one-on-one conversations with everyone and integrates this information for feedback to the team.
	• Consider forced negotiation.	• Usually in a closed-door setting to resolve especially difficult differences of opinion with a directive that resolution is a must.
	• Use a team Web site or collaborative virtual space, a team center.	• To share ideas and information, formally and informally, and to create a virtual context that team members have in common.
		• Helps reinforce team identity.
	• Encourage company networking.	• Helps team obtain a broader perspective on the task and perhaps a more comprehensive solution or buy-in of important stakeholders or other groups outside the team.
	• Encourage customer networking.	• Helps the team stay abreast of changes in contexts by involving credible customers to obtain their points of view about the task and their suggestions for possible solutions.
		• Provides shared focus to integrate differences of opinion in the team.

(*Continued*)

Table 16.2. Summary of Learnings (*Continued*)

Integration: To sustain development in GVTs, or even accelerate it, teams need to engage consistently and frequently in integration processes and avoid processes that can lead to disintegration.

Key Learnings	Action Steps	Results
	• Do not ignore incompatible work processes that are culturally based.	• Avoids creating tension, confusion that can stymie progress on task.
	• Watch for member withdrawal or infrequent or sporadic participation.	• Nips disintegration early and avoids disruption that can slow development.
	• Do not engage in secret operations.	• Avoids creating suspicion, feelings of exclusion, power imbalance, anger, hurt, and distrust among team members.
	• Do not allow communication to lapse or become sporadic.	• Keeps people from drifting to local priorities to the detriment of the common team task.
	• Resist personal blaming when things go wrong.	• Avoids relational conflict and competition that diminish trust and the collaboration necessary to successful development.

boundaries. The leader of the HTM team picked team members who knew one another, had the ability to work with diverse people, and were at a high enough level in the company to command both respect and resources. The reorganized CC team, however, had members who had been working well in the French context but were not necessarily suited to the demands of the global work they were being asked to do. They were also competing with each other for position and power, which reduced trust and their willingness to share information and collaborate to define their task and project plan. The CC team members also spanned hierarchical levels and grappled with disagreement and ambiguity about who should lead and be on the team.

One other influential developmental factor in team start-up, which often goes unrecognized, is geography. In the Celestial French team and the HTM-TP8 team, there were two major clusters of people: one in the United States and one in France. These clusters each had their own claims to authority because they were close to either the customer or corporate headquarters. This situation created an issue of power imbalance in the team that slowed team development. The TP8 team had the additional complexity of two opposing power bases created by a conflict stemming from differences in occupational cultures of engineering and marketing that were also aligned with the geographical clusters, engineering in the United States and marketing in France. In the Ramtech CPS team, senior managers deliberately selected members who were scattered geographically and not near the company's headquarters, eliminating the power imbalance that could have slowed their development. This was very important for the Ramtech CPS team since any slowdown would have significantly hindered their chances of completing their task since they had only two months together as a team.

Enriched Start-Up

The early processes of teaming can jump-start a team and help them take advantage of the positive initial conditions set by senior managers. In the stories of the Ramtech CPS team and the HTM-TP8 team, we can see that both teams began their work together in face-to-face immersion training that served as a sort of incubator to help them integrate quickly as a team. The early time together, away from their regular jobs, allowed the team members concentrated time together to engage in shared sense making around their task, define specific roles and responsibilities, and get to know one another personally in informal social settings. The immersion training included a business simulation in the case of the Ramtech CPS team to help align team members in their thinking about their own task and how their task fit with the strategic direction of the company. Both teams also received cross-cultural training to help them recognize differences and similarities and then target specific areas for negotiation. The training helped team members set norms for communication and expectations for each other in their virtual work. Overall, the face-to-face immersion training provided the clear direction, strong interpersonal relationships, and collaboration skills the team needed to sustain their virtual work and withstand the environmental influences in their multiple contexts that could have caused the teams to stall in their development or to disintegrate.

The Ramtech CPS team and the HTM-TP8 team each had a cross-culturally skilled, trained facilitator to help with their initial negotiations. The facilitator would stay with these teams as a full member, watching out for potential changes in context that could lead to disruption in development and for disintegrative processes. Having a competent professional facilitator helped integrate the relationships among team members as they worked within their multiple contexts, helping them stay on track so they could spend their limited and valuable time on accomplishing their task. The Celestial French customer team also had a skilled facilitator assigned to the team; however, he did not work with the team as a whole to build alignment and collaboration among the members until the crisis that occurred in the videoconference forced the issue. He was also perceived initially by the original French team members as aligned with the new American leader and hence part of the U.S. camp.

Two other early processes are worth noting because they illustrate specific examples of teaming behaviors that are especially helpful for GVTs: round-robin sense making and creating a team logo and slogan. In the Ramtech CPS team, the members spent quite a bit of time going around the table taking turns telling stories about their experiences with the SAP software and what they knew about it. These stories, like those of our three teams, helped team members transfer knowledge quickly about the expertise each of them was bringing to the team and about the characteristics and peculiarities of context they would need to address in devising a solution for SAP implementation. The knowledge gained in round-robin storytelling helped the team identify and capitalize on their expertise quickly, as well as avoid costly mistakes that could have derailed their efforts at SAP implementation and led to the team's failure to accomplish its task.

The immersion training for the HTM-TP8 team included an exercise requiring the members to develop a logo and a short slogan for the team that would convey to people both inside and outside the team what the team was all about. The logo helped the team members develop an identity they could share and brought them closer together since the exercise forced them to reveal information about themselves, their values, and their attitudes and negotiate a reason for being that was both inclusive and common. The team members referred to the slogan to help them stay aligned and focus on their core task when they were not together. They often referred to it at the start of an audioconference and included it in their internal and external documents. The logo and slogan were shortcuts that enabled the team members to communicate quickly and directly among themselves, with other groups in the company, including senior managers, and with their customers.

The Celestial French customer team did not have such an enriched environment when they began their life as a global team. Senior managers did not provide the team with any initial training similar to that received by the Ramtech CPS or the HTM-TP8 teams because the managers considered the French customer team to be ongoing, having been formed for quite some time. Team members largely ignored incompatible perspectives and work processes and either withdrew or participated only sporadically in team interactions until a crisis forced them to acknowledge their differences and communicate openly with the help of their facilitator. The team might have had a better start and avoided the disruptions that slowed their development if they had spent some time together face-to-face to re-form and reintegrate as a team rather than fall back into camps going their separate ways.

Integration Processes

In all three case illustrations, we can find examples of positive, integrative processes that helped the teams advance to maturity. The Ramtech CPS team and the HTM-TP8 team used the information technology available to them to communicate frequently and appropriately, given their communication objectives. The Ramtech CPS team relied heavily on audioconferencing and e-mail communication because both of these technologies were familiar and easy to use. In their two months together, they could not afford to spend time learning to use new or more complex technology that may have impeded their development. HTM-TP8 did their work together in the early 1990s, when sophisticated technologies were not available to them. However, they worked on specific, manageable tasks by regularly scheduled audioconferences, using a flexible agenda format they had negotiated previously to accommodate differences in communication style and preferences. They also had a structured process for following through on agreements they made in their audio meetings and keeping in touch by e-mail and fax between these conferences to track progress or relay new information. The Celestial French customer team, following their videoconference crisis and the crisis caused by reduced sales volume, began to use collaborative Web technology to share ideas, processes, and information about what they were doing in their respective contexts. Although this technology had been available to the team members early on, they never made use of it. Their Web-based team center was designed for collaboration that required them to share information openly. Prior to the videoconference crisis, it is likely that team members did not trust one another sufficiently to feel comfortable with this degree of collaboration. There was also too much complexity in the team's early teaming process to take on the additional complexity of sophisticated information technology that would have required more time and effort to learn new skills.

The HTM-TP8 team established quarterly face-to-face meetings in addition to the meetings they held virtually to keep them integrated as a team, particularly in relationship to each other, and to tackle sensitive, complex issues that would have been difficult to manage through restricted, structured, mediated communication. They rotated meeting sites to help maintain the power balance in the team and learn about one another's contexts. The Ramtech CPS team also concluded their work with a week-long face-to-face session when they needed to make the difficult and strategic decisions about how to resolve the SAP problem and present their politically sensitive solution to senior managers. The Celestial French customer team made significant progress in their development when they met together six months after they were reconstituted as a global team and spent time fostering their relationships with one another, as well as working on their task.

In all three cases, there were several positive integrative communication processes the team members and their facilitators employed to keep the teams moving forward. In the HTM-TP8 team, the facilitator, and later the members themselves when they became familiar with the strategy, regularly stopped their discussion to check for shared understanding of key points. The Ramtech CPS team members continued the practice of storytelling they had begun in their initial immersion training to surface differences, provide updates about events in their respective contexts, and explore possible solutions to their problems. All three teams used language strategically in virtual and face-to-face communication to help them stay integrated. They relied on technical language that was commonly understood to communicate quickly without sacrificing shared understanding. The HTM-TP8 team allowed communication, written and oral, in both French and English to maintain the balance of power in the team and ensure that nonnative speakers of English would not be disadvantaged. The Celestial French customer team used a food metaphor everyone in the team could relate to and commonly understand to talk about their work and integrate their two competing projects.

Both the HTM-TP8 and the Celestial French customer teams had significant internal conflict to overcome before they could fully collaborate. In their stories, we can identify processes the teams used, generally with the help of their facilitators or leaders, to provide added impetus for integration when challenges stemming from cross-occupational conflict (HTM-TP8), unspoken tensions resulting in open conflict (Celestial French customer), or changing industry and business conditions in the marketplace (Celestial French customer) threatened to disrupt development. In the HTM-TP8 team, the leader forced negotiation by locking feuding team members in a room and not allowing them to come out until they had reached agreement. The team leader also used the strategy of partnering the engineering and marketing representatives on the team to work on a customer problem they both considered important, focusing them on a higher-order goal that needed their collaboration to achieve. This partnering strategy gave both team members a shared history and stories they could tell together that furthered the team's development by adding knowledge and reinforcing their collaboration. In the Celestial French customer team, the facilitator engaged in shuttle diplomacy to smooth feelings and gather facts, which he used to help the team members understand one another's positions and contexts, setting them on the road to collaboration. The team relocated some of its core members together in France as a measure to keep the team from disintegrating entirely and to help them learn more about each other, the French customer, and what each team member could contribute to the team task, all information that is implicit and difficult to convey without being there.

To keep apprised of their ever-changing contexts, the teams in our stories engaged in processes designed to monitor what was happening in the organization that might affect their work and throw the team off-track, hindering their progress. The Ramtech CPS team engaged in company and customer networking to obtain information from credible sources and then collectively integrate the information and come to a shared understanding about how it could help them in accomplishing their task. The team members were able to obtain a broader perspective on their task and a more comprehensive solution adapted to their multiple contexts, which contributed to their success. The Celestial

French customer team temporarily redefined their task from one of developing a new global market strategy to one of increasing sales volume to match the changing business conditions and priorities of the French customer. This reversion to more familiar ground reduced the complexity in the team at a time when they were about to disintegrate. The redefinition of their task reenergized and unified the team by drawing on commonly shared, preexisting expertise and focusing on an urgent business problem the team members could all understand and collaborate to resolve.

Processes that can hinder ongoing development were evident in the Celestial French team during the period following the company reorganization and customer merger. For example, a subgroup in the team developing a pilot project kept other members in the dark about their actions and in the process created suspicion, feelings of exclusion, and in-group versus out-group factions, resulting in power imbalances, anger, hurt, and distrust among team members. This process threatened to tear the team apart. Because there was distrust, the team members engaged in infrequent and closed communication. They avoided discussion that could have brought the tension to the surface and allowed them to resolve their differences earlier in their development process, before they resulted in the videoconference blow-up. The infrequent communication also kept people focused on local issues to the detriment of the common team task, further reducing trust and increasing in-group versus out-group conflict. When conflict finally did surface, team members resorted to personal attacks, and the team facilitator was not able to address the situation adequately until after the videoconference (using shuttle diplomacy) because he was connected only by audio link and could not observe the interaction in the videoconference.

Implication for Practice

We place our emphasis on development processes because managers and team members can do something about them. Developmental processes involve managing people, social relationships, task, contexts, and time. These components interact dynamically in the process of development, which means that it is difficult to know just how the process will unfold over time as contexts shift, people and their relationships change, or the nature of the task is altered by changes in business strategy. The team may not be able to exert much control over many of the factors outside the team, such as a reorganization or economic slowdown. However, if managers and team members pay close attention to the processes of GVTs, particularly those that help team members keep abreast of changes and integrate their work across multiple contexts, they can foster development and increase their level of performance (Gluesing, 1995, 1998). GVTs are all about integration. It is our experience that teams that engage in integrative processes consistently throughout the formation and ongoing development of the team will be more likely to reach maturation and perform effectively to achieve their task.

References

DeSanctis, G., and Poole, M. S. "The Hidden Complexity in Advanced Technology Use: Adaptive Structuration Theory." *Organization Science,* 1994, *14,* 157–176.

Earley, P. C., and Gibson, C. B. *Multinational Teams: A New Perspective.* Mahwah, N.J.: Erlbaum, 2002.

Fineholt, T. A. "Global Software Development, Productivity and Trust in Virtual Teams at Lucent Technologies." Paper presented at Effective Virtual Teams Conference, Collaboratory for Research on Electronic Work, School of Information, University of Michigan, Oct. 2000.

Gersick, C.J.G. "Time and Transition in Work Teams: Toward a New Model of Group Development." *Academy of Management Journal,* 1988, *31*(1), 9–41.

Gersick, C.J.G. "Marking Time: Predictable Transitions in Task Groups." *Academy of Management Journal,* 1989, *32*(2), 274–309.

Gluesing, J. G. "Fragile Alliances: Negotiating Global Teaming in a Turbulent Environment." Unpublished doctoral dissertation, Wayne State University, 1995.

Gluesing, J. G. "Building Connections and Balancing Power in Global Teams: Toward a Reconceptualization of Culture as Composite." In T. Hamada (ed.), "Anthropology of Business Organizations." *Anthropology of Work Review,* 1998, *18*(2), 18–30.

McCollom, M. "Reevaluating Group Development: A Critique of the Familiar Models." In J. Gillette and M. McCollom (eds.), *Groups in Context: A New Perspective on Group Dynamics.* Reading, Mass.: Addison-Wesley, 1990.

McGrath, J. E. "Time, Interaction, and Performance (TIP): A Theory of Groups." *Small Group Research,* 1991, *22*(2), 147–174.

Tuckman, B. W. "Developmental Sequence in Small Groups." *Psychological Bulletin,* 1965, *63*(6), 384–399.

CHAPTER SEVENTEEN

Closing the Time Gap in Virtual Teams

Janice A. Klein, Astrid Kleinhanns

The competitive business environment is forcing every organization to try to do more with less. Employees are being asked to squeeze more tasks into their workday. The result is a constant juggling of projects. Attention is typically focused on the immediate, short-term tasks at hand. Projects that need advance preparation or that are requested by someone from a remote location get the backseat to local firefighting. Because being a virtual team member is typically just one more activity that must be managed along with other local tasks and responsibilities, local priorities end up interfering with full participation in virtual teams (Klein and Barrett, 2001). Virtual team leaders must find ways to make their teams a top priority. Their task becomes one of capturing a team member's mind-share (Gayeski, 2000). In other words, virtual team leaders need to engage more of the attention of their team members whose focus is diluted by their other tasks and priorities. As one team leader noted, "I see my role as helping to capture mind-share. It's like market share, but with mind-share,

---

This chapter stems from a team effort that has provided inputs from academic and industrial perspectives. Although the research team has studied numerous companies with locations across the globe, this chapter is the product of interviews with over seventy-five members of nine virtual teams from one global high-technology firm. To protect the anonymity of the interviewees, all references to gender are masculine. We thank Betty Barrett, Feniosky Pena-Mora, and Sanjeev Vadhavkar for their insights and assistance in many of the interviews cited. The chapter also benefited from the feedback and suggestions of Betty Barrett, Dan Klein, Bill Hanson, Catherine Cramton, and Susan Cohen.

I want to know that people think about the things that they're working on, and I want their attention to be focused on the priorities for the team."

Capturing team member mind-share is a problem whether a team is colocated or virtual, but virtual teams make the task more difficult because of the "out-of-sight, out-of-mind" syndrome. Even if a team is colocated, there is usually a gap between time available to focus on team activities and the time required to accomplish the team's objectives fully. The lack of physical proximity and the increased cultural diversity of virtual teams make this task more complicated.

As companies expand into global markets, virtual teams are being formed to leverage local expertise and enhance capability by integrating cross-functional, cross-cultural, and cross-organizational know-how and experience. The benefit of a team is not derived merely from the presence of diverse intelligence; it is created within a collaborative team effort that results in a better outcome than the best individual team member could achieve alone. Teams that accomplish their task by splitting it into individual team member assignments and accountabilities are pseudoteams and miss out on the most important asset of a team: the synergy created by team member interaction. The key is to create this synergy, but to do it as quickly as possible to avoid requiring even more time in team members' busy schedules. In the words of one virtual team member, "In my mind, an effective team is one that can tap the collective intelligence, the different points of view, and work their way through those things—and bring their unique skills and capabilities to bear, but do it fast. Do it as quickly or approaching what it would take just one person to do it."

Virtual team collaboration requires a combination of synchronous and asynchronous work. When team members are squeezed for time, both modes of work suffer. Local priorities override any time that team members had planned to devote to team assignments (asynchronous work) and distract team members during team meetings (synchronous interaction). The result is ineffective collaboration that ultimately requires more time to accomplish the team's goals. As shown in Figure 17.1, a vicious cycle is set in motion that leads to a continual widening of the gap, with team members spending less time on team activities that they view as an inefficient use of their time.

This chapter draws on in-depth case studies from a multiyear project investigating virtual teams to explore factors that impede full contribution to virtual teams. We conclude with a set of tactics and techniques that team leaders can use to minimize the time gap and maximize team member mind-share.

TEAM COLLABORATION

If one individual had all the knowledge required to accomplish a task, there would be no need for teams. Furthermore, if the only objective were to gather the input of diverse opinions, that could be accomplished by one individual's

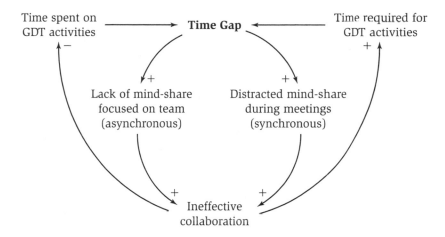

Figure 17.1 The Perils of Time Pressures.

Note: The arrows signify a positive or negative causality. For example, ineffective collaboration leads to more time required to accomplish GDT activities, while team members are less willing to spend time on GDT activities if they perceive that time is being spent on ineffective collaboration.

collecting the thoughts of multiple people and then summarizing them in an integrated report. The true value of teams is through the synergy, or shared creation (Hackman, 1987; Schrage, 1989; Fisher and Fisher, 1998), that results from gathering the work of diverse team members, that is, a sharing of minds, and building a synergetic output. As shown in Figure 17.2, effective team collaboration is a three-step process of collecting, integrating, and then building on individual inputs (Gibson, 2001).

Input

At the individual level, each team member brings to the team individual experiences and knowledge. The first step toward synergy is to share this diverse intellectual capital at a team level. This can be done synchronously in a virtual or face-to-face meeting or asynchronously using e-mail or some other form of communication. But when time is at a premium, asynchronous processes are more efficient because participation can occur in parallel.

Integration

Once the various inputs have been shared, they must be integrated and shared with the rest of the team. This process is more than just summarizing because integration entails finding how those inputs fit together to create a mosaic of diverse but integrated ideas. Once again, this can be done synchronously or asynchronously, but it does not necessarily require the effort of the entire team.

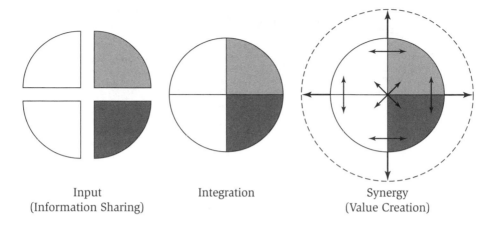

Input
(Information Sharing)

Integration

Synergy
(Value Creation)

Figure 17.2 The Three Phases of Team Collaboration.

To save time, one individual can be assigned the task of integrating the diverse inputs into a whole that is then shared with the team.

Synergy

The third and most important step is mutually reflecting on the individual inputs to create a synergetic output. While the first two phases can be done individually and shared asynchronously through technology, the third phase is a collaborative team effort that is based on iterative feedback loops among the team members. This iterative process of mutually reflecting on each other's input is a collaborative team effort that creates synergy based on a complementary set of knowledge and skills. Although it is possible to do this third phase asynchronously, it is much easier to create synergy in a synchronous mode. Due to the reciprocal nature of this phase, it will take much longer if done asynchronously and there is a potential loss of momentum because responses may not be made with people in the same frame of mind, that is, there will be a loss of mind-share between responses.

Many team members complain that too much time is spent on merely sharing information in meetings (the input phase) rather than doing truly collaborative work, such as team decision making or problem solving. With limited time and multiple priorities, it is typically difficult to get team members to focus on the team other than during team meetings. As a result, team meetings become the primary vehicle to capture mind-share. With limited time to meet, meetings are held in only the first two phases, although information sharing could be done more efficiently in an asynchronous mode. As one member explained, "In general, the team meetings with all the site representatives take the form of what I would call just information sharing. They are really not a decision meeting."

THE TIME GAP: BARRIERS TO EFFECTIVE COLLABORATION

Each of the three collaboration phases presents different challenges in capturing team member mind-share that threaten team effectiveness. As much as these challenges can be found in both colocated and virtual teams, in virtual teams these challenges differ in intensity and kind from those in colocated teams. Technology-mediated communication combined with variation in site availability of advanced technology resources, a lack of overlapping working hours, local priorities, cultural diversity, and the absence of physical presence as a means of communication make it difficult for virtual teams to achieve effective team collaboration processes. Although working through all three phases of virtual collaboration may take more time, it is critical to attain added value from the team effort. Part of the problem is that most of the team's work is relegated to team meetings. With limited meeting time and tightly scheduled agendas, there is never enough time to make it through all three phases, as this member noted: "Time is of the essence. You have only one hour to meet, only one hour to accomplish so many things. So communication is sometimes sacrificed."

Diverse Members

Effective collaboration requires clear and open communications among team members, the development of a shared understanding relative to team goals and tasks, and a trust among team members that each is committed to and will adhere to team processes (Cohen and Bailey, 1997; Duarte and Snyder, 1999; Fisher and Fisher, 1998). Due to the diversity inherent in a global virtual team, this may mean more time spent to ensure that all voices are adequately heard. One member stated, "In one group, I had a colleague who never spoke, and we would have lost his insight altogether if he had been ignored, so you must ensure that everyone has had their say, and that means sometimes you add an hour for agreement to the meeting time. For example, for a face-to-face, use a four-hour agenda for an eight-hour meeting."

Not surprisingly, many team members are reluctant to spend the extra time, and the lack of effective collaboration ultimately requires more time to achieve the team's objectives. For example, a member explained, "Specific discussion really got bogged down, and it took us three different meetings to get to some level of understanding of what needed to happen. That's partly because people still aren't on the same page as far as purpose is concerned."

Team members who are overloaded with work focus their time on what they think is the essence of their work. Often this means that they limit communication with their peer team members to a minimum. But team members who live in different cultural contexts base their team collaboration on different assumptions, beliefs, and experiences in regard to work, time, and human interaction.

A team that lacks the time to explore and communicate its cultural diversity carefully may find itself caught up in a never-ending circle of misunderstandings, conflict, and frustration. This is illustrated in the following passage: "If I say I am going to deliver the car, then it must have all the attributes I expect and it performs and sticks to what the manual says. Asians want to know how I built the car. I have too many things on my mind to worry about how you resolved the issues of the tires. They want to know how tough it has been for you."

Communications that do not take place face-to-face require more time and attention for individual team members to embrace and decode all nonphysical clues that come or do not come with it. If not dealt with carefully, communication can turn into an explosive undesired baggage, slowing or even stopping the team's success (Hallowell, 1999). Being familiar with the personal needs, concerns, interests, priorities, and fears of the team members is important to fill in and make sense of the gaps of communication caused by the absence of body language, foreign accents, or silence on the telephone. Because global virtual teams communicate in a language that is not the first language for many of the team members, the levels of linguistic capability of the team members may differ in phonics and syntax. Unfamiliar accents and an inappropriate use of vocabulary can make it hard and sometimes impossible to understand each other. One team member pointed out that another team member "is difficult to understand, so he doesn't have that much credibility in the organization. So he'll say something, and no one will listen because they can't understand him and they don't have the social skills to say, 'Hey, I am not sure I caught what you just shared. Can you try again?' They will move on and just ignore it."

Despite recent developments to improve collaborative technologies, the quality of voice and data transmission often accentuates difficulties. Any shortcoming of the technology becomes an added aggravation when time is spent trying to clarify what was said, as is illustrated here:

> The quality of the phone systems is such that sometimes you just can't hear people very well; it's fuzzy, or it's faint or something else, and that exacerbates the language problem. So if someone doesn't enunciate very well or pronounce very well or has problems with vocabulary, it becomes very difficult. The communication process can be tedious. You end up having to make three or four attempts to really understand what the person's trying to say.

After a series of failed attempts of reaching understanding, team members feel frustrated and give up asking. This phenomenon is aggravated by the lack of time because of the need to move on and get things done, as one team member explained: "I can't see you, so I don't know if you are doing it right. I cannot trust that I'm getting the right information or enough information, and I may never be certain, yet we'll just use it. I get tired of fighting and just use the information, so you're cutting a few corners just to make things a little faster."

In addition to cultural and language diversity, teams must also account for diversity in individual cognitive processing (Seagal and Horne, 1997). The time gap that virtual team members face constrains the time needed to think about the team and the task, draft input, comment on input, reflect on the topic, and ask questions for understanding—for example, one team member stated, "Getting information out in time for people to read it, absorb it, understand it, and put it in context. All of that gets sort of added to, in terms of complexity, by being virtual. We never have enough time to create an adequate context and amount of information and get the right kinds of information back. So expectations aren't always clear. Responsibilities aren't always clear."

Time Zone Dispersion

Others have noted the impact of time and space on ease of communications (McGrath et al., 1993; Goodman and Darr, 1996; Cramton, 2001; Hinds, 1999; Lipnack and Stamps, 1997; O'Hara-Devereaux and Johansen, 1994). Here, we explore the impact of time zone dispersion on the time available and required for team collaboration. The teams we have studied have included members in multiple locations throughout North America and Asia, where there is often a thirteen-hour time difference between sites. As a consequence, time zone dispersion is typically a more significant factor than geographical dispersion (Olson and Olson, 2000). As one team member stated, "It is difficult to work over distances. More difficult than distance is the time differential. It is hard to work when one of you is sleepy or needs an answer right away."

With limited time available, team members often leave things for the last minute and assume they can squeeze things in right before a meeting. Virtual teams, however, require advanced lead time to get materials out to remote sites. Team Web sites allow for almost instantaneous distribution of information, but asynchronous work must still be done prior to a meeting to absorb and reflect on the material. If a meeting happens to be on a Monday morning at Eastern Standard Time, North American team members must distribute materials on Thursday so that Asian or Australian team members receive them before their weekend. Even if the preparation time would be required to prepare for a colocated team meeting, the required lead time is typically viewed as additional preparation.

Although some organizations have found ways to capitalize on the time difference to have team members working asynchronously around the clock (Haywood, 1998), time zone dispersion narrows the window for synchronous team interaction while typically lengthening the workday for global team members. Ideally, team members should be able to flex their work hours to accommodate team meetings outside their normal workday, but local job pressures typically require them to work their normal hours and then be available for meetings either before or after their scheduled workday. Virtual team members ascribed these difficulties as follows: "The time differences kill us because we have to wait until 6:00 to 8:00 P.M. and people get burned out. We have local meetings in the morning and global ones at night." "The time of day for the meeting puts someone in the middle of the night: Asians come early, and we stay late. People in North America are ready to go home before the discussion is finished." Late-evening or middle-of-the-night virtual meetings can result in team members' facing sleep deprivation or family interruptions, especially if they join the meeting from home. This often leads to late arrivals or no-shows. For those who do attend the meetings, their mind-share during meetings will most likely be less than optimal. A member commented:

> When you have one person calling in at ten or eleven o'clock at night, another person calling in at six in the morning, and others in between, there are varying levels of attention and engagement on the part of the participants. I've been on both ends of the extreme many times, and I know how hard it is. It's not like when you're in the middle of a normal workday and being engaged in something. It's very different when you have just gotten up or when you're very tired at the end of the day.

The result is that virtual team members view global teams as adding time to an already packed workday; for example, one member said, "It's a bit painful because it means a twelve-hour day. We spend so many hours here—usually two hours extra but maybe extend a half-hour hour to one hour up to four hours for a team each week."

Synchronous and Asynchronous Work

Because team meetings are the most visible part of global team interactions, their effectiveness becomes a measure of the overall collaborative effort. This is unfortunate because the effectiveness of synchronous interactions is dependent on the team's ability to capture team member mind-share for asynchronous work. For teams where synchronous time is limited, it is vital to think carefully about how synchronous time is spent to provide the most value to the team.

Preparation

Another consequence of the time gap is that team members find they often do not have time to prepare adequately for team meetings, for example, reviewing advanced reading material. When this occurs, meeting time is spent reviewing the material, an activity that could have been done asynchronously. The result is that the meeting is viewed as an inefficient use of time for team members who have done their homework and typically leads to frustration. One team member stated, "We could improve if we go to meetings prepared to act on data that we've already read." Another team member commented, "If people don't know the agenda, if shared documents are not there on time, that affects effectiveness. If documents are sent early, it helps to prepare before the meeting. Sometimes we spend time at the meeting just reading, so it helps to read before."

Frustrated team members often become unwilling to devote time outside team meetings to reviewing advanced material because they lack confidence that others will do the same. Furthermore, they are likely to arrive late, assuming that the first part of the meeting was spent going over the advanced reading. All of this fuels their aggravation. But even without the lack of trust, the mere existence of the time gap will often lead to late arrivals or, worse yet, no-shows, as expressed here: "What is consistent is the lack of attendance. It's pretty consistent. They are so busy with so many different things at their site. They've got such huge jobs, and this is just one more meeting they need to attend, and they need to respond to things."

Getting All Members on the Same Page

When teams come together (with or without late arrivals or no-shows), they typically spend time updating each other and making sure everyone understands where the team is at on the agenda, timeline, or deliverable that is on the same page. When tardy or absent team members do arrive, additional time is needed to make sure they are aware of everything that has transpired. These are typically redundant discussions that take further time out of tightly packed agendas. But even with the redundant discussions, there will be missed dialogue that does not get recapitulated. As one team member explained.

> I know that if I miss a meeting, I miss a lot. I can't always pick it up from reading the minutes. A lot of times, you get some discussion in there that's really critical but isn't important to capture in the minutes. But it was good discussion, whether it's explaining somebody's lack of understanding on something and clarifying it. After missed meetings, I've really had to work hard to get caught up because I don't want to fall behind in what's going on. It takes a lot to catch up. So if you miss quite a few meetings in a row, there's no way you can know what's going on.

With the never-ending need to get all team members on the same page, there is limited time in the meeting to move forward, as these team members noted:

> In our environment, where things go so fast and we move quickly, meetings often are used as catch-up time rather than being meaningful sessions when people come together in terms of our ability to move forward. So they are times for leveling people up to the same kind of basic set of assumptions and so forth, and often there is not very much time for moving forward.

We seldom ever get through all the agenda items. A big part of that is because we're virtual, and people need that time to level when they come together. We're trying to get ourselves settled on the right things.

Multitasking

The time gap takes its toll on even the most conscientious team members. Even if they have done all the necessary preparation and arrived on time, their mind will probably still be on all the other tasks they should be doing. In today's busy world, most people have fine-tuned the art of multitasking. It is quite common (and typically required to avoid feedback noise) to mute one's telephone when not speaking. This allows the remote participant to carry on a side conversation or rifle through papers without other participants' hearing or knowing that the team member is multitasking. It is also quite easy for a team member to read and respond to e-mail during meetings. This has become a bit of an epidemic in both virtual and face-to-face meetings where team members have their laptops. Some multitasking is a way to cope with all the redundant discussions, but ultimately multitasking leads to additional redundant discussions due to missed or only partially heard discussions. Multitasking can also distract team members to such an extent that they miss an opportunity to provide valuable input into the discussion (Waller, 1997). This in turn has a negative impact on the overall collaborative effort of the team, as evidenced here: "Local teams are more effective because you know everyone's listening. In virtual teams, people are multitasking—listening for key ideas. We do it because there's a lot of work and not enough time. Time management is an art."

Results of the Time Gap

As shown in Figure 17.3, the source of all the inefficiencies noted above is the gap between the time team members make available for team activities and the time needed to accomplish the team's objectives successfully. The result is both ineffective team meetings and collaboration in general. The worst part is that the inefficiencies aggravate the time gap due to the need to hold more meetings to get the work of the team completed, as one member commented: "We just sort of do what we can in our meetings, and then when we don't get something closed, we hold another meeting."

IMPLICATIONS FOR PRACTICE

The key to more effective team collaboration appears to be finding ways to narrow the time gap through reducing the time required to accomplish the team's objectives or persuading team members to shift more of their mind-share to the team. Seven techniques have been found to capture increased mind-share of their team members.

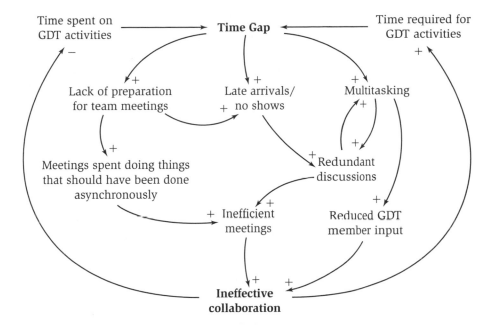

Figure 17.3 Impact of Time Gap on Synchronous and Asynchronous Interaction.
Note: The arrows signify a positive or negative causality.

Enhance the Perceived Value of the Team Collaboration

One counterbalancing force to the time gap is the perceived value of the time and attention team members devote to the collaboration. The decision criteria for time spent on a team's activities are typically a combination of individual choice and priorities set by a team member's manager. Both of these are set, in part, based on a perception of the value of the team effort and whether the team collaboration process is viewed as an effective use of time.

The strategic importance of the task and the amount of attention, support, and resources afforded the team by senior leadership also influence the perceived value of the collaboration effort. Senior sponsorship helps to raise the importance of the work in the eyes of the team members and refocus team members away from the daily tactical demands of their local jobs. As one virtual team member mentioned:

> Often people think, "I don't need to participate in this because I am already more ahead in this area than the others." But it's a give and take; sometimes you are the leader, and sometimes you are the follower. And that's what makes that organization work. You have to approach it from a more strategic point than a tactical point of view. And that has been really hard because most people just think from one day to the next, and they lean back and ask themselves, "In the long run, what does this do for me?"

More important, senior leadership support sends a message to each team member's local site management and peers that the work is important and time should be made available. This in turn helps to align local objectives with the goals of the team and lessen any local distractions or local priority conflicts.

Hence, one of the first priorities for a team leader is to ensure that the team's activities and output are aligned with both local and global objectives. For a team leader, this will entail added time up-front to meet with each team member's local manager and supervisor to get their commitment to support the team effort. If this step is skipped, the time gap will only worsen. A team member noted, "Full willingness and participation need to be ensured, and people need to be engaged. Sometimes their boss doesn't want them involved, so you don't get their support."

Clarify Each Team Member's Role and Purpose for Being Part of the Virtual Team

Teams, both virtual and colocated, tend to mushroom in number. When this occurs, team members begin to question not only the value of the team but also whether their personal participation is needed. It is therefore crucial that each team member know exactly how he or she can best add value to the team. This requires the team to spend sufficient time on clarifying team members' roles, responsibilities, and individual and team accountabilities.

Being aware of the team interdependencies and the importance of one's own contribution to team progress will increase the team member's responsibility to spend sufficient time on the team's task. It is also helpful to show how the purpose and goals of the team link back to the team member's local responsibilities. Team members who see that they will be responsible for implementing the output of the team decision making or that the output will directly affect their daily activities will have more personal investment in the team. This has been particularly evident in several of the team meetings we have observed. Otherwise quiet team members tend to speak up when they see a direct link to their personal accountabilities as stated by this team member: "I think the ones who are always engaged are most affected because the decisions that come down from the team really affect their work at the site. They can't help but be affected by it."

Create Shared Accountability to Team Processes and Protocols

Because a significant amount of the inefficiency created by the time gap stems from team members' not devoting appropriate mind-share to team tasks, it is important to get buy-in from all team members on expected team member behavior and adherence to agreed-on team processes and protocols (Henry and Hartzler, 1998; Gerber and Pennito, 1999). These protocols include expectations around team meeting attendance and punctuality, timeliness of input and feed-back to each other, and advanced preparation for team meetings. The importance of this is illustrated in the following comment:

> It just needs to be laid out really specifically, and I don't think it ever has been really laid out. I'm not certain that it was made crystal clear that this is the expectation of being on this team: "This is what we require of you, and if you cannot make that commitment, maybe you shouldn't be on the team."

> Whereas we might rely on informal and real-time communication mechanisms with the local team, you can't rely on those same mechanisms with the virtual team. You have to have more formal mechanisms, more structured meetings, and that kind of thing.

A laissez-faire attitude toward commitments made to one another will lead to frustration and undermine trust among team members. Unfortunately, it takes only one team member to derail a meeting or become a bottleneck to the team's progress. Team members who fail to uphold their team responsibilities are, in essence, showing disrespect for their fellow team members' time and should be confronted if their behavior becomes habitual (Handy, 1995). Noted a team member, "We decided to expand the team because people really wanted to be on it. They wanted more of a voice. Now that we have expanded it, we don't get the attendance by those people who wanted to be on it. I think that's pretty frustrating."

Shift Work to More Asynchronous Interaction to Make Meetings More Value-Added

With meeting time at such a premium, it is best to use it for work that really needs to be done synchronously. To make synchronous interactions more value-added, teams need to find ways to increase asynchronous mind-share.

Agendas are often so tight that they do not leave time to collect everybody's thoughts and ideas. This should not preclude open dialogue during meetings. The dialogue should be focused on clarifying input that has already been collected by e-mail or electronic bulletin boards. One technique to facilitate focused asynchronous work is to outline specific questions for team members to ponder prior to the meetings, as suggested in the following: "There are too many things on the agenda, and we don't have the quality time to discuss things. Don't just give me all the stuff, but ask me a question, and I'll think about it and then give you my perspective. To get meaningful discussions, it would be good for us to think about those questions ahead of time."

Shifting to more asynchronous work requires that team members find the time to focus mind-share on the team tasks. Most fully intend to devote the time, but all too often, good intentions do not overcome daily distractions. It is therefore useful to provide periodic stimuli to capture team members' mind-share and remind them of their team responsibilities. A little prompting by an e-mail or telephone call will help team members to focus on the team activities and ensure that they update themselves to the same level of information in terms of previous meeting accomplishments or discussions, as well as new developments. But even with the reminders, capturing mind-share can be a struggle that requires perseverance—for example, "Some of the struggles that are current are the lack of participation of some of the members. So, for example, [a team member] sends out a note that asks for input by a certain date, and he gets no input. It's like pulling teeth to get some information."

Although shifting to asynchronous work may appear to just be shuffling activities, overall the team will find they accomplish their tasks in less time and with fewer frustrations, as this member noted: "Meaningful and effective meetings happen only when there's truly been a lot of work and preparation and common agreement and some leveling and all that kind of stuff beforehand."

Encourage Frequent and Continuous Communications Among Team Members

Colocated team members often rely on informal communication in the hallway or the cafeteria to update one another on new developments, brainstorm ideas, clarify misunderstandings, create a shared understanding, and strengthen relationships and trust. In virtual teams, much of this informal interaction is lost unless a conscious effort is made to keep communications flowing among team members on a continual basis. As one team member stated, "If you have a team of people all over the world, there's the complexity of time and the time dimension. You have different time zones to deal with. Communicating is not possible in the same manner as when you're in the same area and working together. You have to come up with different methods of staying in touch with one another."

More frequent communications between individual team members can save significant amounts of time in team collaboration and avoid misunderstandings or conflicts that slow the collaborative team process. Regularly scheduled team meetings can help to set a rhythm for both synchronous and asynchronous work (Maznevski and Chudoba, 2000). In addition, periodic one-on-one meetings between the team members will help to build personal networks, strengthen a shared understanding of their different perspectives, and develop mutual accountability. As relationships are built, team members will feel more obliged to follow up on commitments made to each other. As one member suggested, "I think I have good relationships with people because I have the one-on-ones, I always help out, and I usually deliver on time."

Make Assumptions and Personal Agendas Explicit

Assumptions that are not subjected to a reality check can have a negative impact on the effectiveness of a team collaboration and may lead to disastrously large amounts of time used to identify and clarify false assumptions. It is therefore crucial to virtual teams to regularly check into each other's assumptions and beliefs concerning the team's task and progress. One member explained:

> When I'm physically present with people, I have sort of an intuitive sense about how things are going and whether I need to spend more time on a topic or less time. I find that there's a certain amount of uncertainty I walk away with every time I'm meeting on the phone versus when I'm face-to-face with somebody. Did we really agree on that? Did we really surface all of the issues or questions or concerns that people had?

Virtual interaction, especially audioconferences, presents many opportunities for team members to build subjective assumptions about what is going on at the other end of the line. It is therefore important that the team members get to know each other and gain a mutual understanding of who the other members are and what their personal needs, concerns, priorities, and interests are. Because getting to know one's peers and their idiosyncrasies requires the establishment of trust and positive relationships within the team, many researchers and practitioners believe that face-to-face meetings are critical in the early stages of a team's life (Duarte and Snyder, 1999; Lipnack and Stamps, 1997). Getting to know each other as individuals helps in understanding tone of voice in a virtual meeting or an unspoken agenda. One member suggested:

> Because we've had several face-to-faces, people know each other, and you have a better understanding of who the other person is. When you see them and you talk to them, you can read body language and connect the body language to the voice intonations, and you learn to associate those. So when you talk to someone off-line, you're much more perceptive about changes in tone, speed, and things like that, and you learn to read people better and understand them.

Even after relationships have been built, virtual collaboration creates black boxes that are left open to individual interpretation. Global virtual teams must put extra effort on explicitly communicating things that may not be evident to other team members. This takes time and requires different skills and know-how from the team members than they have developed for face-to-face communication. This is illustrated by the following comment:

> It's difficult for visual people when they get into conceptual differences. I've done this several times, where I've actually verbally described things; I say, "Imagine a picture," and I draw a picture. And that, although tedious, is sometimes the only way that you can get visual people to get it. That doesn't work

very well in a phone-only environment. You have to try to use words to replicate pictures, and that's hard.

Provide a Human Link in the Virtual Environment

Many wishful thinkers believe that virtual communications can supplant human interaction. We have found, however, that the best intentions often go awry due to time pressures, and it is necessary, especially in virtual environments, to add a human link to coordinate and build relationships among virtual team members. Some might argue that an added human link is unnecessary overhead. Our research and that of others (Olson and Olson, 2000) suggest the exact opposite. The facilitators or tactical team leaders we observed provided not only project management coordination, but also helped to build relationships and bridge all the holes found in virtual communications. To be effective in the role, the human link must possess knowledge about the content of the team's work, the processes the team has agreed to use, and the members themselves, that is, their interests, concerns, and priorities. By really knowing the team members, the facilitator can sense and identify when someone indicates doubt or disagreement but does not air it explicitly. The role of the facilitator is therefore to help the team members voice their opinions and help the entire team understand each of the person's viewpoints. For example, one member claimed:

> He's a better facilitator for the team because of the relationships that he's built and the knowledge that he's acquired about the different members on the team. He also had worked with the group, had relationships in place. That makes him more effective in leading the meeting, whether face-to-face or on the phone, but especially on the phone. He's more familiar with the people, and when they say something, he has an idea of some of the unsaid things that might go along with that, what might be going on. He is very much in tune with people's interest in issues. He really understands and has worked hard to build good relationships with the people on the team.

By having created a mutual understanding in the team, a facilitator can move the team forward to produce results, make decisions, and meet the goals. With an established relationship, a facilitator can also help to balance team dynamics and process. This is a role that is often relegated to the team leader, but our interviews suggest that even the team leader is often too busy with local responsibilities to do all the needed coordination adequately. The role of a facilitator or tactical team leader—what we are referring to as the human link—is a key factor in making sure that everything is aligned to make meetings as effective as possible. It is a very process-oriented role that includes organizing the meeting and its logistics, sufficiently preparing team members prior to the meeting, helping the team to gather individual team input, create mutual understanding in the team, and facilitate the meeting toward results.

Final Thoughts

The intent of global teams is to engage the diverse talents of a global workforce but all too often the value of the global team gets lost in the daily juggling of multiple job demands. Many organizations rush to set up virtual teams at the drop of a hat without recognizing the added time demands they require. As a result, being part of a virtual team is often viewed as a distraction to avoid as best one can as opposed to a privilege or opportunity to provide input on a global basis. Organizations must recognize the time demands placed on individual team members and avoid just adding their names to a long list of potential teams. Virtual teams should be formed only when there is a need to create synergy from the diverse contributions of dispersed team members.

When there is truly a need for team collaboration, team leaders need to value the diversity and focus on the mechanisms discussed here to maximize the contribution of all team members. Recognizing that the time gap is a reality of life, team leaders need to emphasize the importance of full participation and dedicated mind-share to achieve the value-added from the team effort effectively and efficiently.

Virtual collaboration is fraught with potential pitfalls, but if it is done right, organizations and team members can reap the benefits of tapping diverse global voices while avoiding the costs and stresses associated with extensive travel or relocation. This requires that organizations begin looking at virtual teams as an investment rather than an expense. Experience indicates that successful virtual collaboration will take more additional up-front time to align priorities, build relationships, and gain shared understanding. It will also require continual reminders to virtual team members that they need to be respectful of each other's time and that time spent doing work asynchronously will make meetings more efficient. In this way, participation in virtual teams will begin to be viewed as part of one's daily activities as opposed to an add-on. In the long run, the added time will lead to a better collaborative output that will help the organization meet its strategic global objectives. This team member captured the essence: "It's all about helping the whole team understand each of the person's viewpoints and seeing it from a different perspective. Yeah, it takes more time, but you end up with a better decision and a better understanding with the team."

Capturing mind-share is the only way that companies will benefit from the use of virtual teams. If team members are not mentally present, organizations waste precious time and the effort of people who already feel stretched to the limit. It is no wonder that employees complain there are too many teams and they do not have time to get any work done.

References

Cohen, S. G., and Bailey, D. E. "What Makes Teams Work: Group Effectiveness Research from the Shop Floor to the Executive Suite." *Journal of Management,* 1997, *23*(3), 239–291.

Cramton, C. "The Mutual Knowledge Problem and Its Consequences for Dispersed Collaboration." *Organization Science,* 2001, *12*(3), 346–371.

Duarte, D. L., and Snyder, N. T. *Mastering Virtual Teams.* San Francisco: Jossey-Bass, 1999.

Fisher, K., and Fisher, M. D. *Distributed Minds: Achieving High Performance Through the Collective Intelligence of Knowledge Work Teams.* New York: American Management Association, 1998.

Gayeski, D. *Managing the Communication Function: Capturing Mindshare for Organizational Performance.* San Francisco: International Association of Business Communicators, 2000.

Gerber, S., and Pennito, J. "Virtual Teams at Work: One Manager's Story." Working paper. Cambridge, Mass.: MIT Leaders for Manufacturing 1999.

Gibson, C. B. "From Accumulation to Accommodation: The Chemistry of Collective Cognition in Work Groups." *Journal of Organizational Behavior,* 2001, *22*(2), 121–134.

Goodman, P. S., and Darr, E. D. "Exchanging Best Practices Through Computer-Aided Systems." *Academy of Management Executive,* 1996, *10*(2), 7–20.

Hackman, J. R. "The Design of Work Teams." In J. W. Lorsch (ed.), *Handbook of Organizational Behavior.* Upper Saddle River, N.J.: Prentice Hall, 1987.

Hallowell, E. "The Human Moment at Work." *Harvard Business Review,* 1999, Jan.–Feb., pp. 58–66.

Handy, C. "Trust and the Virtual Organization." *Harvard Business Review,* 1995, May–June, pp. 40–50.

Haywood, M. *Managing Virtual Teams: Practical Techniques for High-Technology Project Managers.* Boston: Artech House, 1998.

Henry, J., and Hartzler, M. *Tools for Virtual Teams: A Team Fitness Companion.* Milwaukee: American Society for Quality Press, 1998.

Hinds, P. *Perspective Taking Among Distributed Workers: The Effect of Distance on Shared Mental Models of Work.* Palo Alto, Calif.: Stanford University, 1999.

Klein, J., and Barrett, B. "One Foot in a Global Team, One Foot at the Local Site: Making Sense Out of Living in Two Worlds Simultaneously." In M. Beyerlein (ed.), *Advances in Interdisciplinary Studies of Work Teams.* Vol. 8: *Virtual Teams.* Stamford, Conn.: JAI, 2001.

Lipnack, J., and Stamps J. *Virtual Teams: Reaching Across Space, Time, and Organizations with Technology.* New York: Wiley, 1997.

Maznevski, M., and Chudoba, K. "Bridging Space over Time: Global Virtual Team Dynamics and Effectiveness." *Organization Science,* 2000, *11*(5), 473–492.

McGrath, J. E., and others. "Groups, Tasks, and Technology: The Effects of Experience and Change." *Small Group Research,* 1993, *24*(3), 406–420.

O'Hara-Devereaux, M., and Johansen, R. *Globalwork—Bridging Distance, Culture, and Time.* San Francisco: Jossey-Bass, 1994.

Olson, G., and Olson, J. *Distance Matters.* Ann Arbor: University of Michigan, 2000.

Schrage, M. *No More Teams! Mastering the Dynamics of Creative Collaboration.* New York: Currency Doubleday, 1989.

Seagal, S., and Horne, D. *Human Dynamics: A New Framework for Understanding People and Realizing the Potential in Our Organizations.* Waltham, Mass.: Pegasus Communications, 1997.

Waller, M. J. "Keeping the Pins in the Air: How Groups Juggle Multiple Tasks." In M. M. Beyerlein, D. A. Johnson, and S. Beyerlein (eds.), *Advances in Interdisciplinary Studies of Work Teams.* Vol. 4. Stamford, Conn.: JAI Press, 1997.

SUMMARY

The chapter authors in Part Five effectively illustrated the dynamic nature of virtual teams, discussing how process factors contribute to the development of enabling conditions and subsequent virtual team effectiveness. They emphasized several common themes and reiterated features of our design model. Elron and Vigoda, for example, point to the importance of shared understandings, a key enabling condition in our framework, in order to avoid potential dysfunctions associated with different perceptions of politics and influence tactics across cultures. They also add an important nuance in this regard: it may be the subtle cultural differences that are the most insidious in terms of influencing processes. If much culture is shared, small variations in perspectives may become big surprises. Elron and Vigoda also speak to the role of organizational context as a key input condition in virtual teams. They explicitly recommend flat organizational structures to encourage the use of the most effective political processes: rationality, reason, and assertiveness. Finally, they highlight the importance of integrating organizational cultures, given that many norms around politics and influence are developed at that level.

Griffith, Mannix, and Neale discussed several elements of successful conflict resolution that also are addressed in the general design framework and elsewhere in this book. They note, for example, that task-based conflict is often more productive than relationship or process conflict but that team members often misperceive which forms of conflict they are experiencing. Griffith, Mannix, and Neale recommend that one key to breaking this cycle is building trust within the team, which paves the way for members to share and resolve task conflict as task related. This underscores the importance of trust as a key enabling condition in virtual teams. They also suggest that the level of task and relationship was equal in virtual teams and colocated teams when virtual teams structured work to overcome challenges of distance. This is a key point in our design framework: organizational and team-level decisions have an impact on processes and enabling conditions in virtual teams. In order to manage conflict further, Griffith, Mannix, and Neale also discuss the importance of team processes such as direction setting, establishing norms, meeting management, and rewards and recognition, all of them components in the design framework and discussed in earlier chapters in this book.

Klein and Kleinhanns expanded our definition of team process factors to include concerns around how competing priorities (often established as a result of certain organizational structures and team designs) affect virtual team member contributions. They reiterate and elaborate on techniques we included in our design model. For example, they recommend building shared understanding by clarifying each team member's role and purpose for being part of the team and by making assumptions and personal agendas explicit. They recommend techniques for building integration, such as creating shared accountability for processes and protocols and enhancing the perceived value of collaboration. Finally, their technique of encouraging frequent and continuous communication and providing a human link in the virtual environment is likely to go a long way toward establishing trust, our third enabling condition for virtual team effectiveness.

Gluesing and associates also emphasize the important impact that time zone crossing has on process, particularly in global virtual teams. Like Klein and Kleinhanns, they mention cultural and language differences as complicating factors that make integrating ideas difficult, impeding maturation. Their action recommendations based on their three case studies emphasize the importance of several of our input factors in the design framework, including a supportive organizational context and solid team processes such as goal setting, chartering, and communication. They emphasize a set of practices aimed at integration to enable full maturity in virtual teams. For example, they suggest that open communication links with groups and people outside the team, followed by regular sense making and redefinition of task, are key mechanisms for building integration. In some instances, they recommend face-to-face communication to grapple with significant rapid change in the context (such as mergers or business crisis). They echo many of the recommendations provided by Elron and Vigoda, such as establishing power balances. They reiterate suggestions discussed by Griffith, Mannix, and Neale such as regular and frequent communication and sharing of norms and preferences for conflict resolution. Finally, they mention best practices described by Klein and Kleinhanns, such as defining the team task as a high priority and creating opportunities for social interaction. All of these recommendations can go a long way toward a holistic approach to improving process in virtual teams over the course of their life cycle.

CHAPTER EIGHTEEN

The Last Word

Conclusions and Implications

Cristina B. Gibson, Susan G. Cohen

The chapter authors generated many extremely valuable insights and suggestions. We were often awed by their findings, impressed by their interpretations and analysis, and inspired by their recommendations. Our summary is organized into four sections. In this final chapter, we summarize their key learnings, pulling together key themes around the question, "What makes virtual teams special?" We look at the bright side of virtual teaming and highlight the key advantages of this form of organizing, but also temper the good news with some bad news, summarizing the dark side of virtual teams. Finally, we review the most critical recommendations provided by the chapter authors for virtual team leaders, members, and facilitators.

WHAT MAKES VIRTUAL TEAMS SPECIAL?

All of the chapter authors noted that the more that teams become virtual, the more they experience certain unique phenomena that set them apart from teams at the colocated end of the degree of virtuality continuum. We have categorized these phenomena into four broad categories: technological complexity, extensive diversity, dynamic nature of work, and developmental idiosyncrasies.

Technological Complexity

Virtual teams rely substantially more on information technology than colocated teams and use collaborative technology to connect people more so than do colocated teams do. This puts a premium on standardized and efficient storage, retrieval and exchange of knowledge, and technology training. We anticipated that technology would be a critical component of virtual teaming. Yet the chapter authors pointed out the importance of recognizing that virtual teams are not just technological systems; they are sociotechnological systems, that is, social systems completely intertwined with technology systems (Maznevski and Chudoba, 2000). Perhaps as a result, we were surprised to find that use of advanced technologies is relatively uncommon in virtual teams, with most team members preferring e-mail as the primary mode of communication.

Use of technology is complicated by the composition of most virtual teams. We were particularly intrigued by the different norms for how often members should check in for messages by e-mail, voice mail, and an answering service. Furthermore, because different cultures are often involved, silence and lack of responses to communications by technology can have multiple meanings across contexts represented on virtual teams, including indifference, technical failure, discomfort, or confusion. Finally, some members may have access to electronic communication only during certain hours. These features are unique and surprisingly salient in virtual teams that rely heavily on electronic communication.

Extensive Diversity

Perhaps the second most prominent feature of highly virtual teams that sets them apart from colocated teams is that virtuality brings together highly diverse groups, including people from different nations, regions, organizations, and professions. On average, highly virtual teams tend to be more diverse than colocated teams, so we anticipated that differences make a difference, but the chapter authors specifically stressed the importance of differences in context. For example, there are different formal and informal rules that dictate workplace interaction and different policies and government regulations for human resources; moreover, the stability and efficiency of economic and political environments vary greatly among members on a virtual team. Furthermore, virtual teams are embedded within the larger network of an organization or multiple organizations, and they often have members with multiple domains of expertise. Several authors emphasized that the national, organizational, and professional cultures that mingle have their own shared understanding, sense making, beliefs, expectations, and behaviors. On some virtual teams, members share many cultural characteristics; on others, there is a high degree of cultural difference.

A fascinating and somewhat ironic finding is that when members of virtual teams share many cultural characteristics (for example, all are Westernized, or all share the same function), subtle cultural differences may go unnoticed, but then cause real surprises as the team interacts. Thus, members cannot take for granted that other members share their contextual knowledge or have a common frame of reference. They are especially likely to hold tacit knowledge unavailable to others, so context must be articulated for sharing to take place. In fact, the more differences there are represented on a virtual team, the more information there is to be shared. In particular, members need to share more information about context than they would if working in the same location.

Coinciding with cultural differences on virtual teams are differences in the way in which people use language. We were amazed at how subtle yet profound these differences can sometimes be on virtual teams. For example, across cultures, communication varies in the extent to which people use implicit versus explicit language (for example, the use of qualifiers such as *maybe, perhaps,* or *somewhat*), the extent to which messages are context free or context specific, the degree to which messages contain emotional content or a serious tone, and the degree to which informal versus formal channels of communication are used.

Finally, more so in highly virtual teams, it is often necessary to create a hybrid culture, structure, and set of operating policies that represents a compromise among various alternatives preferred by the team. Therefore, cross-cultural skills and training, a learning orientation, lateral understanding, and cross-functional capabilities are critical in virtual teams.

Dynamic Nature of Work

A third set of unique features pertains to the fundamental nature of work processes in virtual teams. With virtuality comes an added degree of flexibility in the type of work that can be accomplished. Although face-to-face teams also perform knowledge work, it is even more likely in virtual teams that knowledge will develop unexpectedly and change over time and that it often involves novel problems, negotiation, and interpretation. Virtual work often needs to be construed as conversation making, sense making, and community making consisting of trade-offs and deliberations (Markus, Majchrzak, and Gasser, 2001). In fact, even the participants may be unknown in advance; perhaps they are unavailable due to other meetings or they may choose not to attend based on other priorities. Therefore, there cannot be a rigid sequence of activities imposed on the work, tools cannot be structured to assume the presence of any given participant, and work structures must often emerge.

We learned from Mohrman, Klein, and Finegold in Chapter Three, for example, that global new product development occurs through a system composed of a set of complex and overlapping task networks, typically linking multiple product lines and several geographies, and that accomplishing the strategic intent of the global firm depends on developing shared meaning to guide sense-making processes in the team. This often occurs simultaneously within and across different parts and level of the system, including in different units or projects and with customers and suppliers.

In addition to placing a premium on dynamic sense making, virtual team collaboration requires both synchronous and asynchronous work. We were intrigued by the finding that creating team output through iterative reflection is often easier in a synchronous mode. In fact, reflection will likely take longer if done asynchronously because responses may not be made with people in the same frame of mind, leading to a loss of mind-share between responses. Surprisingly, in virtual teams, doing and communicating often occur at the same time; for example, a discussion may begin verbally and escalate to sketching on a shared white board.

It was also interesting to note that the type of relationships and linkages that are important in a virtual team depends on which task characteristics are dominant. Some virtual tasks are primarily integration (for example, combining knowledge to develop a new product), others require differentiation (as with customizing for different markets), and still others are learning tasks (benchmarking, for example). Integration tasks require extensive internal social capital, that is, internal networks of relationships. Differentiation tasks require extensive links external to the team, and ties can be weaker. Finally, learning tasks probably require a balance of the two types of networks. Configurations of networks are often combined in virtual teams with varied tasks to achieve the best of all worlds.

Developmental Idiosyncrasies

The fourth category of unique features pertains to the developmental patterns that accompany virtuality. In highly virtual teams, initial structure, start-up, and formation activities are potentially more critical than in colocated teams because they provide common ground needed to bridge differences and develop basic operating structure. Furthermore, given that many factors known to contribute to social control and coordination, such as geographical proximity, similarity in backgrounds, and experience with each other, are often absent in virtual teams, the development of collective trust is critical. This development requires a balance between an optimal level of risk and interdependence. Perhaps somewhat ironically, some minimal level of risk and interdependence is necessary to create opportunities to demonstrate trust. Without any risk or interdependence, trust is not necessary.

Team leaders typically play a key role in the process of balancing risk and interdependence. Interestingly, leaders often emerge in virtual teams even when they are not formally designated. Emergent leaders tend to be rated higher than other members in terms of trust, particularly role performance trust, which involves demonstrating competency with the tasks and behaviors necessary to accomplish team goals. This is gained through reliability, consistency, quality of work, initiative, and experience. Emergent leaders also tend to be rated higher than other members on transformational leadership (influencing through values and ideals, inspirational motivation, intellectual stimulation, and individual consideration).

Beyond developmental issues related to trust, the chapter authors emphasized that in virtual teams, the flow of knowledge and information is related to the development of networks of relationships in the team, particularly the subgroups that often form. Interestingly, if subgroups tend to coincide with the different subtasks of the group (with different types of expertise to apply to different client problems), then knowledge will flow more effectively; if the subgroups do not coincide with subtasks, then knowledge flows are often compromised. This process is complicated by the fact that members of virtual teams are often on their best behavior because they consider themselves something of ambassadors of the groups they represent. Yet, ironically, in virtual teams, crisis and conflict often most clearly signal the need for integration and help to bridge differences represented on the team.

ADVANTAGES OF VIRTUAL TEAMS

When highly virtual teams are implemented effectively, chapter authors found, they bring many advantages to collaborative efforts. In this section, we summarize three major categories of such advantages: innovation and synergy, effort and performance gains, and constructive influence tactics, politics, and conflict.

Innovation and Synergy

When virtual teams bring together representatives from numerous locations, they allow synergetic interaction among parties that might otherwise duplicate effort or even work at cross-purposes. Virtuality potentially increases the number of participants and overall contributions to meetings, and allows members to maintain access to their home computing environment and desktop tools, which facilitates knowledge capture and search. In global new product development efforts, for example, virtual teams facilitate work that occurs across diverse and dispersed knowledge centers. By virtue of different locations, members can tap into multiple sources of information and knowledge, and this broad spectrum of knowledge can be leveraged on behalf of the team and the organization. The process of obtaining information is greatly facilitated by building relationships within and outside the team; members hear about what is important from other people they know, they are alerted to potentially useful knowledge and information, and they interpret meaning in part based on knowledge of its origins. Good relationships with the right people can help team members acquire knowledge and analysis that competitors cannot obtain.

Effort and Performance Gains

If diverse intelligence is leveraged in virtual teams, it allows better outcomes than the best individual team member could achieve alone. Teammates are able to work around the clock without violating the personal time of any one member (Pape, 1997). Virtual teams have a strong potential advantage over colocated teams with respect to their ability to implement decisions because of the strong ties that distributed members can develop locally with clients, customers, and other external constituents. In addition, some forms of electronic media, such as text-based conferencing and discussion groups, have been found to facilitate a more equal and full representation of team member inputs (Tyran, Dennis, Vogel, and Nunamaker, 1992). It is less likely that a vocal and assertive member can dominate a group that relies primarily on text-based electronic media, and virtuality often decreases power and hierarchy issues in teams. Finally, many managers find that performance is easier to document and review in virtual teams, given that most interactions and commitments are archived electronically.

Constructive Conflict, Influence, and Politics

A third important set of advantages accrues regarding processes in virtual teams. For example, relationship conflict, which has demonstrated dysfunctional impacts in teams, is more likely to be filtered out of computer-mediated communication. Furthermore, in virtual teams, communication is often more explicit and therefore may avoid the common problem of misunderstandings found in less explicit forms of communication.

In terms of influence processes, rationality and sanction are used more frequently in virtual teams, and these tend to be the most functional forms of influence. The less popular and socially acceptable influence tactics, such as pressure, sanction, and legitimating, are typically used less frequently because lower familiarity and intimacy serve as gatekeepers to these tactics. Political behavior takes on a more careful and covert form in virtual teams because communication is more frequently documented. Cultural boundaries and differences restrain people from using extremely aggressive influence and politics (Elron, Shamir and Ben-Ari, 1999), and research conducted by the chapter authors indicates that there are fewer stable political coalitions based on cultural subgroups in virtual teams.

DISADVANTAGES OF VIRTUAL TEAMS

No organizational form is perfect. Alongside the benefits, virtuality brings several drawbacks that can constitute major barriers to virtual team effectiveness if they are not explicitly addressed through various design and process techniques.

We examine five categories of such challenges: technology failures, communication mishaps, dysfunctional conflict, inefficient work processes, and challenges to support systems.

Technology Failures

Across members, the quality and capacity of the infrastructure for communication vary, limiting access and the feasibility of high-bandwidth technologies such as videoconferencing. In addition, members often have different formats and protocols for storing knowledge. These variations in availability of advanced technology and resources to support them can cause major communication breakdowns. To complicate matters, most technologies treat knowledge as object (focus on information only) or knowledge as action (focus on collaborative processes only) and therefore fail to support the full range of virtual team activities and needs. In addition, many of the collaborative structures that are referred to as teams are actually communities of practice or work groups and therefore have different technology needs. Even when everyone agrees that the need for a true team structure exists, members rarely share the same computing platform, even within the same firm.

Communication Mishaps

In highly virtual teams, there is less opportunity to engage in informal and social interaction; communication is more formal, and less time is allocated for non-task behavior. Furthermore, involvement in the virtual team is often less central than involvement with a member's local environment, with less emotional attachment, vested interest, and identification. In turn, this means lower familiarity and intimacy and less self-disclosure. English as a second language may exacerbate this and result in less depth and candidness of exchange, which increases psychological distance and fears of misuse, miscommunication, and misinterpretation of knowledge. As a result, there is often a higher perception of risk, which increases ambiguity and complexity of information exchanged.

Even when English is designated as the official language of the collaborative effort and even when sophisticated technologies or translation procedures are used, language presents a key challenge to collective sense-making processes in virtual teams. Because nonverbal communication can be an important source of information when assessing the trustworthiness of a new teammate, the use of text-based electronic communication like e-mail may impede the development of trust in virtual teams.

In addition, communication through text-based media is laborious, and so people tend not to type out details they would communicate verbally (Graetz and others, 1998). As a result, computer-mediated groups have lower communication efficiency than colocated groups (DeSanctis and Monge, 1999). The details, qualifications, social rituals, and cues that reveal meaning are often left out of text messages, and this may hinder interpretation, cohesion, and relationships in virtual teams. Computer-based communication media also eliminate cues about interpersonal affection, warmth, attentiveness, and trust.

Equally as troubling, people who are communicating through technology often are not successful in directing the receivers' attention. In the absence of rich auditory and visual cues such as voice intonation, understanding of complex messages is inhibited, and there is less feedback that information has not been understood. Receivers often fail to let a sender know their perception of the message that was sent. The complex information that is often exchanged in virtual teams is open to many interpretations, particularly across cultures and disciplines, which presents a key challenge in terms of the coding and categorization that must take place if knowledge will be used for collective thought processes. Adjustment to a shared norm of communication may be resented, particularly if that norm is more inclined toward a given culture (for example, Israelis resent having to be more indirect due to the preferred style of U.S. participants).

Finally, virtual teams may need more time to make sure all voices are adequately heard. Differences in phonics and syntax, unfamiliar accents, and inappropriate use of vocabulary can make it difficult or impossible to understand each other. Participants who are not physically located at or near headquarters or with the core of the team may be at a disadvantage because they do not have as many opportunities to participate in informal exchanges. All of these phenomena may interfere with creativity and satisfaction, which are linked to team performance.

Dysfunctional Conflict

A third set of disadvantages revealed by chapter authors pertains to conflict. Although teams experience advantages related to conflict due to the virtual nature of their work, these benefits may create challenges. For example, virtual team members often do not have the opportunity to engage serendipitously in sense making, and communication is often limited to brief episodes; this is efficient in some ways but may potentially increase opportunities for misunderstandings. Consensus is more difficult to reach in virtual teams, particularly in teams working on complex, nontechnical issues (Hollingshead and McGrath, 1995). In addition, conflict is likely to be hidden longer in a virtual team, and there may be higher levels of process-based conflict because members are likely to use different work processes.

Also challenging is that members from different nations are likely to perceive and react to organizational politics differently; thus, what some view as a negative influence tactic others view as fine. This divergence could result in negative emotions and dysfunctional conflict. In a related way, distrust and suspicion often arise between individuals from different cultural groups purely on the basis of group membership. Subgroups often form based on national, organizational, and functional cultures, and perceptions of risk across these subgroups are likely to be superoptimal, prohibiting trust, particularly when members of one subgroup have inadequate information about the other subgroups. Extreme divergence of views is often a reaction to the perceived risk.

Finally, text-based electronic communication makes it more difficult for team members to formulate impressions of their teammates and make inferences about one another's knowledge (Walther, 1993). Thus, virtual team members often err on the side of dispositional attributions, assuming behavior was caused by personality, because they lack situational information and are overloaded, and this may make them less likely to try to modify problematic situations. In sum, colocated teammates can often establish credibility with each other by a process that is not explicitly designed, but virtual team members must create much more explicit routines that will allow this to happen.

Inefficient Work Processes

A fourth set of disadvantages in virtual teams arises due to the logistics of coordinating work processes across locations. In addition to difficulty in reaching consensus, virtual teams may need more time than a colocated group to accomplish the same basic work task, although the likelihood is that they will have less time. They require advanced lead time to get materials out to remote sites, and this is often viewed as additional preparation. Some members may not have time to prepare, and then meetings may be viewed as inefficient by those who did prepare. Virtual teams also need additional time for updates and establishing a common understanding of what has transpired or needs to be accomplished (that is, getting on the same page), which often means redundant discussions and missed dialogue. Equally as challenging, virtual teaming typically lengthens the workday for virtual team members, and time zone dispersion narrows the window for synchronous team interaction. Multitasking, common during meetings, can distract members to such an extent that they miss an opportunity to provide valuable input. Moreover, the focus of virtual team members is often diluted by their local tasks and priorities. If local priorities override time that team members had planned to devote to team assignments or meetings, process loss may result in more time than planned to complete the team's work.

In addition, information is likely to be much more distributed across locations in highly virtual teams than in colocated teams, and thus considerable communication is required to make local information commonly known in the team. The distributed nature opens up the possibility that contextual information will be delayed, overlooked by remote team members, or lost in transmission because of technical or human errors. Perhaps as a result, members tend to take their own context (local situation) for granted and assume others' are similar, and thus do not know what about their context needs to be communicated to others. Virtual team members often complain that too much time is spent on merely sharing information in meetings rather than doing truly collaborative tasks, such as decision making or problem solving. In a colocated situation, it is more likely that team members will be around when changes in requirements are made, so information is likely to be distributed more quickly and with less effort than in virtual teams.

Finally, geographical distance, different contexts, and reliance on technology lead to fewer similarities across members, less open communication and information sharing, and less use of unshared (unique) information and greater possibility of divisive subgroups. Interdependence is often higher within subgroups (for example, within a subset of members who are all from the same organization) than across subgroups. Without opportunities to demonstrate reliability and responsiveness across subgroups, collective trust cannot exist, and a negative cycle of divisive conflict will likely ensue. These conditions mean less shared understanding on the team, and this can result in less predictability, less efficient use of resources and effort, more implementation problems and errors, decreased satisfaction and motivation, and increased frustration.

Challenges to Support Systems

The final category of disadvantages captures difficulties associated with the systems that exist in the organizations in which virtual teams are embedded, including human resource systems and performance management systems designed to define, develop, and review team performance. For example, in virtual teams, there are often vast differences in job design and staffing patterns across participants and partners. Without common support systems, building competencies and expertise is difficult, and this can hamper overall development, knowledge management, and sense making. Furthermore, it is very difficult to determine what is valued by each member in a virtual team, and this is exacerbated by national and cultural differences. These differences make application of traditional motivational techniques extremely difficult in virtual teams. Virtuality may make rewarding individuals (common in many organizations) more precarious due to the increased needs for cohesion, mutual accountability, and interdependence.

Finally, when informal networks of relationships within a team do not coincide with an organization's formal structure, conflict may ensue. Control mechanisms to ensure structural alignment can help, but strict mechanisms like formal contracts appear to signal the absence of trust and can hamper its emergence. Equally as challenging, it is more difficult to assign monetary values to costs and benefits not easily quantifiable in order to determine return on investment in virtual teams, particularly for the ancillary benefits of virtuality.

BEST PRACTICES FOR VIRTUAL TEAM EFFECTIVENESS

The many disadvantages that chapter authors identified may seem to paint a grim picture for virtual collaboration, but quite the contrary may be true. By identifying the key potential challenges, chapter authors call attention to the areas of opportunity for improving virtual team effectiveness. Furthermore, all of the authors were generous in their delineation of strategies, tools, and techniques for addressing the many stumbling blocks in the virtual environment. We summarize these here in the format of best practices for virtual team leaders, members, and facilitators.

Lessons for Leaders

Team leaders often play a key role in ensuring virtual team success. The chapter authors identified numerous behaviors that increase leadership effectiveness.

- *Conduct a limited number of critical face-to-face meetings.* A face-to-face introductory meeting in which members develop a charter, norms, roles, and deliverables is important. At the very least, there should be a one-day video-conference to kick off the team in order to help establish trust that will encourage the recognition of conflict and the use of positive conflict management strategies. Immersion training is an important component of the first meeting and should include a practice task or business simulation to help establish a pilot to learn from and some early successes.

Even after initial formation, maintain a regular schedule of face-to-face meetings, rotating team meeting sites. Encourage and initiate travel by members to other locations. In addition to discussing goals, work processes, and progress, devote time in meetings and during travel to personal network building. In general, the team should meet face-to-face with a regular rhythm, such as every three to four months for two to three days at a time. Gluesing and colleagues recommend that person-to-person interactions, key for sense making, gradually move from ad hoc meetings and informal hallway discussions to a combination of synchronous and asynchronous electronically mediated communication. They further suggest that synchronous interaction (both face-to-face and virtual) be scheduled far in advance.

- *Create goal alignment across organizational boundaries.* Make sure the team's activities and output are aligned with local and global objectives and that from the outset there is strong agreement about high-level goals. Ensure that each location has full input into the processes and systems for defining products, projects, architectures, and strategies, as well as ongoing feedback and influence as work evolves. Pay attention to the larger organization and project structure. Does it support virtual teaming? Elron and Vigoda recommend flatter structures that encourage rationality, reasoning, and assertiveness. They suggest that managers develop and safeguard team structures that are as flat as possible, dividing responsibilities and authority among team members and allowing the teams to decide on their inner dynamics and procedures. Decentralized approaches coupled with explicit leadership roles that address expectations regarding hierarchy and shared norms around decision making facilitate trust and shared understanding. Make sure that equity, fairness, and a sense of procedural justice are maintained across parties involved in the virtual teaming effort.

Lateral communication mechanisms appear to be particularly critical to ensure links among the segments of the organization or project, and smooth lateral flow of information creates optimal levels of risk and interdependence that help to establish trust. Each of the elements of a new product development system, for example, must be aware of and connected to the larger system, and the larger system must be responsive to and able to incorporate the knowledge that is generated in the various subunits.

Finally, the overall business strategy is a key means of aligning the subunits: it relates the loose configuration of teams and projects to the larger system, provides direction and meaning to work, and determines what knowledge needs to be acquired, generated, and leveraged (Zack, 1999). A strategic activity core to building innovative capacities, for example, is determining the role of each of the units and members and what they contribute to the overarching strategy. Knowledge-sharing priorities, encoding (preparing and labeling), and priorities for reuse of knowledge between the team and the firm must also be established. Finally, to build internal team alignment, consider creating a metaphor to talk about the team's task, as well as a team logo, slogan, and letterhead.

• *Develop infrastructure and technologies that connect dispersed members.* The information technology infrastructure is a key part of linking geographically dispersed activities. At the same time, the best infrastructure is the one that goes unnoticed. In general, knowledge repositories and databases that help develop transactive memory systems (knowledge about who knows what) are extremely helpful and can help establish the knowledge competency and expertise needed to build trust. Develop an infrastructure to capture a team's history in order to share conflict management norms and patterns. Also ensure that the team has adequate resources for appropriate technology and meetings. Ensure that task, social, and contextual information is included in the sharing and storage of information.

Chapter authors also note that not all technologies are appropriate for all teams; technology use should be matched to the nature of the team's task, the stage of the team's development, and the broader organizational context. Teams should conduct a technology and infrastructure assessment when deciding on which technologies to use. The transmission capacity (bandwidth), propagation delay (lag between when the information is sent and when it is received), and degree of shared access required are all important considerations. For example, work-sharing software is important if a team needs to build strong internal networks of relationships for integrating knowledge tasks (such as developing a new product). If a team needs to tap into organizational knowledge in a targeted way, access to knowledge-management technology, such as human resource systems, and data warehousing are important tools. If the team focuses on differentiation tasks such as establishing a new market, then issues of firewalls and compatibility with external systems become important. If the team needs broad and diffuse networks for learning, access to news services and search technologies is critical externally.

Knowledge complexity should also guide choice of information technologies. For example, tasks that require the team to generate ideas can be accomplished with a structured chat tool or an electronic meeting room. Tasks requiring virtual teams to resolve conflicting views or interests may need transmission of rich information through sophisticated software such as computer-supported collaborative work technologies. Furthermore, team size must be considered. Larger teams (of ten or more people) are likely to take longer to reach consensus and may constrain the use of certain applications. For example, at the time of this writing, Microsoft Netmeeting cannot support application sharing among more than about seven users. Thus, larger teams may need more sophisticated technology to ease the decision process.

Because knowledge relevance changes so quickly, capturing and coding it may not be cost-effective. Balance costs of capture and categorization to determine the relevance-to-cost ratio. Organizational attitudes and practices toward the security of a firm's information resources must be adapted to allow outside access to knowledge archives. Incremental resource commitments can help to manage some sources of risk and potential mistrust. Stability of processes and routines can also help to build infrastructure and trust. In addition to building relationships inside the team, help the team establish and encourage networks outside the team and with customers to stay on top of changes in context and to serve as backup to share differences of opinion inside the team. If the team needs strong external ties, face-to-face meetings with external constituencies are advised.

Over the life of the virtual team, technology and infrastructure needs will change. Early on, it is best not to use experimental tools that may frustrate people, and it is better not to introduce new technologies when deadlines are imminent or at the final stages of a team's life cycle. Consider introducing the technology for a small pilot project before disseminating it across a range of applications. Another strategy is to introduce collaborative technologies to all employees regardless of virtuality, since many technologies can facilitate colocated collaboration as well as virtual collaboration. It may be useful to perform a technology audit at set points during the team's process to ensure that the technology is matched to the various contingencies and to make certain that new technologies will fit with existing tools. All parties must be convinced that issues of version control, security, and data integrity have been resolved.

• *Establish selection, development, and training programs for virtuality.* Help your virtual teams reach their full potential by carefully selecting partner organizations and units, team leaders, and team members. Firms with a reputation of professional integrity and participants with honesty and fairness are a good place to start. In building virtual teams, recognize the special knowledge, skills, and abilities needed to lead and work virtually. Important knowledge, skills, and abilities include tolerance and understanding of diverse viewpoints, interpersonal and team skills requiring new forms of communication and information sharing, self-regulatory skills, and high levels of comfort with technology hardware and software for managing virtual tasks. For members in leadership roles, reliability, consistency, responsiveness, and ethical integrity are particularly important.

Provide your virtual teams with appropriate training at every stage of team development. Ongoing face-to-face training and learning help to achieve understanding of tacit elements of knowledge and context. Of particular importance is helping your virtual teams build social capital, use technology effectively, overcome cultural differences, and build communities of practice. Communicating effectively using technology means more than understanding how to transfer knowledge and information. Team members also need training as to how to inspire, motivate, mediate conflict, and develop trust through a variety of communication media. For teams that rely primarily on text-based electronic media, training in written communications is especially critical.

Creating learning cohorts in which the same group of employees advance through a sequence of training programs together can help to build formal and informal networks that can be used to promote future knowledge transfer and sense making. Establish subject matter experts to help increase information gathering and direct information flow. Transfers and exchanges of personnel may help accomplish some of the internal transfer of expertise needed to build the overall competencies of the team. Actively rotate people in and out of headquarter locations to develop a working network of contacts and an understanding of the bigger picture. Also, implement team training sessions that coincide with customer visits. These practices all serve to help increase mutual perspective taking, that is, an understanding of how one's own behavior affects those at distant sites with different perspectives. In the initial stages, it is particularly important to have facilitators and trained support staff present during all training to facilitate and solve interpersonal and technical problems. As work progresses, establish some stability of membership in order to create a high level of commitment among a core in the team and to maintain and transfer knowledge, norms, and expertise. Finally, monitor the use of technologies and the effectiveness of training over the life cycle of the team. Consider a measure of productivity costs before and after technology and training implementation in order to justify the investment in collaborative technologies and special programs.

• *Build performance management systems that enable strategic alignment.* Create one or more team performance templates (such as a team "cockpit") to focus virtual teams and their members on important team outcomes and team processes. Careful development of team performance templates helps managers align virtual teams with strategic organizational objectives. Direction, goals, and rewards also help to avoid process conflict and dysfunctional conflict management. Consider complementing the performance templates with a 360-degree evaluation model to provide the developmental feedback for virtual teams and their members that is essential for continuous improvement.

A key decision is whether to pay for skills or performance, or both. The answer should depend on the level of integration needed, the extent of self-management required, the type of team, and the goals of the performance management system (for example, to attract and retain, motivate, promote skills and knowledge development, shape corporate culture, or define and reinforce structure). Paying the individual instead of the job and pay-for-performance approaches that focus on collective performance more than individual performance are potentially the best fit for virtual teams of all types and for multiple performance management goals. It is critical to use valid team performance measures as the bases for team recognition and reward. In the final analysis, calibrate prospective return on investment in virtual teams against prior projects, and emphasize whether a virtual team's charter is consistent with your company's bottom-line objectives.

• *Design dynamic systems responsive to changes across contexts.* Be sure to redefine the task, structure, and policies when conditions change to maintain alignment with organizational strategies, particularly in dynamic environments where contexts change frequently. At a microlevel, this may mean, for example, negotiating a flexible agenda format for meetings. At a more macrolevel, this may mean balancing a globally integrated approach with applications in diverse local and industry markets and across existing and emerging technologies. Technical road maps, system architectures, and standard processes for change management can help to initiate alignment, but these frameworks should be dynamic and should respond to what is learned as team activity evolves. An ongoing process for weaving emergent understandings into the formal framework of the system or project should be developed.

Must-Haves for Members

Of course, team member behavior also makes a critical difference to the success or failure of a virtual team. Chapter authors delineated many techniques members can use to increase their effective participation in virtual teams.

- *Discuss cultural differences and similarities openly.* It is particularly important to understand cultural differences in relation to one's own culture. Identify, discuss, and elaborate on your understanding of your own and others' context, and specifically organizational cultures, given that the political culture of the organization and the influence norms it holds have a strong impact on the intensity of political activity in the team. Such discussions should include both values and work practices. Learn to make inquiries about others' contexts on a regular basis. Discuss cultural differences in influence behaviors openly, and reach a consensus on a comfortable range of such behaviors that are legitimate within the team. In addition to differences, establish similarities across members, for example, perhaps members share the same educational background or goals. Through consistent and sustained information sharing, identify and develop important commonalities that you share with other members.

- *Become familiar with each others' competence and unique personal attributes, and establish trust.* Create opportunities to collect evidence about other members' credibility and trustworthiness. Frequent communication facilitates this. It is important to share each other's view of the team's distributed activities and to invest time in showing goodwill and intimacy. Become familiar with personal needs, concerns, interests, priorities, and fears of team members to fill in communication gaps. Use storytelling to allow for implicit, complex, and contextual information to be shared or round-robin sense making where each member tells what he or she knows about a particular topic. Credibility can also be established through imitation, that is, trial and error that is critiqued by a mentor. Virtual teams with higher role performance trust (based on knowledge of competence, reliability, and consistency) perform better.

- *Communicate frequently using e-mail and other media.* Information exchange, regular and predictable communication, and verbalization of commitment, excitement, and optimism can help build trust. Therefore, communicate frequently with everyone on the team, including one-on-one interactions. In order to notice conflict early and manage it effectively, document commitments through e-mail. E-mail is more effective in increasing the range, amount, and velocity of information and communication of equivocal information (McKenney, Zack, and Doherty, 1992), and asynchronous interaction can help make meetings more value-added. Face-to-face communication is more effective than electronically mediated communication in ambiguous or uncertain circumstances, in socially sensitive conditions, in intellectually difficult situations (Nohria and Eccles, 1992), and for resolving misunderstandings.

- *Plan advanced technology use carefully.* Make sure all members have sufficient access to repositories and adequate bandwidth (computer functionality) to run the collaborative tools that the team selects. E-mail and multipoint audio-conferencing are currently the most widely available, reliable, and cost-effective tools being used by most virtual teams and can be used throughout the entire life cycle of a virtual team. Balance concerns with security and information sharing, and recognize that there are different norms around these issues. Where possible, use multimedia methods of capturing the content of meetings and exchanges, including documents, audio, visual, and databases. Use shared work spaces and Web sites (electronic places that all members can access) to communicate, share, and store documents in order to increase shared understanding and also to help reinforce team identity. Include aspirations, norms, and procedures. Create and integrate search and retrieval processes such as an index of standard key words.

• *Develop communication norms that facilitate technology use and bridge differences.* To minimize process-related conflict, agree on times when it is reasonable to call, appropriate communication media and contact information, documentation procedures, and meeting schedules. Develop protocols for expectations around team meeting attendance and punctuality, timeliness of input and feedback to each other, and advanced preparation. Encourage members to highlight important parts of long messages as well as questions in the body of an e-mail or in a telephone message. Active listening, that is, frequent requests for elaboration and clarification, can help overcome intercultural challenges to building trust. Listening for key ideas and common themes across members is important, as is the ability to frame messages. Framing involves taking the other's point of view.

Responses are equally as important as the original message sent in creating a supportive communication climate that encourages the safety to share ideas early in their development and take risks that lead to innovation. A response is an endorsement that you are willing to take the risk of interpreting the sender's message, supply the missing elements, and make it understandable in your own terms. Responses are trusting behaviors that indicate involvement, which conveys intimacy, affection, and commitment. Following up by accurately repeating a communicator's message in a timely manner can also go a long way to establishing a supportive communication climate in virtual teams.

Philosophies for Facilitators

Team facilitators can be a tremendous asset to virtual teams. Chapter authors mentioned several ways that facilitators contribute to virtual team effectiveness:

• *Provide a human link.* Consider yourself the human link who administers, coordinates, and facilitates meetings and networks. Keep tabs on the effectiveness of communication, and intervene when puzzles, misunderstandings, or problems arise. For particularly sensitive issues, use shuttle diplomacy in which you conduct a series of one-on-one meetings with each member, integrate, and feed back information to the team.

• *Intervene to maintain ongoing communication.* Do not allow communication to lapse or become sporadic. Watch for member withdrawal or infrequent or sporadic participation. Ensure that interaction encompasses task, social, and contextual information, including member whereabouts, availability, progress, local events, personal developments, and deviations from plan. Disseminate information about team members (biographies, resumés, photos, Internet pages) to facilitate development of social knowledge and trust.

• *Minimize politics, identify conflict early, and work to resolve it.* Less socially acceptable influence tactics and high prevalence of organizational politics are related to negative attitudes and behaviors and deficient performance at the individual, team, and organizational levels. Good logic presented in a rational manner is almost always sufficient to run the team. At the same time, recognize that political activities do occur in virtual teams, even if in a milder or less intense manner. Help virtual team members focus on noticing conflict and identifying it in its early stages. Use face-to-face meetings to resolve relationship conflict. Frequently stop discussions to check for mutual understanding of what is being said. Pair up conflicting team members to create partnering. Avoid secretive or selective operations and personal blaming when things go wrong. Encourage team members to give each other the benefit of the doubt.

• *Develop roles, sponsors, and champions that value virtual teaming.* Finally, it is critical to assign experts to particular domains of information, since teams recognize more unshared information when group members are assigned such roles (Stewart and Stasser, 1995). Help to recognize and work with gatekeepers in the set of virtual collaborators who serve as key links between subgroups, bridging differences and filling structural holes. Senior sponsorships help raise the importance of the team's work in the eyes of team members and refocus team members on the work of the virtual team.

FINAL WORDS OF WISDOM

We believe that the vast majority of people involved in collaboration, armed with knowledge of what makes virtual teams special, key advantages and disadvantages, and the most critical tools for improving virtual team effectiveness, have much to gain from virtuality. We have witnessed the benefits of virtual teaming firsthand in our own collaborations and those of our research participants. We have made strides in improving the value proposition of organizational behavior and wish you the same in your virtual endeavors.

References

DeSanctis, G., and Monge, P. "Introduction to Special Issue: Communication Processes for Virtual Organizations." *Organization Science,* 1999, *10*(6), 693–703.

Elron, E., Shamir, B., and Ben-Ari, E. "Why Don't They Fight Each Other? Cultural Diversity and Operational Unity in Multinational Forces." *Armed Forces and Society,* 1999, *26,* 73–98.

Graetz, K. A., and others. "Information Sharing in Face-to-Face, Teleconferencing, and Electronic Chat Teams." *Small Group Research,* 1998, *29*(6), 714–743.

Hollingshead, A., and McGrath, J. "Computer-Assisted Groups: A Critical Review of the Empirical Research." In R. Guzzo and E. Salas (eds.), *Team Effectiveness and Decision Making in Organizations.* San Francisco: Jossey-Bass, 1995.

Markus, M. L., Majchrzak, A., and Gasser, L. "A Design Theory for Systems That Support Emergent Knowledge Processes." *MIS Quarterly,* 2002, *26*(3), 199–220.

Maznevski, M. L., and Chudoba, K. M. "Bridging Space over Time: Global Virtual Team Dynamics and Effectiveness." *Organization Science,* 2000, *11*(5), 473–492.

McKenney, J. L., Zack, M. H., and Doherty, V. S. "Complementary Communication Media: A Comparison of Electronic Mail and Face-to-Face Communication in a Programming Team." In N. Nohria and R. Eccles (eds.), *Networks and Organizations: Structure, Form, and Action.* Boston: Harvard Business School Press, 1992.

Nohria, N., and Eccles, R. "Face-to-Face: Making Network Organizations Work." In N. Nohria and R. Eccles (eds.), *Networks and Organizations: Structure, Form, and Action.* Boston: Harvard Business School Press, 1992.

Pape, W. R. "Group Insurance." *Inc.,* June 15, 1997, pp. 29–31.

Stewart, D. D., and Stasser, G. "Expert Role Assignment and Information Sampling During Collective Recall and Decision Making." *Journal of Personality and Social Psychology,* 1995, *69*(4), 619–628.

Tyran, C. K., Dennis, A. R., Vogel, D. R., and Nunamaker, J. F. "The Application of Electronic Meeting Technology to Support Strategic Management." *MIS Quarterly,* 1992, *16*(3), 313–334.

Walther, J. B. "Impression Development in Computer Mediated Interaction." *Western Journal of Communication,* 1993, *57,* 381–398.

Zack, M. H. "Developing a Knowledge Strategy." *California Management Review,* 1999, *41*(3), 125–145.

SUBJECT INDEX

A

Accommodation, to manage conflict, 345

Accountability: shared, to team processes and protocols, 392–393; of team vs. community of practice (CoP), 294, 295, 298

Active listening, to build trust, 72–73

Aerospace Alliance (pseudonym): communication practices in, 73, 75, 76, 77, 78; description of, 60; negative trust expressions in, 65, 66, 67–68; trust building in, 62, 63–64, 64–65

Affective conflict, 337

Alignment frameworks, integration using, 39, 57n1

Application forms, information about virtual team experience on, 104–105

ASC NewBiz virtual team: complexity of task of, 253–255; culture and language differences in, 246, 247; profile of, 241, 242–243; technology's role in development of, 261–262; work across time zones by, 248

Attributions: contributing to dysfunctional conflict, 411; inappropriate, and information sharing, 223–225

Audioconferencing: lack of visual cues in, 247, 250, 335; team size as problem in, 249–250; by virtual teams doing unstructured knowledge work (UKW), 268–269

Auto Unification (pseudonym): communication practices in, 72, 73, 74, 75–76, 77, 79; description of, 60; negative trust expressions in, 65, 66, 68; trust building in, 63

Avoidance, to manage conflict, 345

B

Background, similar, shared understanding with, 25, 32

Bandwidth, varying capacity and quality of, when doing unstructured knowledge work (UKW), 268–269

Biased discussion, 216–217

C

Calendaring, 269

Case examples: of development of global virtual teams (GVTs), 358–365, 367, 368; of global new product development system, 40–53; hypothetical, of unstructured knowledge work virtual meeting, 266–267; of influence and politics in virtual teams, 318–319; of return on investment (ROI) for virtual teams, 155–173; of technology in development of global virtual teams

429